SEEING
the BIGGER
PICTURE

This book is part of the Peter Lang Media and Communications list.
Every volume is peer reviewed and meets
the highest quality standards for content and production.

PETER LANG
New York • Washington, D.C./Baltimore • Bern
Frankfurt • Berlin • Brussels • Vienna • Oxford

Mark Sachleben AND Kevan M. Yenerall

SEEING the BIGGER PICTURE

American AND International Politics in Film AND Popular Culture

SECOND EDITION

PETER LANG
New York • Washington, D.C./Baltimore • Bern
Frankfurt • Berlin • Brussels • Vienna • Oxford

Library of Congress Cataloging-in-Publication Data
Sachleben, Mark, 1965-
Seeing the bigger picture : American and international politics in film
and popular culture / Mark Sachleben, Kevan M. Yenerall. — 2nd ed.
p. cm.
Includes bibliographical references and index.
Includes filmography.
1. Politics in motion pictures.
2. Motion pictures—Political aspects—United States.
3. Television and politics—United States.
I. Yenerall, Kevan M. II. Title.
PN1995.9.P6S14   791.43'6581—dc23   2011021146
ISBN 978-1-4331-1132-7 (hardcover)
ISBN 978-1-4331-1133-4 (paperback)
ISBN 978-1-4539-0143-4 (e-book)

Bibliographic information published by **Die Deutsche Nationalbibliothek.**
Die Deutsche Nationalbibliothek lists this publication in the "Deutsche
Nationalbibliografie"; detailed bibliographic data is available
on the Internet at http://dnb.d-nb.de/.

The paper in this book meets the guidelines for permanence and durability
of the Committee on Production Guidelines for Book Longevity
of the Council of Library Resources.

Printed in the United States of America

For Angie and Nee

ACKNOWLEDGMENTS

Mark and Kevan wish to thank the following individuals, institutions, filmmakers, and producers for their support, insight, kindness, encouragement, and permission to reprint film images: Bryce Aaronson, Jessica Acheson and Meghan Graham, for their research and technical assistance in finishing the manuscript; John Hoskyns-Abrahall and Mark Martelli from Bullfrog Films, for their persistence and advocacy in securing permission for reprinting film images; Micha X. Peled (*China Blue* and *Store Wars*) and Teddy Bear Films; Marshall Curry (*Street Fight*) and Curt Ellis (*King Corn*); Charles Ferguson, Tammy Klemith, and Representational Pictures (*Inside Job*); the Omni Parker House, Boston; Dr. Christopher Kelley, political scientist, prolific scholar, and dear friend, for his continued generosity in allowing us to incorporate his research and ideas; Dr. Alison Dagnes, Shippensburg University; Dr. Andrew Dudas, Center for Public Management and Regional Affairs, Miami University; Jeremy Larner, brilliant, prescient screenwriter of *The Candidate*, for his kind comments and suggestions; the Northeastern Political Science Association; Dr. Michael Genovese, Loyola Marymount University; Dr. Karen Kedrowski, Winthrop University; Dr. Clyde Brown, Miami University; Dr. Oliver Schulze-Nahrup; Ed Carroll and his family for the pictures from the Rally to Restore Sanity and/or Fear; our insightful anonymous manuscript reviewer; and to all of our esteemed colleagues who have used previous incarnations of our research in their courses.

Finally, a very special debt of gratitude is owed to Mary Savigar, Senior Acquisitions Editor of Media and Communication Studies at Peter Lang. Her patience, support, generosity, and editorial expertise guided this project from initial deliberations to the final product. We could not have asked for a more dedicated, enlightened colleague.

Mark wishes to thank all of his colleagues in the Political Science Department at Shippensburg University for their support and encouragement; John S. Baick, Western New England College, Eric Leonard, Shenandoah University, and Patrick Haney, Miami University, for their comments, observations, and suggestions; his family, especially his mother and father and Richard and Patricia Smith, for their support and interest; and, for Angie, who patiently takes care of everything including proofreading. I owe her a debt of gratitude for everything she does.

Kevan wishes to thank family and friends, especially his father, Dr. Joseph D. Yenerall; Annie and Stevo Parys for their friendship, neighborly camaraderie, love of film, Steeler Sundays, and generous care of our beloved feline, Max; the Carnegie Library of Pittsburgh (especially, the South Side branch), the Pittsburgh Filmmakers, Regent Square Theater, the Oaks Theater, and Landmark Cinemas for facilitating the screenings of independent and foreign films; the Battle of Homestead Foundation; fellow traveler Philip Terman, for his poetry and friendship; Dr. Stephen Maynard Caliendo, North Central College, and the Project on Race in Political Communication; Dr. John Kares Smith, SUNY-Oswego; Dr. Stan Green, Monmouth University; Dr. Scott McLean, Quinnipiac University; The Washington Center for Internships and Academic Seminars, especially Dr. Gene Alpert and Kathleen Regan; the Greater Pittsburgh Literacy Council; university-wide faculty development grants and summer research stipends for support of professional travel and scholarship; and the music, literature, PBS, NPR, C-SPAN, Turner Classic Movies, *Theme Time Radio Hour*, *Daily Show*, and *Colbert Report* that have inspired and sustained me. Most of all, however, I am thankful for the love, compassion, humor, sanity, humanity, and humility of my wife, Nee—the most graceful, big-hearted, beautiful soul I have ever met. As the immortal John Prine sings, "She is my everything."

CONTENTS

Section 1: Setting the Stage

Section 2: American Politics

Section 3: The International Dimension

Section 4 Finishing Up

· SECTION 1 ·

SETTING THE STAGE

· C H A P T E R 1 ·

INTRODUCTION

Film, Television, and Popular Culture:
Frames of Reference, from Water Coolers to War Zones

We love movies. Not only the authors (of course *we do*), but people in general. Measured in attendance, box office receipts, film rentals and sales, column space, academic departments—and myriad exuberant expressions of fandom on the Internet and throughout the universe—film is the most popular art form in the entertainment world. Similarly, television is one of the most accessible, discussed, and well-liked media. Yet while we love our popcorn, comedy, special effects, and welcome diversions from the stress of everyday life, movies and television are also far more than mere escapism and entertainment.

While they are largely commercial enterprises designed to make money, film and television provide millions with common frames of reference—whether they involve life, death, sex, work, religion, spirituality, or politics. And these references, in turn, can provide crucial context and reveal deeper meaning. Add to this medley our enduring fascination with, and passion for, other prominent (and, in some cases, ancient) pieces of the popular culture puzzle—especially, literature and music—and you have an ever-expanding mosaic of art and entertainment that reflects and shapes our collective memory in creative avenues for expressing, confronting, or redefining our fears, hopes, dreams, and fantasies.

In a media-saturated culture such as ours, communication among people often relies on quotes, scenes, and anecdotes from popular films and television shows to share and foster ideas and emotions. Consider Homer Simpson. The bumbling, clueless yet kindhearted patriarch of the longest-running primetime television series in U.S. history has become synonymous with his famous expression, "d'oh!" Using the utterance "d'oh!" for many in our society refers to a boneheaded mistake or misstep that reflects a general lack of common sense or intelligence. Our vernacular contains a wide array of other phrases, culled from film and television, that express meaning, often offering commentary on the human condition.

Moreover, it is hardly just the average citizen at the water cooler who may employ the language of pop culture to express a particular emotion, frame a cause, or define a role. You could be part of the staff of one of the nation's top military leaders. According to a notorious exposé in a popular culture mainstay, *Rolling Stone*, members of the staff of General Stanley McChrystal, then commander of U.S. and NATO forces in Afghanistan, "jokingly" referred "to themselves as Team America, taking the name from the *South Park*-esque sendup of military cluelessness" and "prided themselves on their can-do attitude and their disdain for authority."[1] The raunchy puppet-based film *Team America: World Police* (2004), from the minds of *South Park* creators Trey Parker and Matt Stone, had lampooned American militarism overseas as well as left-wing critics in the entertainment world. An additional signal of the McChrystal camp's deliberate use of the film's moniker as a badge of honor was their wearing of patches emblazoned with "Team America."[2]

Whether it is the global editor at large of Reuters explaining economic anxiety and inequity in income distribution in the United States by citing Willy Wonka and *Charlie and the Chocolate Factory*[3]; a newspaper columnist framing a discussion of U.S. policy in Afghanistan by quoting liberally from Stanley Kubrick's dark Cold War/atomic bomb comedy classic, *Dr. Stangelove*[4], and examining the debate over the environmental consequences of natural gas extraction in the United States by referencing the 1944 film *Gaslight* and the 2010 documentary *Gasland*[5]; or a prominent former New York City public advocate shaping the debate over extending unemployment benefits by citing Andrew Mellon, Herbert Hoover, and *The Simpsons*' Mr. Burns, it is evident that film and television are routinely employed to shape debate, bolster analysis, question authority, explain political phenomena, and reveal ideological preferences.[6] Characters, phrases, and films ingrained in our collective memory provide tools for participation in the political process. How, when, and why we utilize these tools, and to what effect, is of course determined by a variety of dynamics.

Our Mission

We hope in writing this book to tap into the appeal of movies, television, and, on occasion, elements of our broader popular culture to raise interest in the world of politics, and to provide examples of contemporary debates and enduring governmental institutions that warrant the attention of citizens. One of the troubling aspects of our society over the past several decades is the citizenry's declining interest in politics. In a political system where citizens are supposed to be informed and engaged in order to participate in democratic governance, there is an apparent apathy and dangerous cynicism among people to the ideas, institutions, and debates in politics. Many scholars have written extensively about waning civic involvement and the disintegration of institutions necessary to revitalizing our communities, discourse, and politics. Moreover, voter turnout in the United States, even with some recent blips in the positive direction, remains the lowest among industrialized democracies. There is an array of reasons *why* these disheartening dynamics have occurred, naturally— but our central aim is to make politics more accessible, relevant, and, hopefully, even a tad more interesting.

Our fundamental mission in the following pages is to survey several significant political topics across a spectrum of fields in political science. Naturally, given the limitations of space and time, there are numerous subjects that are not covered by this book. Nonetheless, we hopefully raise a diverse array of concerns and questions so that you will be able to make links to other relevant issues and debates. In calling this book *Seeing the Bigger Picture*, we are asking our audience to see beyond the story, film, or specific television clip (or quip). We encourage readers to be a critical audience and ask these deeper, insightful questions: *What are the messages—both implicit and explicit—behind these films? How might they help us understand and explain the governing institutions, political dynamics, and critical debates that shape the complex world in which we live? Have these films and programs altered or reinforced your beliefs, ideology, or political affiliations—and why?*

To help invite these questions and foster greater understanding and debate, the book cites and discusses a diverse array of films and television shows. By diverse, we mean that the book is not limited to the discussion of films from a particular genre, country, or time. We see this as important for a number of reasons, but two are worth mentioning here. Moving images have the ability to transport the audience to a number of different times and places. By examining films and television shows that are not limited to a single place and time, it allows us to examine issues from a number of different standpoints. Second, films from different time periods allow the audience to see how contemporary thinking on certain subjects has evolved. We should not make the mistake in thinking that *all* films and television shows have represented mainstream public opinion, but knowing that a certain film was popular at a certain time allows us to assume that the message of the film perhaps resonated with audiences.

Using a diverse array of films—in style, decade, and substance—does present some challenges. Popular culture seems to crave what is new and what is current. The modern wonders of movie downloads, YouTube, online rentals, cable and satellite programming, DVRs, and the wide reach of DVDs and Blu-ray allow us unparalleled access to a greater array of films than ever before. In the hectic and immediate media-saturated world deluged with multiple formats and ultra-current clips, it is not very often that older films remain in the public consciousness; however, they do serve as a reservoir of cultural memory. In the United States particularly, since most Americans do not deal with languages other than English on a regular basis, there is a great reluctance to engage in films that are shot in languages other than English. Hence access to foreign language films, particularly outside major metropolitan areas, can be difficult. Nevertheless, the movies mentioned in this book are generally available if you are willing to look.[7]

Political Film?

Logic would seem to dictate that, in order to begin a cogent discussion of how film and television can potentially educate, provide context, and spur debate in the political arena, we must first determine what makes a film "political." However, the object of *Seeing the Bigger Picture* is not to define political film. Others, notably political scientists Michael Genovese and Ernest Giglio, have already traveled this intellectual terrain and have provided an enlightened and operational foundation for students and scholars alike.[8] Genovese's framework, for example, suggests that a political film must meet one or more of the following requirements in order to be included in the political film genre:

- The film serves as a vehicle for international propaganda;
- The film's major intention is to bring about political change; and
- The film is designed to support the existing economic, political, and social system.[9]

Giglio builds on this groundwork by offering additional and alternative qualifications (i.e., intent and effect), but ultimately suggests that, despite our best intentions to be systematic in our study of politics and film, the audience's diverse interpretations may make any exact, unambiguous definition unattainable. Indeed, the following chapters will consider a number of films, television clips and animated shorts that have heretofore not been deemed explicitly (or perhaps even implicitly) political.

Therefore the aim of this book is to not necessarily examine strictly *political* films per se, but to use *all* kinds of films to demonstrate concepts and topics in politics. For example, it is difficult to classify the classic Bugs Bunny–Elmer Fudd cartoons of the 1950s as political films. But we will examine one of these films because it helps to reveal some important concepts that have direct political relevance. In that sense, the book omits or scarcely discusses some of the most famous political films ever made in favor of using a wide variety of films to access key topics and debates.

Differences in Film Presentation

A common complaint for many people is that films sometimes look old, even antique. In the age of 60-inch LCD screens, stadium-seating theaters, and digital surround sound this grievance is understandable. Many of us are unaccustomed to viewing other types of films. We, the authors, ask you to make an effort to see some of these films. Once you have become familiar with different media and styles from various eras we think that you will appreciate the differences. It is also worth mentioning some of the history behind these different types of films.

Many have complained, particularly younger people, that they do not like black and white films. It is true that prior to 1950 or so, most films were black and white, and afterwards most films were filmed in color. Television programs sometimes continued in black and white well into the 1960s. Yet, color techniques were widely available to filmmakers from almost the very inception of the medium in the 1890s. (Color television was slow in coming because of the cost of color television sets for the public.) Films like *Nothing Sacred* (1937) and *Gone with the Wind* (1939) were shot in color. However, the technology remained expensive, and World War II necessitated that cost be minimized wherever possible in order to support the war effort.

Yet after the war, there continued to be a number of black and white films. Often this was the choice of the director, the person in charge of actually completing the film, rather than an economic choice. A particularly popular genre of the late 1940s was *film noir*. Literally French for "black film," *film noir* was designed to capture the darkness of life. Directors were interested in portraying humanity's darker sides, hidden temptations, and appetites. Therefore, it seemed a logical choice for many directors to use black and white photography to help accentuate the darkness of their subject. Black and white photography is still used in film on various occasions. Directors who are usually considered artistically inspired have used black and white films to create dramatic effects. Woody Allen used black and white photography in *Manhattan* (1979) and *Stardust Memories* (1980); Martin Scorsese depicted the world of boxer Jake La Motta in black and white in the film *Raging Bull* (1980); and director Gary Ross used black and white photography mixed with color techniques as part of the narrative in the film *Pleasantville* (1998). Joel and Ethan Coen revisited the classic *film noir* genre by employing stylish black and white in their existential work, *The Man Who Wasn't There* (2001). George Clooney's prescient rumination on the media and politics in the Joseph McCarthy and Edward R. Murrow era, the Oscar-nominated *Good Night, and Good Luck* (2005), was presented in smoky, jazzy, and earnest black and white, with original newsreels strategically integrated into the film. And the highly acclaimed German film *The White Ribbon* (*Das weisse Band—Eine deutsche Kindergeschichte*, 2009) used stunning black and white cinematography to evoke the emotional senses of the characters.

Going even farther back in time, there was a period when films had no spoken words. Now commonly known as silent films, most of the time "silent films" were neither silent nor usually black and white. Silent films were almost always accompanied by music in some form or another. Small-town and second-run theaters would employ at least a piano player to accompany the picture, while some of the larger theaters would use full orchestration. Full color was somewhat of a rarity during the silent period but not unknown. However, most films were dyed different colors to enhance the story line. For example, a blue tint usually meant that the scene was taking place at night.

With the 1927 exhibition of *The Jazz Singer*, movie studios clamored to make full-talking pictures. By 1930, although there were a few exceptions, most films were made as talking pictures. Clearly, many people do not see silent films today. However, this book argues that for an understanding of the politics prior to 1930, silent films provide an indispensable resource. Since a number of issues—such as race relations in the United States from the perspective of 1915—are no longer politically acceptable without commentary, films of that era provide a critical background and understanding. Likewise, outside of the United States, after the 1917 Russian Revolution, film in the Soviet Union became an important medium for explaining the themes of the revolution. The films made during this period provide us with an excellent record of how the leaders, and, frankly, many people, saw the problems of the early twentieth century.

This raises an interesting question: Why not just show documentary footage from the time period or subject in question? Documentaries, films that use actual footage of events or attempt to reconstruct events, are an important resource for understanding politics, and the book employs a few documentaries to discuss some topics, especially civil rights and social justice. However, narrative films, films that tell a story, offer the audience an engaging way to look at the topic in question. Using a narrative structure, the director can build suspense, allow for introspection among characters, and engage an audience that might otherwise be uninterested in a subject.

Consider a simple example of how a narrative story might offer more insight: a documentary feature about Rick Blaine (a fictitious character) might discuss his fighting on the side of the Loyalists in the Spanish Civil War, his time in Paris, his move to Casablanca during the Nazi invasion of France, and his subsequent opening of a nightclub there and joining of the Free French. Yet the same story in the context of *Casablanca* allows the audience to see Rick's personal struggle as he decides what should be done. His personal interaction with corrupt French officials, Nazi officers, and the underground that he tries to ignore at first, but is eventually won over by, gives context and meaning to the larger struggle of World War II. The intention of the filmmakers was to suggest that Rick's life and politics mirrored those of the United States.

There is a problem with an overreliance on narrative films, however. Because they are designed to tell a story, the filmmakers have an artistic license to change pieces of the story for dramatic effect. Many very entertaining films offer false premises in their assertions because they are trying to lead audiences down a certain path. The key for us is to understand this and to dissect the ways in which, and the reasons why, this may happen.

Documentary films help us understand problems inherent in narrative films, but they have a problem as well. We should remember that documentaries are not unbiased. Documentary filmmakers make films about subjects they care about, thus they are portraying a point of view that they probably have. This is not to say that a great number of people who make documentaries do not try to be objective, but simply by choosing their subjects, documentary filmmakers are making a choice. The presumption here is that in a free society all voices should have a chance to be heard.

Sometimes it is difficult to distinguish between a film with a point of view and propaganda. Generally propaganda is considered a relatively deliberate attempt to manipulate a debate.[10] This manipulation can include, but is not limited to, a distortion of facts, a disregard for alternative arguments, and general oversimplification of ideas, symbols, and policies. Thus, some films of the Nazi regime in Germany, such as *Triumph of the Will* (1935) and even *Kolberg* (1945), are offered as examples of propaganda.[11] Whether or not some American, British, Soviet, or other films of the period are propaganda is the subject of some debate. This book leaves it for the reader to decide.

Whether propaganda, documentary, or narrative, films from other countries give the audience an opportunity to experience a completely different existence. If film has the ability to transport the viewer to another time and place, then foreign films can make that trip much more realistic. American films about Africa, for example, are filtered through a perception of how Americans think about Africa. However, an African film about Africa is apt to reflect how Africans see their lives, rather than preconceived notions.

It is common for people to say that film transports audiences, but that transportation can be even more realistic with foreign language films. When one travels abroad people in other countries often do not speak English. The temperament and tone of actors in foreign language films are reflected in their own tongues. With many DVDs, foreign language films can be dubbed so that a movie can be seen with an English-language soundtrack. Our preference is to see a subtitled film, but to watch such a film takes some practice. Whichever way you choose to see a film, we want to encourage you to consider these films, because they give a unique insight into how people from other countries and cultures see the world around us: a world similar to ours but often with different interpretations.

Troubling Images

One aspect of concern in a book such as this is to give the reader ample warning of upsetting images sometimes contained in films. Whether it is killing, skinning, and gutting rabbits for furs or meat (*Roger & Me*, 1989), Senator Jay Billington Bulworth's obscenity-laced raps about corporate malfeasance and political corruption (*Bulworth*, 1998), bloody fights and ample sex (*Fight Club*, 1999), or a regiment of American and allied Jews exacting brutal justice on Nazi thugs (*Inglourious Basterds*, 2009), films have the potential to trouble, disturb, and offend. Yet they may also more directly connect us to the world of politics.

Among the most effective films discussing ethnic conflict is the film *Before the Rain* (1994). Unfortunately, some may consider the film to be too overwhelming, the violence or tension too great, to be able to sit through it. The film is graphic and the violence, at times, is unsettling.[12] There is also a brief scene of nudity during the part of the film that is filmed in London, which some may find objectionable. While mindful that certain subjects may be difficult for some viewers to watch, it is difficult to discuss the real tragedy of some situations, such as the former Yugoslavia, without some realization that violence was a part of the problem. Violence and the use of sexual attacks were two of the hallmarks of a conflict that captured the headlines of the world press over and over again in the 1990s. *Cabaret Balkan* (1998) reinforces the complexity and the brutal nature of ethnic conflict in the former Yugoslavia. However, using *Cabaret Balkan* as a film to depict the effects of ethnic conflict to a wide variety of people may be difficult at best. With sexual attacks, murders, and offensive language, it may accurately capture mid-1990s Serbia yet also be too intense for many students and adults. *Ghosts of Rwanda* (2004) may also prove equally disturbing. Our sense is that neither the nudity nor the violence in *Before the Rain* is any worse than most R-rated movies that hit American screens. However, we want to insure that viewers are cognizant of scenes that might be especially troubling and will endeavor to indicate them throughout the book.

Outline of the Book

In order to tackle a broad spectrum of topics, the book organizes sections by expansive themes and chapters by topics. The rest of this section also helps to set the stage. The second chapter of the book examines the liberal ideology—that is, philosophic ideas that form the basis of democracy and market economics. One should not confuse liberalism in the classic sense with the liberal or "left-wing" politics today. There is a distinction between the two. Both Democrats and Republicans in the United States are considered classic liberals, because both embrace the ideas of democracy and market economics. The domestic debate between left-of-center parties and right-of-center parties in democratic governments often focuses on *how* to implement democracy and the proper use of government to deal with the failures of the market. In doing so, the chapter examines what assumptions we make in our political lives. One also should consider how film and television have reinforced these assumptions. As a counter position, the chapter also examines some films that question the assumptions of democracy and capitalism.

The third chapter is an examination of alternative ideologies to liberalism. Perhaps the two greatest challenges to liberalism in the twentieth century were fascism and communism (or Marxism).[13] In examining fascism and communism the chapter focuses primarily on films from the Nazi periods of Germany and the Soviet period of Russia. Yet, it also considers American feature films and documentary films as well. In considering arguments against the two ideologies the chapter examines the anti-fascist American films of the early 1940s, and the Czech New Wave films of the 1960s.

The second section of this book focuses on American politics. The fourth chapter examines the institution of the American presidency. We should be mindful that this is not the only institution in politics—the U.S. Congress, the courts, the parliament, the presidency of France, and the British monarchy, for example, are all vital institutions that film has examined over the years. However, the book chooses to examine the American presidency because of the widespread availability of films and the number of films that have been made on the subject. Moreover, the 1990s witnessed an explosion in the number of presidency films: more than forty U.S. films in that decade dealt with some aspect of the American presidency.

Chapter 5 examines how campaigns and elections have been depicted in films and on television, and draws from a wide array of perspectives to illustrate both the noble and less noble character of elections in a democracy. Chapter 6 deals with civil rights and the search for social justice; here, we consider how commercial films and documentaries have reflected, deflected, explained, and debated racism, the legacy of the Ku Klux Klan, the civil rights movement, and racial profiling. In addition, Hollywood's treatment of homosexuality and hate crimes is examined. Lastly, this chapter uses films and documentaries to examine labor struggles in the United States—from Matewan, West Virginia, to Flint, Michigan, to Austin, Minnesota. Chapter 7 considers the role of media in American politics. Additionally, we will examine the explosion of satire, particularly on American television in recent years.

The final section of this book looks at the international dimension of politics. Chapter 8 examines the issue of war. While theories of war are briefly considered, the thrust of the chapter is a debate on whether war can be averted or if it is sometimes necessary. The chapter then considers the impact of nuclear war and the new faces of conflict: ethnic conflict and terrorism. We also consider the impact of the wars in Iraq and Afghanistan on film, television, and popular culture.

Chapter 9 reviews film's powerful ability to provoke, challenge, and influence the politics of human rights. Included in this chapter is a debate about the efficacy of the death penalty in the United States from the perspective of human rights advocacy. Finally, the book concludes with a chapter that surveys the increasingly important genre of environmental films. In addition to the topic of climate change, the chapter examines issues of pollution and environmental degradation and their impact on the body politic.

As you will have noticed, this volume is a revised edition of our 2004 book. We thought it was a good time to update films and television programs as well as add some additional materials. A lot has happened since the publication of the original *Seeing the Bigger Picture*. For example, the aftermath of the American invasion of Iraq has provided a broad new spectrum of films concerning war, and the financial crisis and meltdown of 2008 have prompted reexaminations of capitalism and financial markets in popular culture. We have also included new chapters on media, human rights, and the environment to reflect the growing awareness and academic research in these areas. Also since the publication of the first edition, we have seen an explosion in the way in which moving images have been delivered to viewers. We are tempted to provide a list of the new technologies but fear that by the time you read this they will be obsolete! One of our goals in this edition was to focus less on specific films and highlight a broad range of films that offer complementary and competing visions of politics. We have also developed a website to provide links to additional material and film clips that will help facilitate the study of film and politics.

Getting Started

We should keep in mind that we live in a media-saturated society. We hope that seeing and discussing these films, programs, and other elements of pop culture will give us a starting point to discuss topics and themes that are important to a participatory society. However, we should always remember that the mere projection of a particular subject, fact, or collection of data that makes it onto the movie or television screen does not mean it is an exact presentation of truth or history. As Oliver Stone's provocative and controversial presidency-centered films, such as *JFK* (1991), *Nixon* (1995), and *W* (2008), illustrate, there is a great tendency to partially fictionalize political stories and situations in order to heighten drama and pose tough, transcendent questions about politics and history. At first glance this appears to be a huge problem; after all, it takes some background knowledge to differentiate between historical fact and artistic license. There is a significant danger in asserting, for example, that the czar and his family were really good people and misunderstood during the Russian Revolution, like in Twentieth Century-Fox's *Anastasia* (1997). Without understanding the actual context of history, the real reasons for the revolution are completely missed. This is why the book attempts to establish a context for understanding films and suggests additional readings in the endnotes, to help viewers gain essential background and context. In a media-saturated society, being able to distinguish between fact and fiction in the media is a skill critical to media literacy and critical thinking.

The popcorn and politics are ready for us to consume. Without further adieu, let's start the show . . . but without losing sight of the *bigger picture*—the political concepts, debates, and challenges that shape our world and warrant our attention.

For links to films, clips, and more information, go to www. seeingthebiggerpicture.net.

Notes

1. Michael Hastings, "The Runaway General," *Rolling Stone*, 1108–1109 July 8–22, 2010: http://www.rollingstone.com/politics/news/17390/119236?RS_show_page=1.
2. Marc Ambinder, "McChrystal's 'Team America,'" *The Atlantic*, July 15, 2010: http://www.theatlantic.com/politics/archive/10/07/mcchrystals-team-america/59841. According to multiple responses to Ambinder's original posting, the patches were readily available to all and were not specially made for McChrystal's team. And indeed it was revelations in *Rolling Stone*, a popular culture magazine with significant roots in the San Francisco coun-

terculture of the late 1960s, that ultimately led to President Barack Obama relieving Gen. McChrystal of his duties in Afghanistan, reasserting the principle of civilian control over the military, and nominating General David Petraeus, then the head of the U.S. Central Command, to replace McChrystal.

3. Chrystia Freeland, global editor at large for Reuters, interviewed by *Newsweek* editor and *Need to Know* co-host John Meacham. Transcript of PBS's *Need to Know*, July 9, 2010: http://www.pbs.org/wnet/need-to-know/uncategorized/need-to-know-transcript-july-9-2010/2473/.

4. For Afghanistan, McChrystal, and *Dr. Strangelove*, see Tony Norman, "Learn to Stop Worrying and Love the War," *Pittsburgh Post-Gazette*, June 29, 2010: http://www.post-gazette.com/pg/10180/1068909–153.stm.

5. The environmental impact of gas drilling in the Marcellus Shale, misleading or fooling people in terms of public health concerns, and the salience of the 2010 documentary *Gasland* are discussed in Tony Norman, "We're Becoming Victims of a Shale Game," *Pittsburgh Post-Gazette*, July 10, 2010: http://www.post-gazette.com/pg/10190/1071417–153.stm?cmpid= bcpanel1.

6. Former New York City public advocate Mark Green appeared on MSNBC's *Hardball with Chris Matthews* to debate extending unemployment benefits with Mark Sherk of the Heritage Foundation, a conservative think tank. See transcript of *Hardball with Chris Matthews*, July 12, 2010: http://www.msnbc.msn.com/id/38222246/.

7. See the filmography provided in chapter 12; there are many websites to help locate films sources, including http://www.imdb.com and this book's webpage, http://www.seeing thebiggerpicture.net.

8. Ernest Giglio, *Here's Looking at You*, 3rd ed. (New York: Peter Lang, 2010); Michael Genovese, *Politics and the Cinema* (Lexington, MA: Ginn Press, 1986). Giglio discusses at length in his text Dr. Genovese's groundbreaking efforts at defining political film, and then offers an alternative definition that includes studying the film's *intent* and *effect* to determine whether or not it is truly political. At the same time, Giglio advises that, despite all of the noble and systematic efforts to define political film, any one precise definition may be too elusive and doomed to failure. As Giglio suggests, "In the final analysis . . . the political character of a film may lie in the eye of the beholder rather than any textbook definition" (Giglio, 35–36). See also Ernest Giglio, *Here's Looking at You*, 3rd ed. (New York: Peter Lang, 2010).

9. Genovese's political taxonomy cited in Giglio, *Here's Looking at You* (2000), 23.

10. For a more complete definition and analysis of propaganda, see Bruce L. Smith, "Propaganda," in *The International Encyclopedia of the Social Sciences* (New York: Macmillan, 1968). For further reading consult Jacques Ellul, *Propaganda: The Formation of Men's Attitudes* (New York: Knopf, 1965); and Garth S. Jowett and Victoria O'Donnell, *Propaganda and Persuasion*, 3rd ed. (Thousand Oaks, CA: Sage, 1999).

11. For an in-depth view of German propaganda, see Randall Bytwerk's collection of Nazi and East German propaganda: http://www.calvin.edu/academic/cas/gpa/.

12. One scene that is unsettling is near the beginning of the film where the Macedonian paramilitaries use a cat for target practice with their automatic weapons.

13. Francis Fukuyama, *The End of History and the Last Man* (New York: Free Press, 1992). Fukuyama argues that a liberal ideology is the final form of human government and that

its last two significant universal challenges were fascism and communism in the twentieth century.

CHAPTER 2

LIBERAL IDEOLOGIES

Democracy and Capitalism

Introduction

One of the early scenes of the classic comedy *Monty Python and the Holy Grail* (1975) finds King Arthur searching the length and breadth of Britain for knights who are willing to join him at his court in Camelot. Set in AD 932, the film is a parody of the tales of the knights of the Roundtable, using modern references and outrageous situations to poke fun at the tales that are so often told with such reverence. As Arthur approaches one castle he asks a peasant who lives in the castle. He is told that no one does. The peasant, Dennis, goes on to tell the king that they have no lord, but instead live in a communal cooperative based on democratic socialist ideas. Another peasant, an old woman, asks who Arthur is. He tells her that he is King of the Britons. She remarks that she had never voted for any king. Arthur replies that kings are not elected; that he was chosen king when the Lady of the Lake held aloft Excalibur, signifying by divine providence that he was to be king. Dennis argues that strange ladies hanging around in ponds, distributing swords, is no way to form a government. Instead, Dennis says, supreme authority comes from a mandate from the masses.

Traditionally what we in the modern era think of as democracy stems from a rational philosophy of good governance and a liberal philosophy about the rights of humans. Rational thinking in bringing order to a chaotic world depends on accessing the wants and needs of the governed. At the same time, liberal writers insist that individuals have an inalienable right to participate in matters that affect them. Since each person is deemed capable and rational, each should have some say about the rules affecting their lives.

Throughout North America, many people typically think of the development of liberal democracy as a particularly American phenomenon. However, democratic thought and practices developed in several parts of the world, each taking on nuances relevant to local situations. The most recognizable examples of the development of democracy outside North America are clearly France and Britain. The eighteenth century saw the rise of rational and liberal thought among the French elite, culminating in the French Revolution in 1789. In Britain, the progression of parliamentary sovereignty, and in particular the dominance of the House of Commons—the body that represents the general population—signaled the dominance of participatory government. As inquisitive citizens and students of politics, we should be mindful of other democratic experiences as well. Iceland, for example, has had a parliament, the *Althing*, that has met for well over a thousand years.

In the twentieth century, many scholars began to assume that liberal politics (*democracy; self-government*) matched or even fostered liberal economics (*capitalism*).[1] Others suggested that the opposite was true, that capitalism fostered democracy. Certainly by the end of the century there appeared to be a high correlation between the two. But scholars remain divided on the exact nature of the relationship between capitalism and democracy. On the one hand, some intellectuals and academics have argued that capitalism, which has a tendency to accumulate wealth in the hands of a few, has a propensity to undermine democratic societies because those with more money have a disproportionate amount of political power. On the other hand, Milton Friedman, economic advisor to the Reagan administration and libertarian/conservative icon, has argued that democracy corrupts capitalism by allowing people to elect politicians who might interfere with the market. Friedman argues that politicians will be tempted to intervene in the market in order to satisfy the desires of the electorate, and thus, stay in power.[2]

The relationship between democracy and capitalism is an intriguing problem for scholars and policy makers. Evidence suggests that the relationship is complicated and varies depending upon many factors. Certainly there is no logical reason why one could not exist without the other. Regardless of the relationship, both capitalism and democracy point to a theoretical tradition that emphasizes the role of the individual.

In this chapter, we will explore how democracy (i.e., mass participation and majority rule) and capitalism (i.e., the free market economy) have been portrayed on film, with special attention to some of the central questions, themes, and concerns revealed in each slice of popular culture. While the chapter considers films that are supportive of democracy and capitalism and films that are critical of each, it should be noted that the political positions of some of the films are rather ambiguous, and, moreover, as with myriad movies considered in this text, the most salient or precise political messages may be either implicit, or woven into broader story lines or subtexts. As you read about the diverse films we include in this chapter, consider the significant political messages they convey. *What do you believe are the most enduring attributes of democracy and capitalism, and which concerns and criticisms of the liberal economic and political order present the greatest immediate and long-term challenges to the human condition? Do you agree or disagree with their perspectives? Do they reinforce or challenge your political beliefs and values?* Then consider what other messages about democracy and capitalism, admittedly often implicit or ambiguous, are present in films, television programs, or other aspects of popular culture you may be familiar with, but are not considered in this chapter.

Democracy

The Films of Frank Capra

Over the course of his career, Frank Capra (1891–1962) made a number of films that praised the democratic impulses and institutions of his adopted country, even as he used his artistic vision to criticize the excesses, imperfections, and corruption that occasionally threatened its future. Born in Sicily, Capra embraced the individual freedom and participatory processes present in the United States, and, in several films, used a stock character—the everyman— to promote democracy and fight for the good of the masses. Capra's "everyman" protagonists—whether named Jefferson Smith (a boyish U.S. senator in *Mr. Smith Goes to Washington*), George Bailey (a small-town, populist savings and loan operator in *It's a Wonderful Life*), or even Grant Matthews (an independent-minded industrialist and presidential candidate in *State of the Union*)—were idealistic and honest, often to a fault, and used politics, or at a minimum their livelihood, to battle entrenched, selfish interests. In Capra's films, which were frequently sentimental and patriotic, these antagonists were media moguls, conniving businessmen, greedy financiers, or wayward politicians. The everyman that battled these frequently undemocratic and always corrosive forces, even if naïve or without wealth, worked feverishly to defeat the manipulation of the masses and make life better for everyday Americans. In short, in most of Capra's body of overtly and implicitly political films, activism, idealism, political participation, and trust in the common sense of the American people were the weapons wielded to slay the corrupt giants.[3]

Mr. Smith Goes to Washington

Clearly Frank Capra and Twentieth Century-Fox understood the message they were trying to convey in the classic political drama Mr. Smith Goes to Washington (1939). The trailer to the film used the famous radio commentator H. V. Kaltenborn to promote the film. Mr. Kaltenborn proclaimed Mr. Smith a significant film because it emphasized "democracy in action." The film follows the journey and political awakening of wide-eyed idealist Jefferson Smith (James Stewart), a midwestern everyman and hero of the "Boy Rangers" appointed to fill a vacancy in the U.S. Senate. Smith, a popular patriot who can recite Lincoln and Jefferson by heart, arrives in the nation's capital starry-eyed and in awe of Washington's sacred monuments. However, a cynical, hard-drinking journalist and Jim Taylor's vile, graft-hungry political machine quickly shake the spirit of the fledgling senator. The media has fun smearing Smith as a lightweight cornball, and it doesn't take long before the jaded politicos stop the junior senator's initiatives. When Smith proposes legislation to build a national Boy Rangers camp in his home state, the Taylor machine, along with their chief political crony—the once-noble public servant Senator Paine (Claude Rains)—use their power and persuasion to try and kill the legislation. The new Boy Rangers camp would be built on Willet Creek, an exploitable location where a pending dam project engineered by the corrupt Taylor (Edward Arnold) and Paine would bring huge profits to Taylor and his minions. When the Taylor machine fails to dissuade Smith from pursuing his Boy Rangers camp, they manufacture allegations to ruin his reputation and, later, manipulate the media to brand the idealistic senator an enemy of the common man who delays anti-poverty legislation and profits from the pennies, nickels, and dimes sent in by the masses to fund Smith's proposed camp.

Distressed and depressed, Smith returns to the hallowed ground of the Lincoln Monument for solace and inspiration. He is reborn and revitalized after a meeting with Abe, and returns to the Senate to fight the corrupt Taylor machine. With the support of his assistant, Saunders (Jean Arthur), Smith embarks on his Herculean task: to expose the corruption of the political machine and keep the powers that be from taking action to expel him from the Senate. In the famous climax of the film, an exhausted-yet-determined Smith uses the *filibuster*—the process of "talking a bill to death"—to maintain the Senate floor and keep the nasty Taylor machine at bay. Capra, through radio commentator Kaltenborn, uses the occasion of Smith's filibuster to praise U.S. political institutions, criticize undemocratic regimes, and promote the idea of "democracy in action":

> This is H. V. Kaltenborn speaking. Half of official Washington is here to see democracy's finest show, the filibuster: the right to talk your head off; the American privilege of free speech in its most dramatic form. The last man in that chamber—once he gets and holds that floor, by the rules—can hold it and talk as long as he can stand on his feet, providing always, first, that he does not sit down; second, that he does not leave the chamber or stop talking. The galleries are packed. In the diplomatic gallery are the envoys of two dictator powers. They have come here to see what they can't see at home: democracy in action.[4]

It is the most famous filibuster in Hollywood history, and Smith's honesty, tenacity, and use of U.S. political institutions ultimately rule the day, as Senator Paine cracks under the weight of guilt and corruption. It is perhaps more than a tad ironic that the filibuster—a fundamentally anti-majoritarian process of "talking a bill to death"—is used to celebrate the American experiment in representative government. The filibuster has been used, for example, to thwart federal civil rights legislation—and other substantive policies—for decades. Thus, in practice, it is not necessarily the friend of the "little guy" or the majority. And its use in recent legislative sessions has actually *increased*. Indeed, as congressional scholar Norman Ornstein of the American Enterprise Institute noted during the second year of the Barack Obama presidency, "The filibuster, once rare, is now so common that it has inverted majority rule, allowing the minority party to block, or at least delay, whatever legislation it wants to oppose."[5] Yet, in accordance with long-standing Senate rules, the only way to stop a senator from holding the floor indefinitely is to invoke cloture. To do this is no small task: senators must first submit a petition—which requires the signature of at least sixteen members—for a cloture vote. Then, at least sixty senators must vote for cloture, and thus, end debate.

The vital and ever-germane debate over the democratic nature of the filibuster aside, *Mr. Smith* stands as an explicit example of promoting political participation in representative government and celebrating democracy. The monuments and participatory political institutions housed in Washington, D.C., are revered. And, in the end, the ruthless Taylor machine is defeated neither by bullets nor a *coup d'état*, but by embracing the opportunity to speak one's mind, without fear of repression, in the sacred chambers of American representative government.[6]

Revisiting Mr. Smith: The Satire of The Simpsons

The 1991 *Simpsons* episode "Mr. Lisa Goes to Washington" is an example of a humorous retelling of the heroic, romantic *Mr. Smith* story. In doing so, Matt Groening's landmark long-running animated series offers its trademark subversion and biting sociopolitical commentary. It both embraces *and* lampoons the romantic patriotism of the 1939 Capra classic. In this installment of the series, Lisa Simpson, second grader—and resident over-achieving intellectual and environmentalist in the Simpson clan—writes a patriotic essay for a contest advertised in the journal *Reading Digest* (needless to say, a delightful spoof of the once-iconic publication *Reader's Digest*). Lisa ultimately wins the local Springfield competition of the "fiercely patriotic" essay contest and earns an all-expenses-paid trip to Washington, D.C. for herself and her family. There, she will compete with other young Americans for the national essay contest championship.[7] During the essay competition sequence, we hear flashes of several speeches, and most of the essay excerpts poke fun at the "fiercely patriotic" genre of such contests. In one infamous contest speech, notorious Springfield Elementary bully Nelson Muntz offers this zealous stream of jingoism:

> So burn the flag if you must, but before you do, you better burn a few other things! You better burn your shirt and your pants! Be sure to burn your TV and car! Oh, yes, and don't forget to burn your house because none of these things could exist without six white stripes, seven red stripes, and a hell of a lot of stars![8]

During the Simpsons' time in the nation's capital, there is both a playful fondness for and updating and lampooning of Jefferson Smith's unwavering reverence for the nation's monuments and government buildings. There is also heavy criticism of the American populace, which, not unlike other *Simpsons* episodes, is often portrayed as disinterested, lethargic and politically unsophisticated.[9] Times have clearly changed. Here the sheer awe and idealism present in *Mr. Smith* have turned to angst, contempt, and some sly (if very brief) sexual imagery: Homer loudly boos the IRS building (the stuffy IRS bureaucrat opens the window and retorts, "Oh, boo yourself"); Marge giggles at the Washington Monument, finding it to be quite phallic in nature; and the Simpsons stay at the Watergate, the hotel/condominium complex which serves as the enduring symbol of political corruption that brought down the Nixon presidency. The American voter is also portrayed as apathetic, if not downright pathetic. When the Simpsons get a special VIP tour of the White House (Homer asks the tour guide what VIP stands for), the family does not find activism or vigorous dissent alongside Pennsylvania Avenue. Instead, as the Simpsons enter the White House, we see several lollygagging, lethargic "protesters" sitting on the curb—or lazily walking and whistling along—with signs that read, *"Things Are Fine," "No Complaints Here,"* and *"No Opinion."*[10]

And in the most direct send-up of Mr. *Smith*'s veneration of political institutions and leaders, Lisa visits the Lincoln Monument to seek inspiration and solace after witnessing her congressman, Rep. Bob Arnold, take a bribe. But instead of being able to conduct a solemn conversation with the sixteenth president, Lisa finds every manner of citizen crowded at the monument, hurling petty, picayune questions at Honest Abe. Her serious concerns cannot be heard over the cacophony of selfish, petty Americans, who treat the hallowed grounds as a crude self-help line. Lisa then takes her shattered faith in American democracy to the Jefferson Memorial, seeking advice and inspiration. When she arrives and tells Thomas Jefferson that she has a problem, the Jefferson statue replies, "I know, the Lincoln Monument was too crowded!"

Lisa's witnessing of raw corruption in Congress forces her to rip up her old, fiercely patriotic essay and craft a new speech to reflect her disgust with Rep. Arnold's bribery. Her new entry is called "Cesspool on the Potomac." (According to her father, Homer, this essay was not as "crowd-pleasin'" as her first *Reading Digest*–winning essay.) In her vastly revamped speech, Lisa offers this brutal assessment of the state of the Union:

> The city of Washington was built on a swamp some 200 years ago and very little has changed; it stank then and it stinks now. Only today it is the fetid stench of corruption that hangs in the air.[11]

In the end, however, Rep. Arnold is arrested in a sting operation, and young Lisa Simpson's faith is apparently restored—at least for the time being. As such, the Simpsons poke good-natured fun at the more sentimental and simplistic aspects of Capra's Mr. *Smith*.

State of the Union

Frank Capra returned to the theme of noble public servant in 1948's *State of the Union*. This time, however, the honest "everyman" does come from the same humble beginnings as patriot Jefferson Smith. Here, Grant Matthews (Spencer Tracy) is a wealthy industrialist and political outsider who seeks the presidency in order to battle corruption and work like the dickens for the majority, not the special interests. His democratic crusade is seriously compromised, however, by his chief campaign sponsor, the cold, calculating, and fabulously wealthy newspaper magnate Kay Thorndyke (Angela Lansbury), with whom he has had an affair. This is never explicitly stated, but there is ample innuendo throughout to suggest that this is the case. This reality makes this Capra protagonist more flawed than previous incarnations of the honest everyman or outsider, à la Jefferson Smith, or George Bailey from *It's a Wonderful Life* (1946).

As the ebullient Matthews loses his way, becoming more and more controlled by the advisers and image makers provided by Thorndyke to manipulate the public, and caving in to the narrow special interests in order to win their support at the nominating convention, he begins to misplace his moral and political compass as well as faith in himself. The conclusion of the film is a paid radio program, broadcast live from Matthews's home. It is a carefully orchestrated, slick production and is meant to show family unity in the face of rumors concerning Thorndyke and Matthews. Grant's wife, the dutiful Mary (Katharine Hepburn), is painfully forced to grin and bear the phony arrangement, tolerating the presence of the scheming Thorndike in her own home. Witnessing the pain and anguish of his wife, Matthews regains his sense of crusading, democratic spirit, throws off the shackles of the image makers and politicos, and blows the whistle on this absurd and staged media circus masquerading as authentic political event:

> I had the right idea when I started to talk to you people of America. The idea that you voters, you farmers, you businessmen, you working men, you ordinary citizens of whatever party, are not the selfish ones that venal politicians make you out to be. I thought I could speak my piece straight-out and forward. I thought I could tell you that this country of ours is young, it's not old, that we've just begun to grow. That all we need is courage, and from out of that courage could come a greatness greater than we ever dreamed. I wanted to tell you that we Americans are the hope of the world, and the secret of our great plenty is freedom, and we've got to share that secret and all that plenty with the other nations of the world.

> I withdraw as a candidate for any office, not because I'm honest, but because I'm dishonest. I want to apologize to all the good, sincere people who put their faith in me and I want to apologize to my wife.[12]

Matthews's final speech presents several recurring Capra themes: the transcendence, if occasional imperfection, of America's political process and gov-

erning institutions; the unvarnished power of individual liberties, such as freedom of expression, in a democratic system; and, perhaps most of all, a belief in
the wisdom and governing ability of everyday American people. Self-
government is sacrosanct, even during challenging times. And, as in H. V.
Kaltenborn's criticism of "dictator powers" in the filibuster scene in Mr. Smith,
in Matthews's climactic soapbox address and confessional we see a direct attack
on communism and fascism—two ideologies in competition with liberalism.[13]

Why We Fight

Such faith in people, democracy, and a diverse pluralistic society (though note
Matthews's belief that there should not be Machiavellian *exploitation* of racial,
ethnic, or class divisions) is also exemplified in Capra's famous Why We Fight
films. Why We Fight, a seven-part series of so-called information films, was produced from 1943 to 1945 and sponsored by the federal government. The
movies were explicitly used as a recruitment and propaganda tool during World
War II. The seven films in the Why We Fight series[14] discuss the necessity of U.S.
involvement in the war, and, to varying degrees, celebrate the "melting pot"
theory of the United States. This perspective, present in several of the films,
suggests that whether you are a farmer, immigrant factory laborer, rich or poor,
black or white, Catholic or Protestant, cosmopolitan East Coaster or rural resident, you could—and *must*—unite and work together to win the war. And,
moreover, it is the belief in the superior form of self-government that separates
the American experience from other political systems. Capra's series suggests
that, in theory and practice, *all citizens* can and do participate in the system of
representative government, and as such pluralism is an attribute of, not a hin-
drance to, the American way of life.

Capra's Why We Fight films were a seminal tool used by the U.S. government to maintain unity, promote the war effort, celebrate our social and political fabric, and support the notion that the liberal ideologies of political
participation (democracy) and economics (capitalism) were superior to communism, fascism, or any other system of government. How better to achieve this
mission than to bring notable Hollywood directors on board to use the most
popular art and entertainment form to make their case? This direct
Hollywood–Washington political connection also included the likes of the singular icon of American animation, Walt Disney, who used federal largesse to
keep his studio afloat in the 1940s. During World War II, Disney—"despite a
passionate opposition to socialism and to any government meddling in free
enterprise"—used money from the federal government to produce a plethora

of propaganda and military training films.[15] In this short period of time, government contracts for these pro-American films constituted 90 percent of
Disney's studio's output. Disney's propaganda and military training films included such titles as *Food Will Win the War*, *High-Level Precision Bombing*, and a *Few
Quick Facts About Venereal Disease*.[16]

Looking back at the romantic, often idealistic films of Frank Capra, rife with
witty repartee and selfless, big-hearted citizens ready to do the right thing for
the nation, one might ponder how far modern films are from the unabashedly
pro-democratic sentiments espoused by the native Sicilian. While *Mr. Smith*
glorifies and sanctifies the symbols of U.S. government and mass participation—
such as the Washington Monument, Lincoln Memorial, and White House—
some modern films have offered rather lukewarm or ambivalent messages about
such things. Some have taken a more ominous or confrontational tone, and at
least anecdotally, Americans have responded favorably to negative perceptions
of democratic and political symbols. The summer sci-fi action smash
Independence Day (1996), for example, features a scene where alien intruders
blow up the White House. As was widely reported in the American press at the
time, some thrilled audiences cheered at the sight of the "People's House"
being smashed to smithereens. The sci-fi blockbuster is but one example of how
a slew of Hollywood's films have treated monuments, symbols, and Washington
itself since the 1970s, but it is perhaps a prescient one. For better or worse,
Capra they are not.[17]

The West Wing: "Decisions Are Made by Those Who Show Up"

An Updated, Sophisticated Capra for the Clinton and Bush Years

Like a modern day Frank Capra, Aaron Sorkin's popular and critically praised
political drama, *The West Wing* (1999–2006, NBC)—a program with unprece-
dented real-world connections to the American presidency—presented the
viewing public with plotlines that routinely celebrated diversity, pluralism,
enlightened citizenship, and the finest (if quite imperfect) aspects of democratic governance.[18] Throughout its seven seasons, the show promoted the para-
mount importance of direct political participation, and frequently did so in an
explicit manner. Consider this rallying cry for political engagement from White
House press secretary C. J. Craig (Allison Janney) at a jam-packed "Rock the
Vote" rally in Cambridge, Massachusetts:

Twenty-five years ago, half of all eighteen to twenty-four year olds voted. Today it's 25 percent. Eighteen to twenty-four-year-olds represent 33 percent of the population but only account for 7 percent of the voters. Think government isn't about you? How many of you have student loans to pay? How many of you have credit card debt? How many want clean air and clean water and civil liberties? How many want jobs? How many want kids? How many want kids to go to good schools and walk on safe streets? Decisions are made by those who show up. You gotta rock the vote![19]

Sandwiched in between sets by musical acts Aimee Mann and the Barenaked Ladies (it *was* a Rock the Vote benefit concert, after all), Craig's message from the fourth-season episode "College Kids" (2002) is a paean to participatory democracy and reflects one of the show's persistent themes: if *you* do not roll up your sleeves and play the noble and necessary game of politics, politicians and public policy will leave you behind. Vigilant civic engagement is mandatory for a functioning republic. Rock the vote, indeed.

The Noble, Democratic Everyman Returns: "Mr. Willis of Ohio" and "The Short List"

In the episode "Mr. Willis of Ohio" from the show's inaugural season (1999), the Wednesday night drama, channeling Capra, celebrates the profound impact and positive difference one person can make within the democratic institutions of government. Here the Capra archetype, the everyman, is "Mr. Willis"—an African American social studies teacher from Ohio who has replaced his late wife, Janice Willis, in the House of Representatives. Shortly after taking office, the plain-spoken midwestern educator and newest member of the House of Representatives is one of three swing votes on the Commerce Committee who can help, or prevent, the Bartlet administration from getting a sampling provision for the census approved and, in the process, pass the latest appropriations bill. Initially, Willis is not sold on the Bartlet administration's rationale behind census sampling. He believes it may be too slanted by partisan considerations. In the end, however, after extensive negotiations with White House communications director Toby Ziegler (Richard Schiff) and personal reflection, the Ohio teacher sides with the president and votes for the appropriations bill. Rep. Willis's decisive vote in the Commerce Committee, and his very ascension to the position of congressman, simultaneously celebrate two potential attributes of participatory democracy. First, the notion of inclusion in a pluralistic system—that teachers and minorities can serve in the highest levels of governance—is promoted. Second, Rep. Willis uses his power not for personal gain or petty politics but for public service in the grandest sense: putting country and what is right above all tactical, political considerations. He votes for the bill because he believes it is best for the country. His decision to follow conscience and the public good over crass, partisan politics is reflected in the following exchange between Toby Ziegler and Rep. Willis:

> TOBY: I was wondering, what changed your mind?
> MR. WILLIS: You did. I thought you made a very strong argument.
> TOBY: Thank you. . . . I'm smiling because . . . well, around here the merits of a particular argument generally take a backseat to political tactics.[20]

This simple, kindhearted teacher, much like the benevolent everyman Jefferson Smith from years past, represents the machinery of representative government being used by everyday Americans for the noblest purposes.

Also from the first season, "The Short List" celebrates the ability of regular folks—in this case, minority citizens, who, historically, have had the socio-economic deck stacked against them—to rise to greatness and serve the public in a democratic system. This hour in the life of a fictional television presidency follows President Bartlet's (Martin Sheen) attempts to nominate a new Supreme Court justice. Initially, the president and his advisers zero in on Peyton Cabot Harrison II (Ken Howard), who is seen as a safe, moderate, credentialed, and confirmable—if rather uninspiring—choice for the highest bench in the land. But it soon becomes apparent that the rich, stuffy elitist judge does not share the administration's view on a constitutional right to privacy. In fact, he doesn't believe that such a fundamental right exists. Rather than take the safe road with the wealthy, white Harrison—"of Phillips Exeter and Princeton, a Rhodes Scholar, editor of the *Harvard Law Review* and dean of Harvard Law School"—Bartlet and his team decide to take a huge political risk by choosing a Hispanic from New York City, Justice Mendoza (Edward James Olmos), to serve as an associate justice of the U.S. Supreme Court.[21] Mendoza— a graduate of "P.S. 138 in Brooklyn, CUNY, and the New York Police Academy," who worked his way through law school by serving in the NYPD and as assistant DA—is a liberal judge far more in sync with Bartlet's views on privacy.[22] Mendoza, unlike Harrison, believes that mandatory drug tests would constitute an illegal search and, as such, would be unconstitutional. With the choice of Mendoza, we once again see *The West Wing* celebrate a system where people from humble beginnings have the chance to make a difference, where they can serve honorably in the most powerful political institutions in the world.

Current Events: Keeping the Masses Informed

Another aspect of *The West Wing* that smacks of unrepentant pro-democracy sentiment is its ongoing attempt to further public dialogue and debate on a wide array of contemporary public policies.[23] One of the chief tenets of *majoritarianism* is the belief that the masses, not just the elites, should be engaged and informed. Press Secretary C. J. Craig's comments at the Rock the Vote rally, cited at the outset of this section, clearly reflect this view. Moreover, in addition to the plotlines from its seven seasons of work, *The West Wing* used its nascent online presence to register voters ("rock the vote") and promote an engaged citizenry. Starting in the fall of 2002 with their two-hour season premiere, "20 Hours in America," NBC's official *West Wing* web page featured links to political issues raised in each episode of the new season. Those visiting the program's home page back in the fall of 2002, for example, came across this message: *"Find out more about each week's political, economic, social, and 'hot' topics. Click here for information and links to related online sites."*[24] A mere two episodes into the 2002–2003 season, "The West Wing Hot Topics" web page featured substantive links to web pages dealing with the economic, social, and political issues and institutions raised in the episodes "20 Hours in America" and "College Kids"—among them: Title IX (equality for women in collegiate athletics), NASDAQ, the Department of Labor, the New York Stock Exchange, Farm Aid, the U.S. Department of Agriculture, the Commission on Presidential Debates, and Rock the Vote.

But informative web sites aside, in the final analysis there was no more consistent place to receive the egalitarian message that one person can make a profound difference in the engines of democracy than the show itself. "Two Cathedrals" (2001), season 2's dramatic cliffhanger, imagines the recently deceased Mrs. Delores Landingham (Kathryn Joosten), the president's secretary, discussing the challenges faced by Bartlet and the nation. Because he was not forthright with the American people about his multiple sclerosis, the president's popularity has plummeted; a media feeding frenzy has descended on the White House, and his own party hints that they no longer want him as their standard bearer. Bartlet laments his situation and ponders his political future. Should he seek another term? Is he finished? What about the problems of the country? Can he still earn the trust of the American people, lead, and make a difference? After his conversation with Mrs. Landingham, the answer is clear:

BARTLET:	Give me the numbers.
MRS. LANDINGHAM:	I don't know the numbers, you give them to me.
BARTLET:	How 'bout a child born in this minute has a one in five chance of being born into poverty.
MRS. LANDINGHAM:	How many Americans don't have health insurance?
BARTLET:	44 million.
MRS. LANDINGHAM:	What's the number one cause of death for black men under 35?
BARTLET:	Homicide.
MRS. LANDINGHAM:	How many Americans are behind bars?
BARTLET:	3 million.
MRS. LANDINGHAM:	How many Americans are drug addicts?
BARTLET:	5 million.
MRS. LANDINGHAM:	And one in five kids live in poverty?
BARTLET:	It's 13 million American children. Three and a half million kids go to schools that are literally falling apart, we need 127 billion in school construction, and we need it today.
MRS. LANDINGHAM:	To say nothing of 53 people trapped in an embassy.
BARTLET:	Yes.
MRS. LANDINGHAM:	You know if you don't want to run again, I respect that. But if you don't run because you think it's gonna be too hard . . . or you think you're gonna lose . . . well, God, Jed, I don't even want to know you.[25]

As the series concluded its prime-time run in 2006, it was fitting that, given *The West Wing*'s embrace of American exceptionalism, pluralism, and the necessity and nobility of self-government, the newly elected president who succeeded Jed Bartlet was a Hispanic American. In the series' final episode, "Tomorrow" (2006), Rep. Matthew Santos (Jimmy Smits), a Texas congressman and military veteran, was sworn into office. The march toward progress in a democratic America where anything is possible—at least on television—was on full display. It was, as *Mr. Smith*'s radio correspondent H. V. Kaltenborn said, "democracy in action."

Capitalism: Liberal Economics

The United States emerged from the Second World War as a country unrivaled in its economic position in the international arena. Although roughly 400,000 Americans lost their lives in the cataclysmic conflict, these numbers were negligible compared to what other major combatants had lost. European and Asian countries had the war fought on their own terrain; Britain had received substantial bombing of its infrastructure during the war, and six or more years of war had worn down the other major powers. Secured by two oceans, sustained by stable political institutions, and fueled by an expansive free market economy anchored by a massive industrial base, the United States entered the postwar era with its infrastructure in place, a dominant military deployed, and preparing a world order for the postwar era. During the war, the United States had already taken steps to devise a postwar world in which key economic and political issues would be addressed.

During the war the United States caucused with its major allies to hammer out an economic plan for recovery and maintenance. One of the primary lessons learned from the prewar years was that a volatile economic environment led to political instability and war. In Germany, the fall of the democratic Weimar Republic was attributed to massive hyperinflation and severe economic depression. In Japan, the military was allowed to seize control of the government in an effort to modernize and develop the country to make it a major economic power. In both cases, the lessons learned were that the economic instability and lack of development in relative comparison to other powers led Germany and Japan to pursue a belligerent policy in order to achieve their goals. The Conference at Dumbarton Oaks in 1944 sought to establish institutions[26] that would help regulate the world economy and promote economic growth and development.

As the emerging economic giant of the postwar era, the United States and its film industry were only too ready to promote the capitalistic economic values espoused by American society. Generally, American political and corporate leaders sought to make the values of economic liberalism and free trade the primary driving force of international economic policy following the war. Time and time again during the war, films and popular culture touted the benefits of free markets and democracy. Films such as *Lifeboat* (1944) and *Mr. Smith Goes to Washington* (1939) latently and blatantly gave the audience an explanation as to why democracy and the workings of government are so important. Other films, such as *It's a Wonderful Life* (1946), celebrated the idea that working hard and being honest leads one to economic security (if not super-wealth) and happiness.

The primary tenents of economic liberalism are found in the writings of some eighteenth- and nineteenth-century economists, particularly David Ricardo and Adam Smith.[27] Both of these economists theorized that if states would allow markets to develop autonomously, without undue interference and with as few barriers as possible, they would maximize their own efficiencies.

Doing so would create more wealth, which in the end would benefit all. Hence, liberals base their analysis on three assumptions: first, individuals are the principal actors in the economy; second, individuals—who are able to conduct cost-benefit analyses and choose between competing economic options—are capable of making rational decisions; and third, individuals will ultimately make decisions that will maximize their benefits and minimize their costs.[28]

Hollywood was only too ready to help promote liberal economics, and educate the public about the benefits of free trade and capitalism. Using film shorts, which were commonly shown before feature films prior to the advent of television, major studios offered their interpretation of capitalism. In *Stuff for Stuff* (1949), the filmmakers argued that there was a need to rebuild the economic and political infrastructure of Europe following the Second World War in order to secure the prosperity of the entire world. *Stuff for Stuff* argues the logic behind this theory by reviewing economic history. In ancient Egypt, according to the film, people began to conquer the elements. With the invention of the plow, one person could begin to feed many people. With surplus commodities, people were free to engage in other types of commerce. Trade allowed for the development of wealth. The film traces the development of trade and prosperity through the Greeks, Spanish, Portuguese, and English.

The film portrays history very specifically, for example, when, in 1914, the Germans made a bid for world domination and countries began to become aware of how interdependent they were as each was drawn into the First World War. After World War I, the United States replaced Britain as the leading economic power. During the Great Depression, the cessation of two-way trade took its toll on the economic prosperity of the world. By not trading with one another, orders between countries were canceled. By canceling orders jobs were lost, and out-of-work citizens meant that a pool of people was susceptible to radical ideologies. *Stuff for Stuff* calls on the people of the world to accept the ideology of free markets, as "Civilization will be destroyed . . . unless undeveloped areas are developed . . . unless destroyed areas are rebuilt . . . and developed areas are allowed to engage in two-way trade."

Another form of the short subject is the ever-popular cartoon. *When My Ship Comes In* (1934) is a Betty Boop cartoon set during the Great Depression of the 1930s. In the cartoon Betty fantasizes about what she could do to help people during the economic tough times. With a snappy little song of the same title, Betty daydreams that she wins a million dollars. Rather than saving the money for herself, she elects to spend all of it on materials. By purchasing items she stimulates the economy. Each item she buys requires people to make it, and people to sell it. When she buys the goods, the merchant and the manufacturer make money, which they in turn use to purchase items, which helps out other merchants and manufacturers. Betty's purchases create wealth far and wide. At the end of the cartoon Betty imagines the map of the United States as a machine—as more money is fed into it, the more the machine revs up, and soon it runs at full steam.

A slightly different embracing of the merits of consumption in revving the engines of capitalism is expressed in the final installment of Capra's seven-part series of propagandistic informational films, *Why We Fight*. In *War Comes to America* (1945), Capra reminds Americans not only about the transcendence of our sacred secular documents, shared values, melting pot of immigration, and superior political system, but how our unrivaled wealth and possession of sought-after material goods buttress our strength as a country. For example, American prowess in terms of car and radio ownership (among other contemporary goods of great status) is explicitly cited as evidence of the superiority of our system of economic liberty. In short: capitalism creates comfort, fosters entertainment, and makes life better.

In the mid-1950s the famed cartoon director Friz Freleng directed a trilogy of cartoons that were designed to be lessons on economics and capitalism. Freleng was the head of the Warner Brothers cartoon department from 1933 to 1963, when the department was closed down. A longtime friend of the more famous animator Walt Disney, the two had worked together in Kansas City, and Freleng briefly worked for Disney when he first arrived in Hollywood. Although overshadowed in name recognition, Freleng would direct and/or animate over 260 cartoons for Warner Brothers, produce the Pink Panther television series in the 1960s, and win several Academy Awards.

In 1954 Freleng directed *By Word of Mouse*, which had an American mouse lecturing his European counterparts on the fundamentals of American economics. The next year, Freleng directed *Heir Conditioned* (1955), which stars Sylvester the Cat and Elmer Fudd. Sylvester is the beneficiary of an inheritance, and Elmer is the financial advisor who explains the benefits of investing rather than spending the inheritance. Elmer convinces Sylvester that by investing his money he can increase his standard of living. To close out the trilogy, Freleng directed *Yankee Dood It* (1956), which is a film about the methods of capitalism.

While most of us assume that cartoons are purely entertainment, there has been a long history of education and propaganda as well. Warner Brothers cartoons are especially known for their biting satire and social commentary. A casual glance at a program of Warner Brothers cartoons (such as Bugs Bunny, Daffy

Duck, Foghorn Leghorn, Sylvester and Tweedy, etc.) reveals references to popular culture and a critique of American life in the 1930s, 1940s, and 1950s.
Warner Brothers cartoons would use catch phrases from radio programs like the
Fibber McGee and Molly Show (1935–1959) and television programs such as *This
Is Your Life* (1952–1961). The social commentary of the studio was particularly vociferous during the war. And during the Great Depression, several cartoons
addressed the issue of poverty.[29] Given the time period of their popularity,
roughly 1935–1960, the cartoons were instrumental in advocating free market
economics to the American moviegoing public.

Raising Concerns about Democracy

It is a well-worn commentary that the framers of the U.S. Constitution were
wary of an unrestrained public, a tyranny of the masses, running the affairs of
state. The Constitution, in its original form, established some institutions,
such as the Senate and the presidency, as being indirectly elected, or in the case
of the Senate, selected, to assuage these fears. It was not until 1913 that the
Senate was directly elected. Concerns about the full participation of the electorate can be demonstrated in the films of the silent period. The question of
women's suffrage was addressed in films such as *When the Men Left Town*
(1914).[30] Seen from today's perspective, these films might seem silly and inef-
fectual. But the concept of women gaining the vote, kicking the men out of
town, and then society falling apart, as the plot of *When the Men Left Town* suggests, was a serious comment on the state of full suffrage in the early part of the
twentieth century.[31]

Much more recently, HBO's ambitious Prohibition-era drama set in
Atlantic City, *Boardwalk Empire*, which premiered with great fanfare and critical praise in 2010, further reflects the fears, prejudices, and culture of the male-
dominated power structure of this period. Through their snide remarks, boorish
behavior, and everyday actions, many of the male titans of politics, business,
and bootlegging (often one and the same) share deep-seated concerns about the
soundness of allowing women to vote, believing that their intellectual and emotional temperament is suspect, thus extending the notion that suffrage was at
a minimum foolish, and potentially, quite dangerous.[32]

Likewise, a similar scenario, painted in less comedic terms than *When the
Men Left Town* and with significantly less sex and violence than cable television's *Boardwalk Empire*, was presented to the country in *Birth of a Nation*
(1915). Directed by the famous and important director D. W. Griffith, *Birth of*

a Nation was the first large-scale American blockbuster and took filmmaking to new heights. There is no doubt as to the importance of *Birth of a Nation* in film history; however its message is certainly more controversial than those dealing with the suffrage of women. In Griffith's film, it is implicitly and explicitly argued that democracy should not have been expanded to include voting rights for black Americans. The newly freed slaves are portrayed as wholly incapable of an educated vote, as the film portrays them as ignorant, slovenly, lazy, and unable to understand their own, let alone the nation's, best interests.

The story takes place before, during, and after the American Civil War, and focuses on two families, the Stoneman family from the North, and the Cameron family from the South. In the film, during the Reconstruction following the war, all males of the Southern society, including the African Americans, are enfranchised to vote. In what is purported to be a historical reenactment of the events, African Americans take control of the Senate in South Carolina. The film focuses on some fairly shocking stereotypes of how African American politicians behave in the Senate. Politicians, with no shoes on, are seen with their feet propped up on their desk; several senators are eating fried chicken in the chambers; and others resort to drink before engaging in important votes. Griffith's message is unmistakable: there are some segments of society—in this case, African Americans—that are clearly not ready or able to be entrusted with the power of voting or legislating. Instead of suggesting that all people are cognizant of their best interests, and then able to exercise their rights in a free society, Griffith is arguing that the freed slaves are not capable of that knowledge. Thus, expanding democracy—and placing the decisions of state in the hands of the unsophisticated or intellectually deficient—leads to undesirable consequences.

Likewise, Gregory La Cava's *Gabriel over the White House* (1933)—produced by none other than the persistently political newspaper magnate William Randolph Hearst (the primary target of Orson Welles's 1941 classic, *Citizen Kane*) and distributed by conservative Louis B. Mayer's studio MGM[33]—provides moviegoers with another cautionary critique of democracy. In *Gabriel*, the message is clear: democracy and a separated system of checks and balances are ineffective and impractical in times of economic crisis and national emergency.[34] Presidential candidate Judson C. "Judd"/"Major" Hammond (Walter Huston) is an opportunistic playboy, telling the masses whatever it takes to get elected. Once in office, he takes a hands-off, laissez-faire approach to a deepening depression and has no intention of addressing unemployment and racketeering by implementing massive government programs. But things change:

while driving recklessly, President Hammond is in a near-fatal car crash and descends into a coma. Unbeknownst to the public, he is visited and resuscitated by the angel Gabriel, who transforms a selfish, weak chief executive into an assertive, determined leader.

Blessed by this new spirit, the president dismisses his cabinet, institutes martial law, defies and overwhelms Congress at every turn, and demands that allies repay their World War I debts immediately (he brazenly threatens them with war if they do not settle up their debts). In addition, he tramples on civil liberties and decisively sends the full might of the U.S. military after mobsters and bootleggers, court-martials them and then sentences them to death, and in one of the more outlandish scenes in any political film, has the mobsters executed—gunned down just outside of the Statue of Liberty. The message here is unambiguous: public consent and the machinations of representative government may be alright when things are fine, but to fight bootleggers, keep our allies and enemies in line, and defeat depressions, we should empower a benevolent dictator to take the reins of power and act according to his own vision. Democratic institutions, civil liberties, and checks and balances are ineffective in the face of such dire threats.

We turn now to the year 2054, when the Justice Department's new "pre-cog" anti-crime program is wildly popular with the American people. This is the setting for the summer 2002 blockbuster *Minority Report*, a futuristic political thriller directed by Steven Spielberg. In the film, Detective John Anderton (Tom Cruise) is the chief of the Justice Department's new "Pre-crime Unit" and serves alongside the program's director, Lamar Burgess (Max von Sydow). Together, they help execute a new anti-crime program that uses three genetically altered humans who can see into the future to prevent murders. How does the elite anti-crime unit function? Armed with the expert cognitive ability of the genetically altered "pre-cogs" and modern computerized technology, the crime unit uses the pre-cogs' reports to see what crimes *will be* committed in the future and then uses these reports to arrest the suspects *before* they commit a crime. Preemptive justice, indeed.

The American public, scared of violent crime and impressed by the seemingly flawless work of the Pre-crime Unit, votes to dramatically extend the scope and power of the anti-crime program. Through the completely democratic process of the plebiscite, the people give Director Burgess more authority to expand and execute the program. Yet several troubling questions arise: What happens if the system is not foolproof? What if the pre-cogs and their reports can somehow be manipulated by humans so that innocents can be arrested for crimes they have no intention of committing? At its very core "the movie presents us with a classic totalitarian trade-off, upgraded by technology and the paranormal: Would you surrender a slew of civil liberties for a world without crime?"[35]

Dubbed "a fabulous, witty totalitarian nightmare" by Salon.com, *Minority Report* offers an ominous glimmer into what horrors can arise when vast, unchecked police power—explicitly backed by popular will—is given to a select few under the guise of security.[36] Indeed, as it turns out, the Pre-crime Unit *is* manipulated and abused by forces within the program, and soon Detective Anderton finds himself the target of someone's high-tech scheming. He is on the run, fighting for his life, while trying to determine how such an advanced system could be used for evil purposes. The horrific abuse of the popular futuristic pre-cog Pre-crime Unit provides us with a potentially sober lesson about democracy: what the majority wants—and indeed *votes for*—is not always what is just or sound . . . or even *democratic*. Democratic decisions can prove to be most insidious if they empower opportunistic individuals with their own agenda or sinister intent. Released in the year after the September 11, 2001, terrorist attacks in the United States—and with the passage of legislation designed to fight terrorism and ensure security, such as the popular Patriot Act, still fresh in citizens' minds—many found the screening of the fantasy sci-fi political thriller to be especially timely.[37]

Critiquing Capitalism: The Consequences and Limitations of Deregulation, Competition, and Efficiency

In the fall of 2008, as the U.S. presidential election entered the homestretch, the global financial system, and perhaps the U.S. economy as well, appeared on the verge of collapse. Storied staples of the investment banking, business, and home mortgage worlds—such as Lehman Brothers, Bear Stearns, Merrill Lynch, Fannie Mae and Freddie Mac, and insurance giant AIG—were on the brink of or had reached financial ruin. The Dow Jones industrial average plunged nearly 800 points in one day in September, the largest single drop in history up to that point.[38] What policies precipitated this calamitous jolt to the financial services industry and free market economics itself?

Inside Job (2010), earning a spot on many critics Top Ten lists and described by *New York Times* film critic A. O. Scott as "a meticulous and infuriating documentary about the causes and consequences of the financial crisis of 2008," stands as perhaps the definitive cinematic exposé of the nexus of factors that drove the global financial meltdown.[39] Directed by political scientist and film-maker Charles Ferguson, this landmark film argues that the deregulation of the financial services industry in the 1980s and 1990s, coupled with the resultant explosion of complex and risky financial instruments (such as derivatives, credit default swaps, and subprime mortgages) and the cozy relationship between economists and policy makers cheering less governmental oversight of such hazardous practices, led to the financial crisis. *Inside Job* methodically covers some policy and political terrain featured in other films; yet it does so with a more potent, accessible mix of economic context, political science lec-ture, and humor or what one critic asserted was outrage built on "reason, research and careful argument."[40]

Leslie and Andrew Cockburn's documentary *American Casino* (2009), for example, stands as a searing indictment of unscrupulous business practices and unfettered capitalism, reviewing the roots and consequences of the calamitous, cascading subprime mortgage and home foreclosure crisis, which played an inte-gral role in the financial meltdown.[41] Illustrating how aggressive lenders delib-erately targeted minority populations for risky subprime mortgages—African Americans and Hispanics, for example, were found by the Federal Reserve of San Francisco to have been four times more likely than Caucasians to be sold subprime loans—the film catalogs the painful human costs of the subprime explosion.[42] Also, arguably Michael Moore's most personal film to date, *Capitalism: A Love Story* (2009) deals with the deregulatory policies of the 1980s–2000s, the subprime loan phenomenon, the incentivizing of greed and unnecessary risk within the financial services sector, and the disastrous conse-quences for everyday Americans.

The Global Financial Crisis and Deregulation: An *Inside Job*

An image from Charles Ferguson's widely praised docu-mentary Inside Job *(2010); from left to right: Henry "Hank" Paulson, Secretary of the Treasury under President George W. Bush and former CEO of the investment firm Goldman Sachs; Ben Bernanke, chairman of the Federal Reserve; Timothy Geithner, former chair of the New York Federal Reserve and later Secretary of the Treasury under President Barack Obama.*

Political scientist–turned–filmmaker Charles Ferguson details the deregulation of the financial services industry, the pernicious influence of economists, and the crop of complex, risky financial instruments that resulted in a global financial meltdown. Through interviews, data, and a review of the economic-political history of the 1980s–2000s, he catalogs the lack of oversight from the Federal Reserve, a corrosive Wall Street culture, and the incentivizing of greed that he believes destabilized an international financial system that had been relatively secure until the regulatory regimes imposed in the wake of the Great Depression were weakened.

Bleak Rural and Urban Landscapes: "Where Life Is Cold and Kin Are Cruel"[43]

Winner of Grand Jury awards for best picture and best screenplay at the Sundance Film Festival, *Winter's Bone* (2010), directed by Debra Granik and based on the book by Daniel Woodrell, presents a bleak Hobbesian universe where basic survival is the eminent concern, and human beings will do seemingly inhumane things to earn a living—even if it means murdering or torturing family members or leaving a teenager to tend to her mentally ill mother and two fatherless children in the hinterlands.[44] This is the desolate rough-and-tumble reality of winter in the Ozarks of Missouri, where jobs and hope are nonexistent and the leading industry is the methamphetamine trade. And it is the backdrop of economic despair, brutal violence, and familial hostility that plague the resilient seventeen-year-old heroine, Ree Dolly (Jennifer Lawrence), left to fend for her family of two younger siblings and an incapacitated mother.

With her father, a former (or current?) meth cooker, missing, it is up to Ree to find out if her father is dead or alive, as the sheriff informs her that their house and land will become the state's unless her father emerges to attend his court date, or Ree can provide definitive physical proof that her father is deceased. With homelessness and starvation around the corner of an already hardscrabble life, Ree encounters varying layers of intrigue and levels of hell as she seeks family assistance in finding her father. Yet her extended family is in the only homegrown industry in the region that generates a profit, and they are not anxious to compromise their trade. The film is, as the *New York Times'* A. O. Scott deemed it, a "regional-realist morality tale,"[45] but it could easily also be viewed, by extension, as a dark fable of the cruelty of desperate capitalism in severely impoverished areas, of the horrors individuals (cousins, aunts, uncles, neighbors) will visit upon their own flesh and blood in order to beat down unfriendly competition and maintain their illicit income. As such, *Winter's Bone* can be seen to critique pure laissez-faire economics by suggesting that, absent an adequate social safety net to offset the miserable economic conditions, the search for a steady stream of cash in an anarchical, distressed countryside—the marketplace—leaves a trail of shattered lives and people living on the margins of society.

Geographic and economic desolation, generational poverty, and the desperate measures brought on by harsh times also dominate *Frozen River* (2008). The setting of the barren, ice-cold New York–Quebec border, alongside a Mohawk reservation, serves as a metaphor for the bleak economic situation of the film's characters. Ray Eddy (Melissa Leo, in an Academy Award–nominated performance) is a newly single mother of two sons after her gambling-addled husband absconds with the family vehicle and what little petty cash existed and she faces the minimum wage dead end of clerking at the local dollar store. Unable to pay the heating bills for their current modest domicile, let alone save money for the quality mobile home they have hoped for, and needed, for years, Ray becomes part of an immigrant smuggling operation along the frozen St. Lawrence River.

Films like *Frozen River* and *Winter's Bone* depict an economically, emotionally, and physically cold universe, where decent jobs, goodwill, generosity, and hope are in short supply. Women like Ree and Ray, the films' protagonists, are resilient, hardworking, and incredibly responsible; yet they face omnipresent economic upheaval and a level of unfairness that, for some, may reveal the limitations of the liberal economy. Individual initiative, efficiency, and incredible persistence may never be enough to provide for your family, or even yourself. This is a message that also runs through Stephen Frears's 2002 dark urban thriller, *Dirty Pretty Things*, set in a London where recent immigrants struggle to survive by working long hours in hotels or in the black market economy of sweatshops and prostitution, even stumbling upon an illicit operation involving the sale of human organs as they toil to get by. Moreover, these are themes that are not exclusive to the big screen; such messages run through popular music as well. From the Appalachian ballad tradition to the tale of the desperate, impoverished South Dakota farmer who kills himself and his family in Bob Dylan's *Ballad of Hollis Brown* (1963), or John Mellencamp's *Jackie Brown* (1989), popular culture has addressed what some consider the all-too-real shortcomings of capitalism.[46]

Another film, *Store Wars* (2001), raises questions about the desirability of unchecked capitalism in small-town environs—in this case, the further expansion of the world's largest retailer, Wal-Mart. The film is a documentary set in the small town of Ashland, Virginia, just outside of Richmond. The film chronicles a year in the political life of the city as the world's largest retail chain petitions for a store to be built there. Two opposing sides quickly coalesce regarding whether or not Wal-Mart should be allowed to build. One side favors the development because it is seen as a way to bring jobs to the area, increase the visibility of Ashland, and give citizens access to products at a lower cost. Those opposed to Wal-Mart coming to town, who dub themselves the "Pink Flamingoes," fear that the increase of traffic will destroy the small-town atmosphere of Ashland, and that the service-sector jobs created will come at the expense of higher-paying jobs lost in the town's smaller businesses that Wal-Mart would force out of business.

Ashland's political leaders are at a loss for what to do. Initially their primary concern is the traffic problems a new Wal-Mart would create for the town. The proposed development is huge compared to the town's ability to supply infrastructure. As citizens become organized, they voice concerns about the economic and political impact on Ashland. Wal-Mart provides an information video on the positive impact it has had on Tappahannock, Virginia. A delegation from Ashland makes the trip to Tappahannock to discuss the issue with local political and business leaders. Business leaders tell them that Wal-Mart's presence has led to all of the small, locally owned enterprises going out of business. The argument used by those who opposed Wal-Mart is that profits made by local businesses are recirculated within the community, while profits made by Wal-Mart are taken back to Bentonville, Arkansas, the corporate headquarters of the retail chain.

Wal-Mart's first proposal to build in Ashland is turned down by the planning commission. The commission felt that the proposed development did not adequately address the traffic and infrastructure concerns and also did not believe that the megastore would fit in with the quaint, small-town charm that Ashland was supposed to invoke. The celebration among the Pink Flamingoes is muted. They understand that the rejection is really an invitation to restate the proposal. A few months later Wal-Mart submits another plan that incorporates some of the city's concerns, scaling down some of their initial designs. Additionally, in the spirit of the town's quaintness, the new proposal calls for the store to be decorated in yellow and green rather than Wal-Mart's more commonly used red and blue.

The new proposal solves many of the concerns the city council, mayor, and planning commission had with the original proposal. The Pink Flamingoes become even more active and begin lobbying city council members directly. One commissioner tells representatives of the organization that even if all the residents of Ashland signed a petition against Wal-Mart, he would still vote for the proposal because he thought it was in the best economic interests of Ashland. Wal-Mart intensifies its lobbying efforts, even as many town residents remain skeptical and hostile. At a town meeting, a lawyer representing Wal-Mart insisted on the corporation's right to buy property and build where it wanted. A member of the audience, quoting Sam Walton's (the founder of Wal-Mart) autobiography, asked about his pledge not to locate a Wal-Mart in any town that did not want one. Meanwhile, a full-page advertisement taken out in the local newspaper by Wal-Mart touted the benefits of a new superstore. Included in the ad was a reference to alleged positive economic impact that new Wal-Marts bring to an area, with a prominent citation of a 1995 study coauthored by an economics professor at the University of Massachusetts-Dartmouth. However, when a supporter of the Pink Flamingoes called the professor for clarification, the scholar stated that the conclusion of her study was precisely the opposite: that employment levels *did not* increase under such circumstances, and at best new Wal-Marts had no economic impact on affected areas.

One of the significant points of *Store Wars* is how divided a town can become over economic and quality-of-life issues. As bitterly contested elections for mayor and the city council are set to take place shortly before the final decision on whether or not to approve the proposal, a strong slate of candidates opposed to the development emerges. However, the city council, in a lame-duck session, votes to approve Wal-Mart's development plans.

About the same time that *Store Wars* was released, Wal-Mart had not only become the largest employer in several U.S. states but was the largest private employer in the entire country. In Pennsylvania at that time, for example, where Wal-Mart possessed ninety-four discount "supercenters" and twenty Sam's Clubs warehouses, the retail chain employed over 39,000 people.[47] Ashland's store, therefore, stands as a link in an ever-expanding chain of unrivaled retail power, and the documentary stands as an engaging study of corporate and citizen power at the local level.

The Economic, Political, and Aesthetic Impact of Wal-Mart: *Store Wars* (2001)

Citizens gather at local government meetings in Ashland, Virginia, to voice concerns over a proposed Wal-Mart supercenter in their neighborhood.

A chronicling of local grassroots responses to a Wal-Mart supercenter in small-town Virginia, Micha X. Peled's documentary raises questions about the consequences of the liberal economy and large retailers on small neighborhoods. Will Wal-Mart bring needed jobs, low-cost goods, a steady stream of tax revenue and convenience—or will it breed low-paying jobs, unwanted congestion, and a loss of neighborhood identity?

South Park and *Frontline* Ask: Is Wal-Mart Good for America?

Who are the economic winners and losers as Wal-Mart contin- ues to thrive and expand? Are human beings primarily con- sumers or workers—or are we both, equally? Who ultimately has the power to affect Wal-Mart's business practices?

One traditional "highbrow" network and the public affairs documentary program *Frontline,* PBS's award-winning documen- tary series; and one notoriously and unabashedly "lowbrow" ani- mated series from Comedy Central, Trey Parker and Matt Stone's landmark potty-mouthed series, *South Park, each* in their own way seek to answer these, and other, salient questions about the form of modern capitalism exhibited by the retail behemoth.

Frontline's "Is Wal-Mart Good for America?" (2004) exam- ines a host of issues concerning the real-world impact of Wal- Mart in the United States—specifically, Wal-Mart's effects on the quintessential midwestern towns of Wooster and Circleville, Ohio. In so doing, *Frontline* examines some of the negative con- sequences of the retail giant's liberal economic model, undergird- ed by advances in innovation, outsourcing, efficiency, and customer satisfaction.[48] Modern liberal and libertarian econo- mists provide data and analysis, and interviews with Ray Bracy, Wal-Mart's vice president for federal and international public affairs, and Jon Lehman, a former seventeen-year Wal-Mart vet- eran–turned–critic–and–labor organizer, provide additional con- text.[49] Key concepts such as *creative destruction, opening price points,* and *push-and-pull production models* are defined and applied to Wal-Mart's practices and their impact on consumers and workers in the United States.

Save Us from Ourselves! *South Park*'s Libertarian Methodology in "Something Wall-Mart This Way Comes"

A predominantly libertarian perspective concerning Wal-Mart's benefits and drawbacks is provided in Trey Parker and Matt

Stone's 120th episode, "Something Wall-Mart This Way Comes" (2004). In the suburban Colorado hamlet we find the frequently sheeplike townspeople, including Stan Marsh's father, Randy, obsessed with Wall-Mart's low prices and abundance of . . . well, cheap items.[50] Soon, the local stores shut their doors as all the townies, and Wall-Mart champion Eric Cartman, head to the big box store. Depressed, the townspeople then decide to boycott Wall-Mart in order to bring life back to their downtown stores. Soon enough, however, human nature and rampant consumerism return as the locals are sucked back to the megastore, unable to follow their own directive to avoid Wall-Mart. *Can "the Wall-Mart" be defeated? Have the fate of small-town stores and a way of life been sealed by some insidious corporate force, or "heart"?* Parker and Stone make the case that the nefarious "heart" of Wall-Mart, which sucks consumers in like mindless drones, is . . . low and behold . . . ourselves! Rational individuals act according to what they want, and that is why this particular superstore (or *any* store, for that matter) will succeed.

David Fincher's controversial $63 million sex- and violence-dominated sociopolitical statement *Fight Club* (1999), starring Gen-X box office draws Brad Pitt, Edward Norton, and Helena Bonham Carter, while ostensibly an action-rife, darkly humorous exploration of maleness in modern America, concurrently draws serious attention to the darker, more extreme impulses of capitalism: materialism and corporate manipulation run amok.[51] Driven to spend inordinate and irrational amounts of money on cars, clothes, furniture, and household minutiae, American males Tyler Durden (Brad Pitt) and "the Narrator," Cornelius (Edward Norton), realize that they, like other men of their generation, have become slaves to corporate manipulation and mindless materialism, buying "shit that they don't need" from catalog after catalog and trendy store after trendy store.[52] They have become part of the ever-expanding consumer class, wedded to Starbucks, Viagra, Calvin Klein, Tommy Hilfiger, DKNY, IKEA, and endless amounts of the "right" fashion, food, furniture, beverages, perfume, and household amenities that we are told (*and convinced*, via omnipresent advertising and corporate values) we need.

For iconoclast Tyler Durden, the crisis of modern American manhood is not caused by Great Depressions or foreign wars but by "a spiritual war" brought on by consumerism and the false belief—broadcast ad nauseam on television and everywhere in American capitalist society—that everyone will become rich if they work hard enough. This is a hyperactive capitalism gone crazy. Americans work all day so that they can buy at night and on the weekend, trying to move ever closer to the unattainable nirvana of purchasing power and possessions. We have become, in Durden's words, pathetic slaves with "white collars." To combat this predicament, the radical Durden, along with his "protégé"—the narrator, Cornelius—channel their aggression about the state of affairs and their programmed minds into secret male societies known as "Fight Clubs": gatherings of men where folks batter each other senseless. Later, the two men and their minions engage in smart-ass shenanigans, pranks, and small-time terrorism designed to disrupt the ongoing capitalist, consumerist slavery. Eventually the group's activities, dubbed "Project Mayhem," turn darker, ultra-violent, and illegal, and include the planned destruction of the major credit card companies. Why credit card companies? So we can, in Durden's words, "erase the debt and start at zero."

Project Mayhem is financed in a variety of ways, but soap is the essential component of the Fight Club economic engine. Stealing cellulite leftover from liposuction, the members of Fight Club use the fat to make expensive, trendy, soap ($20 a bar) that quickly becomes extremely fashionable at department stores. Thus, the renegades literally sell fat back to the weight- and image-conscious consumers of America. As the narrator states, they were "selling rich women their own fat asses back to them." The angst of Durden and the narrator is also driven by the injustice that they see. For example, the narrator's work is basically concealing routine—and severe—corporate malfeasance. His company produces faulty car parts but, regardless of the numerous fatalities and injuries caused by their faulty products, they fail to correct them because their cost-benefit analysis reveals that it is cheaper to keep making the shoddy, life-threatening parts and pay (mostly) paltry settlements than to correct the mistakes. The narrator uses damning information he has culled from years as an insurance adjuster for the company to blackmail his corporate bosses, his silence shrewdly traded for money to finance the anti-corporate Project Mayhem of Fight Club.

Released in the fall of 1999, *Fight Club* raised eyebrows, provoked a great deal of criticism, and, ultimately, underperformed at the box office in its U.S. release. Opening to U.S. audiences on October 15th, just a few short months after the shooting rampage at Columbine High School in Littleton, Colorado, one prominent film critic asserted that, after the first twenty-five minutes or so, "the movie stops being smart and savage and witty, and turns to some of the most brutal, unremitting, nonstop violence ever filmed."[53] He continued:

> "Fight Club" is the most frankly and cheerfully fascist big-star movie since "Death Wish," a celebration of violence in which the heroes write themselves a license to drink, smoke, screw and beat one another up.
>
> Sometimes, for variety, they beat up themselves. It's macho porn—the sex movie Hollywood has been moving toward for years, in which eroticism between the sexes is replaced by all-guy locker-room fights. Women, who have had a lifetime of practice at dealing with little-boy posturing, will instinctively see through it; men may get off on the testosterone rush. The fact that it is very well made and has a great first act certainly clouds the issue.[54]

With negative, seemingly contradictory reviews such as this, and with the legacy of the Columbine massacre still fresh in the minds of many, the edgy, unique, pervasively violent, ultimately anti-corporate and materialist tale suffered at the box office, grossing a less-than-expected $37 million in the United States.[55] Did the film deserve such criticism? Did its message get bogged down in a barrage of sex and violence? Is *Fight Club* a penetrating, agitating film with a serious political edge, or is it, as the famous *Chicago Sun-Times* film critic Roger Ebert suggested, merely a violent, misogynistic "thrill ride masquerading as philosophy"?[56] You be the judge. But whatever your analysis of the sex, violence, and its merit (or lack thereof), the film's political connotations and cultural commentary on modern American maleness, consumerism, corporate manipulation, and capitalism run amok are unmistakable. And perhaps, a tad unsettling.[57]

An International Economy? Globalization and Liberalism

The imperatives of an international economy in the modern era demand that countries open their markets. An emphasis on reducing barriers to goods coming into a country, especially tariffs (or taxes), has meant that materials produced by smaller manufacturers are often at a disadvantage to larger, more efficient manufacturers. This is because the larger manufacturers have an economy of scale that makes their production much cheaper than smaller manufacturers. Often this means that multinational corporations can lower their prices so much that small manufacturers cannot sell their products at a profit.

By opening their markets, countries are no longer able to protect some of their most vital industries. There have been calls to protect the cultural industries of some countries. For example, there have been movements in the past to have the French government protect their film industry by requiring a certain percentage of movie screens to show French-language films.[58] Some would argue that this leads to a situation where economically disadvantaged cultures might be pushed out of the arena by wealthier and seemingly more influential societies.

Increased global interaction and globalization allow for an exchange of ideas and cultures that has never existed before. As this book demonstrates, foreign films, once only seen in major metropolitan areas of the United States, are now available around the country by way of the Internet, DVDs, and cable and satellite television. American film, television shows, music, and literature are available in nearly every country in the world. Sometimes this interaction provides us with learning situations; sometimes it presents us with entertaining situations.

At the beginning of the film *The Gods Must Be Crazy* (1980), Xixo (played by N!xau) is walking in the Kalahari Desert when a strange animal flies over the sky. Xixo, a member of a small Bushmen tribe in Botswana, has never seen a white man or technology; moreover, nor does he know anything harder than the scrub wood that is occasionally found in the Kalahari. As the strange animal flies overhead, it drops something from the sky that is at once beautiful and the hardest thing Xixo has ever seen. The animal flying overhead is in fact an airplane, and the wonderful, beautiful, hard object that Xixo believes the gods have given him is a Coca-Cola bottle. After the bottle causes great trouble among the members of his clan, Xixo sets off on a journey to throw the bottle off the edge of the world. During this sojourn he encounters a world that he never knew existed, and the resulting culture shock, both for him and those he encounters, provides audiences with one of the classic comedies of the art house circuit.

Another film with a similar theme is the first film ever made in the country of Bhutan, *Phörpa* (*The Cup*). Made in 1999, the film is based on a true story of two Tibetan Buddhist monks who are avid soccer fans and go to extraordinary lengths to watch the 1998 World Cup final from Paris. The young monks go through a great deal of difficulty, not the least from the elder monks in the monastery, and obstacles to pull off their plan to watch the Cup final. While funny and sweet, the movie also says a lot about the world in which we live. Tibetan monks, in some of the most remote regions of the world, are interested in a soccer game that is played halfway around the world. The interaction between cultures is significant.

However, it would be a mistake to think that all of the effects of liberal economics and globalization are sweet and funny. Several scholars and pundits, notable among them Thomas Friedman, Benjamin Barber, and Ignacio Ramonet, have debated the benefits and drawbacks to globalization. The one conclusion that they seem to come to is that there are both benefits and drawbacks.[59]

Closer to home and praised as "pop culture to salve national wounds that continue to fester in the real world," *Up in the Air* (2009), Jason Reitman's successful follow-up to the smash hit *Juno* (2007), features Ryan Bingham (George Clooney) as a hired ace from an Omaha company that specializes in firing workers.[60] Companies, to save face and money, have now "outsourced" the very process of downsizing and counseling workers to "termination engineers" like Bingham. In the modern economy, it is not painful enough just to *lose* one's livelihood; now workers must suffer the *extra indignity* of an impersonal firing at the hands of a complete stranger. Yet Bingham, who focuses on accumulating frequent flyer miles and elite status at hotels, may himself be expendable in the current rush to save money and register profits at all costs. Coworker Natalie Keener (Anna Kendrick)—"a presumed human-resources expert who, having come of age in front of a computer, has no grasp of the human"—is pioneering a process to make Bingham obsolete by implementing the downsizing of workers via videoconferencing.[61] Rational attention to cost-cutting, or efficiency, maximizes profits. Yet the march toward efficiency has its human costs, and *Up in the Air* reveals the emotional and psychological toll of this "throw away" economy, where individual workers matter less and less. And as Ryan's and Natalie's lives reveal, they are not immune to the corrosive effects of this phenomenon, as the fixation on efficiency, profits, and lack of empathy moves from our business models to our everyday interactions.

Guerilla filmmaker Michael Moore's documentary *The Big One* (1997) follows the controversial satirist and social commentator on his nationwide book tour in support of his 1996 bestseller, *Downsize This! Random Threats from an Unarmed American.*[62] Moore, the man behind 1989's lauded *Roger & Me*, which cataloged the disastrous effects of GM layoffs in the Flint, Michigan, area in the 1980s, uses his book tour to examine downsizing and economic misery in the 1990s. As he trots from bookstore to theater to university campus to radio show—and hotel to airport to hotel—he runs into Americans who have been downsized (or fired) in the midst of national prosperity. From Centralia to Rockford, from Milwaukee to Minneapolis, and many places in between, Moore chastises corporations for laying off workers in times of rising profits, presents corporations with checks for their first hour of Mexican wages, criticizes a welfare-to-work program in Wisconsin, and asks Pillsbury—on a "Post-It Note"—why they need millions of dollars in federal subsidies to promote their "Doughboy" overseas. In Des Moines, Iowa, he shows solidarity with Barnes & Noble employees who work to form a union, and at the Mall of America outside Minneapolis, he finds a murderer who worked for TWA while in prison. It turns out that, across the country, prisoners perform labor for severely reduced wages.

All of these experiences on the road in the United States reinforce Moore's central interpretation of what he sees as the darker, or more extreme, side of liberal economics: that many corporations do not care—but should care—about the health and well-being of their employees; and, moreover, that the social contract demands that people should not lose their jobs when they are productive and the company is doing well. It is a theme accented at length in his first film, *Roger & Me*, and *The Big One*, while essentially a series of pit stops on a promotional book tour, echoes the same message.

While Moore provides the audience with some comic and entertainment relief, such as a visit with Cheap Trick's Rick Nielsen, where Moore does his best Bob Dylan impersonation, these are merely entertaining distractions from the heart of the film, which asks the fundamental question: *What is the human cost of the global liberal economy—both here in the United States and around the world?* In the spirit of this question, Moore winds up at a Nike protest in Portland, Oregon, where the shoe giant's corporate headquarters are located. Activists came to protest working conditions at shoe factories in Vietnam and Indonesia. Unlike GM CEO Roger Smith, who never agreed to a significant sit-down with Moore in *Roger & Me*, Philip Knight, the CEO of Nike, actually *invites* Moore to his home to discuss his inclusion in the "corporate crook trading cards" section of Moore's *Downsize This!* When they meet, Moore presents Knight with two airplane tickets to Indonesia so that he and Knight can inspect the factories where Nike shoes are made. Knight politely declines the invitation. Throughout their discussion of Nike's factories and corporate citizenship, Knight is affable and accommodating to his muckraking guest but clearly does not share Moore's view that fourteen-year-old girls should not be working in Indonesian factories making Nike shoes. He also rejects Moore's contention that Americans would, if paid a decent wage, manufacture shoes in the States. In the end, their views of the global economy and the social contract are obviously not in sync, though Moore does get Knight to match his $10,000 gift to public schools in Flint, Michigan.

One critic's review of *The Big One* summarizes opposing interpretations of corporate responsibility and the costs of globalization: "Moore's overall conclusion: Large American corporations care more for their stockholders than for their workers, and no profit level is high enough to satisfy them. If he'd been able to get more top executives on camera, I have a feeling their response would have been: 'Yes. And?'" [63]

In the final analysis, these closing remarks get to the heart of *The Big One* and the issues it raises. What should the proper balance be between workers' rights, wages, health and safety standards, and environmental standards, on one hand, and efficiency, profit, and affordable goods on the other? Would it be better to pay workers in the Third World higher wages and pay more for shoes here at home so that the workers would take home more money? Are corporations doing underdeveloped states a favor by taking jobs to countries starved for economic investment? Who benefits more from the economic relationship in globalization: the corporations, the American consumers, or the workers in factories—whether in Indonesia, Vietnam, or China? Clearly, *The Big One* is a vehicle for Moore's perspective. Twelve years later, Moore revisited the theme of the role of corporations in modern economic life in his film *Capitalism: A*

Our Jeans, Their Lives:
The Faces of Globalization in *China Blue* (2005)

In these images from the award-winning documentary China Blue *(2005),* teenage Chinese factory workers Jasmine and Liping use clothes pins to keep awake so that they meet their production quota
and are not fined by their boss; another image shows them keeling over from exhaustion due to the
strenuous work and long hours.

Directed by Micha X. Peled, and winner of Amnesty International's
Human Rights Award, *China Blue* (2005) takes an unflinching look
at globalization through the lives of teenage female factory workers who work day and night to make blue jeans. Shot clandestinely and under difficult conditions, Peled's film exposes the conditions
under which many of the clothes sold in Western countries are produced, revealing the human costs of the liberal economy.
    You can learn more about this film and Peled's other documen-
taries at teddybearfilms.com and seeingthebiggerpicture.net.

Love Story (2009). Even critics of Moore were impressed by his exposé of the
excesses and corruption of capitalism to the extent of ruining individuals'
prospects of economic success. The film ends with a plea from Moore to return
to the roots of democracy (rule by the people) and a social contract based on
shared prosperity and sacrifice rather than rule by an extreme form of deregu-
lated capitalism.[64]

Conclusion

The United States, as the most prosperous and powerful country in the world for the latter half of the twentieth century, frequently saw its values and world-view displayed on the screen. Even before the Second World War, the United States had a domestic audience sufficient to insure that its film industry could out-produce any of its rivals in Europe. Consequently, the American film industry became the standard by which other industries were measured. As this chapter has indicated, however, there have been warnings about the excesses or limitations of both democracy and capitalism coming even from the United States. Other parts of the world have been less sure about the assumptions that capitalism and democracy necessarily go hand in hand.

For example, Fritz Lang's 1927 science-fiction masterpiece *Metropolis* depicted a world of the year 2026, where growing disparities between haves and have-nots lead to a physical separation between the two. The haves lead an idyllic life in the Metropolis above ground. They are blessed with a lifestyle of wealth and leisure, largely unaware of the plight of those who live below the city. The have-nots, workers who live underground and run the city, work themselves to death in service to the Metropolis. While they are indeed employed, they are little more than automatons. The workers are forced to operate machinery in perpetual motion, in dangerous circumstances, and often die at their workstations. In one scene of the film, in the eyes of a person who lives above ground, the machinery is transformed into an altar for human sacrifice, where individuals are forced into the interior of the machine that resembles people being dumped into a volcanic pit.

By the end of the film, labor and management are reconciled by the love of a daughter of the underworld and the son of those who live on top. Interestingly enough, both fascists and communists claimed the film. In fact, it was also said to be Adolf Hitler's favorite film, although both the director of the film, Fritz Lang, and the author of the novel, Thea von Harbou, claimed that Hitler misunderstood the meaning of the film.

Some films, as this chapter has indicated, provide a clear message as to how society should be governed, and what ideology should be the driving force: liberalism, fascism, or communism. Other films, such as *Metropolis*, provide a seemingly ambiguous message. That being said, *Metropolis*, Fritz Lang, and Thea von Harbou centered the story on the domestic relationship of capital and labor. While claiming no particular ideology, the film nevertheless focuses the attention of the audience on a particular relationship within society. It is important to remember that films, documentaries, and television programs each carry a message, stated or unstated. If they had no story to tell, no message to convey, then the piece or work would not have been made. Consider how films with no apparent political message might have one anyway. The next time you sit down to watch a film or television program consider the following questions: *Does the film implicitly or subtly support capitalism and democracy? Are the characters motivated to go out to shop and accumulate goods? Do they complain about, or to, their elected representatives, even in an offhand manner?* If so, then note that this is a subtle, albeit substantial, reinforcement of the current political-economic system. Our job as citizens and purveyors of popular culture is to discover and consider all of these messages and discuss their application and relevance to the real world of politics, policy, governmental institutions, and international relations. Whether you are watching film classics, PBS, prime-time television, HBO, Comedy Central, YouTube, or sitting at the multiplex with a bucket of delicious, buttery popcorn, this critical approach to studying film and our world will set us on the intellectual path of truly seeing the bigger picture.

Notes

1. For an exploration of the relationship between capitalism and democracy, see Gabriel A. Almond, "Capitalism and Democracy," *PS: Political Science and Politics* 24, no. 3 (September 1991): 467–74.
2. See, for example, Milton Friedman, *Capitalism and Freedom: Fortieth Anniversary Edition* (Chicago: University of Chicago Press, 2002), and Milton and Rose Friedman, *Free to Choose: A Personal Statement* (New York: Harcourt Brace, 1980).
3. For more about the films and life of Frank Capra, consult Charles J. Maland, *Frank Capra* (Boston: Twayne Publishers, 1980); Raymond Carney, *American Vision: The Films of Frank Capra* (New York: Cambridge University Press, 1986); and Leland A. Poague and Frank Capra, *Frank Capra: Interviews* (Jackson: University Press of Mississippi, 2004).
4. Transcribed from the film.
5. Norman Ornstein, "A Filibuster Fix," *New York Times*, August 27, 2010: http://www.nytimes.com/2010/08/28/opinion/28ornstein.html.
6. The Senate itself has been an evolving institution. The Seventeenth Amendment (1913) established the direct election of U.S. senators. Prior to 1913, senators were selected by state legislators, as mandated by the U.S. Constitution.
7. The essay contest guidelines in *Reading Digest* stipulate that the essay entries be "fiercely patriotic."
8. "Mr. Lisa Goes to Washington"; Nelson Muntz quote from *The Simpsons: A Complete Guide to Our Favorite Family*, ed. Ray Richmond and Antonia Coffman (New York: HarperPerennial, 1997), 63.

9. There are countless scholarly considerations of the *Simpsons*, but one of the most perceptive, enlightened, and exhaustive examinations of the Simpsons' extensive attention to
democratic theory and political participation come from political scientist Fran Moran at
New Jersey City University. See Fran Moran, "Popular Democracy and Citizen Engagement:
Lessons from Springfield," paper presented at the annual meeting of the Northeastern
Political Science Association, Philadelphia, Pennsylvania, November 16–19, 2009. The
paper can be found online at: http://faculty.njcu.edu/fmoran/morannpsa2009.pdf.

10. Richmond and Coffman, *The Simpsons*.

11. Ibid.

12. Grant Matthews's (Tracy's) speech is transcribed from the film.

13. Life does imitate art. Republican presidential candidate Ronald Reagan, himself an actor
before his days as governor of California and later president, channeled the spirit of Grant
Matthews's radio speech from *State of the Union*, when during a debate in Nashua, New
Hampshire, a testy Reagan emphatically stated, "I am paying for this microphone, Mr.
Breen!" See Craig Shirley, "Reagan's Blend of Stagecraft and Statecraft," *Washington Post*
blog, February 25, 2010: http://voices.washingtonpost.com/shortstack/2010/02/reagans
_blend_of_stagecraft_an.html.

14. The films in the *Why We Fight* series are *Prelude to War* (1943), *The Nazis Strike* (1943),
Divide and Conquer (1943), *The Battle of Britain* (1943), *The Battle of Russia* (1943), *The Battle
of China* (1944), and *War Comes to America* (1945).

15. Eric Schlosser, *Fast Food Nation* (New York: Perennial, 2002), 38.

16. Ibid.

17. See, for example, our discussion of Alan Pakula's film adaptation of Bob Woodward's real-
life Watergate saga, *All the President's Men* (1976), in Chapter 7, "Media, Politics, and
Satire."

18. It must be noted that *The West Wing* had a bevy of real-world advisement and gravitas concerning the modern presidency and the American political process. For example, the likes
of Carter pollster Pat Caddell; Clinton press secretary Dee Dee Myers and Gene Sperling,
chairman of the National Economic Council; Reagan press secretary Marlin Fitzwater and
speechwriter Peggy Noonan; and U.S. Senate staffer (Senate Finance Committee) and aide
to Sen. Daniel Patrick Moynihan (D-NY) Lawrence O'Donnell all served as advisers, producers, occasional screenwriters, and, in some cases, even guests on the show. O'Donnell,
who began a stint hosting the program *The Last Word with Lawrence O'Donnell* on MSNBC
in 2010, portrayed President Jed Bartlet's father in the season two closer, "Two Cathedrals"
(2001). See Kevan M. Yenerall, "The West Wing: Left Wing or Right for the Times," paper
presented at the annual meeting of the American Political Science Association, San
Francisco, California, 2001; and Peter C. Rollins and John E. O'Connor, eds., *The West
Wing: The American Presidency as Television Drama* (New York: Syracuse University Press,
2003). There are several stellar chapters in the Rollins and O'Connor volume that are relevant to the topics referenced in *Seeing the Bigger Picture*, especially, but hardly limited to,
the exceptional scholarship of Staci Beavers, Donnalyn Pomper, and Greg M. Smith.

19. Transcribed from *The West Wing*'s season four episode "College Kids" (original airdate
October 2, 2002).

20. Aaron Sorkin, *The West Wing: The Official Companion* (New York: Pocket Books, 2002), 47.

21. Ibid., 62.

22. Ibid., 67.

23. This aspect of the show is discussed in-depth in Chapter 4, "The American Presidency."

24. For the quote, see *The West Wing* home page: http://www.nbc.com/The_West_Wing/index. html. For an index of "West Wing Hot Topics," see http://www.nbc.com/nbc/The_West_ Wing/hot_topics/archive.shtml, or http://www.nbc.com/nbc/The_West_Wing/hot_topics/ index.shtml.

25. The "Two Cathedrals" episode excerpt taken from Aaron Sorkin, *The West Wing Script Book* (New York: Newmarket Press, 2002), 396–97.

26. The United States proposed three institutions: the International Bank for Reconstruction and Development (or World Bank), the International Monetary Fund (IMF), and an International Trade Organization. The proposal for an International Trade Organization never got off the ground, and an ongoing conference called the General Agreement on Tariffs and Trade (GATT) took its place instead. In the mid-1990s, GATT was, in turn, replaced by a World Trade Organization, which took on many of the functions of the originally proposed ITO.

27. Specifically, David Ricardo, *On the Principles of Political Economy and Taxation* (1817); and Adam Smith, *An Inquiry Into the Nature and Causes of the Wealth of Nations* (1776).

28. Steven L. Spiegel and Fred L. Wehling, *World Politics in a New Era*, 2nd ed. (Fort Worth: Harcourt Brace College Publishers, 1999), 260–61.

29. Warner Brothers cartoons also took on other issues as well. The 1936 cartoon *I Love to Sing* is a film about fitting into American culture.

30. See also *How They Got the Vote* (1913) and *When Men Wear Skirts* (1914).

31. A similar film, called *Les femmes députées* (*Women Deputies*, 1912), offered a similar view of the participation of women in politics in France. In this short film, the prospect of two women running for office results in bickering and slapstick. Women's suffrage would not come to France until 1944.

32. *Boardwalk Empire* was created by producer and writer Terence Winter, one of the leading creative forces behind HBO's landmark mob and family drama, *The Sopranos* (1999–2007). The premiere episode of *Boardwalk* was directed by Martin Scorsese. Conversely, films such as HBO's *Iron-Jawed Angels* (2004), starring Academy Award winner Hilary Swank, documented the heroism and real-life struggles of the women's suffrage movement, standing as a dramatic endorsement of the expansion of voting rights in the United States.

33. Louis B. Mayer, a staunch Republican, held the film until President Herbert Hoover (1929–1933), also a Republican, was out of office. MGM released the film when Democrat Franklin Delano Roosevelt (1930–1945) took the reins of power, in large part because the movie is very critical of presidential inaction in the face of a deepening depression. In other words, Mayer and Hearst did not want the film—which advocates ultra-powerful executive action to combat joblessness and racketeering—to be seen as a direct attack on Hoover's performance and policies.

34. *Gabriel over the White House* is also discussed in Chapter 4, "The American Presidency."

35. David Edelstein, "Blame Runner," *Salon.com*, June 21, 2002: http://www.slate.com/id/ 2067225/.

36. Ibid.

37. The Patriot Act, legislation granting the Justice Department increased capacity, power, and latitude to investigate and prosecute terrorism—including, among other items, expanded

wiretapping authority—was passed overwhelmingly in the U.S. House and Senate. In the U.S. Senate, only one U.S. senator—Russ Feingold (D-WI)—opposed the hugely popular measure.

38. Alexandra Twin, "Stocks Crushed," *CNNMoney.com*, September 29, 2008: http://money.cnn.com/2008/09/29/markets/markets_newyork/index.htm?cnn=yes. The 778-point drop on the Dow Jones came after the U.S. House of Representatives rejected a $700 billion bailout plan for the financial services industry pushed by Treasury Secretary Henry Paulson. The plan would later be slightly revamped and would ultimately pass, becoming known as TARP, for the "Troubled Asset Relief Program."

39. A. O. Scott, "Who Maimed the Economy and How," *New York Times*, October 7, 2010: http://movies.nytimes.com/2010/10/08/movies/08inside.html.

40. Ibid.

41. For more on the 2009 documentary *American Casino*, an in-depth examination of the roots and consequences of the subprime mortgage crisis, see: http://www.americancasinothemovie.com/.

42. Andrew Jakobovics and Jeff Chapman, "Unequal Opportunity Lenders," *Center for American Progress*, September 15, 2009: http://www.americanprogress.org/issues/2009/09/tarp-lending.html; Orsan Aguilar, The Greenlining Institute, letter to the editor, "Race and Subprime Loan Crisis," *Sf.gate.com*, December 8, 2010: http://www.greenlining.org/news/in-the-news/2010/race-and-subprime-loan-crisis; see also: http://www.americancasinothemovie.com/synopsis.

43. A. O. Scott, "Where Life Is Cold and Kin Are Cruel," *New York Times*, June 11, 2010: http://movies.nytimes.com/2010/06/11/movies/11winter.html.

44. Daniel Woodrell, *Winter's Bone* (New York: Little, Brown and Company, 2006).

45. Scott, "Where Life Is Cold": http://movies.nytimes.com/2010/06/11/movies/11winter.html.

46. Bob Dylan, "Ballad of Hollis Brown," *The Freewheelin' Bob Dylan* (Columbia, 1963); John Mellencamp, "Jackie Brown," *Big Daddy* (Mercury, 1989).

47. Associated Press, "Wal-Mart Now Pa.'s Biggest Private Employer," *Pittsburgh Post-Gazette*, October 21, 2002: http://www.post-gazette.com/breaking/20021021employp7.asp. "Surpassing steel mills, coal mines, higher education and high technology, the world's largest retailer has taken over as Pennsylvania's largest private employer. . . . Wal-Mart has surged past the University of Pennsylvania, long the state's largest private employer with about 25,000 faculty and staff members, in a state Department of Labor and Industry ranking."

48. *Frontline*, "Is Wal-Mart Good for America?" (WBGH, Boston), November 16, 2004: http://www.pbs.org/wgbh/pages/frontline/shows/walmart/. The entire program can be viewed online at: http://www.pbs.org/wgbh/pages/frontline/video/flv/generic.html?s=frol02p71&continuous=1.

49. Re: Bracy and Lehman, see "Secrets of Wal-Mart's Success" at: http://www.pbs.org/wgbh/pages/frontline/shows/walmart/secrets/.

50. South Park's reigning clown of a father figure, Randy Marsh, has long been portrayed as alternatively impulsive, idiotic, narcissistic, or selfish, even willing to deliberately induce testicular cancer in order to get a prescription for medical marijuana in the episode "Medicinal Fried Chicken" (2010).

51. For the $63 million budget for *Fight Club*, see: http://us.imdb.com/Business?0137523.

52. The quote "Shit that they don't need" is attributed to Tyler Durden (Brad Pitt).

53. Roger Ebert's two-star review of *Fight Club* in the October 15, 1999 *Chicago Sun-Times* is online at: http://rogerebert.suntimes.com/apps/pbcs.dll/article?AID=/19991015/REVIEWS/910150302.

54. Ibid.

55. See: http://www.the-numbers.com/movies/1999/FIGHT.html.

56. http://rogerebert.suntimes.com/apps/pbcs.dll/article?AID=/19991015/REVIEWS/910150302.

57. *Fight Club* is also analyzed in Chapter 3 as an example of proto-fascism in modern films.

58. David Crary, "'Jurassic Park' Fans U.S.-French Fight over Films," *Chicago Sun-Times*, October 21, 1993, p. 34. In a similar story, French farmers have also protested the effects of the United States and EuroDisney on French culture and politics. See Matthew Fraser, "EuroDisney Has to Cope with Irate Farmers, Slack Turnstiles," *The (Montreal) Gazette*, June 29, 1992, p. B1.

59. See Benjamin R. Barber, "Jihad vs. McWorld," *The Atlantic Monthly* 269, no. 3 (March 1992): 50–63; Thomas L. Friedman, "Manifesto for a Fast World," *New York Times Magazine*, March 28, 1999, pp. 40–44ff; Thomas L. Friedman, *The Lexus and the Olive Tree* (New York: Farrar, Straus Giroux, 1999); and Thomas L. Friedman and Ignacio Ramonet, "Dueling Globalizations: A Debate between Thomas L. Friedman and Ignacio Ramonet," *Foreign Policy* 116 (Fall 1999): 110–27 .

60. Frank Rich, "Hollywood's Brilliant Coda to America's Dark Year," *New York Times*, December 12, 2009. http://www.nytimes.com/2009/12/13/opinion/13rich.html.

61. Manohla Dargis, "Neither Here Nor There," *New York Times*, December 4, 2009, http://movies.nytimes.com/2009/12/04/movies/04upinair.html.

62. Michael Moore, *Downsize This! Random Threats from an Unarmed American* (New York: Crown Publishers, 1996).

63. Roger Ebert's review of *The Big One*, *Chicago Sun-Times*, April 4, 1998.

64. For an in-depth analysis of this perspective, see Robert B. Reich, *I'll Be Short: Essentials for a Decent Working Society* (Boston: Beacon Press, 2002).

· 3 ·

ALTERNATIVE IDEOLOGIES

Communism, Fascism, and Authoritarianism

One of the seminal debates in any society is how the society is best governed. Many would argue that in European societies the polities have been moving from a time where one individual served as the sovereign toward an era where the incorporation of all people in the society into the decision-making processes is the norm rather than the exception. Yet debates still occur as to *what decisions* are in the public sphere and which are best left to private individuals. In many societies, those that we tend to think of as "Western," societies are guided by liberal ideologies, meaning a reliance on a market system of economic governance, as well as an understanding that fundamental freedoms and human rights are necessary and proper for the maintenance of good governance in society. In this chapter we will explore two of the more prominent ideologies that challenge these sacrosanct liberal ideals.

In a seminal piece written as the Cold War was coming to an end in 1989, Francis Fukuyama wrote that the world was entering a phase where great battles over ideologies were over. Liberal democracy was "the end of history" because aside from technical modifications, it was a system of governance that could not fundamentally be improved upon.[1] Since that time, Fukuyama's claims have been doubted, but there has been a general acceptance that democracy is the preferred method of governance, perhaps even a right.[2] If one is to consider the course of history, it seems there is an ever-increasing number of people participating in the decision-making process. Once the number of people participating reaches its maximum (all adults), then there is no way to fundamentally enlarge the number of people who participate in society. Fukuyama argues that over the course of the twentieth-century liberal democracy experienced two great challenges: communism and fascism.

This chapter will focus on those two primary philosophical challenges to liberalism, beginning with films that advocate Marxist/communist perspectives, and then examining those that were used to criticize its central tenets. Next, we examine films made by fascist regimes, films that advocate a fascist agenda, and, finally, films that attempted to refute fascist ideology.

Alternative Views: Marxism

Writing in the mid-nineteenth century, Karl Marx observed the growing economic inequality between those who provided labor and those who own capital. Marxists argue that this system of economics was a structurally unfair system, one that privileged those few fortunate enough to own capital such as factories. Those who owned the factories (the bourgeoisie) actually did no work but profited from the hard labor of those (the proletariat) who were employed by the factory. Yet the workers received little for their extensive labor. Most Marxists argued that the relationship between the two classes was parasitic, with the owners living off of the labor of the working classes. Marx argued that the capitalist system was one that would gradually privilege fewer and fewer people while at the same time drive more and more workers to the brink of desperation.

Thus, Marx predicted that history was moving toward a time when workers would finally unite and revolt against the upper classes, later creating a system of governance that would be fair to workers. Since everyone would then be a laborer, a classless society would emerge. Marx had originally thought that the workers' revolution that was to come would occur in an industrialized society where the inequalities between the labor and capital classes were most pronounced. He observed the conditions many workers experienced, some of which were captured in Victorian novels. For instance, Charles Dickens's *A Christmas Carol* (1843), which has been filmed several times and performed on countless stages throughout the Western world, illustrates the very difficult lives of British workers and the capitalist calculations of owners during that era.[3] Yet, the first successful Marxist, or communist, revolution occurred in imperial Russia, a largely agricultural state that lacked significant industrialization.

Adhering to Marx's ideas, Vladimir Lenin, the leader of the Bolsheviks (or "Reds"/communists), expounded on Marx's central theory by adding the concept of imperialism. Imperialism meant that, in order for capitalism to continue, it would necessarily have to expand in order to gain access to increasing capital and markets. In order to do this, capitalists would use the state to create and exploit colonies, using force if necessary, and extract their cheap labor and raw materials while procuring potentially lucrative markets for their products, thus insuring the protection of the capitalist class's interests.

After the Russian Revolution of 1917, the Bolsheviks would use the relatively new medium of cinema to "educate" the population. While many of the films of this period are considered propaganda, there is general agreement that the films produced during the silent era of the Soviet Union (roughly 1917 to 1930) are some of the most imaginative and innovative films ever made. Early Soviet cinema also visualized the ideals of a workers' revolution most clearly. In many ways it is unfortunate that these films are not more widely known because they are excellent commentaries about the Soviets' view of the world in the first thirty years of the twentieth century.

Consistently ranked among the top ten films ever made, *Potemkin* (or *Battleship Potemkin*, 1925) tells the story of the failed 1905 Russian Revolution. The film, made in honor of the twentieth anniversary of the event, recounts the story of the battleship *Potemkin*, which, while in the Black Sea, has a mutiny break out. Sailors are given maggot-infested food for their rations, and when some of them protest, the captain orders the protestors to be shot. One sailor, Vakulinchuk, implores those who carry the rifles not to follow orders, noting that they would only be shooting their brothers. The sailors lower their weapons and join in a general mutiny against the imperial czarist officers. During the struggle for the ship, Vakulinchuk is killed; however, the mutiny is successful.

The sailors take the body of Vakulinchuk to Odessa, where the citizenry of the city come to pay respects. While a crowd is gathered on the steps heading down to the sea, a czarist militia appears and begins shooting. A massacre occurs, and in particularly moving imagery, even babies and old women are deliberate victims of the massacre. The *Potemkin* returns to the sea to face a group of battleships sent to subdue it. As the sailors ready the guns of the *Potemkin*, they signal the other ships not to fight but instead to join them. Faced with a destructive battle the other ships relent and add their support to the *Potemkin*. The film ends with the jubilant crews of all the ships cruising off to face their adversaries.

Potemkin may be the best example of Marxist filmmaking achievement. Note that there is no real protagonist in the film other than the Russian people (thus putting the collective ahead of an individual). The only other potential protagonist is Vakulinchuk, who is killed off early on as a sacrifice for the good of the people. Also, coming just eight years after the revolution, the film serves as a historical document and a reminder to citizens (and others) of the brutality of the czarist regime. In the famous Odessa Steps sequence, one of the most famous and important scenes in film history, director Sergei Eisenstein focuses on the viciousness of the regime by using a baby carriage to symbolize the innocents. Also, the officers in the navy are particularly brutal and dismissive of the needs of the sailors. Audiences at the time would have recognized that the officers were from the upper class and the sailors were drawn from the working class. Eisenstein is making a comment on how the aristocracy and the upper class in general (the bourgeoisie) favor their own selfish economic interests, and primarily treat workers, the masses, and the nation, with contempt and disregard.[4]

Part of the appeal of the early Soviet cinema was the use of innovative editing techniques. The use of these techniques is evident in the work of Eisenstein, especially in the creation of the Odessa Steps sequence. Esther Shub, one of the early female pioneers in world cinema, would use old newsreel footage and archival footage to create a commentary on the czarist regime before the revolution and the need for a Marxist revolution in *The Fall of the Romanov Dynasty* (1927).[5] Shub searched the Soviet Union for several films to put together a montage of film to create a historical film document of the events from 1912 up to the 1917 revolution organized to create a communist commentary on the events. Shub's efforts are particularly noteworthy not only because of the statement she made about the czarist regime and the necessity of the Bolshevik revolution, but for the fact that she probably saved a number of scenes that would not have otherwise been seen by people today.

Shub creates a number of running themes through *The Fall of the Romanov Dynasty*, the most prevalent of which is the opulence of the czar and the aristocracy juxtaposed with the poverty of the average Russian citizen. The film opens with documentary footage, shot by the czar's own cameramen, of the celebration of the tricentennial of the Romanov Dynasty. The film employs title cards to raise questions as to why some Russians (the czar and his court) are allowed to enjoy such privilege and wealth, while in the meantime newsreel footage shows peasants suffering from various natural disasters, such as floods and drought, and barely eking out an existence. In a particularly biting commentary, Shub depicts a party on a cruise liner on the Black Sea where members of the court are having a dance. Shub next shows footage of peasants suffering from a drought who are on the verge of starvation. Title cards explain the desperate situations in which the peasants find themselves; when the footage cuts back to the dance on the cruise liner, a title card reads, " . . . and the aristocracy dances on."

Regardless of how one views Marxist ideology, it is hard to deny that both Eisenstein and Shub created films that make an impassioned argument for the necessity of revolution against the czarist regime. Both provide evidence of the brutality of the czarist rule and the need for a new order within the Russian society. However, where many departed from this assessment was how society should be ordered after the fall of the czar. Many Russians thought the aristocracy and merchant classes were complicit in the subjugation of the Russian people.

Reactions to the Russian Revolution: From Sympathy to the Red Scare

By the 1930s revolutionary experiments in the Soviet films were over. The film industry in the Soviet Union turned primarily to a reconstruction of revolutionary events in terms of social realism, such as in *Lenin in October* (1937) and *Lenin in 1918* (1939).[6] Of course outside the Soviet Union there were immediate reactions to calls of worldwide revolution. Many are familiar with the more blatant anticommunist films of the 1950s; however, "red scare" films have their genesis in the late teens and 1920s in American film history. Later, in the 1950s, Hollywood would develop a more uniform, sophisticated response to a perceived communist threat. Europeans would offer a more subtle critique that would even come from communist societies themselves.

Hollywood would begin reacting to the Russian Revolution almost immediately. In the same year as the revolution, 1917, the American film industry would produce a number of films about the subject. Two of the more prominent were *The Fall of the Romanoffs* (1917) and *The Rose of Blood* (1917); copies of neither of these films survive today. These films would concentrate on the events in Russia at the time and were not specifically critical of Marxism *per se*. Instead the Soviet Union was used as a backdrop of drama, terrorism, and political intrigue. Later films would focus more on the stereotypes of the regime rather than the revolution itself. These films usually portrayed the excesses of the regime by a few less than honest characters, with Marxist followers depicted as criminals, simpletons, or dupes. In *The Tempest* (1927), a John Gilbert vehicle, the film took viewers "inside" the Soviet Union to show the brutality of the communist regime.

However, during the Second World War, because of the wartime alliance between the Soviet Union and the United States, American films occasionally reflected some of the perspectives of the Soviet leadership. In *Mission to Moscow* (1943), former ambassador Joseph E. Davies, whose memoirs the film was based upon, offers an apologist's view of the Soviet system. The film gives a Soviet view of the war and attempts to garner support for the Soviet Union as an ally. The controversial film even goes as far as offering a sympathetic view of the Soviets' army purges of the 1930s. Other films, such as *Tender Comrade* (1943), directed by the later-blacklisted American filmmaker Edward Dmytryk (later member of the "Hollywood Ten"), portrayed collectivism in action in everyday life. The film tells the story of five women, whose husbands are engaged in war duties, sharing a house together. The women use democracy to run the house, however Jo Flanagan (Ginger Rogers) sets about organizing the house, providing moral chats to keep everyone devoted to the war effort and the missing men. It is debatable whether the film actually intended to espouse a communist philosophy or was simply urging cooperation among civilians during wartime, but nevertheless the film would later become controversial during the "red scare" of the 1940s and 1950s.[7] Dmytryk a child of Ukrainian immigrants raised in California, would later serve time behind bars for being an uncooperative witness before the hostile House Un-American Activities Committee (HUAC). A leftist politically, Dmytryk, was briefly a member of the Communist Party during World War II, and later, after serving in prison, "named names," cooperating with HUAC's investigation of perceived and real communist sympathies in the entertainment industry.

Soon after the death of President Franklin Roosevelt and the end of World War II in 1945, relations between the Soviet Union and the United States, once-staunch allies in the fight against Nazi Germany, fascist Italy, and the empire of Japan, frayed considerably. Competing values, economic systems, and ideologies—namely liberalism and Soviet communism—vied for moral superiority and world prowess. Severe disagreements and misunderstandings over several pressing issues—especially the shape of postwar Europe and, specifically, control of Eastern Europe—fostered increasing hostility and contempt between the superpowers. In the midst of this ideological warfare, both states readied and expanded their conventional and nuclear arsenals[8] and embarked upon forty-five years of expensive, nerve-racking "Cold War."

In the meantime, Hollywood film studios also entered the ideological fray of the Cold War, using their arsenal of writers, producers, and directors to promote liberalism and Western-style capitalism and denigrate communism. Responding to the extensive and, at times, violent labor struggles between Hollywood studios and the writers and actors guilds in the late 1940s, the growing animosity and distrust between the U.S. and the U.S.S.R., the political ascendance of HUAC, and, by 1950, the war in Korea and the loss of American lives, film studios produced a series of films condemning communism and warning of its insidious spread in the United States. Thus, studio heads were not driven entirely by altruism and ideology—be it absolute faith in individual liberty or the gospel of the free market—but by the shifting winds of domestic politics, business interests, and blatant opportunism. In this new era, out were the unabashedly pro-Soviet films—such as the propagandistic *Mission to Moscow* (1943), which had been produced with active support from the Roosevelt administration—and in were movies that featured American innocents duped by the vicious lies of communism.[9] The message of these films is clear: the vigilant rooting out of subversives, socialists, and communists at home is vital to winning the worldwide war against communism.

Amid this ideological warfare, Americans were encouraged, via a variety of new movies, to stand guard against the poisoning of children's minds, to be wary of academic elites and others indoctrinating students with Karl Marx's theories, and, if need be, to turn in family members suspected of being traitors to capitalism and American values. From the late 1940s through the mid-1950s, Hollywood produced a plethora of frequently propagandistic anticommunist "red scare" films that reflected the paranoia and hysteria concerning real and imagined domestic communist subversion and the fear of worldwide communist domination. A slew of films—such as *The Iron Curtain* (1948), *The Red Menace* (1949), *I Married a Communist* (1949), *I Was a Communist for the FBI* (1951), *Big Jim McLain* (1952), *My Son John* (1952), and, to a lesser and more curious extent, *Invasion of the Body Snatchers* (1956)—represents this genre of political films.

Yet, this genre of political storytelling was not limited to motion pictures. For instance, *I Was a Communist for the FBI* was also a radio drama starring Dana Andrews. The radio program used formulaic plot devices for seventy-eight episodes in 1952 and 1953. *Big Jim McLain* (1952), starring film icon John Wayne, highlights many of the plot devices inherent in this genre of movies and remains a quintessential "red scare" anticommunist film. Directed by Edward Ludwig and produced by John Wayne and Robert Fellows, *Big Jim*

McLain is a blatant propaganda tool for HUAC. Made with the U.S. government's explicit enthusiastic cooperation, through the participation of HUAC, the film stars Wayne as Jim McLain, a HUAC investigator who, along with his partner (James Arness), is sent to Hawaii to break up the communist infiltration of a longshoreman's union. Not unlike other red scare films, the communists are portrayed as sleek, well-dressed, occasionally effeminate sophisticates (some with decidedly Eastern European accents) who are willing to murder and drug innocents and even sacrifice their own "comrades" if it advances their worldwide crusade. The film is also unabashedly anti-intellectual. At the film's start, determined, patriotic HUAC investigators at a congressional hearing grill suave economics professors about their communist beliefs, only to be thwarted by the university intellectuals exercising their Fifth Amendment right to protect themselves against self-incrimination. McLain scoffs at these un-American tactics, chastising the professors for "hiding behind the Constitution" just so they can continue to manipulate and poison the minds of American students. Some film critics have argued that the movie gives the impression that the sacred liberties in the Bill of Rights are reserved only for certain Americans.

As in other classic red menace movies of the era, *McLain* features parents who cooperate with HUAC investigators and willingly turn in their children who have been brainwashed by the communists and have become Soviet agents. In this film, the parents are retired, God-fearing, working-class people who have settled in Hawaii after years of toiling for modest wages in San Francisco. They think it is their duty to inform HUAC of their son's descent into communism. What makes *Big Jim McLain* unique among this group of films, however, is the prominence and drawing power of its leading man. While the vast majority of the red scare films featured moderately famous and B-movie Hollywood players, *Big Jim McLain* featured a bona fide Hollywood superstar— "The Duke," John Wayne. This immediately gave the film stature, and an audience, other red scare films could only dream of. Moreover, while most of the aforementioned anticommunist films were mildly successful, *McLain* was a major box office success. With a budget of $800,000, the Wayne–Fellows-produced *McLain* grossed over $2.4 million dollars, earning a very healthy profit.[10]

In the sci-fi Cold War classic *Invasion of the Body Snatchers* (1956), alien seedpods infiltrate Middle America, quietly turning the citizens of Santa Mira into heartless, loveless drones. Released in the midst of anticommunist panic, the political implications would seem to be clear: the pods represent the communist menace, calmly and deliberatively turning trusted neighbors into uncaring communists. This development is especially alarming, as the neighbors look the same, dress the same, and inhabit the same houses, but something is wrong—*terribly* wrong. Their individuality and vitality have been sapped and been replaced with passionless adherence to the communist cause. One by one, once-vivacious, individualistic Americans are now dressed in the suit of subversive, Soviet skin.

Upon another careful viewing, however, Don Siegel's film may speak to another dynamic in postwar America. Rather than solely espousing the fear of insidious, Godless, soulless communism taking over the bodies of everyday suburban Americans, the film may very well be an *indictment* of Eisenhower-era conformity, McCarthyism, and mindless anticommunism. In this interpretation of the film, the pods that take over innocent Americans do not represent the evil of *communism* but, rather, the peril of *anticommunist conformity* run amok. Political scientist Phillip Gianos advances this alternative, an increasingly accepted theory of the film's political message, believing that *Invasion of the Body Snatchers* is "an allegory on another cold-war era concern: the drive toward a dehumanizing conformity in behavior and orthodoxy of thought in the service of opposition to communism."[11] Indeed, as Gianos points out, this was the interpretation that the film's director, Don Siegel, attributed to his film, "arguing that the film was designed as a warning about the price in freedom to be paid by demanding political and social orthodoxy."[12]

Similarly, political scientist Ernest Giglio includes *Body Snatchers* in the category of fifties films that indirectly question the pervasive anticommunist hysteria of the day. While there were few films that dared to overtly criticize the red scare and McCarthyism, *Body Snatchers* is cited as a movie in a category of films that "challenged the communist paranoia and the effects of McCarthyism allegorically, expressing . . . condemnation of HUAC and the blacklist in plots that dealt with subjects ranging from space aliens to westerns."[13] The pods, therefore, represent "the three dominant forces of the fifties: conformity, paranoia, and alienation."[14] While saturated in American popular culture at mid-century, the fifties sci-fi classic with powerful political undertones has remained popular with subsequent generations of moviegoers. Gianos asserts that the film's staying power—it was remade in 1978, 1992, and 2007—is due, in large part, to the story's enduring appeal and its applicability to the politics and concerns of Americans on both sides of the ideological spectrum; "its attractiveness both to those who see the film as anti-Communist allegory and those who see it as a cautionary tale about conformity—and 'anti-anti' Communist fable."[15]

Indeed, other later films would dare to directly criticize and lampoon McCarthyism and anticommunist conformity as well as self-serving, cynical politicians who propagated fear and paranoia to further their careers. John Frankenheimer's chilling Cold War political assassination classic, *The Manchurian Candidate* (1962), is a perfect example. In one famous scene, the loudmouthed McCarthy-esque Senator Iselin (a hilarious James Gregory) rants and raves on the Senate floor about the growing number of communists serving in the U.S. government. However, when pressed by reporters outside of Senate chambers for more specifics, Sen. Iselin responds by giving several different numbers of communists. He finally settles on one number to suit his domineering political operator and wife (Angela Lansbury): 57. Why 57 communists? Because he tops his hamburger with Heinz's 57 Ketchup at dinner the night before his next anticommunist diatribe![16] This snippet from the movies mirrors the historical record of—and is clearly an indictment of— Senator Joe McCarthy, who, during a famous speech in Wheeling, West Virginia, in 1950, made headlines by claiming he had a list of communists serving in the government. Said McCarthy in Wheeling: "I have here in my hand a list of 205 [card-carrying communists] . . . who are still working and shaping policy in the State Department." Secretary of State George Catlett Marshall was also the target of McCarthy's ire; he asserted that Marshall avidly participated in a "conspiracy so immense and an infamy so black as to dwarf any previous such venture in the history of man."[17] Like the fictional Senator Iselin, McCarthy also occasionally had trouble remembering the *precise* number of communists selling out the United States. But, much like films critical of America's involvement in Vietnam—most of which appeared years *after* the war—it is important to note that it took several years for Hollywood to overtly question and criticize the almost-sacrosanct anticommunist ethos of the late 1940s to mid-1950s. Indeed, identifying communists and furthering the fear of domestic subversion became increasing popular and bipartisan, as evidenced by the passage of the McCarran Act in 1950. Passed over the veto of Democratic president Harry Truman, the McCarran Act sought to restrict the civil liberties of communists, mandating their registration with the government and the revoking of their passports. It also planned for the establishment of concentration camps in "the event of a national emergency."[18]

The Legacy of the Red Scare: HUAC, the Blacklist, and the Hollywood Ten

In 1938, the House Committee on Un-American Activities—in later years also referred to as the House Un-American Activities Committee (HUAC)—was also known to many simply as the "Dies Committee," as the select committee was chaired by Rep. Martin Dies (D-TX). HUAC was formed to probe a variety of dangerous "Un-American" right- and left-wing ideologies and movements, from fascist kidnappers to the Ku Klux Klan. Soon after Dies ascended to the chairmanship of the committee, however, the targets became increasingly left-wing individuals and groups, especially those associated with President Franklin Roosevelt's (in office 1933–1945) New Deal programs.[19] What was the legislative basis for the congressional examination of subversive groups? Specifically, the new House committee was authorized to—"from time to time"—conduct investigations of

> the extent, character, and objects of un-American propaganda activities in the United States, (2) the diffusion within the United States of subversive and un-American propaganda that is instigated from foreign countries or of a domestic origin and attacks the principle of the form of government as guaranteed by our Constitution, and (3) all other questions in relation thereto that would aid Congress in any necessary remedial legislation.[20]

In particular, Dies and his investigators targeted suspected communist and socialist playwrights, actors, and directors in Franklin Roosevelt's Federal Theatre Project (FTP), part of the New Deal's ambitious Works Progress Administration (WPA).[21] Tim Robbins's film *Cradle Will Rock* (1999), a work of historical fiction, examines this period of political history, and uses in the movie direct congressional testimony from Hallie Flanagan, director of the FTP. *The Cradle Will Rock* not only addresses the congressional investigation of the Federal Theatre Project but delves into several subplots, chief among them the FTP-supported creation and staging of Marc Blitzstein's 1937 left-wing Depression-era musical drama *The Cradle Will Rock*, a play that depicted a union organizing drive in a steel-producing city ("Steeltown, USA"). The play's protagonists included a union organizer, Larry Foreman, and the chief villain was a wealthy, union-busting industrialist named Mister Mister. The drama's title comes from the stirring song sung at the conclusion of the play by the workers.[22] Robbins's film follows the extensive difficulties faced by FTP director Flanagan (Cherry Jones), as well as the challenges faced by the likes of writer Blitzstein (Hank Azaria) and producers Orson Welles (Angus MacFadyen) and John Houseman (Cary Elwes), who were attempting to stage the pro-union musical in the midst of enormous political pressure and threatened (and later, real) censorship. Tim Robbins's *Cradle Will Rock* is unabashedly sympathetic with the government activism of the WPA and the FTP, and, moreover, defends the rights of artists to practice their craft free from government censorship. As such, the film stands as a cautionary tale of how reactionary politics can stifle creativity and forcefully defends the artistic vision and liberal politics of the playwrights, directors, actors, and producers who worked in the Federal Theatre Project.

By the late 1940s, however, as America's World War II alliance with the Soviet Union gave way to the Cold War, HUAC's main targets were no longer New Deal programs (the Federal Theatre Project was eventually discontinued after a series of congressional investigations) but left-wing actors, writers, and directors—some of whom were active in organizing the various unions in the film industry. In October 1947, after several closed-door hearings and investigations over a six-month period, HUAC chairman J. Parnell Thomas began public hearings designed to root out communists in Hollywood. The first to appear before the committee were so-called friendly witnesses trotted out by the motion picture industry to denounce communism and to suggest names of suspected Communist Party members and sympathizers in Hollywood. Witnesses representing "The Motion Picture Association for the Preservation of American Ideals" included actors Gary Cooper and Adolphe Menjou and studio heads Jack Warner, Louis B. Mayer, and Walt Disney. The studio heads were eager to stem the rising tide of unionism and strikes in their industry, and Thomas's hearings served their purpose well.

After the "friendly witnesses" testified, a list of writers and directors who were suspected communists were called before the committee. The first ten of these witnesses were outraged at being called before a hostile, politically charged committee and refused to cooperate with Thomas's inquiry on constitutional grounds. They were later sent to prison for contempt of Congress, and several of them lost years of work in the industry, effectively "blacklisted" by studios and producers. This group of writers and directors became known collectively as the "Hollywood Ten." In alphabetical order, the Hollywood Ten were: Alvah Bessie, Herbert J. Biberman, Lester Cole, Edward Dmytryk, Ring Lardner Jr., John Howard Lawson, Albert Maltz, Samuel Ornitz, Adrian Scott, and Dalton Trumbo. Even actors who were never implicated, but simply made films with blacklisted personnel, would find their careers significantly damaged.[23]

Hollywood eventually directly examined the legacy and fallout of HUAC's hearings and the blacklisting of artists in the poignant dark comedy *The Front* (1976). Directed by blacklisted director Martin Ritt, written by blacklisted screenwriter Walter Bernstein, and starring a host of blacklisted actors, including Zero Mostel (Hecky Brown/Herschel Brownstein) and Herschel Bernardi (Phil Sussman), *The Front* stands as a major achievement: it is the first studio film to directly criticize the blacklist and address its myriad effects on writers, actors, producers, and their families. For instance, in the film, we see how the lack of work, loss of income, mounting depression, and pressure to "name names" causes the talented comedian Hecky Brown, now a blacklisted actor, to commit suicide.

The film stars Woody Allen as Howard Prince, a simple debt-ridden bookie who is a "front" for his friend Alfred Miller, a blacklisted writer. Prince routinely meets with Miller and other blacklisted writers at a local deli, where the out-of-work artists give Prince scripts for television shows. Prince gets a 10 percent cut from each of the scripts and winds up becoming a celebrity as he pads his modest gambling revenue. Even Prince's high school invites the bumbling bookie–turned–star writer back for a school assembly, where he is introduced as a bona fide American success story. The deli scenes have direct political resonance, as the three fictional writers depicted in the film—Herbert Delaney (Lloyd Gough), Bill Phelps (David Margulies), and Alfred Miller (Michael Murphy)—are actually composites of real-life blacklisted writers Walter Bernstein, Arnold Manoff, and Abraham Polonsky, who collaborated on the 1953 Walter Cronkite television segments *You Are There*. It is perhaps poetic justice that in 1977 Bernstein's script for *The Front* was nominated for best screenplay by the Academy Awards and the Writers Guild of America.[24]

In later years Hollywood would revisit many of the same issues addressed in *The Front*, albeit with less critical acclaim. *Guilty by Suspicion* (1991), written and directed by Irwin Winkler and starring Robert De Niro as an unjustly accused communist, attacked the blacklist and its pernicious consequences on writers, directors, and their families. However, the film failed to garner the critical accolades and audience size earned by Ritt and Bernstein's film. A few documentaries do an excellent job of detailing the social, political, and cultural legacy of HUAC's investigations, the red scare films of the late 1940s to mid-1950s, and the blacklist. *Hollywood on Trial* (1976), an Oscar-nominated documentary directed by David Helpern and written by Arnie Reisman, is the most in-depth and impressive documentary of the blacklist era, featuring extensive archival footage of HUAC investigations of 1947 and revealing interviews with members of the Hollywood Ten. *Blacklist: Hollywood on Trial* (1996), premiering on the cable channel American Movie Classics (AMC) and narrated by Alec Baldwin, reexamines many of the themes covered in *Hollywood on Trial*. The documentary earned the President's Award at the 1996 Emmys and the Gold Apple award from the National Educational Media Network, USA.

A Personal Side of the Blacklist:
The Life and Letters of Dalton Trumbo (1905–1976)

As *The Front* (1976) illustrates, often the most penetrating and transcendent political films delve into the personal side of people's lives, examining their humanity and the impact of socio-political dynamics in a very intimate way. Such is the case with the 2007 documentary film *Trumbo*, whose central subject, Academy Award–winning screenwriter Dalton Trumbo, spent eleven months in jail (beginning in 1950) for defying the House Un-American Activities Committee (HUAC), and endured the unofficial blacklist that prevented many left-wing artists from earning a living under their own name.[25] Cataloging personal, family, and professional struggles and successes—as well as the humorous, heartbreaking, and everyday fatherly reflections of the blacklisted writer—the film, based on his son Christopher Trumbo's 2003 play, *Trumbo: Red, White & Blacklisted*, examines Dalton Trumbo's life and ordeals through many of his eloquent letters.

Directed by Peter Askin and based on the aforementioned off-Broadway play, *Trumbo* (2007) features archival footage alongside central dramatic presentations: a bevy of award-winning stars of stage and screen reading Trumbo's own words. The effect is direct and profound. Via the likes of Nathan Lane, Brian Dennehy, Paul Giamatti, Joan Allen, David Strathairn and others, we see and hear Dalton Trumbo, the person, not the symbol, scapegoat, or relic of a bygone era. His humanity, channeled through the actors' reading of his reflections, sheds vital light on the enduring tensions between art, politics, commerce, and family life. As the *New York Times'* Stephen Holden asserts, *Trumbo* "gives you reasons to cheer but also to weep. It makes you lament the decline of the kind of language brandished with Shakespearean eloquence by Dalton Trumbo." The film critic also offered this assessment of the political strife that shaped Trumbo, and the nation, in 1947 and beyond: "If only the movers and shakers of Hollywood 13 years earlier had stood together like the slaves in 'Spartacus' and all claimed to have been Communists, the blacklist might have been averted. But they didn't. Fear can make people instant cowards and informers. Resisting it may be the ultimate test of character."[26]

Challenging Communist Ideology from Within: The Czech New Wave

While the films that confronted communism in the United States tended to rely on scare tactics and overblown characterizations, criticism from within the Communist bloc had to be more muted and subtle. Filmmakers in the Communist bloc had to criticize their regimes and societies surreptitiously. One of the great eras of filmmaking was the Czech New Wave, which flourished in the 1960s and took particular advantage of the loosening of government censorships that culminated in the Prague Spring of 1968. While not being able to attack the communist regime of Czechoslovakia directly, filmmakers like Miloš Forman and Jan Němec used simple stories to explore issues of deeper political meanings. On the surface, one might not see the political significance and in some cases the message of the film is disguised by science fiction or bizarre plotlines, but understanding the context of these films provides a richer appreciation of the work of Czech New Wave directors.

Initially, *Loves of a Blonde* (1965) appears to be a simple tale of a young girl and her adventures following a boy with whom she has spent the night. However, the film is more of an indictment of the monotony of Czech society under the communist regime. As the film opens, Andula is working at a shoe factory in her hometown of Zruč. The manager of the factory is sympathetic to the fact that there are not enough men around for the two thousand or so women who work in the shoe factory. He implores the local military commander to move the base closer to the factory so that the women can meet some men. Initially the military commander balks, arguing that soldiers are needed at the border rather than to entertain young women. The factory manager implores him, asking what good is peace if people cannot live fulfilling lives. The train arrives and off come men who are not very appealing, one of the women comments that the army sent them veterans rather than young soldiers.

At a dance held as a mixer for the women and the soldiers, three soldiers approach Andula and her friends. The women are not really interested in the men, but they are polite, and the encounter results in a comedic exercise. Meanwhile, Andula finds herself drawn toward the piano player, Milda, in the band. She meets him after the dance, and is later seduced by him. After her tryst with the young piano player, she becomes enamored with him and dumps her oft-absent boyfriend.

In a scene that is perhaps telling of the society that Forman is trying to represent, the film depicts how the trappings of democracy can be twisted. After an incident in which Andula's former boyfriend comes to the factory dormitory, the women get a lecture from the housemother about morals. She argues that by "giving into boys," women cheapen themselves and make the prospects of having a happy and fulfilling life with a happy family more remote. After the lecture, two of the women step forward and say that the housemother has made a lot of sense and they propose to take a vote to mend their ways. The women in the dormitory vote to mend their ways without opposition or abstentions.

Seeing her life in Zruc as monotonous, Andula travels to Prague with her luggage to drop in on Milda. When she arrives at Milda's apartment, she finds that she is one in a long line of sexual conquests. She is unwelcomed by Milda's parents. When she returns home, Andula remains upbeat and hopeful of her love life and future. She tells how nice Milda's parents were, and what a great person in particular his father is and how happy Mila was to see her. She whispers to her roommate that she will be making several trips to Prague now, and the close of the film shows her back on the assembly line working on the shoes. While initially we might think that Andula is naïve, one could argue though that she is coping with her plight as optimistically as possible.

Forman has said that he got the idea of *Loves of a Blonde* when he was driving home one night and saw a young girl on a street corner in Prague with her bags. When he stopped to see why she was there she confessed that she had traveled to Prague to find a young man whom she had met in her village and had slept with. However, the address he had provided was false.[27] While the film focuses on the love life of the blonde, Andula, Forman is also commenting on the society in which she exists. Andula's isolation and her reliance on married men, one-night stands, and absent boyfriends for company are a function of her employment. She works in a factory of all women, remote from social functions. In the scene where the women are subjected to a lecture on morals, we presume that the women who propose the vote to mend their ways are operatives. The vote is an opportunity to publicly shame the women into changing their behavior. Clearly no one is going to vote against higher morals, and the vote is essentially meaningless. But, in the end, those in charge can argue that they have provided a democratic "choice" for the women in the dormitory. Similarly, the Czechoslovak government at the time argued they were giving citizens a democratic "choice," although the Communist Party ran unopposed in elections.

Miloš Forman's next film went farther in its criticism of the ineptitude and banality of Stalinist regimes. *The Firemen's Ball* (1967) is again on the surface a simple tale of a party for a former fire chief. But the conformity of the society and the inability of the bureaucracy to rationally organize society are at the heart of the film. The main plotline of the film is a party to award the former fire chief a golden axe in recognition of his years of service. The occasion is his eighty-sixth birthday, even though his eighty-fifth birthday would have been more appropriate, but as one reviewer observed, "procrastination is important to any functioning bureaucracy."[28] Yet, before the awarding of the gifts and the raffling off of various prizes, the firemen are called away on a fire.

One of the funniest scenes of the film features another old man in the town, whose house is burning down and the firemen arrive to extinguish the flames. The man is sitting in a chair in front of his house, in the snow, watching the house burn when his neighbors come out and decide that he should be turned away from the house so that he does not have to watch it burn. The neighbors then decide that since it is cold they should move the man closer to the house so that he does not get cold. Forman is making a comment here about the society's inability to make decisions that are rational. Instead of the neighbors taking the old man inside, to offer him comfort, they search for an idea that is relevant to the man yet does not put any burden on themselves. The entire film demonstrates the discouragement of individual thinking under a totalitarian regime and calls into question the ability of the Communist Party and the Czech society to make substantive decisions without needless bureaucracy and rhetorical assertions.

Miloš Forman

Forman may be the most celebrated director to emerge from the Czech Republic. After he immigrated to the United States following the Soviet invasion of Czechoslovakia in 1968, Forman went on to direct a series of highly acclaimed films. Taken by themselves, the films are some of the most celebrated films of the past several decades. Taken together, and considering his biography, Forman's filmography may provide an interesting body of work to consider.

His parents were killed in a Nazi concentration camp outside Prague during World War II. After attending film school in Prague, Forman made two of the most important films of the Czech New Wave: *Loves of a Blonde* (1965) and *The Firemen's Ball* (1967). Both films ran into trouble with government censors, and some volunteer firefighters in Czechoslovakia reportedly were offended by the ineptitude of the firemen in *The Firemen's Ball*. Although this story may be propaganda produced by the communist Czechoslovak regime.

Consider some of Forman's U.S. films:

One Flew over the Cuckoo's Nest (1975): Nominated for nine Academy Awards, and winner of five, including best picture and best director. The film examines the abuses of authority inside a mental institution. Lead actor Jack Nicholson finds that the head nurse is more dangerous than the patients.

Hair (1979): A musical that celebrates individuals' choices and the counterculture. Being drafted into the Vietnam War interrupts the happiness and contentment of the protagonist.

Amadeus (1984): The phenomenally successful film biography of Wolfgang Amadeus Mozart examines the unique individuality of the great composer. The film was nominated for eleven Academy Awards and was the winner of eight, including best picture and best director.

The People vs. Larry Flynt (1996): A highly controversial film, which examined the right of the famous pornographer and his exercise and defense of free speech. The film used the tagline, *"You may not like what he does, but are you prepared to give up his right to do it?"* Forman was again nominated for an Academy Award for best director.

In the first two films listed here, the director examines the abuses of authority. In the latter two films, Forman examines the exercise of free expression, whether emanating from an eighteenth-century composer who was censored because of his operas' subject matter or a twentieth-century pornographer. Forman did receive a great deal of criticism for his vigorous defense of the free speech of the latter individual, Larry Flynt. For further reading, consider Forman's reasoning behind taking on the controversial film project *The People vs. Larry Flynt*. For Miloš Forman's address to the National Press Club, see http://www.mit.edu/activities/safe/writings-/people-v-flynt.

Notice that neither of the two Forman films reviewed here attacks directly the regime in Czechoslovakia at the time. They are simple stories of everyday life, the life of common people in Czechoslovakia, which have overtones
that go to the heart of Czech society. Behind the story is an exploration of the
one of the most sensitive debates of the late 1960s in Czechoslovakia. When
the end of Stalinism in the Soviet Union and the progress of de-Stalinization
throughout Eastern Europe occurred, the question became what should be
done with those who committed the brutality of the 1950s, particularly those
who were still in power. *The Firemen's Ball* was released in December 1967, just
a few weeks before the Antonín Novotný regime was to be replaced by the more
liberal Alexander Dubcek regime, which ushered in what became known as the
Prague Spring.

Perhaps the most bizarre film discussed in this book is *A Report on the Party
and the Guest* (*O slavnosti a hostech*, 1966). While the narrative and plot seem
rather odd, understand that director Jan Němec was making a very pointed criticism of the Czechoslovak regime while at the same time not directly mentioning politics at all. The film is not designed to be bizarre simply for the sake of
being weird: it was the only way for the filmmaker to address his concerns about
the nature of the communist government in Czechoslovakia. While the *New
York Times* named it one of the top ten films of the 1960s, Czech president
Notovný declared the film "banned forever." As the film opens, a group of people is having a picnic. Each agrees that it is a beautiful day and the food is delicious. The group reminisces about their previous outings and what their host
has done in the past. One remarks, "Remember the time he had the wine?"
Imperceptibly to the picnickers and the viewer, a man comes out of the woods
with a bottle of wine.

Prague Spring

During most of 1968 Prague flourished under increasing political and economic liberalization. Journalists, writers, and academics were given enough freedom and were allowed to speak
about the abuses of the past. Television shows, newspapers, and
commentators outlined the excesses and abuses of the Stalin and
the Novotný regimes. As the liberalization continued, other East
European regimes, and, most important, the Soviet Union, worried about the end result. Questions were raised as to whether
Czechoslovakia would even remain a member of the Warsaw

Pact (the defensive organization of European communist countries). Finally in August 1968, Warsaw Pact troops, led by the
Soviet Union, invaded Czechoslovakia to replace the Dubcek
regime and restore a more hard-line government whose policies
would be more in line with that of the Soviet Union.[29]

The new regime in Czechoslovakia was decidedly more hard
line. Protests against the invasion were mounted but were no
match for the heavily armed forces of the Warsaw Pact. There
were various acts of resistance at the time and commemorations
that have marked the invasion since:

- A student, Jan Palach, self-immolated (set himself on
  fire) in January 1969 on Wenceslas Square, the main
  square in Prague, to protest the reinstitution of press
  censorship. A memorial to his sacrifice was permanently
  established after the fall of communism.
- Jaromír Jágr, arguably the most famous hockey player
  from the Czech Republic, who grew up under the communist regime, wore the number 68 throughout his
  career to commemorate the death of his grandfather in
  1968, as a political prisoner.[30]
- The film *Fantastic Planet* (*La planète sauvage*, 1973) was
  made in France by Czechoslovak animators. The story, set
  in the future, recounts how humans are the pets of a
  much larger creature known as the Traags; it is seen as
  a metaphor for the Czech relationship with the Soviets.
- The film *The Unbearable Lightness of Being* (1988), and
  the novel on which it is based, is set in the midst of the
  Prague Spring. The film explores the ability to maintain a
  lifestyle and privacy in the midst of the Soviet-led invasion.
- Jan Němec, director of *A Report on the Party and the
  Guest*, revisited the events of 1968 in his 2009 film *The
  Ferrari Dino Girl* (*Holka Ferrari Dino*). Němec uses footage
  he shot during the 1968 resistance to the invasion inter-
  cut with contemporary footage to tell the story of how
  he smuggled the film out of Czechoslovakia to the West.

The communist regime would come to an end during the Velvet Revolution of 1989 after peaceful street protests led to the party leadership resigning; on January 1, 1993, Czechoslovakia would peacefully be split into two new countries: the Czech Republic and the Slovak Republic.

Later in *A Report on the Party and the Guest*, the group is making their way through the forest when a strange man (Rudolf) approaches them and asks if they are enjoying their outing. Rudolf is very insistent upon gaining the group's attention, but he makes the group feel very uneasy. Soon a number of severe looking men come out of the woods and prevent the group from reaching their destination. Eventually, they lead the group to a clearing in the forest where Rudolf reappears and forces the group to conform to his wishes. The men bring a desk and chair to the clearing, where Rudolf sits and directs the group to organize, à la a communist apparatchik. Members of the group attempt to address him, but Rudolf only responds when they are organized, as he desires them to be organized. Finally, the intellectual of the group organizes them, dividing men from women by an imaginary line, and addresses Rudolf with the deference he is seeking. When one of the men refuses to be bound by imaginary walls and incoherent rules, he attempts to run away, only to be stopped by Rudolf's men and roughed up. One can understand the scene as the history of authoritarianism (fascism) in Central Europe. The group is forced to conform to the whims of Rudolf (note the similarities to Adolf). When people resist, violence is deployed to bring them back into line. The group is finally "rescued" by the "host," who represents the Communist Party and demands obedience from all.

The point of director Jan Němec is that the communist government, and its insistence that everyone belong to the "party," is just as authoritarian as the fascists. While the story on the surface is seemingly very bizarre, what Němec is portraying is a very clear indictment of the way repression was used in Czech society during the Notovný regime. *New York Times* film critic Vincent Canby noted that the picnickers collapsed in the face of a smiling tyrant, "with only the vaguest suggestion of menace—and meeting only the slightest resistance—the host assimilates the picnic."[31] The story is even more poignant when one realizes that director Evald Schorm, whose film *Return of the Prodigal Son* (1966) was banned by the government at that time, played the role of the unhappy guest. The film is a study in conformity in the face of oppression and brutality. Ultimately the film is an explanation of how and why the Stalinist regimes managed to stay in power without significant opposition.

After the Soviet invasion of Prague in 1968, many film directors that made up the Czech "new wave" left out of fear. Both Forman and Němec left for the United States shortly after the invasion. Forman continued to make films in the United States, capturing Oscars for films like *One Flew over the Cuckoo's Nest* (1975) and *Amadeus* (1984) and receiving accolades for the politically charged *The People vs. Larry Flynt* (1996), a spirited biographical sketch of the life, times, and travails (including landmark free speech court cases) of the peculiar pornographer and First Amendment crusader Larry Flynt. Němec lived in relative obscurity for a time in the United States but returned to the Czech Republic after the collapse of the communist government in 1989. Since his return he has made a handful of films in his home country.

The collapse of communist governments in Eastern Europe in the grassroots "people's" revolutions of 1989 meant that filmmakers were now able to openly criticize governments. Curiously, about a decade after the fall of communism, there was a wave of reconsideration of the communist past and a critique of the increasing capitalism of the present. People did not necessarily miss the repression present in communist regimes, but rising unemployment, a decline in the social safety net, increased drug use, and rampant consumerism clearly created, among some, a longing for the past. In eastern Germany, this phenomenon became known as *ostalgie* ("nostalgia for the east"). An extremely popular film that captured this nostalgia was *Good Bye Lenin!* (2003), in which a young man attempts to preserve the illusion that the German Democratic Republic (GDR, East Germany) still exists so that his very sick mother—now awakened from a coma induced *before* communism's fall—will not become too upset. The film was an attempt to point out that not everything from the GDR was bad; reunification of East and West Germany meant that most things from the East disappeared almost overnight. The counterpoint to this argument can be found in the Academy Award–winning film *The Lives of Others* (2006), a powerful film examining the life of an East German secret policeman who eavesdrops on the life of a playwright sympathetic to socialism. A key point to this fascinating and highly entertaining thriller is that the GDR was so paranoid that it was even willing, through its secret police, the *Stasi* (1950–1990), to spy on and repress its supporters and drive them to opposition. For many opponents of the East German communist government, it is difficult to romanticize such a regime.

Alternative Views: Fascism

Fascism finds its roots in the 1922 parliamentary crisis in Italy. When the institutions of the Italian state were seemingly paralyzed, an attempt to stream-line and make the state more efficient was introduced. Many people saw it as an economic alternative to both liberalism and Marxism. Fascists argued that the community has the right to determine what the national interests are. To that end, the conflicting interests of workers, owners, technicians, and the state should be brought together under a single unit, operating under the control of the public, called "the corporation." The use of strikes or lockouts is to be for-bidden. Ultimately, the primacy of the expert and the technician should out-weigh the desires and needs of politicians. Consequently, the divisiveness of politics should be replaced by the unity of expertise. However, fascists seemed to be more interested in building power than in building theoretical coherence.[32]

While the examination of fascist forms of governance begins with Italy, it is ultimately applied to several totalitarian regimes that sacrifice individual lib-erties in lieu of efficiency and national prosperity. The most famous examples of fascist regimes tend to be Germany under the Nazis (1933–1945), Spain under Francisco Franco (1936–1975), and Italy under Mussolini (1922–1943). There are four main tools of powers that fascists attempted to develop and refine: charismatic leadership, single-party rule, terror, and economic control.

During the Nazi regime, the German film industry was under the control of Minister of Public Enlightenment and Propaganda Joseph Goebbels. Yet unlike the Soviet Union, the German film industry was not nationalized until 1942, almost a decade after the Nazis had come to power and three years into the war. The German government was more interested in the populace being entertained,[33] provided that entertainment was in the form of escapism, than being educated about the benefits of National Socialism.[34] Thus, films concern-ing fascism are relatively rare even from the most recognizable fascist regime. That being said, both Fascist Italy and Nazi Germany, like their Soviet coun-terparts, recognized the utility of film as a propaganda tool.

Films that carried the message of National Socialism to the masses gener-ally fell into one of a number of categories: newsreels, historical dramas of great national leaders or events, films that glorified the Nazi regime, or racial pro-paganda. The most recognizable film that touts a fascist ideology is *Triumph of the Will* (1934), which was filmed by the famous and controversial female director Leni Riefenstahl. The film purports to be a documentary of Adolf Hitler delivering a speech to the Nuremberg Party Convention; however, the entire event was staged for the camera. Complete plans for marches, parades, and architecture were drawn up in advance.[35] The opening of the film depicts Hitler arriving on an airplane in Nuremberg, almost as if he were a god descending from the clouds to address the convention. While the speeches made at the convention were designed to appeal to emotion rather than intellect, officials of the day thought the film effective enough to have it banned in Britain, Canada, and the United States.[36]

Propaganda

The prospect of being manipulated, especially by governments, was something that a number of writers worried about in the middle of the twentieth century. There is no doubt that world events helped to shape many writers' fears. The ability of Soviet and Nazi propaganda to mobilize people worried a number of writers. What is interesting, and what makes propaganda still relevant, is not that writers necessarily feared individual regimes, but that these regimes demonstrated how easily people could be manipulated. Thus, George Orwell demonstrates how propaganda shapes politics in his novels *1984* and *Animal Farm*; Ray Bradbury speculates how the manipulation of people could have dire consequences in novels such as *Fahrenheit 451*; Aldous Huxley examines the effects of brainwashing in *Brave New World*.

Part of the difficulty of studying propaganda is to define what exactly constitutes propaganda. One definition is that it "is the deliberate and systematic attempt to shape perceptions, manipulate cognitions, and direct behavior to achieve a response that furthers the desire of" those who propagate it.[37] Michael Balfour offers that propaganda is the act of inducing people to leap to conclusions without adequate examination of the evidence."[38] Nevertheless, partisans might argue that propaganda is in the eye of the beholder.

And consider these additional definitions of propaganda:

"Propaganda is the relatively deliberate manipulation of symbols (words, gestures, flags, images, movements, music, etc.) of other people's thoughts or actions with

> respect to beliefs, values and behaviors which these people ('reactors') regard as controversial."[39]
>
> Propaganda "consists of recreating certain events in order to illustrate a thesis or, in the face of certain events, to let one thing go in order to accentuate another."[40]
>
> The difficult matter of determining what is persuasion and what is propaganda is left to those who analyze and engage in such discussions.

What may be surprising to many people is how fascism has crept into societies and films outside of Germany over the years. In the depths of the Great Depression some Americans were actively seeking alternative forms of government to help relieve the dire economic crisis of the 1930s. As seen in the film *The Nazis Strike* (1943), a number of Americans were in attendance at a huge rally for the German-American Bund in Madison Square Garden. In fact, there were several rallies during the late 1930s that supported Germany, Hitler, Nazism, and fascism across North America.

Many Americans in the 1930s were looking for ways to escape the economic deprivations that were brought on by the Great Depression, and some were willing to sacrifice individual liberties for economic well-being. One such suggestion is found in the 1933 film *Gabriel over the White House*. In the film a playboy president, Judson C. Hammond (Walter Huston), leads a reckless lifestyle while the country suffers through seemingly endless economic strife. After suffering a near-fatal automobile accident, Hammond has a remarkable recovery and sets about to solve the problems of the country. The president assumes almost dictatorial powers, dismissing his cabinet and ignoring Congress, creating jobs for the unemployed and threatening countries that owe the United States money into reducing their arms and paying off their debt. In one notorious scene almost unbelievable in its brashness, federal agents raid the headquarters of gangsters in New York, take the criminals outside, and line them up along the wall, using machine guns to carry out instant death sentences. As the federal agents begin firing, the camera pans up to the Statue of Liberty, which overlooks the executions. In the end, the film suggests that the angel Gabriel had inhabited the body of the president to solve the problems of the United States, giving the impression that there was indeed divine backing of this ideology.[41]

Even in recent years, there has been an examination of fascist-type governance that does not necessarily reflect the negative attitudes often displayed in films associated with the Nazi regime. Susan Sontag argued that popular culture, after the Second World War, had become increasingly fascinated with fascism, and it increasingly had an impact on popular culture.[42] Other scholars have argued that popular culture has covert references to fascism.[43] The Paul Verhoeven film *Starship Troopers* (1997) depicts Earth in the near future in a world that fights alien bugs from half way across the galaxy. As the film opens, a news report/commercial over a worldwide news service gives an overview of the war with the "bugs" of the Klendathu system. The news update tries to get volunteers to sign up for the infantry in order to fight the bugs, saying, "Service guarantees citizenship."

The film then tells in flashback, beginning a year earlier, how the war with the bugs came about. The story opens in a high school classroom where a history teacher summarizes the lessons of the year. He reminds students that the failure of democracy was the overreliance on social scientists that led the world to the brink of chaos. "Veterans," whose identities are left open, seized power and imposed a stability that lasted for generations. The earth society is based on the idea that only citizens are allowed to vote and participate in the body politic, because citizens are willing to fight and die in defense of it while civilians were not. Violence and naked power are seen as the ultimate, supreme authority from which all other authority is derived. The teacher asserts that naked power has solved more issues throughout history than any other method. The emergence of a strong leader who uses power to solve society's problems is seen as a strong narrative in fascist thinking. Scholars have pointed to more recent films such as *Fight Club* (1999) and *The Matrix* (1999) as examples of the fascist strongman tendency.[44]

Starship Troopers (1997) chronicles the development of the students in the classroom in their pursuit of military careers. Throughout the film, the students espouse different reasons for joining the military. Some of the students want to start families; some want to enter politics; others want to escape poverty, and all of them see the military as the only way to achieve any status in the society. The military, which is particularly brutal, serves its interests, and there are some hints that it has fostered the war with the bugs. While most of the film falls in an action-adventure, or sci-fi genre, the opening sequences that detail earth society provide a backstory that touts some of the detriments of a fascist society but also point to some of the perceived benefits as well.

The film received some criticism from the press because of its perceived pro-fascist sentiment.[45] Although to be fair, it seems there is a muted effort to lay out how a fascist form of government can lead to a violent and militant society. Yet, any anti-fascist message is deemphasized in the film in order to concentrate on special effects and building a feeling of animosity toward the bugs. In the end, the film provides a fairly sympathetic portrayal of fascist ideology and reasoning with the debate in the classroom, with little or no real debate to the contrary.

Alternatively, there have been plenty of films that have decried fascism as a nefarious, or even evil, form of government. A number of wartime propaganda films during the 1940s took their shots at Germany and Italy. The ever-popular cartoon short features are an excellent source of anti-fascist rhetoric. Unfortunately a number of these films dwell on personalities or racial stereotypes rather than an exploration of why fascism is perceived to be "bad." Animated shorts such as *You're a Sap Mr. Jap* (1942) starring Popeye, *Herr Meets Hare* (1944) starring Bugs Bunny, and *The Spirit of '43* (1943), where Donald Duck has a nightmare about living in Nazi Germany, are all examples of this type of cartoon. However, as forms of propaganda, this type of cartoon was highly effective, if not always particularly accurate.

A more serious attempt to educate Americans about the methods and results of fascism is the Disney-produced short *Education for Death* (1943). Although there are some comical propaganda scenes, the message of the short is that the fascist government's control of the upbringing of German children leads them to be militaristic and intolerant.[46] The film *Blockade* (1938), produced prior to the Second World War and focusing on the Spanish Civil War, is a warning to democratic countries about what fascism might bring. But like many films of this genre, the film focuses on the tactics used by fascist forces in war rather than ideology. The film offers a strong condemnation of blockading a town (Castelmare) in order to starve it into submission and the bombing of civilian areas from the air.[47] What is missing from the film is a critique of fascist thinking. Perhaps this is, in part, because fascism had less ideological thought and writing behind it than democracy or capitalism.

The Spanish Civil War (1936–1939)

The Spanish Civil War is seen by many as the ideological prelude to the Second World War. The war started as a rebellion by monarchists and fascists against the government of the Spanish Republic. The government was supported by leftist governments around the world (especially Mexico and the Soviet Union), while the rebels were supported by fascist governments in Germany, Italy, and Portugal. Thus, the civil war took on the dimensions of a proxy war, especially between Germany and the Soviet Union.

The cause of the Republic was joined by many volunteers from around the world, including from the United States, who were dubbed the Abraham Lincoln Brigade.

The war ended in 1939 with a victory by the rebels and led to the dictatorship of Francisco Franco, who ruled Spain until 1975. After his death, democracy was restored to Spain.

The Spanish Civil War plays a very important role in popular culture. Several prominent writers covered the war including George Orwell and Ernest Hemingway. Hemingway's classic novel *For Whom the Bell Tolls* is set in the midst of the civil war and mirrors the author's experiences.

Some films about the Spanish Civil War are:

For Whom the Bell Tolls (1943): Starring Gary Cooper and Ingrid Bergman, this adaptation of Hemingway's novel was released during World War II because of the obvious parallels to the fight against Nazi Germany. In the film, American Robert Jordan is sent on a dangerous mission and reconsiders his life and his ideological beliefs.

Blockade (1938): Made while the Spanish Civil War was going on, the film stars Henry Fonda and Madeleine Carroll. The story focuses on the blockade of the town of Castelmare where the town's residents are being starved and bombed into submission. Made prior to the Second World War the film was designed to raise sympathy for those who were opposed to fascism.

The Spanish Earth (1937): A rarely seen, early documentary that chronicles the civil war, it was one of the first films to document the atrocities of war.[48]

Other films have tackled the same subject in much more subtle ways. For instance, the British film *It Happened Here* (1966) explores the hypothetical result of Germany winning the Second World War. The film explores what life would be like in 1960s Britain under a Nazi regime.[49] Directors Kevin Brownlow and Andrew Mollo's film explores the hypothetical effects of a fascist government on everyday life in Britain, using the tagline, "The story of Hitler's England." American films such as *I Was a Captive of Nazi Germany* (1939), *Confessions of a Nazi Spy* (1939), *The Man I Married* (1940), and *Hitler's Children* (1942) all used similar techniques as the red scare films to make their not-too-subtle points. Some of the best anti-fascist films came from the American government–produced propaganda films such as *Why We Fight: The Nazis Strike* (1943). However, perhaps the most damning of all the anti-Nazi films is *Judgment at Nuremberg* (1961). In this film of more than three hours, the war crimes trial at Nuremberg in 1948 is re-created with incredible effectiveness.

Conclusion: Ideologies, Film, and the Future

Most of this chapter has focused on the two primary challenges to democracy in the twentieth century; it is difficult to discern, with certainty, what ideologies might emerge as the dominant ideological challengers as the twenty-first century continues to unfold and impossible to know what films might be made to catalog these dynamics. Some scholars, as well as elected officials, academics, and pundits in the United States, have suggested that religiously based ideologies will challenge and transform democratic societies in the future.[50] A few, especially on the political right in the United States in the years since the September 11, 2001, attacks in the United States, have focused on the phrase "Islamo-fascism"—their juxtaposition of certain strains of Islam with authoritarian, fascist ideologies. For example, in 2007 conservative speakers and college students joined forces for an "Islamo-Fascism Awareness Week" on 114 U.S. college campuses, with panels featuring speakers such as Ann Coulter, former U.S. Senator Rick Santorum, and film and culture critic Michael Medved, among others.[51] It is worth noting that religion and ideologies are different. Religion provides a set of principles designed to provide an individual with a way to achieve a preferred afterlife (heaven). Ideologies are a set of principles designed to organize a community. Religious ideologies are an attempt to systematize principles in order to re-create the afterlife on Earth.

While many people's attention would turn to political Islam, there are examples of popular culture that depict ideological predilections of other religions. *The Handmaid's Tale* (1990), based on Margaret Atwood's novel of the same name, depicts a near-future America in which environmental devastation and political crises lead to the overthrow of the United States. The Republic of Gilead is governed by a theocratic military dictatorship based on a strict interpretation of Old Testament teachings. In the dystopian novel and film, women are subjugated and religious dissent quashed. The goal of the society is to produce more children in order to defend both religion and the country.

The discussion in this chapter has focused on a number of films; however, we encourage you to think about other films. What has not been addressed is how often ideologies are embedded in films without ever being discussed. Notice that several American films presume liberal intentions; for example, the town meeting is a standard setting in the television program *The Simpsons*. When a narrative film provides a dilemma or group decision, scenes often include some kind of voting procedure or attempt to achieve consensus. The film *Lifeboat* (1944), directed by Alfred Hitchcock and discussed in the chapter on war in this book (Chapter 8), follows this pattern more decidedly than others; when a decision is to be made by the group, the members of the lifeboat take a poll over what to do. Often Americans take this for granted, but still it is an expression of ideas about how we govern ourselves. We encourage you to be perceptive viewers of film, ever mindful of the subtle articulation of ideology. As you watch films, consider: *What is the ideology being advanced, and how and why did the filmmakers include these perspectives?*

Yet films in other parts of the world do not necessarily follow American or liberal political practices; often films from the Soviet Union have imbedded ideas about collectivism and socialist norms. When watching movies from other parts of the world, especially non-Western films, we encourage you to consider: *What underlying or covert ideologies might be present yet not readily apparent? What ideologies stand as direct or indirect challenges to democracy and capitalism?*

Notes

1. Francis Fukuyama, "The End of History," *National Interest* 16 (Summer 1989): 1–31.
2. See the Universal Declaration on Democracy adopted by the Inter-Parliamentary Union, September 16, 1997: http://www.ipu.org/Cnl-e/161-dem.htm.
3. A sampling of the many film and television incarnations of Dickens's *A Christmas Carol* include productions from 2009, 1988, 1984, 1971, 1962, 1951, 1938, among others. Even

Mister Magoo (voice of Jim Backus), the famous cartoon miser, played Scrooge in a classic animated version, *Mister Magoo's Christmas Carol*, in 1962.

4. For further reading, see Richard Taylor, *The Battleship Potemkin: The Film Companion* (New York: I. B. Tauris, 2000); and Herbert Marshall, *The Battleship Potemkin* (New York: Avon Books, 1978).

5. For a review of the work of Esther Shub, see Vlada Petric, "Esther Shub: Cinema Is My Life," and "Esther Shub's Unreleased Project," *Quarterly Review of Film Studies* 3, no. 4 (Fall 1978): 429–56.

6. David Cook, *A History of Narrative Film* (New York: W. W. Norton, 1981), 314.

7. Ginger Rogers's mother and manager, Lela Rogers, later testified before the House on Un-American Activities Committee and argued that Ginger was duped into making the film, not realizing the perceived communist overtones. It appears that Lela Rogers did not have much knowledge about communists or communism as she was successfully sued for libel by a playwright and producer in 1947. See Frank Marshall, *Film Study: An Analytical Bibliography*, vol. 2 (Cranbury, NJ: Associate University Presses, 1990); and Griffin Fariello, *Red Scare: Memories of the American Inquisition, An Oral History* (New York: Norton, 1995).

8. The Soviet Union became a nuclear power in 1949.

9. In fact, during the famous late 1940s hearings of the House Un-American Activities Committee (HUAC), 1943's *Mission to Moscow* was cited as an example of Hollywood's—and the Roosevelt administration's—pro-Soviet subversion and tendency to sugarcoat, and even promote, communism. HUAC's criticism of the film, Franklin Roosevelt, and former U.S. ambassador to the U.S.S.R., Joseph E. Davies, led to the eventual blacklisting of *Mission to Moscow*'s screenwriter, Howard Koch. Koch later moved to England, and, along with his wife, found some success as a writer overseas.

10. Ron Briley, "John Wayne and *Big Jim McLain* (1952): The Duke's Cold War Legacy," *Film & History* 31, no. 1 (2002): 28. Briley discusses Wayne's influence on the film, and his box office drawing power, in detail.

11. Phillip A. Gianos, *Politics and Politicians in American Film* (Westport, CT: Praeger, 1998), 140.

12. Ibid.

13. Ernest Giglio, *Here's Looking at You*, 3rd ed. (New York: Peter Lang, 2010), 113.

14. Ibid.

15. Gianos, *Politics and Politicians in American Film*, p. 140.

16. In the DVD version of the film, this scene is entitled "207 Commies, 1 Idiot!"

17. William H. Chafe, *The Unfinished Journey* (New York: Oxford University Press, 1991), 105.

18. Ibid.

19. Rep. Dies had strong connections to the Ku Klux Klan, who welcomed (and cheered) the congressional committee's new focus on exposing and defeating left-wing "subversives."

20. Investigation of Un-American Propaganda Activities in the United States. United States House of Representatives Resolution 282 (76th Congress), 1940.

21. It is not insignificant to note that the Texas Democrat (who served from 1930 to 1945) had become increasingly antagonistic to FDR's New Deal programs. For example, Hallie Flanagan was brought before Dies's committee to respond to allegations that the FTP was overrun with left-wingers who sought to propagate FDR's liberal social welfare policies with taxpayer dollars.

22. Bruce I. Bustard, *A New Deal for the Arts* (Washington, DC: National Archives and Records Administration, and Seattle: University of Washington Press, 1997), 94–95.

23. Elizabeth G. Pontikes, Giacomo Negro, and Hayagreeva Rao, "Stained Red: A Study of Stigma by Association with Blacklisted Artists during the 'Red Scare' in Hollywood, 1945–1960," *American Sociological Review* 75, no. 3 (June 2010): 456–78 .

24. Bernstein was not the only blacklisted individual to earn kudos for his work on *The Front*. Zero Mostel garnered a nomination for best supporting actor from the British Academy of Film and Television Awards (BAFTA). The British Academy of Film and Television Awards, founded in 1947, are the major film awards held in Great Britain. In 1969 Mostel was nominated for best actor in a musical or comedy for his role in Mel Brooks's *The Producers*.

25. Trumbo was awarded Oscars for screenwriting for *Roman Holiday* (1954) and *The Brave One* (1957)—but not until decades later. Due to the blacklist, both films were penned under different names. Writing credit for *Roman Holiday* was attributed to the purely fictional "Robert Rich," while the writer of *The Brave One* was listed as Ian McLellan Hunter (a British screenwriter and friend of Trumbo's). Trumbo was later presented the Oscars in 1975 (*The Brave One*) and, posthumously, in 1993 (*Roman Holiday*). Stephen Holden, "When an Eloquent Voice Was Stilled in Hollywood," *New York Times*, June 27, 2008: http://movies.nytimes.com/2008/06/27/movies/27trum.html.

26. Holden, "When an Eloquent Voice": http://movies.nytimes.com/2008/06/27/movies/27trum.html.

27. This account was taken from James Reid Paris, *Classic Foreign Films: From 1960 to Today*, (New York: Citadel Press, 1993), 94.

28. Renata Adler, "The Firemen's Ball," *New York Times*, September 30, 1968, p. 60.

29. For an excellent account of the events leading to the fall of the Novotný regime and the Soviet invasion and its aftermath from an American perspective, see Alan Levy, *So Many Heroes* (Sagaponack, NY: Second Chance Press, 1980). See also Robert Littell, ed., *The Czech Black Book* (New York: Praeger, 1969).

30. Scott M. Reid, "Border Wars Spill onto Olympic Ice," *Orange County Register*, February 20, 2010.

31. Vincent Canby, "A Report on the Party and the Guests," *New York Times*, September 28, 1968, p. 37.

32. Although there is some evidence to suggest that fascism attempted to link itself to a consistent theory. For example, theorist Giovanni Gentile sought to link fascism with Hegelian idealism. For a discussion of the nontheoretical aspects of fascism, see Einaudi, "Fascism," in *The International Encyclopedia of the Social Sciences* (New York: Macmillan, 1968), 336.

33. For a discussion of German escapism in films during the Nazi period, see Richard Traubner, "The Sound and the Führer," *Film Comment* 14, no. 4 (July–Aug 1978): 17–23, and "Berlin II—The Retrospective," *American Film* 4, no. 7 (May 1979): 67–69.

34. Cook, *History of Narrative Film*, p. 312.

35. See Siegfried Kracauer, *From Caligari to Hitler: A Psychological History of the German Film* (Princeton: Princeton University Press, 1947), 300–303.

36. David Cook, *A History of Narrative Film*, pp. 311–12.

37. Garth S. Jowett and Victoria O'Donnell, *Propaganda and Persuasion*, 3rd ed. (Thousand Oaks, CA: Sage Publications, 1999), 4.

38. Michael Balfour, *Propaganda in War, 1939–1945* (London: Routledge & Kegan Paul, 1979), 421.

39. Bruce L. Smith, "Propaganda," in *International Encyclopedia of the Social Sciences* (New York: Macmillan, 1968).

40. Michel Delahaye, "Interview with Leni Riefenstahl," in *Interviews with Film Directors*, ed. Andrew Sarris (Indianapolis: Bobbs-Merrill, 1967), 392–93.

41. The film is in the tradition that the United States understands itself as the exemplar of a Godly country. It is based on the tradition invoked by John Winthrop in a sermon ("A Model of Christian Charity") in 1630 in which he compares the colonies in America to the "City on the Hill" referenced in Matthew. See John Winthrop, "A Model of Christian Charity," in *The Norton Anthology of American Literature*, ed. Ronald Gottesman (New York: Norton, 1979).

42. Susan Sontag, "Fascinating Fascism," in *Under the Sign of Saturn* (London: Vintage, 1980), 73–105.

43. Benjamin Noys argues that the myth of wartime fascist resistance is used just as fascists would do in popular culture, essentially creating the idea that fascists were victims. See Benjamin Noys, "Fascinating (British) Fascism: David Britton's Lord Horror," *Rethinking History* 6, no. 3 (2002): 305–18. Bulent Diken and Carsten Bagge Laustsen argue that films like *Fight Club* are examples of microfascism, where an individual in today's society no longer has clear authority figures that they can look up to, and men in current society "are a generation of men raised by women" (Diken and Laustsen, 350). For Diken and Laustsen, a primary message of *Fight Club* is that capitalism provides too much pseudo freedom, for example, the freedom to consume (352). See Bulent Diken and Carsten Bagge Laustsen, "Enjoy Your Fight!—'Fight Club' as a Symptom of the Network Society," *Cultural Values* 6, no. 4 (October 2002): 349–67. Andrea Slane has argued that fascism has been decoupled from its historical meaning in a way that is almost ironic; movements that those who believe in democracy as the right to free expression are described by extreme right-wing groups as "fascists." See Andrea Slane, *A Not So Foreign Affair: Fascism, Sexuality, and the Culture Rhetoric of American Democracy* (Durham: Duke University Press, 2001).

44. Jennifer Barker, "'A Hero Will Rise': The Myth of the Fascist Man in *Fight Club* and *Gladiator*," *Literature/Film Quarterly* 36 no. 3 (2008): 171–87.

45. See, for example, John Griffin, "*Starship Troopers* a Vulgar Shockfest of Teens vs. Bugs," *Montreal Gazette*, November 7, 1997, p. D2; and Ron Weiskind, "Brave New Bugs: 'Starship Troopers' Probes a Future of Fascism and Pest Problems," *Pittsburgh Post-Gazette*, November 7, 1997, p. 4.

46. The more comical *Der Fürher's Face* (1942), also produced by Disney, has Donald Duck living in Germany so that Americans could appreciate the benefits of living in a democratic society. The Soviet animated short *What Hitler Wants* (1941) portrays Germans as brutal and envious of Russian lands and bounty.

47. Picasso's famous painting *Guernica* is based on the bombing of civilian targets by fascist forces during the Spanish Civil War.

48. Other films include *Land and Freedom* (1996), *Pan's Labyrinth* (2006), and *Soldiers of Salamina* (2003).

49. Of course, this is an interesting idea that many people have played with in literature. Take, for example, the novel by Robert Harris, *Fatherland*, which tells the hypothetical story of

Adolf Hitler's seventy-fifth birthday celebration in 1964. Even George Orwell's *1984* is based on the assumption that the aftermath of the Second World War continues for some forty years. Another film that imagines an alternative scenario is *A Very British Coup* (1988), which tells the fictional story of a socialist British prime minister who faces a military coup after advocating nuclear disarmament and open government.

50. See Samuel P. Huntington, "The Hispanic Challenge," *Foreign Policy* 141 (March–April 2004): 30–45. See also, for example, the rhetoric of "Islamo-fascism" in Steven Stalinski, "The Meaning of 'Islamofascism,'" *The New York Sun*, May 24, 2006: http://www.nysun.com/foreign/meaning-of-islamofascism/33302/.

51. For "Islamo-Fascism Awareness Week" on college campuses in 2007, see the Terrorism Awareness Project at: http://www.terrorismawareness.org/islamo-fascism-awareness-week/.

·SECTION 2·

AMERICAN POLITICS

· 4 ·

THE AMERICAN PRESIDENCY

There are so many political institutions worldwide that it hardly seems fair to focus on one.[1] Yet despite the importance of Congress and the Supreme Court to the American political system, and various parliaments, prime ministers, executives, and tribunals to political systems around the world, one office has garnered a disproportionate share of attention on film and television: the American presidency.[2] It is probably a safe assumption that the presidency has been the one U.S. governmental institution that has been depicted the most on screens around the world. Here, we will focus on the American presidency, charting how the institution has been portrayed in the past and in the films of recent decades. We will also consider how films have depicted real, as opposed to fictitious presidents. In order to trace evolving perceptions of political institutions, Robert Brent Toplin has noted that historians often examine how presidents have been portrayed in films and other art forms. Within this chapter we will do the same by focusing on the institution of the American presidency.[3]

We can identify a distinctive change in the tenor of films that depict the presidency. This change was most dramatically seen at the end of the twentieth century. The institution came under fire as film portrayed the presidency in a largely negative light. Juxtaposed to this negative image was NBC's celebrated drama *The West Wing*. With its sweeping musical score, patriotic images, and attention to passionate, enlightened, well-intentioned public servants, *The West Wing* stands as a grand exception to the seemingly seismic shift toward a more cynical and negative depiction of the presidency. Martin Sheen's dignified president (Jed Bartlet), the epitome of erudition and political valor, was neither a shyster, sycophant, nor sexual deviant. As you consider the array of films in this chapter, in your personal collection, or at the box office, and dissect their implicit and explicit political messages, be conscious of *how* the institution of the presidency has been presented; what these depictions may reveal about the public's expectations of the modern office, and the political and social fabric of the country; Hollywood's bottom line in green-lighting these projects; and the consequences these portrayals may have for the body politic and its evolving perceptions of a traditionally venerated institution.

Films in the 1920s, 1930s, and 1940s regularly featured some depiction of the presidency. However, in later years, passion for producing such films seems to have faded somewhat. And while Hollywood never outright abandoned presidency-themed films (there was a slew of presidents in the Cold War movies of the 1960s), decades later, there was clearly something of a renaissance of presidency films in the 1990s. The proliferation of this decade's movies featuring presidents is a trend that, beginning with Ivan Reitman's Capra-esque box office hit *Dave* (1993), showed little sign of reversing itself. In fact, as one columnist joked, the period between 1993 and 1997 brought the moviegoing public "more Presidents onscreen than, say, strippers and volcanologists combined."[4] Yet such a statement, however tongue-in-cheek, is actually remarkably accurate when considering the barrage of films that featured, in major or significant supporting roles, the president of the United States.[5] Running the genre gamut from thrillers, comedies, and box office hits to B-movie, straight-to-video wonders, these films exemplified Hollywood's renewed fascination with the politics and personalities consuming and inhabiting the White House.

The Pre-1990s Hollywood Presidency: President as Redeemer and Hero

By and large, with a few notable exceptions of course, American films prior to the 1990s presented a very positive portrayal of both individual presidents and the institution of the presidency. Presidents were commonly depicted as steadfast and heroic in times of crisis and common men who rose to uncommon greatness. Even when presidents were initially depicted as flawed or less than extraordinary, they often, when faced with certain serious situations, could rise to the occasion and redeem themselves and the country. Moreover, the presidency was generally a revered institution, one that—even if occasionally threatened by conniving, self-serving special interests or disingenuous presidential hopefuls—would ultimately regain or retain its prestige and honor. In short, on screens throughout the country, the president was more often than not a *redeemer and hero*, and the office he inhabited was sacred and renowned. Many prominent films illustrate variants of these themes, including: *Gabriel over the White House* (1933), *Young Mr. Lincoln* (1939), *Abe Lincoln in Illinois* (1940), *Yankee Doodle Dandy* (1942), *Wilson* (1944), *State of the Union* (1948), *Sunrise at Campobello* (1960), *PT-109* (1963), *Fail-Safe* (1964), *The Best Man* (1964), and *Seven Days in May* (1964).[6]

The Prototypical Hollywood Presidents Emerge: Henry Fonda, Fredric March, and Spencer Tracy

The positive image of the presidency was reinforced by Hollywood through the deliberate and skillful casting of certain A-list actors. In particular, three legends of the silver screen—Henry Fonda, Fredric March, and Spencer Tracy—stand out as the prototypical heroic Hollywood president (and presidential candidate) through their memorable onscreen performances in the 1930s, 1940s, and, especially, in the 1960s.

Henry Fonda, having already portrayed the revered Abraham Lincoln in John Ford's *Young Mr. Lincoln* (1939), was perhaps the perfect choice to play the chief executive of the United States, for example, in Gore Vidal's play-turned-movie *The Best Man* (1964), a leading presidential candidate. Fonda, as Secretary of State William Russell, the principled progressive, intellectual presidential candidate in *The Best Man*, ultimately takes his name out of the running at the Democratic National Convention, even as he is the front-runner, when he realizes that a mud-slinging battle and crafty innuendo campaign engineered by his chief rival—the demagogue Sen. Joe Cantwell (Cliff Robertson), whose tactics and ruthlessness recall the red scare mongering of real-life Sen. Joseph McCarthy—would demean the country. Rather than take America down the road of personal scandal and vitriolic campaigning, he opts for the high road. Thus, in this campaign for the highest office in the land, Russell's principled departure from the race proves that he is definitely "the best man." The political process, the presidential campaign, and the presidency remain dignified thanks to the actions of William Russell; however, as noted by the title, perhaps the country did not get the "best man."[7] Outgoing president Art Hockstader may have been a cagey, street-smart old codger willing to use hardball tactics, but, in the final analysis, his aim was pure and his intentions virtuous.

Further cementing Fonda's image as "the best man" was his earnest portrayal of the president of the United States in Sidney Lumet's stirring Cold War drama *Fail-Safe* (1964). As a nuclear first strike is accidentally triggered by the United States against the Soviet Union, it is up to the president to prevent the attack and convince the Russians that the launch was entirely a mistake. Sweating it out in intense negotiations in a closed room, accompanied only by his special assistant Buck (Larry Hagman), Fonda's president is steadfast under the most intense anxiety humanly possible, negotiating one-on-one with the Soviets in order to prevent a pending nuclear holocaust. Ultimately, the president ignores advice from the Pentagon and from the hard-nosed, realist Groeteschele (Walter Matthau)[8] to use the opportunity as a fortuitous sneak attack to roll back the Iron Curtain and insure American military and ideological supremacy for generations. Fonda's president in *Fail-Safe* displays humility and sincerity and condemns the arms race that has triggered the imminent nuclear Armageddon that haunts the entire film.[9]

Fredric March, as the honorable and earnest President Jordan Lyman, advanced the positive image of the presidency in John Frankenheimer's *Seven Days in May* (1964). Faced with a near-certain right-wing *coup d'état* masterfully engineered by the sinister Gen. James Mattoon Scott (Burt Lancaster), President Lyman courageously stays and fights the plot until the bitter end, using close aides and friends, such as Sen. Raymond Clark (Edmond O'Brien) and the ever-faithful Col. "Jiggs" Casey (Kirk Douglas) to firmly exert civilian control over the military and thus thwart the coup. Again, the American movie audience is reassured by the onscreen presence of a strong, steadfast leader and virtuous, if slightly imperfect, presidential aides in the midst of national chaos and constitutional crisis.

In Frank Capra's *State of the Union* (1948), Spencer Tracy portrays Grant Matthews, an aviation tycoon and idealistic Republican candidate for president who pledges to use blunt talk ("plain ordinary garden-variety honesty," in his words) to solve the problems of the day. However, Matthews is quickly swayed by crooked and ambitious politicos, namely his political adviser (Adolph Menjou), and a power-mad newspaper tycoon with whom he has had an affair (Angela Lansbury), to abandon his pledge of probity and refrain from criticizing entrenched interests, such as big business, labor, and farmers, that he will need to secure the nomination. However, as perhaps inevitably in a Frank Capra film, Matthews returns to his values and leaves the race, swayed by the devotion and encouragement of his wife (Katharine Hepburn).[10] Moreover, Matthews assures a live nationwide radio audience that—while he is no longer a presidential candidate in *this* election—he will be going to *both* party conventions to make sure the candidates are accountable to the people's interests. By withdrawing from the race and maintaining his integrity and principles, Matthews upholds the sanctity and integrity of his candidacy and the presidency, and strengthens an electoral process in serious need of cleansing.[11]

However, there are some notable and comedic exceptions to these generally positive portrayals of the presidency. Not all presidents or presidential candidates were Fondas, Marches, or Tracys. *Tennessee Johnson* (1942), *Dr. Strangelove* (1964), and *The President's Analyst* (1967), for example, are a few that stand out in this regard. Andrew Johnson, as the beleaguered and impeached seventeenth president, is depicted as a court-martialed slovenly drunkard in *Tennessee Johnson* (1942). The president of nuclear-doomsday America is portrayed as a peculiar, macho, mentally unstable, and occasionally impotent zealot in *Dr. Strangelove* (1964). On a softer note, the portrayal of President Andrew Jackson in *The Gorgeous Hussy* (1936) is one of an eccentric individual who has the best interests of the common man at his core; however, his quick tongue gets him into trouble with more seasoned politicians. Jackson is portrayed as flawed but with a heart of gold.

But even in the darker films that point out the chief executive's imperfections and personal failings, the presidency does not completely sink into the depths of utter depravity. For example, *Dr. Strangelove's* president, Merkin Muffley (Peter Sellers), may be rather intellectual and egg-headish (note his uncanny resemblance to Adlai Stevenson, who was the Democratic Party's presidential nominee in 1952 and 1956) in the midst of a nuclear crisis, but a devious criminal he most certainly is not. *Strangelove*, Stanley Kubrick's dark, absurd, and humorous treatment of the nuclear age and presidential leadership, stands in stark contrast to the other Cold War–era films that deal with the same subject. As previously stated, the presidents in *Fail-Safe* (Fonda) and *Seven Days in May* (March) are reasonable and seasoned public servants who fare pretty well in the midst of national emergency. Thus, satirical send-ups of the Cold War and the nuclear age, such as Kubrick's black comedy, largely reflect "a certain levity of outlook" evident in other films during this period that questioned the merits and morals of the Cold War.[12]

For most of the history of popular film in the United States—from the 1930s to the 1990s—the prevailing image of the office and the individual presented to the American public (and, in many cases, the world) was a positive one. The likes of George Washington, Abraham Lincoln, Franklin Roosevelt, and Woodrow Wilson—as well as many of Hollywood's fictional presidents— were treated with the utmost respect on screen. Aside from a few notable exceptions, the president and the presidency received reverential treatment from Hollywood. In those films that showcased the flaws of human nature specifically, and the U.S. political system generally, the dignity and goodness of the office ultimately prevailed, even if wayward people did occasionally roam its corridors of power. Such was the case, for example, in 1933's *Gabriel over the White House*.[13] And Hollywood succeeded in establishing a few prototypical heroic presidents—Henry Fonda in *Young Mr. Lincoln, The Best Man,* and *Fail-Safe*; the stoic, diligent, and dignified Fredric March standing up to ideological belligerence and a military coup while preserving civilian control of the military in *Seven Days in May*; and the sincere and crusty-yet-civic-minded Spencer Tracy in *State of the Union*—who largely depicted the institution and individual presidents in a favorable fashion.

Despite entering an age of cynicism, filmmakers and viewers still have an appetite for unabashedly upbeat biographies, which celebrate the country's presidential heritage. *Truman,* premiering on HBO in 1995, starred award-winning Chicago theater veteran Gary Sinise as the plainspoken, bespectacled thirty-third president, and Diana Scarwid as Bess Truman. The tagline for the film, "A Simple Man. . .A Legendary President," sums up the biopic's positive treatment of the feisty Missourian. Whether winning World War II, rising from obscurity through the Pendergast political machine, firing the immensely popular Gen. Douglas MacArthur, or chewing out a reporter for criticizing his daughter Margaret's singing—Harry S. Truman is primarily depicted as a heroic, honest, plainspoken, tells-it-like-it-is leader. He may be occasionally uncouth or ill-tempered but is nearly always unflinching in the face of grave challenges.

Action-Hero and Action Series Presidents, Demographic Shifts, and Positive Portrayals

In the summer blockbuster *Independence Day* (1996), Bill Pullman portrays Gulf War veteran and alien-blasting President Thomas J. Whitmore, a chief executive who helps save the United States and the world from certain annihilation at the hands (or antennae?) of sinister aliens by personally manning a F-18 fighter jet and fighting the extraterrestrial menace. In another summer action-infused blockbuster, Air Force One (1997), perennial top-draw Harrison Ford is President James Marshall—"a blend of Han Solo, Woodrow Wilson and Jackie Chan"—who saves his plane, family, and several members of the press corps and cabinet from death at the hands of a terrorist (Gary Oldman) and his fellow sadistic henchman who hijack Air Force One as it prepares to leave Kazakhstan.[14] Then-president Bill Clinton could not have imagined a more flattering portrayal of an American chief executive. Indeed, a year before the film's release, Clinton himself gave Harrison Ford a tour of Air Force One in August 1996 while vacationing in Jackson Hole, Wyoming.[15] However cartoonish and embellished, both Pullman's and Ford's action-hero presidents stand as examples of principled, heroic figures that harken back to a less cynical age. Television has also used the action series format as vehicle to provide positive and negative depictions of the American presidency.

Fox's action series 24 (2001–2010), featuring the terrorist-hunting protagonist and federal agent Jack Bauer (Kiefer Sutherland), included multiple presidents (nine) over the course of its prime-time tenure, including decisive and honorable as well as conniving and indecisive chief executives. With its attention to global and domestic terrorist threats, interrogation techniques and torture, national security policy, and international law, the program took on special significance and scrutiny in the post–September 11, 2001, era, often earning the admiration of conservatives while displeasing liberal viewers. Yet the show is just as notable, or notorious, for featuring two African American presidents and one female chief executive. Similarly, this expanded demographic imagining of the office was reflected in the short-lived ABC drama Commander in Chief, starring Geena Davis as President Mackenzie Allen, the first woman to serve as president of the United States. While she ascended to the office upon the death of the president rather than through the electoral process, President Mackenzie Allen represented—until President Allison Taylor (Cherry Jones) on 24 (2009–2010)—the only prominent prime-time television president who was not a man. Likewise, 24's President David Palmer (Dennis Haysbert) became the first nonwhite commander-in-chief, and then NBC's The West Wing featured the historic election of a Hispanic, Rep. Matthew Santos (Jimmy Smits), in 2006, during its final season.

An unambiguously positive depiction of the presidency is Rob Reiner's The American President (1995). In the film, President Andrew Shepherd (Michael Douglas), a widowed father, commences a relationship with the attractive environmental lobbyist Sydney Ellen Wade (Annette Bening). The president faces opposition from Senate majority leader Bob Rumson (Richard Dreyfuss), who espouses family values and patriotism in criticizing the president. Written by Aaron Sorkin, creator of the presidency drama *The West Wing* and screenwriter of, among other politically themed films, *A Few Good Men* (1992), the movie is significant in that both the president and most of his closest White House aides[16] are portrayed in a glowing manner. They are dedicated to their jobs and care passionately about public policy. As president, Shepherd does not relish or exploit for political gain an attack on a Libyan terrorist base, and furthermore, he refuses to bow to the pressure from conservative politicians and end his relationship with Wade. At the film's dramatic conclusion, the president announces at a live, unrehearsed press conference that he will fight for gun control and environmental legislation, two pieces of legislation that he previously abandoned due to political pressure and compromise.[17]

Shysters, Sycophants, and Sexual Deviants: Negative Images of the Presidency

In "Mrs. Robinson," one of the standouts from the soundtrack to the classic *The Graduate* (1967), Paul Simon and Art Garfunkel capture the national *zeitgeist*, famously lamenting the disappearance of baseball great Joe DiMaggio from the national scene. Reflecting on the negative depictions of the presidency that emerged in the films of the 1990s, it may well be prudent to mourn: "Where have you gone Henry Fonda, Fredric March, and Spencer Tracy."

In the taut political thriller *In the Line of Fire* (1993), the comments, inferences, and innuendoes of veteran Secret Service agent Frank Horrigan (Clint Eastwood) clearly indicate that he finds the current president to be all pomp and circumstance and no substance. Horrigan, who had protected JFK in 1963, remains haunted by the events in Dealey Plaza in Dallas as he is harassed by a maniacal would-be assassin (John Malkovich) who threatens the new president (Jim Curley). Yet, it is abundantly clear that the weathered agent has little to no regard for the current chief executive. When asked to remember that he willingly lied on several occasions in order to protect Kennedy's sexual liaisons some thirty years earlier, Horrigan responds, "That's different. I was different. *He* was different. *The whole damn country* was different." Moreover, the jaded agent no longer bothers to get to know the presidents he protects, as he may find out "they're not worth taking a bullet for." In addition, in this new era, it seems that not even the president's security detail is above crude political and image manipulation: Horrigan complains that female Secret Service agents are now assigned to the president merely to energize "feminist" supporters.

The big screen version of John Grisham's novel *The Pelican Brief* (1994) is illustrative of the trend towards gloomy assessments of the White House and its most notorious inhabitant. Here, the president (Robert Culp) is engaged in sordid and criminal activity, actively subverting the FBI's and CIA's investigations of anti-environment, big business campaign donors directly tied to the assassination of two Supreme Court justices. In his attempts to cover up the scandal and bury a legal brief implicating his rich benefactors, the president and his chief of staff (Tony Goldwyn) enlist the support of a secret supra-governmental association of thugs and killers. Car bombs, top-notch surveillance, and shootings are routinely provided by the covert cabal. Likewise, in the film adaptation of Tom Clancy's *Clear and Present Danger* (1994), the president (Donald Moffat) is hardly a candidate for inclusion on Mount Rushmore. This chief executive is dishonest and shows contempt for the nation's veterans, planning and executing covert military operations in South America to settle a personal vendetta with drug lords rather than protecting the nation's security. In the meantime, brave military veterans and protagonist Jack Ryan (Harrison Ford) are left for dead in an operation that the administration denies ever transpired. When Jack Ryan finally confronts the wayward president about the crimes he has committed in the name of national security, the president yells, "How dare you come in here and bark at me like I'm some junkyard dog—*I'm the President of the United States!*" Ryan, indignant and utterly disgusted with the lowlife president before him, bellows, "How dare *you*, sir!"

During the 1990s, it appeared that even lighthearted, innocuous comedies were not above portraying presidents as scheming, murderous jerks or just plain peculiar characters. In the buddy comedy *My Fellow Americans* (1996), two flawed former presidents (James Garner and Jack Lemmon) redeem themselves by thwarting power-grabbing and money-laundering schemes engineered by the slick, crooked President Haney (Dan Aykroyd) and his seemingly befuddled (but also crooked) vice president, Ted Matthews (John Heard). In this film, like several others, the thugs enlisted by the president are not above murder or planting evidence. In Tim Burton's campy *Mars Attacks!* (1996), however, Jack Nicholson is a wacky commander-in-chief who is *not* engaged in murder, extortion, or private gain—but *is* an all-around bizarre alien-battling and gambling chief executive (who also uses recreational drugs). The trend continued into the new decade when the short-lived cable-television series *That's My Bush*

(2001), a spoof of sitcoms from *South Park* creators Trey Parker and Matt Stone, ridiculed the then-sitting president.[18]

In 1997, a slew of sexually deviant presidents and close associates hit the screen with reckless abandon. In *Murder at 1600* President Jack Neil (Ronny Cox) is a weak but fairly honest chief executive, but his rich, spoiled playboy son likes to sow his wild oats by engaging in rough sex on the floor of the Oval Office—and on the presidential seal, no less. While neither the president nor his son is ultimately guilty of the murder that soon takes place at the White House, they are surrounded by treacherous, back-stabbing aides, especially the national security adviser (Alan Alda) and the director of White House security (Daniel Benzali), who vie for advancement at the expense of others. *Absolute Power*, released in the early months of 1997, features perhaps the reigning king of sexually deviant, depraved presidents, President Alan Richmond (Gene Hackman). Richmond's dirty talk–laced sexual tryst with the wife of a loyal supporter (E. G. Marshall) ultimately leads to her death when the encounter turns ugly and rough. The Secret Service, sworn to protect the president's safety at all times, shoots the president's paramour as she tries to stab the overly aggressive Richmond with a letter opener. In addition, the B-movie fare *Shadow Conspiracy*, also from 1997, is rife with an evil shadow government threatening to rise to power, including a duplicitous chief of staff (Donald Sutherland) and vice president (Ben Gazzara). Not surprisingly, bombs, murders, and car chases follow those who try to expose the crimes committed by those in and around the White House.

The year 1997 turned out to be a high point in the cinematic cynicism about the office of the presidency. The big screen was filled with scandal-ridden, sex-addicted chief executives. The ultra-cynical farce *Wag the Dog* is probably the epitome of this trend. After the president's sexual liaison with a Girl Scout in the Oval Office is exposed, a cunning White House aide (Anne Heche), cagey spin doctor (Robert De Niro), and Hollywood producer (Dustin Hoffman) are called in to create and orchestrate a fake war (the chosen opponent is Albania) to divert attention from the scandal. In addition to producing their own propaganda—such as bogus video clips of Albanian refugees (they were actors shot on a sound stage!)—the PR gurus then hire country legend Willie Nelson and blues-gospel great Pops Staples to write catchy songs to sway the American public in favor of the war. The images, songs, sound bites, and chicanery work like a charm: the press and the public buy and digest the war story hook, line, and sinker and the president hangs on to power.[19]

"Warm. Direct. Straightforward. Sincere. Comforting." This was how John Travolta described President Bill Clinton, whom he had personally met twice prior to portraying him (or rather, a fictionalized facsimile) on the big screen in *Primary Colors* (1998).[20] Though Travolta has commented that he hoped the moviegoing public would view the Bill Clinton he created on screen as a "very caring and genuine character, flawed but real and wonderful,"[21] and while White House press secretary–turned–television pundit Dee Dee Myers commented after seeing the film that, "It's really not half-bad for the president"— and generally good reviews notwithstanding—the depiction of presidential candidate Jack Stanton is hardly flattering.[22] In many ways the film is, as director Mike Nichols asserted, essentially about "honor."[23] And in nearly all of the tests, the lead character—the smooth-talking presidential candidate Jack Stanton (or, Bill Clinton)—fails. From impregnating a young African American girl, to a string of other marital infidelities, to his (and his wife's) decision to use damaging information to blackmail and destroy a rising competitor (Larry Hagman), Stanton displays a penchant for half-truths, cover-ups, and dirty tricks. His attributes—empathy, love of public service, and mastery of policy— ultimately cannot make up for the dearth of character.

One may characterize these films as simply entertainment. And as the success of big budget summer blockbusters and the health of box office receipts generally indicate, Americans value their escapism. However, in a culture saturated in electronic media, with images and sounds bombarding us from every direction, it seems pertinent to ask: Are there long-term or substantive problems with portraying the presidency in a negative light? Does exposure to negative portrayals of the presidency lead us to take an irrationally jaded or jaundiced view of the office and those who inhabit it? Will such views affect our voting levels, willingness to participate politically, or understanding of a complex institution? Are we, or can we, be unduly swayed by films' portrayals of the presidency—or do we have an automatic switch that allows us to keep the facts from the fun and fiction? Given the myriad ways audiences may react to the same themes and realities, the jury is out. Yet there is no denying that the portrayal of presidents towards the end of the twentieth century was markedly different from those earlier in the century.

There is another strategic element concerning recent Hollywood renderings of the presidency that warrants mention. It is increasingly evident that, in addition to the shysters, sycophants, and sexual deviants occupying the Oval Office, deviancy, criminal behavior, and general ineptitude are every bit as common in the men and women who *advise and counsel* the president. The following films, running the gamut from comedies to dramas to thrillers, illustrate this trend.

In *Naked Gun 21/2: The Smell of Fear* (1991), real-life chief of staff John Sununu (Peter Van Norden), in addition to President George H. W. Bush (John Roarke), is portrayed as seemingly inept and prone to kowtow to business interests that threaten the environment. Ivan Reitman's Capra-esque box office smash *Dave* (1993) finds the chief of staff (Frank Langella) and press secretary (Kevin Dunn) overseeing a massive conspiracy, placing a nidwestern everyman, Dave Kovic (Kevin Kline), in the White House when the real president, Bill Mitchell (Kevin Kline), suffers a massive stroke during a sexual encounter with a White House aide (Laura Linney). While Dave and the White House press secretary eventually find an honorable way out of the conspiracy and cover-up, the power-hungry, conniving chief of staff continues the cover-up, and even attempts to blackmail Dave en route to running for president himself.

As we have seen, *The Pelican Brief* (1994) depicts a scheming chief of staff (Tony Goldwyn) at the vortex of executive corruption, engineering an elaborate illegal cover-up for the president nearly entirely by himself. Likewise, in *Clear and Present Danger* (1994), it is not only the president, but also his chief of staff, who masterminds cover-ups and illegal activity. The aforementioned *In the Line of Fire* (1993) not only suggests that the current president is of questionable character, but his domineering chief of staff (actor-turned-politician Fred Dalton Thompson)[24] is recalcitrant and shortsighted, blatantly placing crass political considerations above the security of the president. When asked by Secret Service agent Horrigan (Eastwood) to consider limiting the president's public appearances due to the serious threat posed by a menacing assassin, he scoffs as the thought of frisking "people going into $10,000-a-plate dinners," suggesting that fewer presidential appearances "would be political suicide." After all, comments the chief of staff, he had already helped to narrow the president's deficit in the polls to a measly five points. Election-year politics take precedence over the safety of the president.

Canadian Bacon (1994), a satire written and directed by Michael Moore, finds a "touchy-feely" president (Alan Alda), a bumbling, gung-ho general (Rip Torn), and an ultra-cynical chief of staff (Kevin Pollack) seeking to divert attention from a stagnant economy, poverty, and pollution by creating an arms race and going to war with Canada. Far more serious and sinister, however, is President Richmond's (Gene Hackman) chief of staff, Gloria Russell (Judy Davis), in *Absolute Power* (1997), a sycophant who uses two Secret Service agents and members of the FBI to do whatever it takes (including attempted murder) to cover up the murder of the deviant president's lover. Further evidence of deceptive, villainous, and/or traitorous chiefs of staff includes *Shadow Conspiracy* (1997) and *Wag the Dog* (1997). In *Murder at 1600* (1997), most of the evil and illegalities are perpetrated by the national security adviser and director of White House security, and in *Primary Colors* (1998), campaign staff, aides, and friends of candidate Jack Stanton assist in the bribing and dirt-digging designed to protect their boss.[25]

In addition to being portrayed as sycophants, cover-up experts, and overly ambitious jerks, several films portray top White House officials as less than qualified. In many of the aforementioned films—especially *In the Line of Fire*, *Clear and Present Danger*, *Absolute Power*, and *Murder at 1600*—ineptitude ruins even the best attempts at a cover-up. Even in the big budget blockbuster *Armageddon* (1998), starring action movie staple Bruce Willis, the president (Stanley Anderson) and his top Defense Department adviser, Gen. Kimsey (Keith David), make the hasty (and wrong) decision to fire nuclear weapons at an incoming meteor, and in the process nearly destroy all of life as we know it. It takes a NASA official (Billy Bob Thornton) *outside* of the president's inner circle to make the correct decisions. Moreover, in the end, a gang of Joe six-pack oil-drillers and petty criminals turn out to be more dedicated and shrewd in their efforts to stop the deadly Texas-sized meteor than the White House and all of its key advisers (one of whom—the top science expert to the president—received "a C- in astro-physics," according to one of the NASA officials).

Explanations for the Negative Portrayal of the Presidency in Hollywood

After the release of 1997 box office hit *Air Force One*, *Newsweek* reporter Howard Fineman pondered that "it may say something about the state of America—or Hollywood—that it took a Japanese studio (Sony) and a German-born director (Petersen) to bring to the screen a creature that we Americans can barely imagine: a president as hero."[26]

Considering the avalanche of 1990s films portraying presidents and the presidency in a negative light, it may not be much of a stretch to concur with Fineman's sentiments, as well as those of former Bill Clinton aide George Stephanopoulos, who asserted that the "new presidential thrillers have a common premise: crime and corruption are routine at the highest levels."[27] It is clear from this survey of American film that a variety of comedies and dramas alike have chosen to depict the presidency as running amok with ambitious, duplic-itous, self-serving, and, at times, sexually deviant criminals. These figures are also generally portrayed as more incompetent and less honest than those out-side the Washington, D.C., corridors of power. What did this trend mean, if anything, for citizenship and public perceptions of our most fundamental gov-ernmental institutions? Why did such a shift occur and why should it merit our attention? Scholars and public servants offer several suggestions on how to go about answering these questions:

> *George Stephanopoulos:* In an era when journalism employs the techniques of fiction ("The Agenda," "Blood Sport") and novels employ the techniques of journalism ("Primary Colors"), it's not surprising that movies are doing the same thing. . . . But what looks true on the screen is rarely what's happening behind the scenes.[28]

> *Michael Sragow:* It's true that American movies are largely about escape. But that's what American public life has been all about, too—form and symbol over substance, and the orchestration of video-images rather than truth-telling.[29]

> *Christopher Sharrett:* Cinema as amusement, rather than springboard for audience debate, always will separate our films, and our art over all, from that of Europe and the rest of the world.[30]

It is hard to deny that there has been, in the not-too-distant past, a seis-mic shift in the way that the president and the institution of the presidency have been portrayed by Hollywood. In the first three-quarters of the twentieth century, the typical portrayal was of a president who was rational, trustworthy, and prone to do the "right thing." The outliers were those films that showed the presidency as "cartoonish" or deviant. At the end of the twentieth centu-ry the exact opposite seemed to be true: it was rare to find a movie that depict-ed the institution of the presidency in a consistently positive, let alone heroic, light. The norm was to depict a president or his advisors as miscreants, perverts, or, at the very least, self-absorbed Machiavellian calculators. The question remains: Why did this shift occur, and what effect does it have on the public's attitudes toward the presidency?

Journalist Richard Lacayo, of *Time* magazine, noted, with a touch of irony, that despite Bill Clinton's friendship with Hollywood elite, it did not translate into positive portrayals when it came to films.[31] In a description of the change in presentation of the presidency, Mr. Lacayo picks up on the same themes that we have addressed. However, Lacayo points to Watergate and the release of *All the President's Men* (1976) as the turning point in which the president is por-trayed as a villain. Yet the film largely reaffirmed what the public had already been led to believe—that checks and balances ultimately will rein in a politi-cal actor who usurps his constitutional authority. It should also be noted that political scientists were themselves reevaluating the notion of executive power after the revelations of Watergate.[32] *All the President's Men* was a depiction of an actual event and, as such, fails in its comparison to the movies released in the 1990s; however, it did open the door to films that overtly questioned the president. Nevertheless, it is better classified as an outlier in the pre-1990s model of the presidency.

So why did Hollywood alter its depiction of the presidency in such a dras-tic way in the 1990s? One possible hypothesis is that with the end of the Cold War, there was no longer the need to show a president as a cool, calm, ratio-nal actor with the nerve and wisdom of Solomon. This hypothesis holds that since the United States was now lacking an enemy, Hollywood could now make films that closely examine the executive branch. It is easy to see a close con-nection in proximity to the end of the Cold War and the onslaught of nega-tive movies about the presidency. But the Cold War, on its own, does not seem to be a sufficient reason to explain this shift. A better explanation has to do with the very nature of the media, both as a result of the consolidation of cor-porate ownership in the 1980s and as a shift in professional norms of what is considered "newsworthy."

The Clinton Era and the Media's Focus on Character

After Watergate, the media became both obsessed with the "character" of our elected officials and cynical regarding politics. As political scientist Thomas Patterson has argued, the press focuses on character as a keystone to leadership, even though the public tends not to view it as one of the more important attributes when coupled with a candidate's stand on the issues or experience and qualification.[33] Character was the issue that drove front-runner Gary Hart from the Democratic primaries in 1988, and character was an issue that dogged Bill Clinton from the primaries of 1992 to his impeachment in 1999, and beyond. Indeed, the drama of his impeachment and "Monicagate" in 1998–1999 brought the question of presidential character to the fore. Thus, Bill Clinton has arguably allowed Hollywood to pre-sent the question of "what if?" According to this line of reason-ing, *if* a president can indeed be a flawed character, what

possible negative (i.e., nefarious, perverted, malevolent) consequences might result? Further, as political communications spe-
cialists have argued, the media now have a story line in which
politics is portrayed as a strategic game in which winning tends
to trump the public good.[34] During the course of the Clinton presidency, polls seemed to register the media's concentration on the
character issue. When asked about Bill Clinton's performance as
a president, the American public tended to give him relatively
high marks. However, when asked about Bill Clinton as a person, his poll numbers were dismal.[35]

Add to this seemingly paradoxical mix of public opinion the
stream of numerous sensational allegations involving devious
cover-ups in the death of Clinton White House counsel Vincent
Foster, and one finds additional media obsession with the issue
of character. Clinton critics and certain media outlets—especially Moral Majority founder Rev. Jerry Falwell (who sold anti-
Clinton videotapes during his *Old Time Gospel Hour*) and the
conservative *Pittsburgh Tribune-Review* (owned by staunch conservative and Bill Clinton–critic Richard Mellon Scaife) and its star
journalist Christopher Ruddy[36] (who featured several lead stories
on the subject)—have asserted that Foster's death was not a suicide, and that the White House engineered an intricate plot to
kill the White House counsel and then cover it up. Such allegations have turned conspiracy theories concerning Vincent Foster's
death and the former First Family's personal and public peccadilloes—both real and imagined—into somewhat of a cottage
industry.[37] Could the persistent rumors and coverage of these allegations surrounding the Clintons' business and extramarital relations have given Hollywood the means and context to direct their
attention to an executive branch that has given way to the "dark
side of the force"?

"Priming" and the Hollywood Presidency

Flawed characters make great subjects for books and for movies, and Hollywood has used this as a springboard to produce a number of reasonably profitable movies that have dominated the post-1990s model. But does the presentation of these movies have any effect on how the public perceives a traditionally venerated institution? We argue that, just as a perceptively negative bias toward politics in the media has done much to shape the public's attitude towards politics,[38] the manner in which the presidency was portrayed in the 1990s also shaped the public's attitude towards the executive branch. Thomas Patterson refers to this process as "priming," which he defines as "the capacity of the press to isolate particular issues, events, or themes in the news, as criteria for evaluating politicians."[39] He suggests that when primed, the public will view politicians and candidates in the manner in which they have been portrayed by the media. For example, Patterson points out that, "A *Times Mirror* poll in May (1992) showed that half of the public believed Clinton was not trustworthy. There was only one way they could have come to this conclusion; the media, in effect, had said so. Clinton had been unknown to the general public a few months earlier."[40]

Can this priming effect be extended to Hollywood? In the 1990s, former Bill Clinton aide George Stephanopoulos noted that in the absence of a Soviet threat, "we can fantasize about the enemy within. After all, conspiracy theories. . .are now part of the popular imagination."[41] Such conspiracy theories help feed the public's imagination that something sinister may be going on inside the White House. If the media have already primed the public to be largely negative and cynical towards politics,[42] then Hollywood has engaged in reinforcing such views, further priming an audience willing to believe that corruption and deviousness are rampant inside the Oval Office. Further, the drive in the media towards "infotainment"; the rise of ideological and often strident web logs, or "blogs"; the punditocratic, partisan cable television networks; and the popularity of (largely conservative) talk radio have pushed legitimate news stories aside for cryptic and sordid tales about our elected officials, including the institution of the presidency, regardless of whether the allegations are true or not.[43] To borrow from Richard Harwood's lambasting of the media and apply it to Hollywood: "Their failure to put things in perspective is perhaps their greatest sin."[44]

Portraying Past Presidencies:
Mixed Messages and Complex Characters

While the aforementioned films present fictitious presidencies from recent decades, other films have addressed actual past presidents, their administrations, and the central scandals, policies, and/or political dynamics that defined their tenure. Oliver Stone's *JFK* (1991), *Nixon* (1995), and *W* (2008) and Steven Spielberg's *Amistad* (1997) are a few examples of such films. The depictions of the presidents in these films are much more nuanced and provide both positive and negative attributes, and thus the overall presentation of the presidency is mixed, and some would argue more realistic. *JFK*, while unabashedly romantic in its fondness for Kennedy, particularly his policies and leadership, is entirely about the thirty-fifth president's assassination in Dallas on November 22, 1963, the subsequent investigation, and the Warren Report. A key point of the film is an explanation of the various conspiracy theories (such as those advanced by New Orleans D.A. Jim Garrison) that shed doubt on the veracity of the Warren Report. The only real portrayals of the presidency as an institution are the negative innuendoes concerning former JFK vice president Lyndon Johnson's willingness to engage in a full-scale war in Vietnam in the aftermath of Kennedy's death. In fact, pressure from the military-industrial complex, an informal alliance between those who produce weapons and those who procure weapons,[45] is explicitly tied to LBJ's decision to appease the Pentagon (and shadowy defense contractors) by enlarging the conflict in Southeast Asia. This message is conveyed by LBJ's conversation in a smoke-filled military-planning room, assuring generals, "You'll get your damn war" in Vietnam.

For a link to the so-called Zapruder film of the assassination of President Kennedy, go to www.seeingthebiggerpicture.net.

In the presidential psycho-history *Nixon* (1995), Anthony Hopkins portrays a haunted, embittered thirty-seventh president, and Stone goes to great detail to present nearly all of the presidential aides, rogue players, and other key Watergate and Washington players who dominated Nixon's presidency and political life. Perhaps surprisingly, given Stone's past movies, outspokenness, and penchant for (generally) left-wing politics, *Nixon* is largely a film that explores the psychological motivations of the president. Hence, the conclusions drawn by the film are reminiscent of classic tragedies. The film is a complex presentation of Richard Nixon that is "appalling and strangely moving"; a vision of "a man whose private and public demons bring him down with an almost Shakespearean thud."[46]

While Stone does not gloss over the sins, cynical political maneuvering, or neuroses of the oft-vilified president—the "Checkers" speech, divisive campaign tactics, and paranoid, profane rants about the Kennedys and other political rivals—there is also ample and overt sympathy for the hardships endured by the Whittier college graduate and Quaker from Yorba Linda, California. For example, considerable screen time is devoted to Nixon's humble upbringing and devout mother, the loss of his older brother to tuberculosis, and the condescension and prejudice endured at the hands of the Yale and Harvard elite when he sought a position in a prestigious law firm. Stone himself has commented that Nixon, like "every one of the protagonists" in his films, "goes through a crisis of conscience and ultimately achieves some form of enlightenment through the travails of this life."[47] Ultimately, the image of the presidency in this film is quite varied; there is extensive evidence of lawlessness, selfishness, and self-induced wounds—yet there is also room for empathy and redemption.

For a link to Richard Nixon's "Checkers" speech and other political speeches, go to www.seeingthebiggerpicture.net.

Based on the historical record, *Amistad* (1997) offers contrasting depictions of two nineteenth-century presidents, Martin Van Buren and John Quincy Adams, and their respective roles in protecting or opposing slavery. The film follows the legal case of slaves as they attempt to gain freedom after their ship, *La Amistad*, is captured off the U.S. coast. Van Buren (Nigel Hawthorne) is presented in a negative light, as he and his close advisers, especially Secretary of State Forsyth (David Paymer), attempt to aid Queen Isabella II of Spain in her quest to retain the slaves. In large part, Van Buren and his advisers take this approach due to crass political considerations, as Southern states threaten to deny Van Buren the Democratic nomination for a second term if he does not intervene to uphold the principle of slaves as property. When it appears as though the slaves may win their freedom, the president intervenes and has the case taken to the Supreme Court. John Quincy Adams, conversely, is portrayed favorably as an old antislavery crusader and statesman who, when called upon by abolitionists, lawyers, and supporters of the slaves, gives an impassioned plea for the slaves' freedom before the Supreme Court. Some critics have charged that Hollywood's version of real-life events in *Amistad* takes too many liberties with the historical record and perhaps applies the norms of twentieth-century politics to a far different age. Yet, ultimately, whether or not the filmmakers tried to do this is up to the viewer.

The Presidency on Television

Television has had a much different history in its portrayal of the American presidency. Starting in the 1950s, the American president and the office of the presidency have been regularly featured on television, but usually in terms of news rather than storytelling. Presidents have used the medium of television as a vehicle to impart important messages to the American public, and in some cases, the world. Some events surrounding U.S. political history are etched in the American mind because of television. President Kennedy's announcement of the Cuban Missile Crisis, President Nixon's resignation from office in the wake of the Watergate scandal, President Johnson's dramatic announcement that he would not seek reelection at the end of a speech on Vietnam, and President Reagan's comments memorializing the Space Shuttle *Challenger* astronauts are all examples of how presidents have used the medium in an effective manner. Similarly, the presidential debates between Kennedy and Nixon in 1960, the annual broadcasts of the State of the Union address, and news footage of the assassination attempt on President Reagan are all examples of events in which television pictures have helped shape the American public's image of the presidency.

For links to historical presidential addresses and more, go to www.seeingthebiggerpicture.net.

While presidents appear almost daily on news programs across the television dial, it is relatively rare that presidents have been seen on regular entertainment programs. Yet there have been a few instances when the presidency figures prominently on television screens. One memorable example was when President Nixon appeared for a few brief seconds on the 1970s hit *Laugh In*, saying simply, "Sock it to me?" The presidency has also figured prominently in programs that have had quite a short history. A 1977–1978 television program called *Carter Country* fictionalized the hometown of President Jimmy Carter during his first year in office. Similarly, prior to the September 11, 2001, terrorist attacks in the United States, Comedy Central's *That's My Bush* fictionalized and satirized the presidency of George W. Bush. Shortly after leaving office, former president George H. W. Bush appeared on an episode of *Saturday Night Live* hosted by his perennial comedic nemesis Dana Carvey.

Presidential *candidates*, however, at least in recent years, have not been as reticent to use pure entertainment to their advantage. As the past several election cycles illustrate, candidates have increasingly turned to late night comedy to get their message, or at least image, out to the masses. Some of the more high-profile examples include:

- Bill Clinton playing the saxophone on *Arsenio Hall*;
- George W. Bush nagging David Letterman about his heart surgery;
- Al Gore bringing his own Top Ten list to read on the *Late Show with David Letterman*;
- John McCain and Barack Obama appearing on the daytime talk show *The View*;
- Democrat Al Gore and Republican George W. Bush appeared on NBC in prime time to introduce *Saturday Night Live's* 2000 "Presidential Bash," a collection of twenty-five years of presidential parodies and political sketches; and
- Presidential and vice presidential candidates Sen. Barack Obama, Sen. Hillary Clinton, Gov. Sarah Palin, Gov. Mike Huckabee, Sen. John McCain, Sen. George McGovern, Rev. Jesse Jackson, and even Vice President Al Gore have all either appeared on or hosted *Saturday Night Live*.

Yet despite these examples of presidential *candidate* appearances, regular appearances by *sitting* presidents on purely entertainment programs have been extremely rare. That is until 2009, when Barack Obama appeared on the *Tonight Show with Jay Leno*, and then in 2010, when he appeared on *The Daily Show with Jon Stewart*, becoming the first sitting president to appear on that landmark program. And so by the early twenty-first century the reluctance of major presidential candidates to appear on television programs had passed. Rather than portraying an image of earnestness and deliberation (as in classic Hollywood films), candidates seemed more interested in portraying themselves as regular Americans.

The West Wing (1999–2006): Television's Positive (and Often Realistic) Portrayal of the American Presidency

While many of Hollywood's examinations of the modern presidency have been anything but flattering or inspiring, television provided one grand exception to this trend in the Clinton and Bush era.[48] Earning an army of Emmys, the prestigious George Peabody award, and named "TV Show of the Year" by *Entertainment Weekly* in its inaugural year, NBC's political drama *The West Wing* was praised in many media circles for its prime-time family friendliness. Its mature consideration of important policies, as well as the behind the scenes drama of presidential politics, gave rise to discussions among politicians, academics, radio personalities, and columnists.[49] Its portrayal of the inner-workings of the presidency and treatment of controversial issues, including the death penalty, school vouchers, and gays in the military, mirrored policy debates in the country.

To make sure that the show presented an authentic rendering of White House politics, institutional dynamics, and bureaucratic snafus, *The West Wing* received consultation from prominent White House and Washington insiders, from both political parties and from the executive and legislative branches.[50] Nonetheless, this did not insulate the show from allegations of ideological heavy-handedness and bias. Indeed, *The West Wing* was often a lightning rod of controversy, as some accused the show of a pervasive liberal bias. Nevertheless, the show was considered influential. Indeed, in a speech before the National Press Club in 2000, Majority Leader Tom DeLay (R-TX) derided NBC's celebrated series as more "left wing" than "West Wing."[51]

Media praise for *The West Wing* focused on the ethical questions that the characters faced that mirrored what real policy makers must contend with.[52] Former Clinton press secretary Mike McCurry asserted that *The West Wing* is "the only television show" that he watched, and commended the popular program for treating "those who work in politics. . .as human beings."[53] Media scholars applauded the drama's ability to "complement journalism by offering an entertaining reality of the White House that sharpens the image of the presidency and national politics."[54] Syndicated columnist and former Clinton

White House aide Matthew Miller praised the show for providing a truer rendition of White House service and politics than most journalists,[55] while Jay Rosen, chairman of New York University's journalism department, suggested that The West Wing "conveys a truth about the White House that we don't get from other sources," especially because the "humanity of the participants" in the White House gets lost in the vast majority of the media's coverage.[56] And the show's detailed attention to the complexity of developing and implementing policy impressed those inside the power corridors of Washington, D.C. For example, Clinton Secretary of State Madeleine Albright offered a ringing endorsement of The West Wing after an episode from season one dealt substantively with the intricacies of India–Pakistan relations and the ongoing conflict in Kashmir.[57]

West Wing aficionados included Republican public servants as well as Democrats. Reagan and Bush press secretary Marlin Fitzwater was an enormous West Wing enthusiast and was brought on as a consultant for the show's second season (2000–2001), as was Reagan and Bush speechwriter Peggy Noonan. Fitzwater gladly climbed aboard the NBC vehicle to offer insight into White House–press relations and presidential governance in general and had high praise for the show and the program's creator, Aaron Sorkin, telling PBS's Terence Smith, "I like it because I think it accurately portrays so many of the aspects of the White House that people never get to see and can't know about. . . . Aaron Sorkin is brilliant. The way he captures attitudes and nuances of issues and people's attitudes toward each other in the White House is truly remarkable."[58]

Amidst the positive feedback from politicians, academics, television critics, and the American public, a deluge of awards, statuettes, and critical acclaim rolled in. Yet beyond winning the prestigious Peabody award in each of its first two seasons and receiving an avalanche of Emmy and Golden Globe nominations, perhaps most important were the size and enthusiasm of weekly audiences glued to their television sets: an average of thirteen million Americans tuned in each week to follow the political, policy, and personal twists and turns that enveloped President Jed Bartlet (Martin Sheen), Chief of Staff Leo McGarry (John Spencer), Communications Director Toby Ziegler (Richard Schiff), Deputy Communications Director Sam Seaborn (Rob Lowe),[59] Deputy Chief of Staff Josh Lyman (Bradley Whitford), Press Secretary C. J. Craig (Allison Janney), and Presidential Assistant Charlie Young (Dule Hill).[60]

Alternatively, some saw The West Wing as an overly sentimentalized depiction of how policy is actually made.[61] Several prominent Republican politicians and strategists, as well as media critics and academics, charged Aaron Sorkin's program with painting a grossly unfair and one-sided picture of the White House, national politics, and social issues that aggressively highlighted and praised liberal policy positions, demonized conservatives, and even challenged America's core values. Conversely, television critics more concerned with quality entertainment than ideological biases chastised *The West Wing* for being sappy, sentimental tripe that was heavy on stirring musical scores, hokey idealism, and moral uprightness.[62]

During his "Challenge of Cultural Renewal" address at the National Press Club in Washington, D.C., in 2000, House majority whip Tom DeLay, the third-highest ranking Republican in Congress, declared his disdain for entertainment that mocked Christianity, religious conservatives, and American values. Asserting that "the American people are trying to resist a cultural *coup d'état*—a revolution launched by a privileged few who are determined to discredit and, ultimately, replace core American traditions."[63] DeLay offered this assessment of the media in general and *The West Wing* in particular:

> In short, in the name of liberation, the fashionable elite created their own perverse ideology; in the name of "tolerance," they are profoundly intolerant. . . . The media show this disdain for faith by the way they depict religious conservatives: as either hypocritical totalitarians on shows like NBC's "The West Wing"—or as "poor, uneducated and easy to command," as *The Washington Post* once put it.[64]

Republican strategist (and 2000 McCain campaign adviser) Mike Murphy blasted the show for demonizing conservatives while canonizing liberals, and columnist and Bush and Reagan White House veteran James Pinkerton complained of a brazen liberal bias, scoffing, "there's always an ideological hit there someplace."[65] Moreover, charged Pinkerton, creator Aaron Sorkin was "a liberal who believes in liberals," whose scripts religiously follow a smug "Republicans bad, Democrats good" plotline.[66]

Yet it was not only stalwart Republicans who were critical of the Wednesday night drama. Other complaints were not centered on any liberal hijacking of American values but of basic believability. Caryn James, chief television critic for the *New York Times*, found the show "wildly uneven" as it all too frequently shifted from complex sequences to "scenes of Martin Sheen making the right moral decision with the music swelling in the background."[67] Even prominent Democrats (themselves avid *West Wing* devotees) found certain small institutional aspects of the fictional White House—such as the GQ-like appearance of nearly every low- or high-level White House staffer, and the size and comfort of the offices—to be unrealistic. And then there was the matter of the show's presentation of issues, which one film historian asserted was presenting "a Hollywood political agenda sometimes so powerfully and passionately" that it was "offensive."[68] To illustrate his point, scholar Peter Rollins cited what he viewed as an unfair caricature of the religious right in the pilot episode, a treatment that he believed went "overboard" in its criticisms of religious conservatives.[69]

Conclusion

For over a century, films and popular culture have been used to critique, glorify, vilify, lampoon, and analyze presidents and the presidency. For the first half of the twentieth century and more, the majority of these offerings, whether biopics or other feature films, were quite lavish in their praise of presidents. The office and its inhabitants were presented in a most positive light, and often featured classic leading men tackling the role of president or presidential candidate. Later, with the advent of the Cold War, and the post-Vietnam era, Hollywood became far less generous to American chief executives. Many of the most extreme examples of this trend arrived in theaters throughout the 1990s, when a majority of movies released in that decade depicted a White House run amok by shysters, sycophants, and sexual deviants.[70]

At the same time, we also see a tale of two presidencies, as television has not fully embraced wanton cynicism. On the one hand, NBC's *The West Wing* humanized the White House in the Clinton and Bush era, offering a sympathetic portrayal of public servants and prescient insights into the everyday workings of the presidency, from the press room, to the war room, and all the pollsters, pundits, policies, filibusters, and bureaucratic inertia in between. On the other hand, during the George W. Bush administration, British cinema and television became increasingly hostile toward the institution of the American presidency. No doubt this was due, in part, to the unpopular policies of the Bush administration. Nevertheless, the films *Love Actually* (2003) and *In the Loop* (2009) depicted Britons reacting against a self-assured, yet completely misinformed, American president. The controversial film *Death of a President* (2006) used archival footage and computer-generated images to create a faux documentary about an imagined assassination of President Bush. While not advocating assassination, the film does question the policies of the administration by suggesting they were responsible for the assassination.[71]

Where does all of this leave us? The office of the president of the United States is the most high-profile political institution in the world, and the president is the singular leader with which most viewers can readily identify. As such the office and its occupants—the president as well as the First Family, members of the cabinet, and numerous advisers—have been praised and ridiculed, presented as average Joes, uncommon heroes, or devious miscreants. The questions that we should ask are: *What are the factors that influence these diverse portrayals? What role, if any, do scandals, political culture, the 24-hour mediated presidency, and basic free market economics play in crafting these depictions?* And, finally, *what cumulative effect do these messages have on our perception of the presidency?* With a rich history of diverse portrayals and discernable themes, the presidency is poised to remain relevant to the big and small screens, providing fertile ground for future films and wider commentaries on our times.

Notes

1. The genesis of this chapter dates to Kevan M. Yenerall and Christopher S. Kelley, "Shysters, Sycophants, and Sexual Deviants: The Hollywood Presidency in the 1990s," *White House Studies* 3, no. 3 (2003). Earlier working versions of this research appeared under the following titles at two conferences: "Shysters, Sycophants and Sexual Deviants: The Hollywood Presidency in the 1990s," paper presented at the Images of American Presidents in Film and Television National Conference, Westlake Village, California, November 10–12, 2000; and "Shysters, Sycophants and Sexual Deviants: How Hollywood Depicts the Presidency in the 1990s," paper presented at the annual meeting of the American Political Science Association, Boston, Massachusetts, September 3–6, 1998. The authors gratefully acknowledge Christopher S. Kelley for his scholarly insight and contribution.

2. Take, for example, the institution of the British prime minister, which one could argue is a high-profile and important office. Nevertheless, films about the office tend to either be historical or biographical in nature, for example, *Disraeli* (1929), *Young Winston* (1972), and *The Iron Lady* (2011), rather than creating a fictional occupant to advance a political story. There are, of course, exceptions, such as *Love Actually* (2003) and *In the Loop* (2009).

3. Robert Brent Toplin, ed., *Hollywood as Mirror* (Westport, CT: Greenwood Press, 1993), vii.

4. Bruce Handy, "Acting Presidents," *Time*, April 14, 1997, p. 99.

5. Including *In the Line of Fire* (1993), *Dave* (1993), *Clear and Present Danger* (1994), *The Pelican Brief* (1994), *Canadian Bacon* (1994), *My Fellow Americans* (1996), *Mars Attacks!* (1996), *Wag the Dog* (1997), *Murder at 1600* (1997), *Absolute Power* (1997), *Amistad* (1997), *Shadow Conspiracy* (1997), *Deep Impact* (1998), *Armageddon* (1998), and *Enemy of the State* (1998).

6. For a categorical breakdown of past presidents portrayed on film, see: www.seeingthebiggerpicture.net.

7. It should also be noted that President Art Hockstader (Lee Tracey, who garnered a best supporting actor nomination) ultimately chose to endorse and fight for Russell's nomination

at the convention, even as the president's policies and decision-making style more closely mirrored those of conservative Cantwell. Yet, President Hockstader could not stomach the utter deviousness of Cantwell's below-the-belt tactics, and he did everything he could—before dying during the party's convention—to see that "the best man" would secure his party's nomination. Gore Vidal's play *The Best Man* staged yet another successful revival on Broadway in the fall of 2000. Charles Durning (President Hockstader) and Spalding Gray (William Russell), among others, led the star-studded cast. While the play ran during the heat of the 2000 presidential election, Vidal did not alter the script to critique Vice President (and distant relative) Al Gore and Gov. George W. Bush or to reflect the times.

8. The character Groeteschele, a professor of international relations, hard-core realist, and Pentagon adviser, was based on Henry Kissinger.
9. George Clooney reprised Fonda's role in a made-for-television version of *Fail-Safe* in 2000.
10. John H. Lenihan, "Hollywood Laughs at the Cold War, 1947–61," in *Hollywood as Mirror*, ed. Robert Brent Toplin (Westport, CT: Greenwood Press, 1993), 141.
11. See Lenihan, "Hollywood Laughs at the Cold War," p. 141; and Richard Lacayo, "All the Presidents' Movies," *Time*, March 16, 1998, pp. 72–73.
12. Lenihan, "Hollywood Laughs at the Cold War," p. 140.
13. In *Gabriel over the White House* (1933), a playboy bachelor president (Walter Huston) is transformed (with the aid of some divine intervention—in this case, the angel Gabriel) into an energetic crusader, albeit one who declares martial law and suspends crucial civil liberties, who engineers a massive government employment plan, decisively and violently rids the country of bootleggers, and brings all of the nations together for a peace treaty. In essence, the film advocates a benevolent dictatorship in times of great national turmoil, such as the Great Depression.
14. Howard Fineman, "Last Action President," *Newsweek*, July 21, 1997, p. 66.
15. Harrison Ford in real life is an avid amateur aviator. See Tyson V. Riniger, "Harrison Ford: The Role of a Lifetime, Harrison Ford Takes on the Ultimate Advocacy Role Promoting and Educating the Public About the World of Aviation," *Private Air Magazine* (November–December 2006): 83–86.
16. In the film, the president's aides were portrayed by Michael J. Fox, David Paymer, Martin Sheen, and Anna Deveare Smith. Michael J. Fox would subsequently portray a similar character on the television series *Spin City* (1996–2002); the latter two would go on to portray characters in Sorkin's *The West Wing*.
17. It should be noted that Sorkin's *The West Wing* (NBC, 1999–2006) also included a dramatic, consequential live press conference from a president in the season two closer (and cliffhanger), "Two Cathedrals" (2001).
18. From *South Park* creators Trey Parker and Matt Stone, the series ran for eight episodes during the spring of 2001 and used actors to impersonate real individuals, including President George W. Bush; his wife, Laura Bush; political strategist Karl Rove; and actor Charlton Heston. The show was canceled prior to the September 11 terrorist attacks because of poor ratings. See John M. Higgins, "Comedy Central Impeaches Bush: Parker and Stone's Controversial Sitcom Loses the Popular Vote," *Broadcasting & Cable*, August 6, 2001, p. 12. Another program, *Lil Bush* (2007–2008), again on Comedy Central, but this time animated, depicted members of the Bush administration as children and ridiculed the intentions and intelligence of the now-former president.

19. Michael Moore's comedy *Canadian Bacon* (1994), a rare commercial film from the famous documentarian, also features a fake war per se when the sitting president (Alan Alda) has his generals and political aides drum up a bogus war with Canada to divert attention from sagging polls and a stagnant economy.

20. Tom Junod, "Our Man in the White House," *Esquire*, April 1998, p. 70.

21. Lacayo, "All the Presidents' Movies," p. 73.

22. Dee Dee Myers quoted in "Primary Reaction," *U.S. News & World Report*, March 9, 1998, p. 15. For a positive appraisal of the film and Travolta's performance in particular, see Eric Pooley, "Tale of Two Bills," *Time*, March 16, 1998, pp. 62–63.

23. James Kaplan, "True Colors?" *New Yorker*, March 2, 1998, p. 24.

24. Fred Thompson was later a Republican senator from Tennessee (1995–2003) and, briefly in 2008, a presidential candidate. Thompson has extensive Hollywood–Washington connections, appearing in several major films in the 1980s and 1990s, and as a lawyer on the Senate Watergate Committee.

25. It should be noted, however, that the moral center of *Primary Colors* is Stanton scandal-cover-upper-extraordinaire Libby Holden (a brilliant Kathy Bates), who ultimately rejects the politics of innuendo and scandal mongering, and takes her life when the Stantons reveal their willingness to acquiesce to sheer gutter politics.

26. Howard Fineman, "Last Action President," p. 67.

27. George Stephanopoulos, "White House Confidential," *Newsweek*, May 5, 1997, p. 34.

28. Ibid.

29. Michael Sragow, "Gross Projections," *Mother Jones*, January 1990, p. 24.

30. Christopher Sharrett, "Cinema's Social Conscience," *USA Today*, January 1991, p. 31.

31. Lacayo, "All the Presidents' Movies," p. 72.

32. Arthur M. Schlesinger, *Imperial Presidency* (Boston: Houghton Mifflin, 1973).

33. Thomas Patterson, *Out of Order* (New York: Vintage, 1993), 194.

34. See, for example, Joseph N. Cappella and Kathleen Hall Jamieson, *The Spiral of Cynicism: The Press and the Public Good* (New York: Oxford University Press, 1997).

35. Gallup Poll, "Clinton's Personal Characteristics," January 1, 1999: http://www.gallup.com/poll/trends/ptimage.asp.

36. Christopher Ruddy, *The Strange Death of Vincent Foster: An Investigation* (New York: Free Press, 1997).

37. For a detailed discussion of this "cottage industry" from a former insider, see David Brock, *Blinded by the Right: The Conscience of an Ex-Conservative* (New York: Crown, 2002). According to Brock, *The American Spectator*, The Federalist Society, and Richard Mellon Scaife were among the seminal movers and shakers funding politically motivated investigations of the Clintons' sexual, political, and financial relationships.

38. Patterson, *Out of Order*.

39. Ibid., p. 196.

40. Ibid.

41. Stephanopoulos, "White House Confidential," p. 34.

42. See the scathing attack of the press in Richard Harwood, *Citizens and Politics: A View from Main Street America* (Dayton: The Kettering Foundation, 1991).

43. For example, note the believability not just of the average person but also of legitimate news outlets of the boorish behavior of the Clinton administration as it left office in January 2001.

News stories were rampant of the pilfering of Air Force One, lewd photos left in the copying machines, computers damaged, and phone lines cut. These wild allegations, widely echoed in national media outlets, never were confirmed.

44. Richard Harwood, "The Alienated American Voter: Are the News Media to Blame?" *Brookings Review* 14, no. 4 (September 22, 1996): 32.

45. See Chapter 8, "War and Terrorism," for a further discussion of the concept of the military-industrial complex.

46. Stryker McGuire and David Ansen, "Stone Nixon," *Newsweek,* December 11, 1995, p. 66.

47. Oliver Stone, "A Filmmaker's Credo," *The Humanist* (September/October 1996): 5.

48. An earlier version of the *West Wing* section of this chapter was presented at the following conference: Kevan M. Yenerall, "The West Wing, the Presidency, and the Classroom: Left Wing or Right for the Times?" paper presented at the annual meeting of the American Political Science Association, San Francisco, California, 2001.

49. See, for example, "The Challenge of Cultural Renewal," Tom DeLay's speech at the National Press Club on May 4, 2000; several NPR segments (from *Fresh Air* to *Weekend Edition*); and lengthy coverage in the now-defunct media journal *Brill's Content*, in Salon.com, the *Washington Post*, CNBC's *Headliners and Legends* television program, and even editorial pages of major newspapers. Members of the cast have visited the Clinton and Bush White Houses, lobbied members of Congress, and were even the topic of outgoing press secretary Joe Lockhart's satirical video sketch at the 2000 White House Correspondents' Dinner. In terms of treatment by academics, see Peter C. Rollins and John E. O'Connor, eds., *The West Wing: The American Presidency as Television Drama* (New York: Syracuse University Press, 2003). The book was the end product of several scholarly panels devoted entirely to *The West Wing* at the Presidents in Movies and Television National Conference, sponsored by the Film & History League, held in Westlake, California, November 10–12, 2000. Terence Smith of PBS's *NewsHour with Jim Lehrer* has devoted significant on-air time to *The West Wing*, including revealing interviews with Sorkin, Marlin Fitzwater, and director Thomas Schlamme. See: http://www.pbs.org/newshour/bb/media/july dec00/westwing_10–4.html, and http://www.pbs.org/newshour/media/west_wing/sorkin. html. In terms of its "prime-time family friendliness," *The West Wing* was praised by the "Family Friendly Forum" for its lack of explicit sex and violence. The "Family Friendly Forum" is "a collaboration of 48 major advertisers created to encourage networks, studios, and production companies to create and air more programs during prime time that are relevant and interesting to parents and children." See "'Gilmore Girls,' 'Malcolm' Win Family Nods," *Atlanta Journal-Constitution*, August 3, 2001. See also Aaron Sorkin, *The West Wing Script Book* (New York: Newmarket Press, 2002).

50. Included on the list of advisors to the program were Democratic Senate staffer Lawrence O'Donnell, Clinton press secretary Dee Dee Myers, Carter pollster Pat Caddell, Clinton economic policy adviser Gene Sperling, and Reagan and Bush speechwriter Peggy Noonan and press secretary Marlin Fitzwater.

51. Tom DeLay, "The Challenge of Cultural Renewal," speech delivered at the National Press Club, May 4, 2000. The speech can be found in its entirety via C-SPAN's video archive/library at: http://www.c-spanvideo.org/program/TheChalle. DeLay argued that *The West Wing* was yet another exercise in cultural imperialism from liberal Hollywood elites hostile to core American values.

52. Peter Ames Carlin, "'West Wing' Gives New Meaning to Link between TV and Politics," *Portland Oregonian*, July 24, 2001.
53. Matthew Miller, "The Real White House," *Brill's Content*, March 2000, pp. 88–95+, esp. p. 90.
54. Donnalyn Pomper, "On *The West Wing*: White House Narratives That Journalism Cannot Tell," paper presented at the Images of American Presidents in Film and Television National Conference, November 10–12, 2000, Westlake Village, California.
55. Miller, "The Real White House."
56. Ibid., p. 113.
57. Pomper, "On The West Wing."
58. Terence Smith interview with Marlin Fitzwater, *The NewsHour with Jim Lehrer*, September 8, 2000, PBS online: http://www.pbs.org/newshour/media/west_wing/fitzwater.html.
59. Sam Seaborn (played by Rob Lowe) left the Bartlet White House to run for Congress in the fourth season (2002–20003). Seaborn was replaced by Will Bailey (Joshua Malina).
60. The numbers of viewers varied from week to week, obviously. Season two's two-part premiere, "In the Shadow of Two Gunmen," drew well over twenty million viewers.
61. John Carman, "Absurdity Dominates Fall Lineup," *San Francisco Chronicle*, August 1, 2001.
62. For example, Caryn James, chief television critic of the *New York Times*, and John Carman of the *San Francisco Chronicle*.
63. Tom DeLay, "The Challenge of Cultural Renewal," speech delivered at the National Press Club, May 4, 2000. See: http://www.c-spanvideo.org/program/TheChalle.
64. Ibid.
65. In a 2000 episode of Matt Lauer's *Headliners and Legends* devoted to *The West Wing*, Republic strategist and chief McCain 2000 aide Mike Murphy (also a part-part-time guest host of CNN's *Crossfire*) criticized and mocked the show for being overly simplistic by portraying Republicans as ghouls and Democrats as unimpeachable and squeaky-clean. For Pinkerton's criticism of the show on ideological grounds, see Miller, "The Real White House," pp. 90, 113.
66. Miller, "The Real White House."
67. Ibid., p. 113.
68. Film scholar Peter C. Rollins' critique of *The West Wing*–see: John Matviko, "Organization's First Conference–A Major Success," *Rewind: The Newsletter of the Film and History League* 1, no. 1 (March 2001). For more on the conference and related criticism of *The West Wing's* politics, see also: Jennifer Ruark, "Hot Type," *Chronicle of Higher Education*, January 5, 2001, p. A18.
69. See Rollins' comments in *Rewind* and Peter C. Rollins and John E. O'Connor, eds. *The West Wing: The American Presidency as Television* Drama (Syracuse University Press, 2003).
70. Yenerall and Kelley, "Shysters, Sycophants, and Sexual Deviants."
71. See Sarah Lyall, "For a British TV Movie, a Very Real President Is Shot," *New York Times*, September 2, 2006.

· 5 ·

CAMPAIGNS AND ELECTIONS

Hollywood and the film industry in general, not unlike myriad commercial interests, civic-minded citizens, and advocacy groups across the United States, have played a consistent role in the electoral process. The film and entertainment community's engagement in conventional forms of political participation—fund-raising, issue advocacy, producing commercials and propaganda films, crafting images, honing messages, and fielding candidates—has been evident in American campaigns and elections since the time of silent films and the World War I era. Elected officials from the entertainment industry have included the likes of U.S. Senators Fred Dalton Thompson (R-TN) and Al Franken (D-MN); Republican mayor of Carmel, California, and silver screen legend Clint Eastwood; and U.S. representatives Helen Gahagan Douglas (D-CA), Sonny Bono (R-CA), and Fred Grandy (R-IA), among others. And of course Tinsel Town had one of its own, Ronald Reagan, occupy the White House.[1]

Evidence certainly exists of Hollywood having a dramatic effect on specific elections—most notably, an infamous concerted effort by the heads of major film studios to smear and defeat the Pulitzer Prize–winning author of *The Jungle* (1906), Upton Sinclair, during his race for California governor in 1934 when he ran on the EPIC (End Poverty in California) platform.[2] Yet our main focus in this chapter will be not on the industry's long-standing involvement in the political process, but rather, how feature films, documentaries, and television have depicted campaigns and elections. And while explicitly political films make up a small percentage of Hollywood's overall output—some scholars' estimates are 5 to 10 percent, at best—the industry, along with emerging independent filmmakers, has devoted a fair share of these films to the electoral process.[3] Several of these films, whether major studio or independent films depicting fictional campaigns or behind-the-scenes documentaries, examine a number of key dynamics and realities that underlie American elections in the modern media age. Our exploration of campaigns and elections on the big and small screen samples movies, sitcoms, and television segments that present revealing and, at times, controversial portraits of candidates, the American electorate, the media, party machines, racial identity politics, and the overall campaign process.

Reel Candidates: Mayors, Governors, Senators, and Presidential Candidates

John Ford's 1958 black and white classic *The Last Hurrah*, based on the novel by Edwin O'Connor, looks back with fondness on big city machine politics and old-school politicking. The protagonist in this colorful tale of campaigning and patronage is the mayor of a large New England city (assumed to be Boston), Frank Skeffington (Spencer Tracy). Skeffington, who grew up in one of the working- class sections of the city and rose to greatness through hard work and party loyalty, is a back-slapping, big-hearted man of the people who sets aside entire days to meet and greet constituents in his office. The film follows Skeffington's last campaign, a battle against the new television-driven politics and the vacuous, smiling, superficial opposition candidate Kevin McCluskey (Charles B. Fitzsimons). The attractive puppet-like McCluskey uses television ads with his wife and children to promote an image of an upstanding, honest, family man. However, the ad in question—which parodies Richard Nixon's famous "Checkers" speech, among other popular political ads—goes horribly awry when McCluskey's dog barks incessantly and his wife has trouble reading the cue cards. The message is clear: this new breed of image-making political stunt is as staged and fake as the day is long. It is an elaborate, well-lit, slickly produced manipulation of the American voter.

Throughout the film, the ebullient Skeffington shows Adam Caulfield (Jeffrey Hunter), a journalist and the mayor's nephew, the ropes of glad-hand-ing campaigning and constituent politics. In one famous scene, Skeffington takes Caulfield to the wake of local man, "Nocko" Minnihan, and the gathering quickly becomes a political event, as the mayor's attendance brings out various constituencies to impress Skeffington. At face value, this may seem like shameless, heartless politicking. However, Skeffington's presence brings a huge crowd to pay respects to Nocko, which soothes his grieving widow. In addition, Skeffington gives Mrs. Minnihan money to help her along and uses his stature to strong-arm the funeral director into providing funeral services and burial for a minimal fee. In the process, the mayor transforms his nephew from skeptical critic to adoring fan, of both his uncle and his style of old-school big city politicking. When the larger-than-life mayor ultimately loses the election to the clueless-but-media-savvy McCluskey, it signals the end of a type of politics and campaigning once so prominent across the country. With the advent of television and the accelerated use of staged events, calculated confessionals, and carefully planned testimonials, this is a sign of things to come. *The Last Hurrah* clearly presents the positive potential of machine politics and portends the end of an era. While the context is quite different (mayoral politics aimed at helping constituents and winning elections), this celebration of patronage is a far cry from the intensely negative portrayal of the Taylor political machine in Frank Capra's *Mr. Smith Goes to Washington*.

An excellent real-world companion piece to *The Last Hurrah*'s send-up of political ads would be Richard Nixon's notorious 1952 "Checkers" speech. Appearing immediately after the popular *Milton Berle Show*, the beleaguered vice presidential candidate masterfully used his well-placed television slot to defend his usage of a political slush fund provided by supporters and to hurl allegations of impropriety at his Democratic rival. Nixon's television event was a huge success, rallying Republicans and forcing Dwight Eisenhower, the 1952 Republican presidential nominee, to keep the young U.S. Senator from California on the ticket. In the decades since Nixon's prime-time confessional, such direct appeals have become quite commonplace. In the midst of allegations of infidelity in the heat of the 1992 New Hampshire primary, for example, Bill and Hillary Clinton appeared on CBS's long-running news magazine *60 Minutes* in January 1992, after the Super Bowl, to address questions of extramarital affairs. During the interview, Bill Clinton admitted to causing "pain" in his marriage. This real-life scene is repeated in fictional form in Mike Nichols's 1998 film *Primary Colors*, which follows the presidential campaign of a Clintonesque southern governor.[4]

For links to campaign advertisements, films, and speeches, including Richard Nixon's "Checkers" speech, go to www.see-ingthebiggerpicture.net.

In 1972's *The Candidate*, directed by Michael Ritchie and starring Robert Redford in the lead role, there is an explicit connection to the real world of modern American politics. The screenplay was penned by Jeremy Larner, an aide to 1968 Democratic presidential candidate Sen. Eugene McCarthy, who no doubt drew from his experiences as a speechwriter on the campaign trail. "The Candidate" in the film is Bill McKay (Redford), the liberal son of a former backslapping, deal-cutting establishment California governor (Melvyn Douglas). McKay is an activist, antipoverty lawyer who is talked into running against the popular incumbent and U.S. Senator Crocker Jarmon (Don Porter), a race he (early on) figures he has no reasonable chance of winning. McKay enters the race an idealistic individual who speaks his mind and offers substantive policy initiatives. However, as the long-shot McKay begins to rise in the polls and provide a stiff challenge to Jarmon, his team of advisers and image men takes over, molding the once-outspoken, authentic insurgent candidate into a conventional, managed contender who drops his bold proposals and specifics and switches to the safe but cynical terrain of empty slogans and sound bites. He even placates his advisers by trimming his sideburns and hair. As political scientist Ernest Giglio observes, *The Candidate* "warns the audience of the pitfalls of contemporary electioneering where . . . personal appeal is celebrated over intelligence and ethical principles, and thirty-second sound bites are favored over detailed analysis of complex issues."[5]

There is a telling scene near the close of the film; when it appears that the younger McKay wins the election, his father approaches him and says, "Congratulations, son. You're a politician." It appears from his tone and facial expressions that he does not necessarily mean politics in the noble, idealistic sense of unselfish public service. Larner's script is razor sharp and in many ways, prophetic, as it astutely and accurately portrays the rise of the stale, cynical, style-over-substance manipulative direction of modern campaigns in a media-saturated age. In this brave new world, candidates are sold not as intellectuals, diplomats, or policy leaders ready to solve society's pressing problems; rather, they are sold as a commodity the same way we promote soda, toothpaste, snacks, and clothes. It is image, not substance.

In a country with mediocre voter turnout (especially when compared with other industrialized, democratic countries), where healthy skepticism often gives way to wanton cynicism and alienation, and where significant sections of the electorate remain woefully ignorant of the structure and nuances of the political system and public policy, such a scene may unwittingly reinforce the most negative perceptions of politics and our governing institutions. At the same time, however, it is evident that Larner's brilliant, prescient script has the creative finger on the proverbial pulse of many modern American elections. Campaigns have arguably become even more dominated by sound bites, slogans, and 30-second ads, especially in the age of 24-hour media coverage and increased television expenditures by a growing list of "independent" groups (i.e., corporate, trade, ideological, and labor organizations) seeking to influence the outcome of the election. At the same time, a cynical or ratings-driven focus on process, peccadilloes, and the horse race rather than policy substance—often propagated by a frustrated media-fed message-of-the-day drivel from campaigns—can be disastrous for promoting active, informed citizenship and political involvement.[6] We must be mindful that, however accurate the portrait of modern campaigning the film presents, *The Candidate*'s portrayal of politics has potentially dire consequences for two important concepts in democratic societies: that politicians hold the public's trust while in office, and that a political career is an honorable one dedicated to public service and the common good.[7]

The "mock" documentary *Bob Roberts* (1992), written and directed by Tim Robbins, presents an ideological critique of contemporary politics and ambitious, "self-made" men who seek power at any cost. Bob Roberts is a millionaire right-wing ideologue seeking a U.S. Senate seat from Pennsylvania who uses folk songs to express his ultraconservative views. With a harmonica around his neck, Roberts releases albums such as *The Freewheelin' Bob Roberts, Times Changin' Back,* and *Bob on Bob*—and sings songs such as "Drugs Stink" and "I Wanna Be Rich."[8] As is evident from these titles, Roberts throws the liberal, activist edges of the 1950s–1960s folk music tradition on its head. Rather than strumming his guitar to promote racial justice, fight poverty, or end war, the senatorial candidate uses his music and campaign events to attack the poor and homeless, antiwar activists, hippies, and drug use. It is a cynical, media-savvy, full-frontal attack on 1960s idealism and liberalism, and Roberts's message draws young psychotic fans into his corner (including a young, hilarious Jack Black as one particularly loyal follower).

As his campaign against liberal incumbent Sen. Brickley Paiste (Gore Vidal) heats up, Roberts smears him as a womanizer and an out-of-touch-big-government liberal who squanders taxpayers' money on wasteful social welfare and antipoverty programs. When an industrious, activist reporter ties Roberts and close aides to illegal activity, Roberts fakes an assassination and has the reporter framed. In the raging narcissistic, right-wing Roberts, Robbins is able to offer a scathing critique of the views, motives, and effects of conservative politics in 1980s and 1990s America, which were clearly in fashion in the age of Reagan.[9]

Robbins's hilarious send-up of an egomaniac and shameless conservative folksinger-senator had an impact in the entertainment intelligentsia, as indicated by an infamous 1994 *Simpsons* episode about a corrupt campaign entitled "Sideshow Bob Roberts." In this installment of *The Simpsons*, perennial nemesis Sideshow Bob (the voice of Kelsey Grammer) gets out of prison in order to run against longtime incumbent Mayor "Diamond" Joe Quimby, a notorious wheeler-dealer and womanizer. Promoting Bob's release and mayoral candidacy is the blowhard Birch Barlow, a popular conservative radio personality and prominent Republican. Longtime *Simpsons* viewers recognize the Boston–accented "Quimby" as a facsimile for "Kennedy," while Birch Barlow is clearly a prototype for longtime conservative Republican radio king Rush Limbaugh. While Bob handily defeats Quimby, it is later revealed—via a hilarious Woodward and Bernstein–Watergate parody complete with a "Deep Throat" reference and dark parking garages—that the former Krusty the Clown sidekick stole the election with the help of massive voter fraud. In "Sideshow Bob Roberts" we are treated to a number of political and campaign references, from Rush Limbaugh and the Kennedys to Watergate and *All the President's Men*. In addition, the episode's Quimby–Sideshow Bob debate sequence cleverly echoes, in satirical fashion, the 1988 presidential debate where CNN correspondent Bernard Shaw asked Democratic nominee Michael Dukakis if he would support the death penalty if his wife, Kitty, was raped and murdered. Further attention is paid to the 1988 presidential campaigns of George H. W. Bush and Dukakis, when there is a parody of Bush's infamous "revolving door" prison ad.[10] In the end, much like the conservative populist folksinger Bob Roberts, Sideshow Bob will do *anything* to get elected. And like Robbins's film, this installment of *The Simpsons* uses political satire and parody to get its point across. But unlike *Bob Roberts*, "Sideshow Bob Roberts" does so in animated and televised format.

Another classic episode of *The Simpsons* also takes aim at modern political campaigns in "Two Cars in Every Garage and Three Eyes on Every Fish." The episode lampoons the "Checkers" speech, the classic film *Citizen Kane* (1941), and much more. This political tour-de-force from writers Sam Simon and John Swartzwelder premiered on November 1, 1990, just days before the 1990 midterm elections. In "Two Cars" Montgomery Burns, filthy-rich overlord of the Springfield Nuclear Power Plant, is fined millions by a government nuclear regulatory commission for his unsafe, shoddy upkeep of his plant. The state-imposed plant inspection is spurred when Bart Simpson catches a three-eyed fish (who Burns later dubs "Blinky" in "Checkers"-like fashion) in a fishing pond adjacent to Burns's nuclear plant. Depressed at the money he will have to spend to improve his plant and be in sync with the code, Burns lashes out at government safety and environmental standards, and, after complaining to plant employee Homer Simpson about the government fines, he vows to run for governor against incumbent Mary Bailey. From there he can selfishly dismantle the state's nuclear power plant regulations. What follows is a sardonic take on deregulation, as well as the manipulation, management, and attack politics of modern campaigns.

Very much like *The Candidate*, Burns's campaign is completely managed, and he speaks whatever calculated, poll-tested, populist drivel his handlers cook up. Unlike Bill McKay, however, Burns was never an idealistic, attractive, and modestly compensated public servant. He is out to hoodwink and manipulate the public 100 percent, and his cynical, mean-spirited attacks on Governor Bailey and his hilarious off-camera remarks denigrating middle-class citizens indicate just how little regard he has for the public. To cement the notion of overhandled candidates who use trickery and media manipulation, Burns's expensive campaign team consists of "speech writer, joke writer, spin doctor, make-up man, personal trainer, muckraker, character assassin, mudslinger, and garbologist."[11] Completely absent, of course, are legitimate, substantive *policy* advisors. When the frail, hunched, and elderly Burns reviews a campaign portrait that renders him a rugged, smiling, and larger-than-life Davy Crockett–like figure, he exclaims, "Why are my teeth showing like that?" His campaign aide Danielson answers, "Because you're smiling." Burns then responds, "Ah. Excellent. This is exactly the kind of trickery I'm paying you for."[12]

In the grand tradition of prime-time political confessionals-commercials, and in one of *The Simpsons* many moments of unbridled hilarity coupled with penetrating political commentary, Mr. Burns and his campaign team cynically pull off their own shameless "Checkers" moment. The issue of the three-eyed fish, a genetic mutation caused by the plant's pollution, must be neutralized. In an effort to put the contaminated waters and bizarre fish behind him in order to improve his image, Burns uses a paid political commercial to redefine the "Blinky" situation to his advantage: the fish will now be portrayed as a wonder of science rather than a freakish symbol of environmental devastation. As such, the fish is *not* a hideous mutation brought on by irresponsible corporate pollution, claims Burns, but rather, a process of evolution. Burns's perceived weakness will now be a symbol of his strength:

MR. BURNS: I'm here to talk to you about my little friend here, Blinky. Many of you consider him a hideous mutation. Well nothing could be further from the truth. But don't take my word for it, let's ask an actor playing Charles Darwin what he thinks. . . .

DARWIN: Hello, Mr. Burns.

BURNS: Oh, hello Charles. Be a good fellow and tell our viewers about your theory of natural selection.

DARWIN: Glad to, Mr. Burns. You see, ever so often Mother Nature changes her animals, giving them bigger teeth, sharper claws, longer legs, or in this case, a third eye. And if these variations turn out to be an improvement, the new animals thrive and multiply and spread across the face of the earth.

BURNS: So you're saying this fish might have an advantage over other fish [and] that may in fact be a kind of super-fish.

DARWIN: I wouldn't mind having a third eye, would you?[13]

Burns's home run of image and chicanery over reason, splashed across Springfield's television screens (including those at the "Springfield Retirement Castle"), immediately begins to push the nuclear plant owner up in the polls. How effective was the "Blinky" (i.e., "Checkers") defense? Evidence that the Burns stunt hits immediate political pay dirt is provided at the close of his commercial, when a perennial patron of Moe's Tavern, Barney, exclaims, from his bar stool: "Wow! Super-fish!" Then, without missing a beat, Moe the bartender spouts: "I wish government *would* get off my back!" Burns's cynical populism was a smash hit with the gullible public. The political message, delivered with sidesplitting humor, is direct: backed by money, consultants, and television, politicians can easily manipulate the public. Even a super-rich, selfish hermit like the nuclear baron Burns can come across as a populist working to get government off our collective backs. And Mr. Burns's "government-off-our-back" mantra has plenty of precedents in modern politics, perhaps most famously in the 1980 presidential campaign of Republican Ronald Reagan. Throughout his successful run for the White House, Reagan effectively painted government, and its regulatory measures, as an unfair, intrusive force that overtaxed and stifled the entrepreneurial spirit.[14]

But Burns was not done with molding his new man-of-the-people image. With his polls showing Burns deadlocked with Mary Bailey, Marge Simpson's choice for governor,[15] Burns's advisers plan a major publicity stunt. On the night before the election, he will have a staged dinner with an average middle-American family, the Simpsons, which will manufacture his credentials as a friend of the "little guy." Burns loves the idea and devilishly relishes the thought of using the media to fool the mindless sheep watching from home:

> Oh, I get your angle. Every Joe Meatball and Sally Housecoat in the God-forsaken state will see me hunkering down to chow with Eddie Punchclock. The media will have a field day![16]

In the end, however, Burns's campaign falters when Marge Simpson serves the gubernatorial candidate a three-eyed fish for dinner. Burns is unable to stomach eating the hideous creature, spitting it out rather than swallowing.

The television series *Futurama, The Simpson*'s creator Matt Groening's other animated series, followed in the tradition of pointed satire. Between 1999 and 2003, seventy-two episodes of the show were produced.[17] Set in the year 3000, *Futurama* follows the exploits of Philip J. Fry (voiced by Billy West), a pizza delivery guy who is accidentally cryogenically frozen on December 31, 1999, for a thousand years, and wakes up in time to see the dawn of the thirty-first century in New York (built on top of old New York). Fry (which is how he is commonly referred to) works for an interstellar delivery company with a vast array of characters that help guide him through the thirty-first century. And though the stories are set in the thirty-first century, many of the episodes mirror the problems of the later twentieth and early twenty-first centuries, with several of the episodes exploring the nature and difficulties and obstacles of democracy in the modern world.

The sixteenth episode of the series, "A Head in the Polls,"[18] (1999) helps to bear this out. This installment opens with Fry and Bender (a robot) watching television. Lela comes running in and tells them to turn the channel because there was a debate on. After some grousing from Fry and Bender, Lela tells them the debate is important because it could help to determine who will be the next president of the world. Fry wonders why that could possibly matter because they live in the United States. Lela reminds him that the United States is part of the world. Fry comments that he has been gone for a long time, implicitly arguing that in the twentieth century, the United States was not a part of the world, a not-so-veiled criticism of American exceptionalism and ignorance.

The candidates for president are actual clones, citing platitudes and sounding remarkably similar. The writers are suggesting that the choice between the candidates is essentially meaningless, as they are virtually the same.[19] After a discussion of the merits and importance of voting, the crew decides to take Fry to register to vote. Professor Farnsworth, a 147-year-old mad scientist, is very enthusiastic about Fry registering to vote. When asked when he became so interested in voting, the professor replies, "The very instant I got old." This is a reference to those who tend to have the highest levels of voter turnout in American elections; as citizens age, the more likely they are to vote.[20] Fry declares, given the imperceptible differences between the two candidates, that he might join a third party. He is told that only mutants and weirdos join third parties. Again, in the American two-party system, any attempt to form a realistic and viable third party is met with skepticism and derision.[21]

This episode details and critiques a number of issues in recent American politics, including the lack of participation among younger voters. This, of course, has the effect of turning the political discussion into a debate about the desires of those who participate in the process. Further, the two-party system seems to be a particular target for the writers; it is depicted as producing bland politicians who make bland statements so as not to offend any part of the electorate. The result is that the electorate does not care about politics. Appeals to a third-party candidate are probably futile because of the advantages the two major political parties have built into the system. Moreover, third-party aspirants are often portrayed by electoral rivals and the media as out of the mainstream or kooks.[22]

Warren Beatty, no stranger to the political scene, directed and cowrote the political comedy-drama *Bulworth* (1998), with the tagline, "Brace yourself. This politician is about to tell the truth!" Beatty plays U.S. Senator Jay Billington Bulworth (D-CA), who is up for reelection in the fall of 1996. Pictures of civil rights activists and liberals such as Rosa Parks, Angela Davis, Malcolm X, Bobby Kennedy, and George McGovern adorn the walls of his Senate office, but Bulworth is a fraud; he has long since abandoned their principles and progressive policies and has sold his soul to the highest bidder. He is now a moderate "New Democrat" in the mold of then-president Bill Clinton and speaks out against welfare, affirmative action, and government programs designed to fight poverty and make health care more accessible. He is in the pocket of big contributors, such as the health insurance industry, and uses his powerful committee position to kill legislation that would cost such corporations' profits. He spouts pious family values rhetoric while he has a severely strained and phony relationship with his wife (Christine Baranski).

Distressed at the pathetic fake he has become, Bulworth hires someone to kill him so that the insurance money can go to his daughter. However, this sense of impending death has a liberating effect on the depressed senator. Along the campaign trail he begins to rap throughout the Los Angeles area—from posh Beverly Hills fund-raisers to South Central Los Angeles—about the insidious power of big business, media conglomerates, oil companies, and the insurance industry, among others. He chides Hollywood moguls for the steady stream of violent, dumb, and dirty films designed for maximum profitability. He meets and falls in love with an African American woman (Halle Berry), who reminds Bulworth of the devastation of urban centers due to the loss of good-paying manufacturing jobs. And, during an interview with a local reporter, the incumbent senator promotes a concentrated worldwide plan of interracial coupling to help make the world one race and, therefore, break away from the tethers of racism. In short, Senator Bulworth becomes, as one film critic observed, "a gleefully emancipated prankster who says exactly what he thinks and doesn't give a damn about the consequences"[23]

The angry, politically charged, pull-no-punches script may not have led to commercial success—the $30 million movie brought in a gross of about $26.5 million—but the critics paid attention. Bulworth was nominated for an Academy Award, a Golden Globe, and the Chicago Film Critics Association award for best screenplay. And Beatty, along with coauthor Jeremy Pikser, captured the Los Angeles Film Critics Association award (LAFCA) for best screenplay. In the winter of 2000, Beatty, along with billionaire Donald Trump and professional wrestler–turned–Minnesota–governor Jesse Ventura, appeared on the cover of major magazines, presented as potential third-party alternatives to the two-party system. Beatty himself openly considered making a presidential bid with the Green Party in 2000 in order to move the Democratic Party back to its more liberal, activist policy positions of the 1960s–1980s, an agenda clearly at the heart of Bulworth. Ultimately, Beatty decided against such a bid for the White House. While many may be uncomfortable with or unmoved by the obscenity-laced critiques of the U.S. political system and the in-your-face progressive politics, several critics praised Beatty for presenting such an unadulterated dose of political satire.[24]

Real Candidates, Campaigns, and Documentaries:
There's No Such Thing as *A Perfect Candidate*

Another ideological critique of the state of politics, power, and campaigning from the left side of the political spectrum comes from writer-director Michael Moore. In a segment entitled "Presidential Mosh Pit" in season two of his cable television series *The Awful Truth* (2000), the sarcastic guerrilla filmmaker declares that his program will offer an official endorsement to any presidential candidate of *either party* who will dive into his portable mosh pit traveling through the ice-cold Iowa winter. Why a mosh pit as the standard for choosing the next leader of the free world? Because, surmises Moore, as many of the 2000 presidential candidates are so close to each other ideologically, the election and campaign process is a sham from the get-go. Rather than have caucuses or primaries and endure a meaningless exercise, therefore, one might as well use the mosh pit as the new standard for judging candidates. Along the primary campaign trail in Iowa, Moore asks nearly every candidate—from Democrat Bill Bradley to Republicans George W. Bush, Orrin Hatch, and Steve Forbes—to dive into the traveling mosh pit of angry youth. Only one candidate, Republican Alan Keyes, agrees to go "in the pit," and Moore and *The Awful Truth* make good on their election standards and "endorse" Keyes for president.[25]

One of the major concerns when using film to teach politics and provoke discussion and debate is to get beyond—or at least temporarily throw aside—the oft-repeated mantra that all officeholders and candidates are visionless, shameless, plotting scam artists devoted to winning at any cost, public interest be damned. Why? Even amid real scandals and human and political shortcomings, most public servants are performing valuable services and are passionate about bettering communities and the country. And then one considers the notorious 1994 U.S. Senate race in Virginia, and perhaps it is harder to convince Americans of the nobility of public service and the legitimacy of their politicians. Facing this dilemma, the documentary *A Perfect Candidate* (1996) stands as a potential nightmare of sorts for the civic-minded believer in voting, democracy, and the electoral process.

R. J. Cutler and David Van Taylor's revealing documentary of the 1994 U.S. Senate race between Democratic incumbent Charles Robb and Republican challenger Oliver North "has just about everything the modern political circus has to offer: negative advertising, demagoguery, flip-flopping on the issues, cynical manipulation of public opinion, shameless lying and an abject refusal to introduce real substance to an election campaign."[26] The film chronicles the twists, turns, drama, and dirty politics that transpire throughout the election, illustrating how candidates can deliberately contradict themselves and prove uninspiring. Viewers are treated to incumbent Senator Robb's obfuscation when *Washington Post* reporter Don Baker asks the candidate simple, straightforward questions. The film also documents the no-holds-barred, flamethrowing, attack politics of Mark Goodin, Oliver North's campaign director and hatchet man. In the end, as audiences treat their recurring nausea and cynicism, Robb squeezes out a victory, one of the few major Democratic victories in an otherwise Republican year.[27] Summing up *A Perfect Candidate* and the 1994 Senate campaign, *Washington Post* critic Desson Howe asserted:

> If documentary filmmaking is about identifying the truth, no subject could be more invigorating, amusing and frustrating to probe than American politics. . . ."A Perfect Candidate" is serenely damning in its indictment of political campaigns and, by extension, America. Here's a choice, after all, between someone who admits to lying to Congress and someone who can't admit to a hotel tryst with a Playboy model. In the words of a frustrated voter, this election wasn't about which direction Virginia should go in, it was a choice between two diseases.[28]

At the same time, the film is not necessarily a disaster for those who desire a more committed, engaged, and educated populace. The sheer hollowness and meanness of the 1994 Robb–North race could, and should, inspire citizens to take an active role in making sure voters have better, or at least more consistent, inspirational and coherent electoral choices. *A Perfect Candidate* also does an excellent job of revealing Virginia's fascinating political culture. From the Shenandoah Valley to the Atlantic coast, and from the cradle of the Confederacy to the increasingly diverse Washington, D.C., suburbs of northern Virginia, the state features an eclectic mix of cosmopolitan, rural, and conservative evangelical Christian voters, and the film does an excellent job of articulating the political, social, religious, and economic currents that flow across the state and influence election outcomes.

D. A. Pennebaker and Chris Hegedus's *The War Room* (1993), which chronicles Bill Clinton's 1992 bid for the White House, captured the National Board of Review award for best documentary.[29] The film, whose tagline is, "They changed the way campaigns are won," follows the work of the Clinton campaign's inner circle of strategists, pollsters, and media consultants, with special attention given to the rapid-fire response team of James Carville, George Stephanopoulos, and Paul Begala. Determined not to be another Michael Dukakis, the beleaguered 1988 Democratic nominee who was lackadaisical in responding to George H. W. Bush's charges of being soft on patriotism and crime enforcement, the Clinton team hunkered down in its Little Rock "War Room" and gave as good as it got, with a relentless, laser-like focus on the economy. The documentary follows the process of crafting rapid response ads, managing the media, and shaping damage control, from the dark, cold days of the New Hampshire primary to the emotional glow of victory on election night. In doing so, *The War Room*, even several decades later, stands as one of the great documents of modern presidential campaign strategy.

Winner of the audience award for best documentary at the Tribeca Film Festival, and nominated for an Academy Award for best documentary feature, Marshall Curry's simultaneously disturbing, revealing, and engrossing *Street Fight* (2005), produced by political documentary pioneers Liz Garbus and Rory Kennedy, stands as an extraordinary, multilayered achievement in the annals of modern campaign films. Digging beneath the electoral surface to uncover pervasive racial and generational stereotypes and resentments, the documentary chronicles the 2002 all-out battle for mayor of Newark, New Jersey. The race pitted Cory Booker, a thirty-two-year-old Rhodes Scholar and Yale Law School graduate, against Sharpe James, the four-term incumbent.[30] Along the way, we find that the minions of the entrenched incumbent and quintessential old-school machine politician James—who was sixty-six at the time of the 2002 race and was first elected mayor in 1986—engaged in brazen electoral subterfuge and economic and physical intimidation in an all-out effort to maintain power. And while the popular imagination and campaign coverage suggest that modern electoral contests might be won or lost via 30-second ad blitzes on television, Curry's film reminds us that many races are still won or lost in the trenches, that is, *literally*, on the streets.

Yet a large part of *Street Fight*'s enduring relevance centers on its attention to the unique racial dynamics present in a mayoral race between two African American men, James and Booker, from different generations and with different complexions. David Denby, writing in the *New Yorker*, crystallizes the profound racial connotations of the James–Booker brawl, a fierce battle over racial identity, generational leadership, and what constitutes "blackness":

> The movie, which begins a few months before the election and concludes after voting day, is conventional in form. What has fascinated African-American commentators, however, is the way the 2002 race became a testing ground for the political weight of "blackness." Sharpe James, in his youth, struggled as a black man to make his way in politics, yet he ran a racist campaign against Cory Booker. James is dark-skinned, Booker light, and James, in a variety of ways, implied that Booker wasn't really black enough—and that he was Jewish, too, even though Booker is Baptist.[31]

Though Booker ultimately lost the race presented so vividly in *Street Fight*, he would later win the next mayoral election in 2006, and has since gone on to be reelected. He continues to be an outspoken national voice for urban renewal and education reform, whether via innovative policy experiments and private-public partnerships, his omnipresent Facebook page updates, or appearances on political programs such as Bill Maher's *Real Time* on HBO.

A *Street Fight* in Newark

Corey Booker campaigns for mayor of Newark, New Jersey, in Marshall Curry's riveting, intense, and perceptive ground-level documentary of racial and generational politics, Street Fight *(2005).*

Offering an unflinching and, at times, uplifting look at American politics at all levels, the WETA-produced *Vote for Me: Politics in America* premiered on PBS stations nationwide in October 1996. Part of PBS's "Democracy Project"— a "PBS initiative to stimulate citizen engagement in civic life and develop and provide viewers with innovative news and public affairs programming"[32]—the ambitious video was directed by award-winning filmmakers Louis Alvarez, Andy Kolker, Paul Stekler.[33] Like Marshall Curry's *Street Fight*, but without the specific attention to generational and racial politics in one single city, *Vote for Me* goes beyond the horse-race, polls-centered approach to politics and gets close to the action to reveal "how local culture and customs are reflected in our politics"[34] It does this from the New England breeze of Rhode Island, to the streets of Chicago, to the mountains of Asheville, North Carolina. The film shows the everyday aspects of campaigning and governing at the state, local, and national levels, from fixing broken steps, ripping down posters, going door to door, helping shut-ins vote, kissing pigs, answering questions about guns and abortion, going to festivals, and dialing for cash. *Vote for Me* also features revealing interviews with the likes of Rep. Barney Frank (D-MA) and three-term former New York governor Mario Cuomo, among others, who comment on the nature of campaigning and politics in America.

Mr. Smith in Modern Politics

The documentary film *Can Mr. Smith Get to Washington Anymore?* (2006) chronicles the 2004 campaign of the relatively unknown Jeff Smith as he runs for the United States Congress in Missouri. The documentary asks the question of whether, in an age of big money politics and family political dynasties, a highly motivated individual without established connections to political elites can get elected. This film is a challenge to the ideals set forth by Frank Capra's 1939 film *Mr. Smith Goes to Washington* (discussed in Chapter 2).

On the one hand, Jeff Smith faces a difficult uphill challenge in that he is running against Russ Carnahan, whose father was the governor of Missouri and mother was then one of the state's U.S. Senators. On the other hand, Smith was a community activist whose job was adjunct professor of political science at a couple of universities. Smith, although active in establishing some charter schools, has little experience in elective politics. Everyone who meets Smith thinks he is savvy, articulate, and full of intriguing ideas but unelectable. The film opens with Jeff's family members talking about how crazy he was for running. His mother, early in the film, tells him not to ask for a contribution from his aunt and uncle because she does not want them to waste their money. Most of his friends and family see his run for Congress as foolish.

Despite the challenges faced by the election process, the campaign does make headway in the community. The campaign attracts many supporters and generates a positive image. Yet, the campaign continues to suffer from a lack of access to the media. Smith and his campaign team work tirelessly to gain access to and attention from the media; the front-runner, Carnahan, does not show up for debates with other candidates. At one point in the film, a campaign worker accuses a local television station of not covering the Jeff Smith campaign because it is unable to sell the campaign advertising spots.

Can Mr. Smith Get to Washington Anymore? appears, at first glance, to be a cynical film about the lack of access to political power by everyday people. This is the question of the film, but it is not as cynical as one might suppose. The campaign's idealistic journey is full of highly motivated people trying to change the political system and volunteer their time to make it happen.[35] The film does raise questions about the nature of democratic governance in an era of mass communication and big money; however, it seems to suggest that not all is lost, that people still matter. In some ways it affirms the ideas set forth in Capra's sentimental tale but does it in a more realistic, less romanticized, way.

Media Behavior and Candidate Access on the Campaign Trail

The insightful, clever presidential campaign and media travelogue *Journeys with George* (2002) premiered on HBO on Tuesday, November 5, 2002, on the night of the midterm elections of President George W. Bush.[36] The campaign–media diary documentary was directed and produced by Alexandra Pelosi, a daughter of Representative Nancy Pelosi, former Speaker of the House, who shared writing duties with Aaron Lubarskiy. *Journeys* finds Pelosi, a network news producer for NBC—in her words, the "hired help behind the scenes"—on the planes, trains, and buses following then–Texas governor George W. Bush's campaign. On her year-long journey, she files news stories, reports varying versions of his campaign's "message of the day," and works hard to gain substantive, unfiltered access to the candidate, a daunting task that is sometimes accomplished but frequently frustrated. In the early weeks of the campaign, members of the traveling press corps have little to no direct access to Bush; after his decisive loss to John McCain in the New Hampshire primary, however, his handlers change course somewhat, allowing the Republican front-runner to mingle and associate with the traveling media in a more direct and occasionally substantive manner. . .at least for a while.

Eating dreadful turkey sandwiches; catching intermittent shut-eye between photo ops, stump speeches, and rallies; and catching the flu, Pelosi does an excellent job of revealing the daily routines, professional and personal struggles, and petty jealousies of the traveling press corps assigned to a repetitive and, at times, grueling year-long campaign trek. Her witty, wry style shapes an approach that is neither heavy-handed nor frivolous, balancing humor and behind-the-scenes antics with a revealing exposé of campaign tactics and media behavior. In the process, *Journeys* offers valuable insight into the ebb and flow of presidential campaigns and media access, and in this respect, two dynamics and realities are especially noteworthy.

First, while George W. Bush is an affable, personable fellow finding his stride as a campaigner, he becomes remarkably less approachable when Pelosi asks him about his employment of the death penalty in Texas. Indeed, after her capital punishment query, Pelosi finds herself temporarily "on the outs" with the Texas governor, gaining no access for a spell. This leads to the second dynamic, or dilemma, revealed in Pelosi's documentary: How do members of the press perform their public duty—by asking thorough, penetrating public policy questions and disseminating useful political information—without alienating their subject, and thus, displeasing their employers who want access, stories, and the advertising revenue that go along with them? Clearly there is enormous pressure to not offend the candidate and incur his wrath—or, in this case, silence and inaccessibility. Can members of the media serve two masters? What are you to do if your network or paper is displeased with a lack of access and applies pressure? This is a dynamic that Bush and his closest advisers, communications director Karen Hughes and campaign guru Karl Rove, understood and exploited. Yet this phenomenon is more far-reaching than any one campaign team's tactics. The Bush campaign, however shrewd, certainly had no monopoly on using this delicate relationship of conflicting roles and dual masters to their advantage.

At the same, time, periodically keeping the press at bay and taking a bunker-type approach on the campaign trail can sometimes backfire and have disastrous results. For example, many reporters who were not given access to the candidate reported that the 2000 Democratic nominee, Vice President Al Gore, was distant and aloof, while characterizing George W. Bush as easygoing and congenial. As the *New York Times* reported during the 2000 campaign, "Bush 'not only slaps reporters' backs but also rubs the tops of their heads and, in a few instances, pinches their cheeks.'"[37] Most significant, a few major media studies indicated that, as the campaign wore on, Gore received disproportionately negative press coverage.[38] As Jane Hall reported in the *Columbia Journalism Review*, after a brief period of positive coverage after his selection of his running mate, U.S. senator from Connecticut Joe Lieberman, in the summer of 2000, Gore received overwhelmingly negative treatment in the press.[39]

Finally, the media-campaign journal *Journeys with George* implicitly revisits a lingering question that is hardly new to the American political landscape: Do marathon presidential campaigns, which frequently test stamina rather than intellect, and campaigning talent rather than governing skills, really serve the voters and by extension, the nation? Add to this mix the increasing tendency for the media to treat the entire election as a series of games and tactics rather than governing and to focus on "character" at the expense of public policy, and we have a real pickle of a situation.[40] If you look closely enough between the turkey sandwiches and chummy exchanges with George W. Bush, Alexandra Pelosi's easygoing yet penetrating campaign diary presents several vital dynamics and dilemmas that shape media coverage of presidential campaigns.[41] And, in the final analysis, if you want *real* news about candidates and their policies, the campaign bus and "the bubble" is not the place to be.

Parties and Partisanship: Giving Voice to the Individuals and Agents of the Partisan Divide

Alexandra Pelosi traveled to twenty-seven states during the historic 2008 presidential election between Democrat Barack Obama and Republican John McCain, and she pointed her camera and questions in the direction of Republican partisans who supported the McCain–Palin ticket, seeking to understand the range of reasons—political, economic, cultural, religious, and other—*why* these conservative citizens opposed Obama. The cinematic product of this nationwide journey to scores of McCain–Palin rallies and cultural and sporting events (e.g., NASCAR) was the HBO documentary *Right America: Feeling Wronged* (2009), an intense and engrossing presentation of the specific public policies, cultural grievances, and fears that drove roughly fifty-eight million Americans to vote for John McCain over Barack Obama.

In multiple interviews on radio and cable television stations, Pelosi articulated her reasons for wanting to get an unvarnished, nonsuperficial account of these citizens' hopes and fears, passions, and interests—perspectives that she believed all too often were not adequately presented in popular media accounts of the campaign.[42] Moreover, the film stands as an important contribution to the study of the American electorate and contemporary political campaigns in two special regards: one, it serves as an excellent exposé of the agents of socialization that drive millions of American voters, namely family, media, and religion; and two, its attention to the unique role and influence of ideologically driven media and cable news networks, especially, for conservatives, Fox News and talk radio. This means that, in our increasingly fragmented and polarized media and politics universe, millions of Americans may exist within their own self-selected echo chambers that merely reinforce their views.[43] And yet, as media analysis has shown, the title "news network" may be a misnomer when it comes to cable news. One prominent academic examination of Fox, CNN, and MSNBC reveals that commentary, not news, receives the lion's share of on-air time.[44]

Now we return to the topic of third parties in the American political system. Referred to as a "citizen response to major party failure" by prominent political scientists, third parties have a unique history within the American two-party system. Although they very rarely affect election outcomes, third parties serve a variety of vital functions in the U.S. political system, acting as policy advocates and crucial safety valves for those unhappy with the political system and the choices presented by the major parties. Starting, joining, or voting for a third party is a concrete way of expressing discontent and, quite possibly, furthering a specific policy agenda or single issue. A wide range of specific issues have been trumpeted by third parties over the years, including the abolition of slavery and prohibition, women's suffrage, the 8-hour workday, the minimum wage, and an end to child labor.[45]

Yet there are many obstacles faced by third parties. The electoral college, for example, with its winner-take-all system of allocating electoral votes in nearly every state (aside from Maine and Nebraska),[46] discourages third parties from entering the presidential fray. Consider the electoral college performance of Ross Perot in 1992. The Texas billionaire and independent candidate received nearly 19 percent of the vote in the three-way race with Gov. Bill Clinton and President George H. W. Bush, yet received no electoral votes. Moreover, state laws routinely make things difficult for third parties. The Democratic and Republican parties are automatically on the ballot across the country, but state laws mandate that third parties collect a varying number of signatures to get on the ballot in each state. In some states, it is not difficult to collect the required signatures. In other states, however, such as Texas, it can take a Herculean effort and time and money that most people, millionaires or billionaires aside, do not have. In fact, most third-party bids for the White House must employ firms to go out and collect the signatures. In addition, the rules of the Commission on Presidential Debates, a private organization headed by Democratic and Republican Party designates, stipulate that third-party candidates must have an average of 15 percent in five national polls in order to participate in the presidential debates.

The aforementioned obstacles, as well as a host of others, are explored in detail in Al Ward's documentary *I'm on the Ballot*. Premiering on PBS stations around the country in the fall of 2000, the film offered a thorough review of the role of third parties in U.S. history, focusing on the specific parties and candidates vying for attention in the 2000 presidential election. While many years and elections have passed since the film's premiere, rendering a few points moot—most notably material regarding campaign finance law (for example, key regulations were amended in 2002 by Congress and then again by the U.S. Supreme Court in the 2010 decision *Citizens United v. the Federal Election Commission*)—the Commission on Presidential Debates, lack of money (to receive federal matching funds, presidential candidates must first receive at least 5 percent of the vote nationwide), poor media coverage, and other legal and cultural constraints are examined in detail. Ward's work is to be commended for its review of third-party achievements and policy influence and for its fair treatment of all of the major third parties of the era. Candid interviews of the third-party candidates and their supporters allow for students and citizens to be exposed to alternative viewpoints—ranging from the left (Socialist and Green parties) to the right (Libertarian and Constitution parties)—that frequently receive scant attention in the mainstream media.

Airing on October 27, 1996, just days prior to the 1996 presidential election between Bill Clinton and Bob Dole, the presidential election immediately after independent candidate Ross Perot garnered 19 percent of the vote, *The Simpsons*'s Halloween segment "Citizen Kang" critiques the two-party system and, to a lesser extent, the American voting public. In this piece, the aliens Kang and Kodos come to Earth and take over the bodies of Dole and Clinton. While they are aliens, the American voting public hardly notices the difference when the two speak.[47] Apparently the vague pleasantries, banal generalities, and lack of substance spouted by the aliens Kang and Kodos (as Dole and Clinton) are what we are used to. Or, is such nonsense what the unsophisticated public really wants to hear? That is for us to decide. At one point, the aliens marvel at their ability to take over the bodies of Clinton and Dole and hoodwink the citizenry without much of an effort:

DOLE/KANG: Fooling these Earth voters is easier than expected.
CLINTON/KODOS: Yes, all they want to hear are bland pleasantries embellished by an occasional saxophone solo or infant kiss.[48]

One specific exchange highlights the show's criticism of the two-party system. In the scene, the Simpsons are watching the nightly news, chaired by longtime anchor (and stock *Simpsons* character) Kent Brockman:

KENT BROCKMAN: Kent Brockman here, with "Campaign 96: America Flips a Coin." At an appearance this morning, Bill Clinton made some rather cryptic remarks, which aides attributed to an overly tight necktie.

(The scene cuts to the news conference.)

CLINTON/KODOS: I am Clin-Ton. As overlord, all will kneel before me and obey my brutal commands. End communication.

MARGE: Hmm, that's Slick Willie for you, always with the smooth talk.

KENT BROCKMAN: Senator Dole, why should people vote for you instead of President Clinton?

DOLE/KANG: It makes no difference which one of us you vote for. Either way, your planet is doomed! Doomed!

BROCKMAN: Well, a refreshingly frank response there from Senator Bob Dole.

(Before a huge crowd at the Capitol Building, Homer reveals the candidates as space aliens.)

KODOS: It's true we are aliens. But what are you going to do about it? It's [a] two-party system! You have to vote for one of us. . . .

MAN IN CROWD: Well, I believe I'll vote for a third-party candidate.

KANG: Go ahead, throw your vote away! Ah-hah-hah-hah-haaaah![49]

In classic *Simpsons* form, beneath the humor, satire, and Homer's antics, several biting critiques of American politics and the American electorate are presented. First, the "Treehouse of Horror VII" Halloween segment criticizes the lack of choice provided by a two-party system enforced by law, culture, and socialization. The two major-party standard bearers are hardly off the hook in this regard, as the piece lampoons the party nominees, Bill Clinton and Bob Dole, for providing little in terms of inspiration, choice, or specifics. Second, *The Simpsons* is also pointing a finger at the American public for its rather apathetic and unsophisticated approach to politics. An implicit message here is that perhaps change *could* come if voters weren't so easily swayed (or hoodwinked) by candidate image, emotional appeals, infant kisses, and, as is the case in "Citizen Kang," miniature American flags. A vigilant and erudite populace is needed to make a difference and force candidates and parties to speak in a legitimate, inspiring, and substantive "non-alien" language.

Conclusions

As this review of reel and real campaigns and elections demonstrates, documentaries, feature films, and animated humor present ample observations that dig beneath the veneer of electoral politics. *I'm on the Ballot, Futurama,* and *The Simpsons,* for example, ask us to ponder these questions: *What are the obstacles faced by third parties in the United States? Is voting for a third party "throwing your vote away"—or is casting your vote for a third-party candidate an act of conscience and courage that can substantively affect the trajectory of politics and policy? Are there negative consequences of third-party participation?* Moreover, films such as *Journeys with George, The Candidate, The Last Hurrah,* and *Bob Roberts* beg us to consider the centrality and ramifications of the media, political communication, ideology, and image in shaping electoral choices. And, as always, *The Simpsons* considers whether Americans possess the knowledge and sophistication to be active, enlightened citizens. For the health of our democracy, and to better understand the direction of our campaigns and elections, these are certainly questions worth examining.

The cost, length, substance, and endless strategizing of contemporary campaigns provide ripe opportunities for filmmakers to develop compelling stories; we have touched on but a few of these narratives. And while it may be easy to become pessimistic about campaigns, elections are perhaps the most direct, foundational act of political citizenship in a democratic society. To be sure, there are positive portrayals of campaigns and elections (for example, the *Northern Exposure* episode "Democracy in America," or the triumphant documentary of grassroots mobilization *By the People: The Election of Barack Obama*); however, in an increasingly cynical culture and noisy, fragmented, and ideological media environment, citizens often lose sight of the enormous consequence of elections.

Notes

1. Not all actors' campaigns for elected office have been successful, of course. Former child star Shirley Temple (married name Shirley Temple Black) ran unsuccessfully for a Republican nomination for U.S. Congress in California in the 1960s, campaigning on a pro–Vietnam War platform. Liberal Democrat and U.S. representative Helen Gahagan Douglas, a former Broadway and Hollywood star, ran unsuccessfully for the U.S. Senate in 1950, losing to Richard Nixon in a legendary bitter ideological contest. Nixon had labeled Douglas a socialist-communist sympathizer, famously referring to her as "the Pink Lady." Douglas, however, may have had the lasting triumph; her derisive label of Nixon as "Tricky Dick" was a

negative label that followed the future thirty-seventh president throughout his career on the national stage. For more, see Ralph Dannheisser, "History of Actors in Politics Goes Back Decades," November 6, 2007: http://www.america.gov/st/washfile-english/2007/November/20071105201635ndyblehs0.4566614.html.

2. Greg Mitchell, "How Hollywood Fixed an Election, *American Film*, November 1988, pp. 26–31. Special thanks to Miami University political scientist Christopher S. Kelley for suggesting this fascinating case study and insightful article.

3. For the 5 to 10 percent estimate, see Ernest Giglio, *Here's Looking at You*, 3rd ed. (New York: Peter Lang, 2010).

4. For further discussion of *Primary Colors*, see Chapter 4, "The American Presidency."

5. Ernest Giglio, *Here's Looking at You*, 1st ed. (New York: Peter Lang, 2000), 98.

6. It was rumored in 2002 that Redford was collaborating with M*A*S*H screenwriter Larry Gelbart on a sequel to *The Candidate*, with the film following the McKay character years later. See "Redford May Make Sequel to The Candidate," *Teagan Goddard's Political Wire*, October 24, 2002: http://politicalwire.com/archives/2002/10/24/redford_may_make_sequel_to_the_candidate.html.

7. Giglio, *Here's Looking at You* (2000), 94.

8. Bob Roberts's album titles are slyly stolen from legendary Bob Dylan works. In delightful tongue-in-cheek fashion, the right-wing Bob Roberts rips off the classic Dylan albums *The Freewheelin' Bob Dylan* (1963), *The Times They Are A-Changin'* (1964), and *Blonde on Blonde* (1966). All records were released on the Columbia Records label.

9. Sean Wilentz, *The Age of Reagan: A History, 1974–2008* (New York: Harper, 2008). In the fall of 2002, Robbins announced on ABC's morning talk show *The View* that a sequel to *Bob Roberts* was in the works. What would the folksinging conservative be up to next? Why, a presidential run, of course. However, to date, there has been no Bob Roberts sequel.

10. In the 1988 presidential campaign, George H. W. Bush's campaign attacked Democratic nominee Michael Dukakis for his record on crime as governor of Massachusetts. One famous ad that attacked a Massachusetts parole program, and by extension, Gov. Dukakis, featured a revolving door prison with hardened criminals being let out for parole. Willie Horton was a man who, while on parole for murder, raped a woman. A group of Bush supporters, led by Republican political operative Floyd Brown, aired "independent" ads featuring Horton's face and attacked Dukakis as soft on crime. Oliver Stone's psycho-analytical 2008 biopic of George W. Bush, *W*, overtly suggests there was little to no independence whatsoever, and that 1988 Bush campaign manager Lee Atwater reviewed the attack ad in the White House. Likewise, commentary from longtime Republican operative and lobbyist Roger Stone in the 2008 documentary *Boogie Man: The Lee Atwater Story* (2008) indicates that Atwater was directly involved in facilitating the notorious "revolving door" prison ad. Directed by Stefan Forbes, the endlessly fascinating and prescient *Boogie Man* won the Edward R. Murrow Award, the Polk Award for Excellence in Journalism, and the International Documentary Association's Donnet Award.

11. Ray Richmond and Antonia Coffman, eds., *The Simpsons: A Complete Guide to Our Favorite Family* (New York: HarperPerennial, 1997), 38.

12. Ibid.

13. Ibid.

14. Reagan consistently preached the merits of limited government in the economic and regulatory spheres, from his corporate spokesman status to his famous "Time for Choosing" speech on behalf of Barry Goldwater's 1964 candidacy and onward. In his first inaugural address on January 20, 1981, President Reagan stated: "In the present crisis, government is not the solution to our problem; government is the problem." See The American Presidency Project's comprehensive compilation of inaugural addresses. Reagan's first address can be found at: http://www.presidency.ucsb.edu/ws/index.php?pid=43130.

15. Marge is not the only Simpson to support incumbent governor Mary Bailey. Lisa Simpson, the intellectual, agitating second-grade daughter of Marge and Homer, sports a shirt that reads, "If I were old enough to vote, I'd vote for Mary Bailey."

16. Richmond and Coffman, *The Simpsons*, 38.

17. After four direct-to-DVD movies, the series was revived in 2010. The new *Futurama* episodes aired on Comedy Central, whereas the show's original run was on Fox.

18. Written by J. Stewart Burns and Jeff Westbrook; directed by Bret Haaland; originally aired December 12, 1999.

19. This identical argument—that the simple, similar, meaningless platitudes and sound bites spouted by candidates reveal a political and party system void of real choice and authenticity—is also presented in Groening's other series, *The Simpsons*, especially in the 1996 "Treehouse of Horror VII" episode featuring aliens Kang and Kodos as presidential candidates Bill Clinton and Bob Dole. This portion of the episode was titled "Citizen Kang." See our discussion of this episode and its other political messages later in this chapter.

20. The lowest-performing age demographic in modern American elections is the 18–29 cohort, even as turnout in this group has been more favorable in some recent presidential contests. On the whole, middle-aged and senior citizens vote at a significantly higher level than young voters.

21. When the crew arrives to register there are several information booths for various political parties and interest groups. Most reflect a twist on twenty-first century-politics; for instance, the Green Party is designed for beings who are actually green (pigment-wise). The NRA (National Ray-Gun Association) is there advocating the protection of the constitutional right to own ray-guns. Dr. Farnsworth asks what the group is doing to protect his right to bear doomsday devices. The advocate tells him that they want to do away with the three-day waiting period for mad scientists.

22. Witness the candidacy of John Anderson in 1980, Ross Perot in 1992, and Ralph Nader in 2000. Usually in American politics, good ideas introduced by third parties are eventually incorporated into the platforms of one of the two major parties. Because of the first-past-the-post (or plurality) system, voters are disinclined to support third parties, no matter how good their ideas. Thus, only "foolish" people waste their votes on third-party candidates. See, for example, Ralph Nader's critique of the two-party system and the media's narratives in his book *Crashing the Party: Taking on the Corporate Government in an Age of Surrender* (New York: St. Martins, 2002). Third-party candidates' lack of major electoral wins, combined with the ideological purity or absolutism demanded by some of their party platforms, also influences their portrayal in the mainstream media.

23. Edward Guthmann wrote, "Playful in tone but bravely radical in concept, 'Bulworth,' a brilliant political satire by Warren Beatty, is one of the most surprising movies to come out of Hollywood in the past decade. This is Beatty's premise: Imagine a politician who drops his

phony, elect-me facade and decides to spill the blunt, unvarnished truth about race, class and economics." See Edward Guthmann, "Beatty's Rap: Hilarious 'Bulworth'—the Truth Sets a Senator Free," *San Francisco Chronicle*, May 22, 1998: http://www.sfgate.com/cgi-bin/article.cgi?f=/c/a/1998/05/22/DD19624.DTL.

24. See, for example, Janet Maslin, "White Bread Senator Turns Homeboy," *New York Times*, May 15, 1998; and Gary Younge, "Warren Beatty: Rebel with a Cause," *The Guardian*, January 23, 1999.

Guthmann, in his "Beatty's Rap: Hilarious 'Bulworth,'" went on to discuss the political impact of the film:

Beatty directed, produced and co-wrote "Bulworth," and it's doubtful that any other Hollywood power could have put a story like this on the screen—or would want to. A shrewd political observer for decades, Beatty has fashioned a hilarious morality tale that delivers a surprisingly potent, angry message beneath the laughs.

It's a fabulous, bold leap on Beatty's part, and you can feel how much the subject energizes him, just as the novelty of truth-telling invigorates his character and puts a goofy grin on Bulworth's face.

Hollywood rarely embraces political satire on this level—as if it were impolite and would make people uncomfortable—but Beatty's lampoon shows not only how much we need this kind of commentary, but also how entertaining it can be. Beatty also knows how much party politics have ignored racial injustice and uses humor to reopen the discussion.

25. Moore explained the Keyes "mosh-pit endorsement" online. See Michael Moore, "How We Got Alan Keyes to Dive into Our Mosh Pit (and Other Scenes from Our First Week of Shooting)," January 28, 2000: http://www.michaelmoore.com/words/mikes-letter/how-we-got-alan-keyes-to-dive-into-our-mosh-pit-and-other-scenes-from-our-first-week-of-shooting. A portion on this mosh-pit election segment is also viewable online at: http://www.youtube.com/watch?v=8qwDBgNMD7c. See also: www.seeingthebiggerpicture.net.

26. Desson Howe, "A Winning 'Candidate,'" *Washington Post*, July 13, 1996: http://www.washingtonpost.com/wp-srv/style/longterm/review96/perfectcandidatehowe.htm.

27. In 2000, Chuck Robb lost his bid for another term to George Allen.

28. Howe, "A Winning 'Candidate'": http://www.washingtonpost.com/wp-srv/style/longterm/review96/perfectcandidatehowe.htm.

29. *The War Room* was also nominated for, but did not win, the Academy Award for best documentary.

30. See: http://www.marshallcurry.com/streetfight.html.

31. David Denby, "Candid Cameras," *The New Yorker*, March 6, 2006: http://www.newyorker.com/archive/2006/03/06/060306crci_cinema.

32. Go to: http://www.pbs.org/weta/voteforme/about.htm.

33. Their credits include installments in the landmark *Eyes on the Prize* civil rights series.

34. See: http://www.pbs.org/weta/voteforme.

35. Smith loses the election by less than 2 percentage points, but after the film Jeff Smith reconstitutes his campaign team and wins the 2006 election for the Missouri Senate.

36. It was a good night for President George W. Bush and the Republican Party. Republicans regained control of the closely divided Senate and picked up seats in the House of

Representatives. It was only the third time since the Lincoln presidency that the president's party gained House seats in midterm elections, and the first time for Republicans. Nationwide, the country was nearly split down the middle: roughly 40,000 votes would have tipped the balance of power to the Democratic Party. Survey research suggests that a stunning 25 percent of the voters made their choices in the final weekend before the midterm elections or on Election Day itself.

37. *New York Times* content cited in Eric Boehlert, "The Press vs. Al Gore," *Rolling Stone*, December 6–13, 2001. For further evidence of the press's characterization of Gore, see media critic Howard Kurtz's insightful "Media Notes" columns throughout the fall of 2000 in *The Washington Post*. Alexandra Pelosi discussed her film and reporters' perceptions of Gore (as distant) and Bush (as chummy) on Comedy Central's *The Daily Show with John Stewart* on November 12, 2002.

38. For the press's increasingly hostile treatment of Gore, see Jane Hall, "Gore Media Coverage—Playing Hardball," *Columbia Journalism Review*, September/October 2000. Hall's original research and review of the Pew Charitable Trusts and Project for Excellence in Journalism study can be accessed online at: http://www.cjr.org/year/00/3/hall.asp.

39. This dynamic is chronicled in a study funded, in part, by the Pew Charitable Trusts and executed by the Project for Excellence in Journalism. Results of the Project for Excellence in Journalism media study are cited in Hall, "Gore Media Coverage—Playing Hardball": Examining 2,400 newspaper, TV, and Internet stories in five different weeks between February and June, researchers found that a whopping 76 percent of the coverage included one of two themes: that Gore lies and exaggerates or is marred by scandal. The most common theme about Bush, the study found, is that he is a "different kind of Republican."
The survey (which included editorials and news stories) focused on *The Washington Post*, *The New York Times*, *The Boston Globe*, *The Atlanta Journal-Constitution*, *The Indianapolis Star*, the *San Francisco Chronicle*, and *The Seattle Times*. It also included the evening newscasts of the major broadcast networks and talk shows such as *Hardball*, which alone accounted for 17 percent of the negative characterizations about scandal.

40. The media's tendency to cover campaigns using a game schema rather than a governing framework, as well as the focus on "character," is covered extensively in Thomas Patterson, *Out of Order* (New York: Vintage, 1994). The focus on strategy, process, and tactics is also revealed in the fall 2000 study by the Project for Excellence in Journalism. See also Harvard University professor Thomas Patterson's website "The Vanishing Voter Project" (http://www.vanishingvoter.org) and his book *The Vanishing Voter* (New York: Knopf, 2002).

41. Alexandra Pelosi is no stranger to the most serious side of politics. Her work with NBC covering George W. Bush in the 2000 campaign fits right in with the fact that politics is a Pelosi family tradition. Her grandfather was mayor of Baltimore, and her mother, Nancy Pelosi, became the highest-ranking woman in the history of the U.S. House of Representatives. Shortly after the 2002 midterm elections, Nancy Pelosi, then the Democratic Party's Minority Whip, became Minority Leader for the House Democrats, replacing Missouri congressman Richard Gephardt.

42. For Alexandra Pelosi's 2009 interviews discussing her film *Right America: Feeling Wronged*, with Leonard Lopate, see: http://www.youtube.com/watch?v=L78defYvTHE; with Sean

Hannity (Fox), see: http://www.youtube.com/watch?v=TsNcPrCeVSo; with Rachel Maddow (MSNBC), see: http://www.youtube.com/watch?v=ZYCnkI4j1zo&feature=related; and with CNN, see: http://www.youtube.com/watch?v=-RE_t0unx3M&feature=related.

43. Terry McDermott, "Dumb Like a Fox," *Columbia Journalism Review*, March/April 2010. See also analysis of McDermott's provocative *CJR* piece in Jared Keller, "The Outsized Impact of Cable News," *theatlanticwire.com*, March 10, 2010: http://www.theatlanticwire.com/opinions/view/opinion/The-Outsized-Impact-of-Cable-News-2790.

44. McDermott, "Dumb Like a Fox."

45. For further in-depth discussion of these issues and the role of third parties in the United States, see Steven J. Rosenstone, Roy L. Behr, and Edward Lazarus, *Third Parties in America*, 2nd ed. (Princeton: Princeton University Press, 1996).

46. Maine and Nebraska do not use the winner-take-all system employed by the other forty-eight states and the District of Columbia; rather, they utilize a proportional allocation of electoral votes by congressional district. For example in the 2008 presidential election, Democrat Barack Obama won one electoral vote from Nebraska's second congressional district; the other electoral votes from the state went to Senator John McCain, the Republican nominee. See "Make that 365: Obama on Track to Pick Up Nebraska Electoral Vote," *Washington Post.com*, November 7, 2008: http://voices.washingtonpost.com/44/2008/11/make-that-365-obama-on-track-t.html.

47. When he can't recall his name, Homer refers to Bob Dole as "Mumbly Joe."

48. Richmond and Coffman, *The Simpsons*, 211.

49. Ibid.

50. Ibid.

· 6 ·

CIVIL RIGHTS AND SOCIAL JUSTICE

One of the enduring challenges of any polity is to make sure that all of its citizens enjoy, or have access to, the fundamental decency of civil rights, economic opportunity, and social justice. In narrative form, stories told via documentaries, feature films, and other elements of popular culture that depict the quest for political, social, and economic justice are often very compelling. Portraying the search for equality and dignity on the big screen, especially when it is done in a visually appealing manner, allows an audience to sympathize and perhaps even identify with protagonists, whether real or fictional. There are literally hundreds, perhaps thousands, of films and documentaries—and for that matter, novels and songs—that chronicle the plight of people seeking civil rights and social justice in the United States alone. And while the search for equality is hardly limited to American society and the U.S. political system, for the sake of brevity and thematic coherence, we have chosen to focus on films and television programs that examine the ongoing quest for civil rights and social justice in the United States. Within the context of American society and politics, we will highlight a few specific issues, groups, and dynamics. Therefore, in this chapter we explore popular culture that examines the civil rights movement and struggles facing African Americans and Jews, and the depiction of and challenges facing LGBT (lesbian, gay, bisexual, and transgendered) Americans. Finally, we turn to an exploration of American workers, specifically, labor strife and the ongoing pursuit of economic justice as portrayed in film and television.

Racism and the Civil Rights Movement

The issues of racism and the search for civil rights and social justice in the American political system have been addressed on the big screen in a variety of ways. Whether it has involved a glowing tribute to the Ku Klux Klan in the Reconstruction-era South (*The Birth of a Nation*, 1915), the trial of a black man falsely accused of raping a white woman in the Depression-era South (*To Kill a Mockingbird*, 1962), a ritualistic lynching in Depression-era Mississippi (*O Brother, Where Art Thou?*, 2000), the reimagining of the FBI's investigation of the 1964 Freedom Summer murders of three civil rights workers in Philadelphia, Mississippi (*Mississippi Burning*, 1988), the racially motivated bombing of the 16th Street Baptist Church in Birmingham, Alabama, in September 1963 (*4 Little Girls*, 1997), the powerlessness of African Americans to get cabs to stop for them in New York City (Michael Moore's television series *TV Nation*, 1993–1995, and *The Awful Truth*, 1999–2000), a satirical look at what America would look like if the Confederacy had won (*C.S.A.: The Confederate States of America*, 2004), or the ramifications of racial profiling in contemporary America (*Murder on a Sunday Morning*, 2001), commercial films and documentaries alike have provided citizens and students of politics with useful insights and diverse perspectives into the seminal events and sociopolitical realities that have shaped attitudes, actions, and public policy.

As the long, gradual march toward equality continued throughout the twentieth century, the Fourteenth Amendment's guarantees of equal protection and due process eventually became more fact than fiction, and the country's politics, social practices, and values slowly evolved. As the attitudes of millions of Americans on race progressed and key elements of legal, state-sanctioned discrimination were eventually dismantled in the 1960s onward (via the Civil Rights Act of 1964, the Voting Rights Act of 1965, and the elimination of the poll tax through the Twenty-Fourth Amendment), Hollywood's and documentarians' portrayal of African Americans and the depiction of the issues at the heart of the struggle for civil rights evolved as well.

An early—and perhaps one of the ugliest—depiction of African Americans on film came in the form of D. W. Griffith's politically charged silent epic *The Birth of a Nation* (1915).[1] Griffith (1875–1948), a Kentucky native and son of a lieutenant colonel in the Confederate Army, often reminisced that he sat at his father's feet listening to stories about the glory that was the Confederacy. Later in life, remembering these stories, he clearly sympathized with the South, and embraced many of the most insidious, and common, racial stereotypes of his day. Based on Thomas Dixon's (1864–1946) novel and play *The Clansman*, Griffith's controversial film portrays African Americans in the Reconstruction-era South as sexually aggressive, deviant, and barbaric slobs who possess neither the intellect nor civility to legitimately exercise their newly found democratic freedoms. Throughout the film freed slaves terrorize the South, preying on innocent white women and bullying and beating Southerners and their "faithful servants" (passive freed slaves who remained as domestic workers in the home of Southerners) at will.[2] Dixon, an evangelical Baptist minister from the Carolinas, was long obsessed with racial relations, especially the issues of integration, miscegenation, and the perceived oppression of white Southerners in the Reconstruction era. He believed that political equality and the "black menace" threatened the very future of white womanhood, white civilization, and America itself.

It should not be surprising, therefore, that Dixon's story reinforces many of the era's dominant—and most ominous—stereotypes of African Americans. In particular, the film makes the case that the right to vote and hold elected office had been abused by incompetent freed blacks. In one infamous scene, belligerent African American state legislators remove their boots, drink whiskey, and chomp enthusiastically on chicken legs in the chambers of the South Carolina legislature. The film has the black majority pass a law allowing whites and blacks to marry as well as a statute mandating that whites salute black officials on the street. And while Dixon and Griffith depict slaves and servants (the vast majority of whom are portrayed by white actors in blackface) as obedient, moral, loyal, and intelligent, the freed slaves and the ambitious Northern political leader Silas Lynch (who is multiracial) are portrayed in the most negative manner possible. Lynch has an aggressive penchant for white women, as does a freed slave named Gus. In one infamous scene, Gus's primitive and violent pursuit of a white virgin ends in the woman falling to her death from a mountain cliff. She would rather preserve her virginity and purity than give in to the demands of the sexually aggressive black male. At the end of the film, the Ku Klux Klan arrive on horseback to save the South from raping and pillaging at the hands of the freed slaves, Silas Lynch, and pesky Northerners, and in doing so preserve white and Southern heritage and bring justice, hope, and redemption to a "new nation."[3]

The broad political implications of the film are unmistakable. In addition to the glowing portrayal of the Ku Klux Klan as redeemer and protector of the nation, and the film's reinforcement of some of the darkest and most destructive stereotypes of African Americans, Griffith's movie received an endorsement from none other than the president of the United States, Woodrow Wilson. Wilson, a Virginia native and Princeton president who had at times embraced racial segregation, stated that The Birth of a Nation "was like writing history in lightning. . . . My only regret is that it is all so terribly true," and held a private viewing of the film at the White House.[4] It was the first time in the history of the presidency that a full-length motion picture was screened at the White House. Years later, after the film had clearly inflamed racial tensions across the country—at the time of the film's release, for example, the NAACP led boycotts of the film in several major cities[5]—President Wilson distanced himself from his previous effusive praise for the film, calling The Birth of a Nation "an unfortunate production."[6]

Griffith's epic was the highest-grossing motion picture of its time, and it signaled the advent of the motion picture as an art form, political statement, and spectacle, or immensely popular and influential cultural event. The director's grandiose vision, groundbreaking cinematic techniques, budget, and innovative special effects—as well as the decades of raw emotions, picket lines, petitions, and protests that the film has spawned—have cemented the reputation of The Birth of a Nation as one of the most influential and controversial movies in the history of film. As historian Leon Litwak has commented, "With the release of The Birth of a Nation in 1915, the motion picture as art, propaganda, and entertainment came of age."[7] The film would continue to be shown commercially into the mid-1920s, and from the time of its release on February 15, 1915, until 1946, it is estimated that roughly two hundred million people viewed The Birth of a Nation in the United States and overseas.[8] The criticism that Griffith received prompted him to make an even more grandiose film the following year as an attempt to answer his critics. In Intolerance (1916) Griffith tells four simultaneous stories of man's inhumanity to man.[9] Perhaps it says something that this film, with its very different perspectives, and which was touted to be even bigger than The Birth of a Nation, failed miserably at the box office. All the money that Griffith made on The Birth of a Nation was lost in the making of Intolerance; in fact, Intolerance lost so much money that it took Griffith years to pay off his debts, and the production company associated with the film filed for bankruptcy in 1921.[10] After the massive financial losses brought on by the commercial failure of Intolerance, Griffith later rereleased a much smaller, reedited incarnation of the film that centered on just one of the movie's original four stories, entitled *The Mother and the Law*.[11]

By identifying the worldview and key antagonists of the Ku Klux Klan, a riveting scene in the Coen brothers' otherwise delightfully farcical, frivolous, and folk music-driven *O Brother, Where Art Thou?* (2000) simultaneously lampoons the Klan's virulent racism and begs us to remember the horrific, violent legacy of lynching in the United States. In this latter sense, the brief scene stands in the spirit of Billie Holiday's haunting 1939 rendition of "Strange Fruit," the famous anti-lynching song penned by New York City English teacher Abe Meeropol.[12]

In their box office hit, the Academy Award–winning and independent film giants Joel and Ethan Coen replicate Homer's *Odyssey* in Depression-era Mississippi against a backdrop of bumbling convicts, buried treasure, vintage Appalachian music, and a hotly contested governor's race between incumbent Menelaus "Pappy" O'Daniel (Charles Durning) and Homer Stokes (Wayne Duvall). During a massive KKK rally designed to hang a black man named Tommy Johnson (Chris Thomas King)[13]—in which Klan members engage in a militaristic, Nazi-esque march and a strange, almost comical, dance—the grand wizard of the KKK removes his red hood, revealing himself to be none other than Homer Stokes, the leading candidate for governor. After singing the unsettling, eerie strains of the traditional Appalachian ballad "O Death" (sung by Ralph Stanley), the racist charlatan Stokes addresses his minions, proclaiming the enemies of the Ku Klux Klan and preparing his followers for a lynching:

> Brothers! We are foregathered here to preserve our hallowed culture'n heritage! From intrusions, inclusions, and dilutions! Of colluh! Of creed! Of our ol-time religion! We aim to pull color up by the root! Before it chokes out the flower of our culture'n heritage! And our women! Let's not forget those ladies y'all, lookin' to us for p'tection! From darkies! From Jews! From Papists! And from all those smart-ass folk say we come descended from the monkeys! That's not my culture'n heritage . . . and so . . . we gonna hang us a neegra![14]

Through the heroism of the kindhearted but simple protagonists Everett (George Clooney), Delmar (Tim Blake Nelson), and Pete (John Turturro), Tommy is rescued just before he is about to meet his untimely fate. This chilling, ghostly sequence—placed in the midst of otherwise lighthearted cinematic fare—is a vivid reminder of the prominence of the Klan and its impact on Southern politics and culture in the first half of the twentieth century. And while KKK membership dwindled in later years and it became less acceptable to publicly embrace the Klan's views in the 1950s onward, "White Citizens Councils"—Rotarian-styled local organizations antagonistic to integration and federal civil rights law—began to crop up throughout the South, quickly becoming a major political force in state politics. Decades later, in the 1990s, an obscure, political action committee (PAC) offshoot of the White Citizens Councils—the "Council of Conservative Citizens" (CCC)—existed in some areas of the South. Former Senate majority leader Trent Lott (R-MS) and former U.S. Representative Bob Barr (R-GA), among others, were criticized by Democrats and others in the mid- to late 1990s for being associated with the CCC, which was viewed by some in the civil rights community as the not-so-distant political progeny of the White Citizens Councils.[15] Sen. Lott was also criticized by both Democrats and Republicans for appearing to praise the 1948 presidential campaign of South Carolina segregationist Strom Thurmond, who ran on the States Rights or "Dixiecrat" ticket after bolting the Democratic Party when they endorsed a federal civil rights plank in their 1948 party platform.[16]

Though merely a "moderate" hit by Hollywood blockbuster standards, it is worth noting that the Coens brothers' O Brother was the tandem's highest-grossing film up to that time, far surpassing their previous critical successes, including the Academy Award–winning Fargo (1996), among others.[17] They would later find even greater box office success with the likes of No Country for Old Men (2007), their gritty adaptation of the Cormac McCarthy novel, which won the Academy Award for best feature film.

The Broken Code: Battling the Cycle of Racism

Harper Lee's classic novel To Kill a Mockingbird (1962), adapted for the screen by playwright Horton Foote, offers an insightful glimpse into the world of black–white relations and institutionalized racism in the Depression-era South. While The Birth of a Nation glorified the KKK as the saviors of white, Christian America, in Mockingbird principled Alabama lawyer Atticus Finch (Gregory Peck) tackles racism, cultural taboos (white women socializing with black men), stereotypes (African American males as sexual predators with a predilection for white women), and the Southern legal establishment head-on by defending an innocent black man charged with raping a white woman. While Finch's vision of justice and equality under the law ultimately loses to the irrationality of racism and enforcement of the South's long-established code for interaction between black men and white women—as his client Tom Robinson is convicted by a white jury—audiences are presented with a strong, passionate voice against racial injustice and intolerance in an era of Jim Crow segregation. Finch is not only a caring, doting, and widowed father raising two children, but he is willing to be shunned by white elites and spat upon by backward thugs in order to stand up for justice in his small Southern town. In his closing statement, Finch articulates the view that what was really on trial in the trumped-up rape case was the breaking of the time-honored *racist code*— the notion that white women and black men could not have emotional, friendly, or sexual relationships. And, in this case, by socializing, a white woman and a black man dared to, ever so slightly, break that code. *To Kill a Mockingbird* stands as a vivid example of popular literature—and then Hollywood—attacking the legitimacy of the racist code, and remains one of the most influential novels (and films) of our day.[18]

As the years passed by, and the civil rights movement picked up strength through the activism and sacrifice of many citizens, as well as landmark legislation that followed, film and television began to break down the barriers of racism and prejudice at an increased pace. Hollywood saw many productions that challenged racist views. Stanley Kramer's *The Defiant Ones* (1958), starring Tony Curtis and Sidney Poitier; Norman Jewison's Academy Award–winning *In the Heat of the Night* (1967), starring Sidney Poitier and Rod Steiger; and the work of outspoken liberal writer and producer Norman Lear in the 1970s (who pushed the envelope by dealing with myriad aspects of race relations in hit series such as *All in the Family*, *Maude*, *The Jeffersons*, and *Good Times*) are primary examples of this cultural and cinematic evolution. Americans found their popular entertainment on living room and theater screens more willing to challenge the often-unspoken codes of intolerance, fear, stereotypes, and prejudice. Fearful of challenging people's prejudices too directly, sometimes breaking racial barriers was done in an unthreatening manner. For instance, the first interracial kiss portrayed on American television was on the classic science-fiction show *Star Trek*. The kiss was set in the twenty-third century, and against the will of the protagonists; presumably this was thought to be more tolerable to the American audience of the 1960s. Nevertheless, the racist codes, reinforced so blatantly in Griffith's *The Birth of a Nation* and in exclusionary (and legally sanctioned) Jim Crow tactics throughout the South, were increasingly facing stiff and subtle challenges from the world of film and television.

Breaking the cycle of deep-rooted generational prejudice is a central theme of Marc Foster's dark, compelling drama *Monster's Ball* (2001), which presents a harrowing tale of violence and racism surrounding a Georgia family. However, through risk taking, changes of heart, the loss of loved ones at an early age, and a series of tragic and unforeseen events, the cycle of racial hatred and misunderstanding is ultimately broken. Monster's Ball—"whose title refers to the party wardens throw for prisoners on the eve of execution"[19]—concerns the life, times, and tortured family and social relationships of Hank Grotowski (Billy Bob Thornton), a racist, taciturn prison guard who works on Death Row in a Georgia penitentiary. He has a volatile, hostile relationship with his son, Sonny Grotowski (Heath Ledger), who also works at the prison, and he has been taught to hate African Americans by his grotesque, frail father, Buck Grotowski (Peter Boyle). All three Grotowskis live in the same house, all have worked at the prison, and the mix of racism, self-hatred, and dysfunction simmering within its walls ultimately leads to an outburst of violence and tragedy. After a troubling turn of events, Hank begins an intense emotional and sexual relationship with Leticia Musgrove (Halle Berry), an African American woman who, unbeknownst to Hank, is the wife of the death row inmate (played by rap artist and icon Sean "P. Diddy" Combs) who was just executed under Hank's watch.

While Hank loses his son in an ugly and vicious family fight—a confrontational scuffle that tragically spirals into suicide—and faces the pressures imposed by his bigoted, belligerent, and ailing father, he is ultimately capable of breaking the code handed down by his father and so many around him. As both Leticia and Hank reach out for companionship and humanity in the wake of their pain, loss, and crises, they find each other. In the end, through their leap of faith and intense physical and emotional attraction, we see that the code of segregation, handed down from generation to generation, can be broken once again. Hank places his domineering father in a nursing home, and at the close of the film, Hank and Leticia sit beside each other on the steps of their humble home, quietly eating chocolate ice cream and gazing at the stars. Audiences do not know for certain what precisely will transpire in the future, but for now at least, they are one in spirit, and stand ready to stare down the future together.

In To Kill a Mockingbird forty years earlier, it was attorney Atticus Finch who exposed the evils of the existing code of racial relations when a white woman, Mayella, and an African American man, Tom, dared to be attracted to each other. In Monster's Ball, the roles are reversed as a white man, Hank, and a black woman, Leticia, send the code of expected conduct between races, passed down for generations, to the scrap heap of history. This gritty, bleak-but-ultimately-life-affirming journey through life's darkest corners of fear, brutality, prejudice, and dehumanization found itself on many critics "best of" lists. And, at the 2002 Academy Awards, it was a historic night, as, for the first time in the history of film, two African Americans took home the honors for best actor and best actress: Denzel Washington (*Training Day*) and Halle Berry (*Monster's Ball*). In this sense, *Monster's Ball*'s tagline, "A lifetime of change can happen in a single moment," could also be applied to the Academy Awards.

Another film that explores personal growth, nay transformation, in the face of lingering prejudices is *Gran Torino* (2008). While the films we have explored thus far have centered on the legal, social, and cultural aspects of bigotry, segregation, and institutionalized racism affecting African Americans, director-actor Clint Eastwood's critical and box office hit *Gran Torino* largely focuses on relations between white Americans and Asian immigrants. Here Eastwood stars as Walt Kowalski, a retired auto worker in suburban Detroit who is a gruff, grim, and newly widowed Korean War veteran carrying ghosts and guilt from his service in the conflict (1950–1953). Walt is a product of his experiences, geography, and generation, and his bigotry (and in some cases, outright racism) is expressed explicitly, consistently, and creatively. And while Kowalski's prejudices are directed at a range of nonwhite residents, and reflected in slurs, grimaces, and grunts and sighs of disapproval, they are primarily aimed at his Hmong neighbors.

Now a minority in his own neighborhood, Walt's surroundings—the dilapidating homes, dying economy, and his distant, pampered, and estranged children and grandchildren—form a milieu of disconnection and confusion. Yet, bit by bit, as Walt is drawn further into the existence and plight of his Hmong neighbors—fixing plumbing, providing a used refrigerator, attending a communal dinner—he becomes close friends with troubled teen Thao (Bee Vang) and his sister Sue (Ahney Her), serving as an unlikely and crusty fatherly figure. Eventually, through a series of events and tragedies, Walt recognizes the humanity and virtues of his Asian friends, breaking decades of misconceptions, derision, and anger aimed at Asians and others.

The film was an enormous box office success and was largely praised by critics, although a few popular and academic critiques found the film contrived, cynical, or simplistic.[20] While the film is on its face, as *New York Times* film critic Manohla Dargis noted, a "nominally modest effort" that features "unfortunate events, some artful and others creaking with scripted contrivance" that drive Walt's transformation from bitter, dying, lonely racist to fatherly figure, *Gran Torino* reinforces the notion that human connections can dissolve the most rigid and pervasive of racial barriers.[21] The symbolic car at the heart of the film, the Ford Gran Torino—manufactured from 1968 to 1976 by Walt Kowalskis all over Detroit—stands as an automobile "made by an industry that now barely makes cars, in a city that hardly works, in a country that too often has felt recently as if it can't do anything right anymore."[22] Yet, by the film's emotional close, one man's unlikely growth and sacrifice reveal that, however late in life, there are some essentials that we *can* get right, and rectify for both the personal and greater good. The film represents a hope for racial reconciliation in Middle America; one film critic even entitled her review, "Hope for a Racist, and Maybe a Country."[23]

That such unpredictable change can ultimately occur, albeit with a very heavy price to individuals and society, is a view that runs through some of the cinematic veins of Paul Haggis's lauded *Crash* (2004), winner of the Academy Award for best picture and screenplay. Set in contemporary Los Angeles and featuring several interwoven tales of racial prejudice, class entitlement, mistrust, resentment, and implicit racial discrimination learned through experiences and the political socialization process, Haggis's mosaic of modern, multicultural, and divided American society is one where resentments and racism simmer beneath the surface—but never too far. Yet, when our lives literally and figuratively crash into one another—whether we are Hispanic, light- or dark-skinned African American, Persian, white, or other—the mistrust, misunderstandings, and anger are brought to the surface, forcing all of us to confront the wreckage of racial attitudes, stereotypes, and economic realities that have shaped our existence and, perhaps, shattered our lives.[24]

Revisiting and Reimagining the Civil Rights Movement

Mississippi Burning (1988), directed by Alan Parker, and nominated for several Academy Awards, including best picture and best actor (Gene Hackman),[25] stands as Hollywood's definitive, though oversimplified and occasionally inaccurate or misleading, version of the all-too-real 1964 Freedom Summer slayings of civil rights workers Mickey Schwerner, James Chaney, and Andrew Goodman. The three men were SNCC (Student Nonviolent Coordinating Committee) volunteers registering African Americans to vote in Mississippi, part of SNCC's concerted efforts to send idealistic college students trained in the tactics and philosophy of nonviolent civil disobedience to the South to help break down persistent and pernicious Jim Crow barriers at the ballot box.[26]

Among the most common criticisms of the film are that it glorifies, or at a minimum overstates, the scope of the FBI's commitment to the civil rights movement generally, and their dedication to solving the murders, specifically, and, moreover, that it unfairly and inaccurately portrays African Americans in Mississippi as passive, subservient, and lacking brave, outspoken, and effective civil rights leaders.[27] For instance, it is now widely known that not only did FBI director J. Edgar Hoover investigate and maintain files on all of the Freedom Summer volunteers trained at the Western College for Women in Oxford, Ohio, in 1964, but that he wiretapped and initiated intimidating measures against Martin Luther King Jr. . Hoover's penchant for wiretapping and harassing prominent civil rights leaders, especially Martin Luther King Jr. (whom he despised and viewed as an ardent communist and incessant womanizer) has been well documented.[28] In addition, one of the great voices of the civil rights movement was Fannie Lou Hamer, an African American woman from Mississippi who founded the Mississippi Freedom Democratic Party, a movement designed to integrate the all-white delegation at the 1964 Democratic National Convention in Atlantic City. There is also no mention of another great black civil rights leader from Mississippi, Medgar Evers, who was killed by an assassin's bullet in 1963. (Rob Reiner's 1996 film *Ghosts of Mississippi*, starring Whoopi Goldberg and James Woods, chronicles Mississippi's thirty-year investigation and prosecution of Evers's alleged assassin, Byron De La Beckwith; and Bob Dylan's 1963 song "Only a Pawn in Their Game," which he performed at the March on Washington that year, is a powerful rendering of the multilayered tragedy of the murder.) Despite these serious drawbacks, the film's taut direction, powerful depiction of pervasive institutionalized racism in Mississippi, and riveting performances by Hackman, William Dafoe, and Frances McDormand (nominated for best supporting actress), *Mississippi Burning* is a passionate, engrossing affair, and topped many "best of" film lists for 1988.

Moreover, the events leading up to and following the murders, as well as all of the key players in the investigation—including all of the real-life suspects, informants, and political leaders in Neshoba County, Mississippi—are reviewed in startling detail in other, nonfilm sources. Along with the historic voting rights March on Selma, Alabama, in March 1965, the Freedom Summer murders of Schwerner, Goodman, and Chaney—two Jews and an African American—stunned a nation and galvanized the civil rights movement and ultimately led to President Lyndon Johnson's signing of the historic Voting Rights Act of 1965. Among other things, the landmark legislation outlawed discrimination in voting, sponsored voter education and registration drives, and provided federal oversight of elections in areas where less than half of the minority voters were registered to vote. Within five years of the Voting Rights Act, the number of African Americans registered in the South doubled.[29]

Documentaries, by their very nature, often delve into terrain where commercial films—so constrained by formulaic plots and the need to reach large audiences and optimize profits—dare not tread. Thus, for examining seminal political events and their effect on the body politic, documentaries can prove to be especially beneficial. Spike Lee's Oscar-nominated documentary *4 Little Girls* (1997) is an excellent case in point. Lee's moving film tells the riveting true story of the bombing of the 16th Street Baptist Church in Birmingham, Alabama, on September 15, 1963.[30] Four girls attending Sunday school at the church—Denise McNair, Carole Robertson, Cynthia Wesley, and Addie Mae Collins—were killed in the racially motivated bombing, and the eyes of a nation were once again focused on the South. Featuring archival footage, interviews with surviving family members, and contextual commentary from national figures such as Walter Cronkite, Jesse Jackson, Andrew Young, and Coretta Scott King—and a series of intriguing and odd ruminations from former Alabama governor, presidential candidate, and staunch segregationist George Wallace—*4 Little Girls* carefully weaves reflections and realities, articulating the long-standing pain and the impact of the bombing on the slain girls' families and the American family. Clearly, students of American politics cannot understand the evolution and dynamics of the civil rights struggle without grasping the significance of this tragedy and its vital influence on the politics, events, and legislation that followed. Used in the proper context, Lee's documentary can be an invaluable educational tool in understanding the political and cultural dynamics surrounding the search for civil rights and social justice in the early to mid-1960s—including the very real climate of fear propagated by the realities of bombings; indeed, Birmingham was known to many at the time as "Bombingham" due to the persistence of such violence. On several levels, it is one very compelling chapter in the civil rights movement.

The Many Faces of George Wallace, Part I

Spike Lee's *4 Little Girls* (1997)

In the DVD of *4 Little Girls*, the "Making of 4 Little Girls" featurette contains illuminating commentary from director Spike Lee concerning the making of the documentary, with special attention to the details and circumstances surrounding the lengthy and revealing, and at times, bizarre and barely audible, interview with former Alabama governor and presidential candidate George Wallace (1919–1998). George Wallace, whose health was in serious decline at the time of the documentary's filming, is frequently barely understandable through a thick fog of Alabama accent burdened by age and illness.

In Spike Lee's documentary, the frail, aging Wallace attempts to make the case that he was never racist and that, as governor of Alabama, he passed legislation that paid for textbooks for African American students. He also demands to be filmed with his personal assistant, an African American man, at his side.

Evaluating the Legacy of George Wallace

Wallace, like most Southerners of his era, started his political career as a states rights Democrat. However, federal intervention in securing civil rights—as well as law and order issues—caused him to bolt the party in the late 1960s. After losing his first race for governor in 1958 to the race-baiting Governor John Patterson, who was openly backed by the KKK, Wallace confided to advisers that he would never be "out-niggered" again.

When Wallace ran for Alabama governor in 1962 on a staunchly segregationist platform, he won, and became immensely popular throughout the South and a legend in his home state. In his infamous inaugural address on January 14, 1963, Wallace declared, "segregation now, segregation forever." The speech was penned by Asa Carter, founder of a KKK terrorist organization. Wallace went on to serve as Alabama's governor from 1963 to 1967, 1971 to 1979, and 1983 to 1987. And he ran for president in 1968 as a member of the American Independent Party, capturing nearly 14 percent of the popular vote nationwide.

Among other things, Wallace is famous for his stand-off with the Kennedy administration in June 1963 over the integration of the University of Alabama. For more on the Kennedy–Wallace and federal-state showdown over the integration of the University of Alabama, see the 1963 documentary *Crisis: Behind a Presidential Commitment.*

On June 11, 1963, after the federal-state dispute with Wallace over integrating the University of Alabama, President Kennedy addressed the nation from the Oval Office, calling civil rights a "moral issue" as "old as the scriptures" and as "clear as the Constitution" During the June 1963 crisis Wallace stood in the schoolhouse door and famously declared, "segregation now, segregation tomorrow, and segregation forever!"

When the Southern Rock band Lynyrd Skynyrd sing "in Birmingham they love the Governor" in their song "Sweet Home Alabama," they are referring to Wallace.

Racial Profiling and American Justice

Over the years, everyday citizens, law enforcement officials, and presidential candidates alike have addressed the matter of racial profiling. This discussion has arguably only increased in the general populace in the years since the September 11, 2001, terrorist attacks on American soil. Yet even prior to the devastating events of 9/11/01, the matter received considerable attention in the public sphere. For example, during the primaries of the hotly contested Bush–Gore 2000 presidential election, several presidential candidates explicitly addressed the issue of racial profiling, openly discussing their opposition to the practice in speeches, debate appearances, and, in the case of Democratic candidate Bill Bradley, in their official policy platforms and websites. Previously a major topic of concern for a slew of civil rights activists, community leaders, law enforcement, mayors, and members of Congress, the issue now gained national prominence. Bradley, the three-term New Jersey senator and former New York Knicks star, stated that the next president should immediately sign an executive order banning the practice. Other hopefuls—from eventual Democratic nominee Vice President Al Gore, to Republicans such as Senator John McCain from Arizona and Texas governor George W. Bush—also expressed their distaste for racial profiling, even as they did not endorse Bradley's specific executive order pledge. Many years later, the issue of racial profiling remains part of our dialogue over national security and civil liberties, yet it has not been as explicitly addressed by specific political party or candidate platforms.

The Many Faces of George Wallace, Part II

Evaluating the Legacy of George Wallace

Later in life, Wallace disavowed much of his segregationist past and asked for forgiveness from prominent African American leaders. In 1979, for example, Wallace called John Lewis—civil rights pioneer, SNCC (Student Nonviolent Coordinating Committee) leader, and future U.S. congressman from Georgia—to ask his forgiveness for his past actions. Lewis accepted Wallace's apology.

By 1982, when Wallace ran for governor yet again, he actively sought the votes of African Americans throughout Alabama. Wallace addressed the Southern Christian Leadership Conference and pronounced his past stand on segregation in the schools "wrong."

> After a four-year political hiatus, Wallace returns to the Governor's Mansion, defeating his opponent easily, largely with the help of the majority black vote. During what would be Wallace's final term as governor, he appoints a record number of black Alabamians to government positions and establishes the so-called Wallace Coalition, which included the Alabama Education Association, organized labor, black political organizations, and trial lawyers.[31]

To learn more about the life, times, politics, and paradoxes of George Wallace, see the following:

* PBS's *American Experience* documentary *George Wallace: Settin' the Woods on Fire* (2000);
* The website *George Wallace: Settin' the Woods on Fire*: http://www.pbs.org/wgbh/amex/wallace/;
* The TV film *George Wallace* (1997), starring Gary Sinise and directed by John Frankenheimer;
* Dan T. Carter's book *The Politics of Rage: George Wallace, the Origins of the New Conservatism, and the Transformation of American Politics* (Simon & Schuster, 1995).

Murder on a Sunday Morning (2001), directed by French filmmaker Jean-Xavier de Lestrade, and winner of the Academy Award for best documentary in March 2002, presents a compelling and disturbing tale of the real-life consequences of racial profiling in Jacksonville, Florida, in 2000. After the murder of a white female tourist outside of a Ramada Inn, a fifteen-year-old African American male, Brenton Butler, is picked up and eventually charged with first-degree murder. On what grounds was he picked up? Did he confess to the murder? Did he resemble the description of the perpetrator provided by an eyewitness? Were his constitutional rights violated? What was the outcome of the trial? *Murder on a Sunday Morning* answers all of these questions and poses many more as it meticulously follows the events in the immediate aftermath of the murder, examines the evidence at the crime scene, and gives the audience a firsthand view of the prosecution's shortcomings and the strategies of Butler's defense attorneys.

We also see the effects of the trial on Brenton Butler and his family, accenting the psychological toll of the entire ordeal. The documentary allows the audience to see the trial and, in so doing, raises several penetrating questions about the veracity and ethics of the Jacksonville sheriff's office, the prosecution, and the practice of racial profiling. And much like Errol Morris's groundbreaking documentary set in Dallas County, Texas, *The Thin Blue Line* (1988), *Murder on a Sunday Morning* illustrates the significant problems and troubling variables that may arise when first-person eyewitnesses *positively identify* the alleged perpetrator. In Florida, much like in Morris's Texas, the individual identified, apprehended, and charged with murder was, in fact, later found to be innocent. Yet it is clear that not all fifteen-year-old petrified, innocent defendants receive the same kind of advocacy and expertise exhibited by Brenton Butler's crack defense team, led by the unforgettable and indefatigable Patrick McGuinness. Roughly one week after capturing the best documentary Oscar at the Academy Awards, *Murder on a Sunday Morning* finally premiered in the United States, appearing as yet another politically charged installment of HBO's provocative documentary series, thus providing a wider audience for the troubling issues raised by the film.

For a much lighter and humorous (though perhaps no less disturbing or stimulating) approach to examining the state of civil rights and race relations in contemporary America—in this case *de facto*, or nonstate-sponsored discrimination—two television segments from writer-director-producer Michael Moore should promote animated reaction and spirited discussion among viewers. The segments-sketches come from Moore's two forays into television: *TV Nation*

(NBC and Fox, 1993–1995) and *The Awful Truth* (Bravo Network, 1999–2000).

The Awful Truth's sketch "Whitey Can't Ride" (2000) follows Moore throughout Manhattan as he poses as a cab driver who refuses to pick up white people, stopping only to pick up African Americans. Need to get to East 86th Street and Lexington? Moore finds such upper-class white neighborhoods "too dangerous" and leaves all Caucasians on his taxi route stranded without the ride they need. This piece, which runs periodically throughout an entire episode, is an aggressive response and follow-up to his provocative *TV Nation* segment called "Taxi" (1994), in which Emmy Award–winning African American actor Yaphet Kotto (*Midnight Run*, *Live and Let Die*, television's *Homicide*) tries to hail a New York City cab but is routinely passed over for . . . a convicted white felon named Louie Bruno! There are a number of discussions and debates that can follow Moore's use of satire to make a penetrating political statement.[32]

Finally, our previous material in this chapter aside, it is obvious that not all of the feature films, documentaries, and television series that deal substantively with race relations in general, and the related search for human understanding and equality under the law specifically, center exclusively on African Americans. *We Shall Remain* (2009), an award-winning multipart history of the Native American experience in the United States from PBS's *American Experience*, as well as the documentary *Reel Injun* (2010), from the National Film Board of Canada, stand as but two examples of films that explore a range of dynamics and challenges facing other racial groups in the United States.[33] A documentary from Cree filmmaker Neil Diamond, *Reel Injun* premiered on PBS's *Independent Lens* after stints at a series of summer film festivals, and examines Hollywood's depictions of Native Americans via movie clips, interviews, and insights from icons such as Clint Eastwood, independent filmmaker Jim Jarmusch, and prominent author Graham Greene, among others.[34] Likewise, the predominantly critical and undisputable commercial success of Clint Eastwood's aforementioned *Gran Torino*, which dealt with a retired white auto worker's prejudices toward Hmong immigrants in the suburbs of Detroit, illustrates that recent films have examined Anglo-Asian relationships. And Paul Haggis's popular and Oscar-winning *Crash* (2004) transcends the strictly white–black dichotomy to explore racial stereotypes and resentment more broadly. Moreover, the inclusion of actor-comedian Aasif Mandvi to the team of correspondents on *The Daily Show* with Jon Stewart in 2007 allowed for the occasional satire about stereotyping Muslims, while the addition of Olivia Munn as "chief Asian correspondent" in 2009 further expanded the satirical repertoire of racially and ethnically relevant issues. And the work of Wyatt

Cenac (2008–) and longtime special commentator Larry Wilmore ("chief black correspondent") continue to push the envelope, devoting segments to matters of racial and religious bigotry and misunderstanding. Countless other quality provocative works that we do not have the space to adequately address here also address long-standing and emerging realities facing a range of racial and ethnic groups in the United States, and we urge you to seek them out on cable, rental sites and machines, and at your local library, multiplex, and university or community film series.

The Struggle for Civil Rights and Social Justice Continues: Anti-Semitism and Homophobia

Another chapter in the search for civil rights and social justice in the United States involves examining undercurrents of anti-Semitism in America. It may surprise some younger people to learn that two landmark films in this genre come not from the era of the civil rights movement in the 1960s, 1970s, or 1980s but from 1947: Edward Dmytryk's Crossfire and Elia Kazan's Gentleman's Agreement. Both of these highly regarded black and white films address anti-Semitism, and its pernicious effects, head-on. Crossfire follows the murder of a Jewish man by a military man, and the twists and turns of the murder investigation. Boasting a stellar cast—including icons Robert Mitchum, Robert Young, and Robert Ryan, the gritty film noir pulls no punches. It exposes prejudice aimed at Jews and the lengths some will go to both exercise it and cover it up. It should be noted that the original plotline of Crossfire involved the bashing and murder of a gay man, not a Jewish person, but addressing homophobia was deemed too taboo and risqué in 1940s America. Thus, the plot was changed to anti-Semitism in order to adhere to Hollywood's implicit and explicit film codes that kept explicit discussion of homosexuality, and prejudice and violence aimed at gays and lesbians, off of the cinematic table for decades.[35]

Elia Kazan's groundbreaking political drama Gentleman's Agreement (1947), winner of the Academy Award for best picture, follows a newspaperman (Gregory Peck) who poses as a Jew in order to catalog the obstacles presented by this faith. In so doing, he finds that neither his love interest nor the workers at his newspaper are immune to the stereotypical comments and sordid whispering campaigns that lie at the heart of anti-Semitism. Along the way he sees how a Jewish army veteran and a close friend (John Garfield) are challenged to a fight at a restaurant just for being Jewish. He also discovers how hotels, clubs, and resorts find creative ways of keeping out Jews in favor of WASPs (white, Anglo-Saxon, Protestants). And, as he continues his journey as an "undercover" Jew in America, his son (a young Dean Stockwell) is taunted and harassed at school, coming home in tears after being called a "dirty Jew" and a "stinking kyke." In the end, the newspaper series at the heart of *Gentleman's Agreement* speaks for itself, exposing the myriad ways anti-Semitism is executed in the United States, whether in the home, businesses, workplace, or school, making the case that it is always present, but not often discussed openly and truthfully.

For decades, Hollywood's treatment of homosexuality—which was primarily (and deliberately) implicit due to overt and covert production codes and the prevailing social and cultural norms of the age—reinforced negative stereotypes. *The Celluloid Closet* (1995), based on the groundbreaking book of the same title by Vito Russo, uses film clips from one hundred years of film—from the silent era through 1993's *Philadelphia*—to examine stereotypes, recurring images, and the overall evolution of Hollywood's depiction of homosexuality on the big screen. Whether it was as sissy, violent predator; hopelessly depressed loner; or regular, everyday person, the documentary presents these images and stereotypes of gays and lesbians in an alternately vivid, disconcerting, entertaining, and informative fashion. Narrator Lily Tomlin presides over this fascinating, illuminating review of film history that features insight and reflections from influential gay screenwriters and actors, including Gore Vidal, Amistead Maupin, and Harvey Fierstein, among others. In addition, Tom Hanks, Tony Curtis, and several other prominent actors comment on their experiences performing in films that deal, implicitly or explicitly, with homosexuality. *The Celluloid Closet* makes the case that the motion picture industry has moved from covert, disturbing, caricatured, or stereotypical images of gays and lesbians to offering more sympathetic and positive portrayals.

Three examples of the ongoing evolution of popular, mainstream commercial films in portraying more sympathetic views of gay relationships and individuals are Ang Lee's landmark love story *Brokeback Mountain* (2005), Gus Van Sant's political biography *Milk* (2008), and Lisa Cholodenko's *The Kids Are All Right* (2010). Set in Wyoming and based on the award-winning short story by Annie Proulx, *Brokeback Mountain* was nominated for several Academy Awards, including best picture, and won Oscars for best director and adapted screenplay. The movie follows the range of emotional, and as well as familial and societal, challenges faced by lovers Enis Del Mar (Heath Ledger) and Jack Twist (Jake Gyllenhaal) over many years. *Milk* tells the story of the rise and tragic assassination of Harvey Milk (Sean Penn, in an Academy Award–winning performance), the first openly gay elected official in the United States. Van Sant's film trails the New Yorker Milk's arrival in San Francisco to his landmark election as a San Francisco supervisor in the 1970s, only to be killed by disgruntled, jealous, conservative political loner Dan White (Josh Brolin) as he reached the zenith of his political power. While the film follows Milk from camera store owner to social and political agitator to elected official, it also mirrors the awakening of the gay rights movement in San Francisco, California, and the United States.

Finally, the critically acclaimed, touching tale of modern family life *The Kids Are All Right* (2010) presents a suburban Southern California lesbian couple, Nic and Jules (Annette Bening and Julianne Moore), as a "picture of normalcy"; they are, as one critic put it, "loving, devoted, responsible and a bit of a mess."[36] As such, their family is not so much a *gay* couple with children, but rather, a regular nuclear family facing many (but not quite all) of the same domestic and emotional issues (dysfunction, insecurity, career and mood shifts, raising children) that traditional heterosexual couples and their families encounter. Here, the children of the couple desire to learn more about their birth father, Paul (Mark Ruffalo), and the film deals with a host of developments that ensue after he enters the picture. *The Kids Are All Right* strives to tell a universal human tale of marriage and family struggles, not an exclusively gay-only story, as it "starts from the premise that gay marriage, an issue of ideological contention and cultural strife, is also an established social fact."[37]

Brokeback Mountain, Milk, and *The Kids Are All Right* are but three examples in an ever-expanding array of popular culture contributions that have addressed, with varying degrees of seriousness, and via different genres and approaches, the lives, joys, and struggles of LGBT citizens. From *All in the Family, Maude,* and *Soap* in the 1970s, to *Roseanne, Ellen, Rosie O'Donnell,* and *Will & Grace,* to *The L Word, Queer Eye for the Straight Guy, Six Feet Under,* and sitcom powerhouses *Glee* and *Modern Family,* among many others, mainstream popular culture is devoting increasing time to the perspectives, challenges, and everyday social, romantic, and economic lives of LGBT Americans. The range of programming, combined with significant cultural and political shifts, and the ability of the very much for-profit entertainment industry to market its products to niche and expanding markets, has made the more persistent and pernicious stereotypes of yesteryear less likely to be screened in multiplexes and living rooms.

Yet serious obstacles remain for real-life LGBT citizens, even amid pervasive, positive changes in popular culture presentations. Hilary Swank's Academy

Award–winning portrayal of Brandon Teena in *Boys Don't Cry* (1999), as well as the documentary *The Brandon Teena Story* (1998), revealed the tragic consequences of hatred toward and misunderstanding of transgendered people; in this case, Brandon Teena, a transgendered teen in rural Nebraska. Found out to be born female, though she identified as a male, Teena was savagely beaten and murdered in 1993 when her secret was revealed.

HBO Films' *The Laramie Project* (2002), written and directed by Moisés Kaufman, deals with the 1998 murder of gay University of Wyoming student Matthew Shepard. With a cast that includes the likes of Laura Linney, Steve Buscemi, Amy Madigan, Dylan Baker, and Christina Ricci, *The Laramie Project* is based on the play created by Moisés Kaufman and the Tectonic Theater Project based in New York City. After the murder of Shepard, Kaufman and his theater project went to Laramie to discuss with hundreds of townspeople the murder and its ramifications. Did they know Matthew Shepard? Did they know the alleged murderers? How is homosexuality treated in the American West? How did the community respond to this brutal crime? What are the perspectives of clergy in the Laramie area? All of these penetrating questions, and many more, are explored in this play-turned-film. *The Laramie Project* has been performed on stages around the country, from college campuses to major public and private theaters. The HBO film provides a way for folks who may not be regular theatergoers to be exposed to the important social, political, and cultural issues that surround homosexuality, hate crimes, and the specific case of Matthew Shepard. And, the impact of Shepard's death was evident in the legal-political world years later, when, in 2009, President Obama signed into law the Matthew Shepard and James Byrd, Jr. Hate Crimes Prevention Act, legislation that added "federal protections against crimes based on gender, disability, gender identity, or sexual orientation."[38]

An ambitious documentary from rural Pennsylvania stands as a prime example of the ability of film to engage an array of individuals about salient sociocultural and political matters. *Out in the Silence* (2009), from first-time filmmakers Joe Wilson and Dean Hamer, follows the fallout in and around Oil City, Pennsylvania, when a former native and high school graduate of the area, Wilson (now a Washington, D.C., resident), posts his (same-sex) wedding announcement in the local newspaper, the *Oil City Derrick*.[39] The announcement was met with vitriolic letters in the paper, and Wilson later traveled back to his western Pennsylvania roots when it was evident that there were allegations of bullying in the local high school based on students' perceived sexual orientation. The engaging film follows one student's departure from the public high school due to harassment, and the burgeoning local movement to counter LGBT bullying in the schools, and to build a network of support within the greater community.

Met with a recalcitrant school board and the organizational efforts of the Pennsylvania Family Institute, which vigorously opposed extending anti-bullying programs to include LGBT students, Wilson and supporters continue their quest for understanding and proactive steps in rural Pennsylvania schools and communities.[40] Along the way, Wilson and his partner strike up a unique friendship with a local minister and his wife who have very different views on homosexuality and marriage. The reverend had written a letter to the local newspaper opposing their decision to include Wilson's marriage announcement, yet it is clear that, as time and the film progress, the rural, religious heterosexual couple find some common bonds of humanity with the decidedly nonreligious Wilson and Hamer, even as they still adhere to some different perspectives and values concerning sexuality and the definition of marriage. *Out in the Silence* stands as an effective, compelling marriage of storytelling and activism; the documentary skillfully weaves the stories of LGBT struggles for acceptance and common ground in the schools and in the community, and the filmmakers later launched an ambitious nationwide program of screenings and talk-backs, beginning in Pennsylvania and carrying on throughout the United States. Indeed colleges, high schools, churches, and community centers have hosted viewings and discussions, and the film's website includes links for discussion kits to help facilitate learning and engagement.

Which Side Are You on? Workers, Economic Justice, and Labor Struggles in the United States

Another aspect of social and economic justice is the continuing struggle for dignity, workers' rights, and better wages. In examining the plight of the American worker and highlighting decisive, divisive battles between labor and business in the United States, several seminal films—from independent film and documentary giants Barbara Kopple, John Sayles, and Michael Moore—stand out. Kopple's *Harlan County, USA* (1976), winner of the Academy Award for best documentary feature, follows an acrimonious, protracted coal miners' strike against the Brookside Mine of the Eastover Mining Company in Harlan County, Kentucky, and its parent company, Duke Power, in the spring and summer of 1973. Throughout the two-hour documentary, Kopple provides the audience with ample political and historical context for the bitter standoff between the workers' union, the UMWA (United Workers of America), and the coal company, highlighting union struggles and violence that date back to the 1930s. This context arms the audience with important information about the nature of work in the mines (extremely dangerous), mine safety (often poorly regulated), black lung disease, and the disputes and violence between the union and coal company, and within the national union, that complicate and stymie the efforts of Kentucky miners to earn better wages and operate with increased safety, a more democratic and responsive union, and dignity.

Not unlike Herbert Biberman's landmark blacklisted feature film *Salt of the Earth* (1954), which chronicled workers' struggle for economic justice during a zinc miners strike in New Mexico,[41] Kopple's documentary also focuses on the integral role—and plight—of miners' wives during strikes. *Harlan County, USA*, also exposes corruption within the union, as, in 1969, the scandal-ridden UMWA president, Tony Boyle, has the democratic voice of the union, reformer candidate Joseph "Jock" Yablonsky, killed. Yablonsky's murder is a blow to the miners who had been fighting for years for real political power within the union. Kopple also skillfully integrates archival footage of the mines and labor struggles with contemporary images of the miners' homes, poverty, and the general dismal socioeconomic reality. Taken together, these images present viewers with a stark, realistic view of coal miners' lives, where lack of running water, electricity, and adequate health care is commonplace.

As the bitter thirteen-month-long strike continues, the Duke Power Company, which controlled much of the mine operations, employed replacement ("scab") workers and hired gun-toting hooligans to threaten workers and break the will of the strikers. Violence begets more violence, and the already destitute town becomes polarized and shaken even further. The introduction of the hired guns presents local law enforcement and the strikers with further setbacks and dilemmas. In the end, while the struggles of the union and its strikers ultimately pay off—the new contract provided miners with a raise and more power within the mine and union—the film suggests that the struggle for better wages and basic dignity will be long and recurrent and require vigilance: just before the credits roll, the miners strike yet again to protest the coal company's abuse of newly won grievance procedures. As such, the documentary indicates that the struggle for collective bargaining power and rights in the workplace continues.

Writer-director-producer John Sayles's *Matewan* (1987) is a semi-fictional retelling of real-life worker exploitation at the hands of a ruthless coal company in 1920s West Virginia. Sayles acts in the film as well, portraying the local evangelical preacher who is more sympathetic with the coal company than the abused miners and their struggling union. As historian Eric Foner writes, the labor struggles and corporate harassment in the southern West Virginia coal mines depicted in the film culminate in "the Matewan Massacre, a violent (and historically accurate) confrontation in which the town's mayor, seven armed guards hired by the coal operators, and two miners lose their lives."[42] The film, based on this very real massacre and the general labor struggles in the coal mines of West Virginia in the 1920s, depicts what life was like in company towns and company stores owned by powerful coal companies. During this time, mine owners would pay workers in company scrip (money), which could only be used at company stores—a situation that invited corruption, maintaining a seemingly endless cycle of poverty for the workers and profit for the company.

Matewan also examines some of the cynical exploitive tactics routinely used by coal companies to keep the miners and their fledgling unions divided and ineffective. Race and ethnicity play a major role here, as the coal company, aided by hired spies and informants within union ranks, tries to paint the newly arrived black coal miners as intent on stealing white miners' jobs. This is not difficult to do in the midst of a poor and worried population of white miners who are destitute and, in many cases, have been inculcated with racial prejudice handed down through generations. Thus, the context was ripe for fomenting racial resentment, even as workers, regardless of race or religion, faced similar economic injustices in the workplace. In addition, the coal barons also play on ethnic and religious differences to create dissension within the union ranks by pitting Italian immigrants against the native white West Virginians and the African American miners.

While featuring riveting performances by James Earl Jones and Sayles's stalwarts David Strathairn and Chris Cooper, since *Matewan* is a semi-fictionalized account of the coal miners' struggles, Sayles did add two fictional characters. Danny Radnor is a union-supporting miner and boy preacher, and Joe Kenehan is a union organizer and pacifist. Nevertheless, the film covers much of the real-world terrain of labor struggles in 1920s West Virginia. As *The Washington Post*'s film review surmised in the fall of 1987:

> Kenehan has his work cut out for him. He must unite disparate groups into strikers and, when the company forces them into a tent camp in the mountains, keep some very desperate people calm. And this company has not only firepower but eyes and ears in unexpected places.[43]

Sayles's attention to historical accuracy and riveting storytelling provide context for West Virginia politics and concentrated economic power in the

1920s. The combination creates one of the most memorable film experiences documenting labor struggles in the United States. *Matewan* exposes class and racial injustice and poses troubling questions about entrenched political and economic power that many films refuse to touch in such a direct, substantive manner. It allows viewers to be transported to a time and a place that may seem far removed from our own socioeconomic reality; yet, it also reminds us that some similar struggles remain. As Foner asserts in his praise of Sayles's masterpiece, to make *Matewan* during the 1980s, a time in which anti-labor sentiment was prevalent, was already an accomplishment, but

> in the hands of director John Sayles, *Matewan* offers a meditation on broad philosophical questions rarely confronted directly in American films: the possibility of interracial cooperation, the merits of violence and nonviolence combating injustice, and the threat posed by concentrated economic power to American notions of political democracy and social justice.[44]

Yet the profound messages from Sayles's film are hardly restricted to any one or two decades in one particular country; one need only examine the perpetual challenges to cooperation across racial, religious, or class lines not only in the United States but across the globe. Resentments that are fueled by, among other factors, competition, religion, and immigration during hard economic times remain. Whether it is the persistent migrant worker and immigration debate in the United States or the influx of Algerians and North Africans into the economies and societies of Southern Europe, the realities of economic anxiety and racial (and religious) animosities stand as multilayered challenges, even as so much progress has been made in reel and real life.

American Dream (1990), directed by Barbara Kopple, and winner of the 1991 Academy Award for best documentary, chronicles labor struggles and an eventual bitter strike in Austin, Minnesota, during 1984–1986. The site of struggle here is the Hormel slaughterhouse and meatpacking plant in Austin. Hormel, the makers of Spam and a wide variety of meat products, while posting a healthy profit of $29 million in 1984, offered the workers at its Austin plant a contract that cut wages from $10.69 to $8.25 an hour. The contract also cut benefits by 30 percent. Kopple's film documents the ensuing battle of wills between Hormel and the local union, P-9, of the UFCW (United Food & Commercial Workers), who strike in order to win back the wages and benefits. It also chronicles the dissension among local P-9 members as the strike wears on, and, most of all, the rancor and severe disagreements between the P-9 and the international UFCW leadership. Indeed it was a "strike which pitted worker against management, worker against worker and even brother against broth-er."[45]

Refusing to take the salary and benefits cut, local P-9 members, led by pres-ident Jim Guyette and activist public relations guru Ray Rogers—who was hired by P-9 to orchestrate a "corporate campaign" aimed at gaining national solidar-ity and sympathy for the strike—work to organize labor, galvanize their union, and oppose Hormel's cuts. National attention comes to Austin, as Jesse Jackson and other political and labor leaders—including future U.S. senator from Minnesota Paul Wellstone (1991–2002), then a political science professor at Carleton College—come to Austin to rally behind P-9's cause. However, as the strike continues with no end in sight, P-9 suffers a number of mortal blows. Hundreds of Hormel workers in other plants, who, in a show of solidarity with P-9 refuse to cross the picket lines at their plant, are fired. In addition, rancor and disagreements over strategy tactics between P-9 and the international union, led by Lewie Anderson, tear apart any hope of one united union front. In the end, Hormel hires back less than 20 percent of the Austin plant work-ers who went on strike and honored the picket line. But that is not the end of the saga. Ultimately, Hormel contracts out their plant to an independent com-pany and promptly slashes wages to $6 an hour. It is a painful, sorrowful chain of events for the workers and their families, and the film captures the struggles—within the union, among the families in Austin, and between labor and busi-ness—in dramatic fashion.[46]

At the same time, many intimately involved with local P-9 efforts take issue with *American Dream*'s depiction of events. Peter Rachleff's 1993 account of the bitter Hormel strike, *Hard-Pressed in the Heartland*, strongly disagrees with Kopple's version of the strike and its presentation of key players. Rachleff, a his-tory professor at Macalester College in St. Paul, Minnesota, who was actively engaged in strike efforts on behalf of local P-9, finds the final film version of the labor dispute to cast an unfairly negative light on the local P-9, its mem-bers, and its leadership, while praising international UFCW leaders who were, in his mind, destructive to the workers' cause:

> *American Dream* presents the International Union's hatchet man, Lewie Anderson, as a tough-talking, hard-nosed union bargainer in contrast to P-9's leadership and advis-ers who are presented as confused, inexperienced, and out of touch with reality. Worse than these character distortions, *American Dream* also gives Anderson one opportu-nity after another to predict that this strike will fail, without ever exploring the crit-ical role he and the UFCW played in undermining it—in discouraging other unions from sending assistance, in denying P-9 the right to block production at Hormel's seven

other unionized plants, in rejecting P-9's call for a boycott of Hormel products, and in organizing a minority of dissident P-9 members to disrupt union meetings and even to cross sanctioned picket lines. *American Dream* actually implies that the UFCW had the "right" position—not to take on Hormel at all, or to return to work on the company's terms when they began to hire "permanent replacements"—at the same time it whitewashes the union's role in destroying a strike it publicly claimed to support.[47]

Rachleff viewed P-9's intense labor organizing at the local level to be "just what the doctor ordered as an antidote for a moribund labor movement," and was amazed by the "large number of people participating, the involvement of families, the spirit and imagination . . . and the determination not to back down before what appeared to be unreasonable demands being made by a profitable company."[48]

Perhaps no film focused on the plight of deindustrialization has garnered more universal acclaim or provoked as much controversy as Michael Moore's exposé of General Motors' downsizing in 1980s Michigan, *Roger & Me* (1989). Made for a paltry $260,000, *Roger & Me* quickly became one of the highest-grossing narrative documentaries in the history of film. A native of the Flint, Michigan, area, Moore returned to his hometown after an unsuccessful stint as editor at the storied liberal investigative journal *Mother Jones* in San Francisco. His mission? To document the layoffs of thousands of GM workers and the cascading consequences for the local economy, safety, mental health, and overall quality of life. The "Roger" is Roger Smith, then the CEO of General Motors; the "Me" is, of course, Michael Moore.

With no filmmaking experience whatsoever, Moore used personal savings, bingos and other creative fundraising efforts to scrape together the funds needed to make his film. The son and grandson of GM auto workers, both union men from the UAW (United Auto Workers), Moore was especially interested in the plight of GM workers, and his repeated visits to plant closings to chat with workers about their trials and tribulations bear this out. Along his journey to plant closing after plant closing, he points to the increase in crime, the building of new jails, the mass exodus of workers, the evictions of citizens from their homes, depressing parades passing vacant storefronts, the exponential rise of the rat population, and the tough, often-poor-paying jobs that people resort to to make ends meet (Taco Bell, Amway, blood and plasma donations, rabbit butchering, prison guards). And—most of all—he tries to track down General Motors CEO Roger Smith and ask him one question: Why, in a time of profits, is GM laying off thousands of workers, and thus, destroying a city and region?

While he is stymied in procuring a one-on-one meeting with Smith, Moore is granted access to Tom Kay, a spokesman for GM. During their interviews, Kay disagrees wholeheartedly with Moore's belief that GM has a special responsibility to the community in which it operates. This kind of "cradle to grave" care is, according to Kay, not the job of corporations.[49] The corporations are businesses, and, as such, are concerned with one thing: being as efficient and profitable as possible, and if it means laying off 20,000 or 80,000 people in order to achieve such goals, then that's what corporations must do. In the meantime, Kay suggests, there is as much economic opportunity in 1980s Flint as ever before and cites the success of a lint roller company. Not surprisingly, Moore finds this contention to be laughable. As the film's credits roll, Moore points out that Kay was himself eventually downsized.

Although *Roger & Me* was a huge critical and commercial success (at least by documentary standards), obviously vigorous debate remains concerning Moore's progressive view of corporate responsibility and social contract theory. Still others charged Moore with playing too loose with the facts when he cites Flint job losses at 30,000. As Ernest Giglio points out, Flint only lost 3,000–5,000 jobs in the time period examined in the film.[50] Moore has responded that the film gives no specific dates and that his film was meant to convey a larger picture about the broad and devastating effects of layoffs on an entire region (the Midwest) over a decade.[51] The other dominant strains of criticism of *Roger & Me* center around the aforementioned sequencing of scenes, perhaps most notably, the precise timing of Ronald Reagan's lunch with unemployed auto workers and the starting date for the building of the Auto World theme park, which local government officials helped to bankroll in order to spur economic development.

Another line of criticism involves whether or not Moore actually had exclusive one-on-one meetings with CEO Roger Smith outside of the brief encounters featured in the film. The Canadian documentary *Manufacturing Dissent* (2007), for example, a critical look at Moore's filmmaking tactics and veracity in general, asserts that Moore met with Smith on two other occasions, yet deliberately, for dramatic effect, left this footage on the cutting room floor. Moore has denied these contentions. Whatever one's view of these criticisms, allegations, and Moore's underlying message and responses, and regardless of one's politics or interpretation of Moore's work (there tends to be a love/hate reaction to Moore's narrative style, politics, and values, especially in the increasingly polarized political and media landscape of the past few decades), the serious socioeconomic issues he raises via his art should spark hours and days of serious debate and deliberation over corporate and government responsibility in the quest for economic and social justice in America.[52]

More Moore?

In the decades following *Roger & Me*, the always outspoken and controversial filmmaker, satirist, and political commentator (often all three at once) from Michigan, Michael Moore, has gone on to write, direct, and produce films and television programs and author books that examine corporate malfeasance, social and economic justice, unjust wars, race relations, health care, and other themes and policy dilemmas.

These issues and films include gun violence, fear, and an irresponsible, profit-driven media (*Bowling for Columbine*, 2002, Academy Award winner for best documentary feature)[53]; war profiteering and the rush to war in Iraq in the George W. Bush presidency (*Fahrenheit 9/11*, 2004); a comparative examination of the inadequacy, immorality, and incoherence of a for-profit health care industry in the United States (*Sicko*, 2007); and the negative human and economic consequences of a newer, meaner, and more extreme strain of hyper-capitalism (*Capitalism: A Love Story*, 2009).

Moore examined many of the same issues addressed in *Roger & Me* via his satirical television shows on *TV Nation* (1993–1995, NBC and Fox) and *The Awful Truth* (1999–2000, Bravo Network). He has also written books, including *Downsize This! Random Threats from an Unarmed American* (1997), *Adventures in a TV Nation* (1998, coauthored with Kathleen Glynn), *Stupid White Men* (2001), *Dude, Where's My Country?* (2004), and *Mike's Election Guide* (2008).

He has also founded the Traverse City Film Festival, an ambitious yearly screening of films at the State Theatre in downtown Traverse City along the shores of Lake Michigan. According to the festival's website, the Traverse City Film Festival (TCFF) is committed to showing 'Just Great Movies' and helping to save one of America's few indigenous art forms—the cinema. We are committed to showing great movies that both entertain and enlighten the audience. We need movies that seek to enrich the human spirit and the art of filmmaking, not the bottom line. Our goal is for people to leave the theater with the feeling that they just watched something special."[54]

In the meantime, other filmmakers, in addition to Moore, Kopple, and Sayles, have continued to address labor struggles and economic justice in the United States, particularly in the area of blue-collar workers and the manufacturing sector. Kristi Jacobson's *American Standoff* (2002), which debuted on HBO, follows the state of the Teamsters in the early 2000s by examining the union's internal politics under the regime of president James Hoffa and by reviewing their extensive, yet ultimately unsuccessful, efforts in 1999–2002 to unionize the Overnite trucking company. Steven Bognar and Julia Reichert's documentary *The Last Truck: Closing of a GM Plant* (2009), also premiering on HBO, chronicles the daily lives of over 2,500 auto workers in a GM plant in Moraine, Ohio, as their plant closes on December 23, 2008. Filmed as the storied auto giant faced potential bankruptcy, the exposé reveals the centrality of work in defining our everyday existence as well as the scores of industries that stood to disintegrate as auto manufacturing deteriorated in the industrial heartland.[55]

Conclusion

Through his infamous characters and films *Borat* (2006) and *Bruno* (2009), Cambridge-educated satirist Sacha Baron Cohen has revealed his creative and controversial "penchant for exposing the bigotry simmering beneath society's thin veneer of acceptance of diversity."[56] Cohen's openly gay fashionista persona Bruno exposed persistent homophobia, while Borat's journey suggests that xenophobia and sexism remain stubbornly, if uncomfortably, present. Yet as this chapter illustrates, whether it is the legacy of racism, the history of the civil rights movement, anti-Semitism, the depictions of LGBT citizens, labor struggles, or the elusive quest for economic justice, American film and television have long provided a wealth of images and perspectives. These films provoke, challenge, offend, advocate, and, above all, tell the extraordinary stories of ordinary people searching for justice.

Social and political action aimed at aiding this journey and realizing the dream of equality and acceptance has taken a long time and has been fueled by the sacrifices of many. The legitimizing and reinforcing of negative racial stereotypes in early American films such as *Birth of a Nation* have given way to a wide array of artistic expressions that have openly or in more subtle ways challenged the prevailing codes of racism, anti-Semitism, and homophobia. Our examination of film reveals directors and documentarians who continue to ask unsettling questions about our past, present, and future, providing the means by which to debate and discuss our republic's ongoing search for civil rights and social justice: *What was the code of conduct that governed race relations, why did it flourish, and how was it ultimately broken down? Is there, or should there be, a social contract that buttresses our economic system, and if so, what rights and responsibilities do workers and businesses have?* As living, breathing, civic-minded organisms from diverse backgrounds, we continue to debate these questions, and in the process discover more about ourselves and our political past, present, and future.

Notes

1. For an overview of how African Americans have been portrayed in films, consult Ed Guerrero, *Framing Blackness: The African American Image in Film* (Philadelphia: Temple University Press, 1993); S. Torriano Berry and Venise T. Berry, *Historical Dictionary of African American Cinema* (Lanham, MD: Scarecrow Press, 2007); and Donald Bogle, *Blacks in American Film and Television: An Encyclopedia* (New York: Garland Publishing, 1988).

2. "Faithful servant" was the title given to African Americans in *The Birth of a Nation* who remained in some degree of servitude to, or performed household duties for, white families in the South after the Civil War. The film depicts "faithful servants" as loyal, loving, caring, bighearted souls who despise the freed blacks and their Northern "carpetbagger" friends. In fact, in the film, they fight the evil, agitating, and often-sex-crazed emancipated African Americans.

3. As membership in the Klan increased steadily in the 1920s, many would cite the heroic portrayal of the Klan in *The Birth of a Nation* as a contributing factor.

4. Leon F. Litwak, "The Birth of a Nation," in *Past Imperfect: History According to the Movies*, ed. Mark C. Carnes (New York: Owl Books, 1996), 136.

5. In fact, the NAACP would publish a pamphlet entitled *Fighting A Vicious Film: Protest Against The Birth of a Nation*. In the pamphlet the film is referred to as "three hours of filth"; it is available at the Library of Congress website: http://lcweb2.loc.gov/service/rbc/rbc0001/2001/20010102001fi/20010102001fi.pdf.

6. For President Wilson's quote, see Litwak, "The Birth of a Nation," 136–41. As a Southerner who reflected the dominant racial views of his day, Wilson's acquiescence to segregation and racism is certainly understandable, however unfortunate. What is perhaps paradoxical—and

is always cause for discussion, study, and examination—is the fact that Wilson, as architect of the League of Nations and the Treaty of Versailles, was a champion of self-determination, human rights, and international law across the globe. Wilson the idealist, with an almost messianic zeal for self-determination and international peace—vs. Wilson the Southern segregationist who screened and endorsed *The Birth of a Nation*—is one of the more interesting inconsistencies and case studies in American politics.

7. Litwak, "The Birth of a Nation," 136.

8. Ibid.

9. The film portrays the fall of Babylon, the passion of Christ, the 1572 St. Bartholomew's Day Massacre in France, and a modern story of a man falsely accused of murder.

10. Michael Glover Smith, "D. W. Griffith: Opening Act for . . . Bob Dylan?" blog, October 31, 2010: http://michaelgloversmith.wordpress.com/2010/10/31/d-w-griffith-opening-act-for-bob-dylan/. Wark Producing Corporation's notice of bankruptcy, featured in the February 19, 1921, *New York Times*, is cited in Smith's blog entry. Smith is an independent filmmaker and film studies instructor at institutions of higher learning in Greater Chicago, including Oakton Community College, Triton College, Harold Washington College, and the College of Lake County.

11. Ibid.

12. The illuminating documentary *Strange Fruit* (2002), featured on PBS's *Independent Lens*, examines the history of the powerful song, considered by many, including *Time* magazine, to be the most influential song of the twentieth century. The film and *Independent Lens* websites provide additional insight and context: http://www.onierafilms.com/films/sf_desc.html, and http://www.pbs.org/independentlens/strangefruit/film.html. See also David Margolick, *Strange Fruit: The Biography of a Song* (New York: HarperPerennial, 2001).

13. The name Tommy Johnson is a composite of legendary blues artist Robert Johnson (1911–1938) and delta blues artist Tommy Johnson (1896–1956). The mythology surrounding Johnson's stellar guitar playing is that he sold his soul to the devil in return for amazing guitar skills. For more on this matter, see Robert Johnson's classic blues rumination "Cross Road Blues." Johnson, a native of Hazelhurst, Mississippi, died under mysterious circumstances near Greenwood, Mississippi. For more information on Robert Johnson, as well as other American blues legends, see: http://www.thebluehighway.com/tbh1.html.

14. Ethan and Joel Coen, *O Brother, Where Art Thou?* (London: Faber and Faber, 2000), 84.

15. For a fascinating recounting of the wide-ranging political influence wielded by the White Citizens Councils throughout the South in the 1950s–1960s, see former president Jimmy Carter's *Turning Point: A Candidate, a State, and a Nation Come of Age* (New York: Times Books, 1992), which chronicles Carter's first major campaign in Georgia.

16. Running as the States Rights Party, or "Dixiecrat," candidate, Strom Thurmond won the electoral votes in all of the Deep Southern states in the 1948 presidential election, signaling the beginning of the end of the solid, one-party Democratic South that had been the norm since the Civil War.

After 1948, the Democrats' loss of the South at the national level began in earnest when Democratic president Lyndon Johnson lost the South to Sen. Barry Goldwater (R-AZ) in 1964. Goldwater took a states rights approach to civil rights, opposing the 1964 Civil Rights Act, for example, and was enthusiastically endorsed by the Ku Klux Klan. Goldwater rejected and disavowed the Klan's support yet remained steadfast in his opposition to the historic federal civil rights law. For an excellent examination of this matter, as well as the wide-ranging influence of Goldwater on the modern Republican Party, and American politics in general, see the documentary Mr. *Conservative: Goldwater on Goldwater* (2006), directed by Goldwater's granddaughter Julie Anderson.

The debate over the 1964 Civil Rights Act and the proper role of the federal government in enforcing civil rights continues to periodically arise at the state or national levels, even as there has been significant political consensus in favor of the landmark legislation. For example, in the 2010 midterm elections, Kentucky Republican candidate for the U.S. Senate Rand Paul expressed his opposition to aspects of the Civil Rights Act that forbade private businesses from discriminating against customers based on race (Title II). Regarding Rand Paul and the Civil Rights Act, see, for example, his interview with MSNBC commentator Rachel Maddow, "Rand Paul on 'Maddow' Defends Criticism of Civil Rights Act, Says He Would Have Worked to Change Bill," *Huffington Post*, May 21, 2010: http://www.huffingtonpost.com/2010/05/20/rand-paul-tells-maddow-th_n_582872.html. On December 5, 2002, at a one-hundredth-birthday celebration on Capitol Hill honoring outgoing U.S. Senator Strom Thurmond (R-SC), Trent Lott said the following: "I want to say this about my state: when Strom Thurmond ran for president, we voted for him. We're proud of it. And if the rest of the country had followed our lead, we wouldn't have had all these problems over all these years, either." Bipartisan criticism of Lott's statement followed, and, by the end of the year, Sen. Bill Frist (R-TN) had become the White House's choice for Senate majority leader. For Lott's quote, see Ken Rudin, "If Lott Had to Quit over Race Issue, Should Reid?" National Public Radio, January 11, 2010: http://www.npr.org/blogs/political junkie/2010/01/we_wouldnt_be_having_all_these.html.

17. Also of note is the overwhelming success of *O Brother*'s soundtrack, a tribute to vintage Appalachian, folk, country, and gospel music. The Coens and producer T-Bone Burnett introduced millions to the work of the Stanley Brothers (especially Dr. Ralph Stanley), Gillian Welch, John Hartford, and Alison Krauss and Union Station, among many others, and captured the Album of the Year Grammy in February 2002. Two highly successful nationwide concert tours—dubbed "Down from the Mountain"—commenced in the winter and summer of 2002. To date, the *O Brother* soundtrack has sold well over six million copies.

18. For a sense of the cultural impact of the novel, see Julie Bosman, "A Classic Turns 50, and Parties are Planned," *New York Times*, May 25, 2010, p. C1.

19. Desson Howe, "The 'Monster's' Within," *Washington Post*, February 8, 2002.

20. Film critic Mark Harris wrote of the film, "I'm not a fan of Gran Torino, which seems less like a freestanding, credible story than a flimsy pretext for the estimable Clint Eastwood to continue a dialogue with his own past selves about solitude and martyrdom and toughness and misanthropy." See Mark Harris, "What Stars Are For," *Entertainment Weekly*, January 2, 2009: http://www.ew.com/ew/article/0,,20250042,00.html. Political scientist Ernest Giglio's assessment of the film as a rather simplistic fable of white male transformation and leadership can be found in his chapter on race and gender in the third edition of his text *Here's Looking at You*, 3rd ed. (New York: Peter Lang, 2010).

21. Manohla Dargis, "Hope for a Racist, and Maybe a Country," *New York Times*, December 12, 2008: http://movies.nytimes.com/2008/12/12/movies/12tori.html.

22. Ibid.

23. Ibid.

24. In his May 15, 2005 Political Film Society review of *Crash*, Peter Hass wrote, "In 1991, Rodney King asked, 'Why can't we all get along?' He was referring to racial mistrust in Los Angeles, but his query was interpreted as relevant to the United States as a whole. . .in *Crash,* one answer to Rodney King's question appears to be, 'We really do not want to get along,' whereas a possible remedy is that everyone needs to have an epiphany to wake up to the fact that they are ruining their own lives by mistrusting everyone, believing in stereotypes, and directing their frustrations toward others": http://www.polfilms.com/crash.html.

25. Hackman, who portrayed FBI agent Joseph Sullivan, lost out to friend and former roommate Dustin Hoffman, who won the best actor Oscar for his role in Barry Levinson's *Rain Man.*

26. An array of excellent books exists that examine the events, players, and social-political-cultural milieu of Freedom Summer. One that pays special attention to this, through the prism of a few of the 700-plus volunteers on the ground in Mississippi, and their work and challenges on the grassroots level, is Bruce Watson's *Freedom Summer: The Savage Season That Made Mississippi Burn and Made America a Democracy* (New York: Viking, 2010).

27. Concerning the portrayal of African Americans and other criticisms of the film, see William H. Chafe, "Mississippi Burning," in *Past Imperfect: History According to the Movies*, ed. Mark C. Carnes (New York: Owl Books, 1996).

28. Among other texts, see Taylor Branch, *Pillar of Fire: America in the King Years, 1963–1965* (New York: Simon & Schuster, 1999); John Lewis, with Michael D'Orso, *Walking with the Wind: A Memoir of the Movement* (San Diego: Harcourt Brace, 1999); David Halberstam, *The Children* (New York: Fawcett Books, 1999); Ralph David Albernathy, *And the Walls Came Tumbling Down* (New York: Harper and Row, 1989); and Andrew Young, *An Easy Burden: The Civil Rights Movement and the Transformation of America* (New York: HarperCollins, 1996).

29. For a more specific, full, and accurate detailing of the range of issues and events surrounding Freedom Summer and the FBI investigation of the slayings of Schwerner, Goodman, and Chaney, one can consult numerous histories of the civil rights movement. Taylor Branch's exhaustive histories, for example, are one place to turn, as well as a 1994 installment of the ABC television news program *Turning Point*. The episode "Murder in Mississippi: The Cost of Freedom," hosted by Forrest Sawyer, follows on the heels of the thirtieth anniversary of the Freedom Summer, joining SNCC volunteers and their families as they make the journey back to Western College at Miami University in Oxford, Ohio, and Mississippi, to revisit this tumultuous turning point in the struggle for voting rights and equality.

30. Folksinger and civil rights advocate Joan Baez's song "Birmingham Sunday" (written by Richard Farina), which plays over the opening images in Spike Lee's *4 Little Girls*, documents the tragedy of that September morning. The song was included on Baez's 1964 album *Joan Baez/5* (Vanguard Records).

31. See the excellent Wallace timeline provided by the *American Experience* on PBS. *George Wallace: Settin' the Woods on Fire*: http://www.pbs.org/wgbh/amex/wallace/timeline/index_3.html.

32. As we write this, two volumes of Moore's Emmy-award winning *TV Nation* are available on VHS, meaning you may have to find a copy at an excellent public or university library, or

else find the time-traveling DeLorean from *Back to the Future* in order to find a copy. Yet both seasons of *The Awful Truth* are available, in their entirety, on DVD, so that those interested can have the opportunity to discuss and debate the vital issues and questions posed by Moore.

A good companion piece to the two provocative television segments would be Moore's book chapters "Why O. J. Is Innocent" in *Downsize This!* (1996) and "Kill Whitey" in *Stupid White Men* (2001).

33. *We Shall Remain* (2009): http://www.pbs.org/wgbh/amex/weshallremain/.
34. For more on *Reel Injun* (2010), see the film's website at: http://www.reelinjunthemovie.com/site/. Alternatively, see the National Film Board of Canada's website: http://www.nfb.ca/reel-injun/.
35. Commonly referred to as the "Hays Code" (after the code's director, former postmaster general Will Hays), these production codes were the censorship guidelines established by the Motion Pictures Producers and Distributors Association (MPPDA) and enforced by Hays. The MPPDA adopted the code in 1930.
36. A. O. Scott, "Meet the Sperm Donor: Modern Family Ties," *New York Times*, July 8, 2010: http://movies.nytimes.com/2010/07/09/movies/09kids.html.
37. Ibid.
38. Barack Obama, "Remarks by the President at Reception Commemorating the Enactment of the Matthew Shepard and James Byrd, Jr. Hate Crimes Prevention Act," October 28, 2009: http://www.whitehouse.gov/the-press-office/remarks-president-reception-commemorating-enactment-matthew-shepard-and-james-byrd-.
39. See *Out in the Silence* home page: http://wpsu.org/outinthesilence.
40. According to the organization, "The Mission of the Pennsylvania Family Institute is to strengthen families by restoring to public life the traditional, foundational principles and values essential for the well-being of society. We are a research and education organization devoted to restoring these values to our state and nation. We produce policy reports, promote responsible citizenship and work to promote unity among pro-family groups": http://www.pafamily.org/index.php?pID=6.
41. For an illuminating and incredibly detailed academic account of the making and blacklisting of Biberman's *Salt of the Earth*, see James J. Lorence, *The Suppression of Salt of the Earth: How Hollywood, Big Labor and Politicians Blacklisted a Movie in the American Cold War* (Albuquerque: University of New Mexico Press, 1999).
42. Eric Foner, "Matewan," in *Past Imperfect: History According to the Movies*, ed. Mark C. Carnes (New York: Owl Books, 1996), 204.
43. Desson Howe, *Washington Post*, October 16, 1987.
44. Foner, "Matewan," p. 204.
45. From the back cover of the DVD of *American Dream*.
46. The story is reminiscent of GFI America, Inc., a meatpacking firm that recruited illegal migrants in Texas to work in Minnesota. Promised work and housing, when the migrants arrived in Minneapolis they were dumped at a homeless shelter and told to report to work at a meatpacking plant. The homeless shelter provided a place for the migrants to stay but blew the whistle on GFI's plans. See Eric Schlosser, *Fast Food Nation: The Dark Side of the All-American Meal* (Boston: Houghton Mifflin, 2001), 162–63.
47. Peter Rachleff, *Hard-Pressed in the Heartland* (Boston: South End Press, 1993), 5.

48. Ibid.
49. "Cradle to grave" is Tom Kay's characterization of Moore's view that corporations have a responsibility to the communities and the workers beyond the company's bottom line.
50. Ernest Giglio, *Here's Looking at You*, 1ˢᵗ ed. (New York: Peter Lang, 2000), 43.
51. For Moore's response to allegations of inflated or false unemployment numbers, see CNN's *People in the News* profile of Moore, October 2002.
52. For caricatures and criticism (and more!) of Moore, witness South Park's creators Trey Parker and Matt Stone's unflattering depiction in their raucous, puppet-based *Team America: World Police* (2004), and *Airplane* director-producer David Zucker's *An American Carol* (2008), starring outspoken conservatives Jon Voight and Kelsey Grammer. *An American Carol* tells the tale of a slovenly America-and-Fourth-of-July-hating filmmaker, "Michael Malone" (Kevin Farley as a Moore doppelganger), who is visited by the ghosts of patriots and generals as he ponders his next liberal, divisive, anti-American project. See also Mike Wilson's *Michael Moore Hates America* (2004) and Larry Elder's *Michael and Me* (2004).
53. *Bowling for Columbine*, which in part examined the roots and consequences of American violence and obsession with guns, cost roughly $10 million to make and by early 2003 had grossed over $21 million. In December 2002, The International Documentary Association (IDA) named *Bowling for Columbine* the best documentary of all time, and in February 2003, Moore's unsettling film won an Academy Award.
54. Traverse City Film Festival mission: http://www.traversecityfilmfest.org/.
55. See *The Last Truck: Closing of a GM Plant* (2009): http://www.hbo.com/documentaries/the-last-truck-closing-of-a-gm-plant/index.html. Shortly after taking office, President Barack Obama faced a host of decisions concerning the shape, scope, and conditions for any potential continued federal government investment in the ailing American auto industry. For the context concerning the significance and debate surrounding these decisions, as well as the ultimate (as of 2010) success of the government's strongly conditioned investment in the auto industry, see Steven Rattner, *Overhaul: An Insider's Account of the Obama Administration's Rescue of the Auto Industry* (New York: Houghton Mifflin Harcourt, 2010).
56. Robert A. Saunders, *The Many Faces of Sacha Baron Cohen: Politics, Parody and the Battle over Borat* (Lanham, MD: Lexington Books, 2008), 136.

MEDIA, POLITICS, AND SATIRE

I want angry shows.
—DIANA CHRISTENSEN (FAYE DUNAWAY), *NETWORK* (1976)

If we amplify everything, we hear nothing.
—JON STEWART, FROM CONCLUDING REMARKS AT THE RALLY TO RESTORE SANITY
AND/OR FEAR (2010)

Introduction

In our discussion of film and television we often forget the vital importance of the media that deliver the messages. What has been called the Fourth Estate is exceedingly vital to a democratic society. If citizens are to make decisions about pressing, occasionally complex, issues facing their lives and countries, then they must be informed about such dynamics, problems, and proposed solutions. The press serves as the primary institution to help people understand these challenges. While not a formal institution of government, media outlets play an essential role in informing the public. Yet, because the press (especially in the United States) is not a part of government, there is a need to finance these organizations. In order for the press to bring us the news they must generate revenue to survive. This need for profit creates a tension between the need for public information, a public service, and the requirements of business enterprises to make money.

Currently, longtime journalists and media scholars worry about potentially devastating trends. Terry McDermott, a reporter for over thirty years with the *Los Angeles Times*, wrote in 2010 that "news" as it is currently portrayed on cable television is little more than talking. Hosts talk to reporters, guests, and themselves. "The guests are a familiar collection of politicians, political operatives, journalists, some experts, and a group we call expert commentators."[1] However, very little reporting of news actually occurs, as there are very few bureaus and journalists investigating stories. Instead, there is a series of individuals reacting to news events.

There should be no doubt as to the central power media have within a society. The great military tactician Napoleon Bonaparte once noted that "four hostile newspapers are more to be feared than a thousand bayonets." Further, a line written by Edward Bulwer-Lytton in 1839, that "the pen is mightier than the sword," serves as a reminder about the ability of the press to shape public and elite opinion. The founders of the American republic held that a free press was an important check on government—without it, democracy could not thrive. Yet, there is a concern that media outlets could overstep their essential bounds as reliable, responsible watchdogs and informers; after all, if the press is indeed the Fourth Estate, and an unelected institution at that, its powers could potentially exceed those of the more accountable, democratically elected branches of government.

Accusations often fly between media outlets and governments about the proper role of each. There are concerns from governments that newspapers, television, and journalists in general try to alter the public agenda and/or manipulate government policy; similarly, media outlets often claim that the government attempts to unduly influence and/or distort information in an attempt to control a story. Such an example would be the infamous "Friday dump": the government's act of releasing unpleasant, controversial, or embarrassing news on a Friday in order to limit the story's impact. The media's 24-hour news cycle will go straight into the weekend, thereby diminishing negative coverage and public outrage.

Moreover, media organizations are also wary of official government sources, often in cahoots with public relations agencies, deliberately using the unwitting press as vehicles for propaganda—such as the government's controversial practice of producing their own "video news releases" (VNR) for dissemination on national and local television news. These news "reports," while they look and sound like the work of independent television journalists,[2] are actually produced by governmental departments and entities to place a positive spin on specific programs and policies. Indeed, on some occasions local news broadcasts will run the VNR without any editing whatsoever, adding their own "local twist by simply having their own reporter read the script" that the government has provided. If you are watching your local news in Albany and you think you have just consumed an impartial report on the merits of a particular president's education policies, you may want to think again.[3]

There is evidence to support both claims of media manipulation and story management from around the world. The ability to establish the context by which the public understands a problem or issue is a powerful proposition. We can look back at the Spanish-American War (1898) as an example of where the so-called Yellow Press framed incidents in Cuba in an attempt to drum up support for a war against Spain with the objective of trying to seize some of Spain's colonies.[4] Yet, writers and journalists like Upton Sinclair, working at roughly the same time, used their talents to help expose the excesses of industrial life. Specifically, Sinclair's revelations of the meatpacking industry in his novel *The Jungle* (1906) led to reforms within the United States.[5]

In the early days of movies, the world of journalism often provided the kind of drama that is useful for films. Because journalists are uncovering stories, there is an element of tension and storytelling that is conducive to filmmaking. During the golden age of Hollywood, films often depicted a gritty, but exciting, world of truth seeking, as depicted in such films as *His Girl Friday* (1940), *Gentleman's Agreement* (1947), and *Call Northside 777* (1948). Sometimes ethical, determined, and civic-minded journalists would be up against powerful interests, like organized crime or corrupt politicians, as in *Afraid to Talk* (1932) and *Deadline U.S.A.* (1952). As time has passed, however, films have become increasingly more cynical about the profession of journalism.

The Media and Film: Ethics and Responsibility, Private Profit or Public Interest?

There has always been a tension between what a free press should do: Is it an institution that protects the public's interest, or is it an entity that is (and should be) solely driven by profit? After all, unlike news enterprises such as the British Broadcasting Corporation (BBC) or the Canadian Broadcasting Corporation (CBC), which are public entities funded by the government, media outlets in the United States are businesses that require profits to be accrued to shareholders. Advertising and ratings must produce profit, not merely inform the electorate. This tension even existed during the golden age of Hollywood. For example, in *Nothing Sacred* (1937), Fredric March stars as a reporter who seeks to reestablish his sullied reputation by proposing a series of stories about a doomed young woman named Hazel (Carole Lombard) who is sick with radium poisoning. March's newspaper provides a last fling for Hazel; the only problem is that, unbeknownst to the newspaper, Hazel does not have a fatal condition. The dilemma presented in the film is: Should the newspaper be intimately involved with covering a story that benefits them financially but is ultimately untrue? A similar conundrum is found in the popular Oscar winner *It Happened One Night* (1934), directed by Frank Capra. Clark Gable plays Peter Warne, a reporter who is ordered to cover Ellie Andrews (Claudette Colbert), a socialite who is running away from her wedding. Warne is torn between his duty to cover the story he is assigned and protecting the privacy and desires of the woman he has fallen in love with.

Both *Nothing Sacred* and *It Happened One Night* are screwball comedies that use very serious topics to humorous effect. Nevertheless, both are statements about journalistic ethics, and the proper balance between what the public *wants* to know and what they *need* to know. *Meet John Doe* (1941), also directed by Frank Capra, is a much more serious examination of the tensions between private profit and public responsibility. In the film, in order to keep her job, a reporter publishes a fictitious letter stating that the author will kill himself to protest society's ills. The reporter (Barbara Stanwyck) and her editor hire a down-on-his-luck man (Gary Cooper) to impersonate John Doe, the author of the letter. As the story grows in the public's imagination, the letter and John Doe spark a political movement, which is ultimately manipulated by the newspaper and existing political interests. Like most Capra films, the story ends on a hopeful note with faith in common people restored. Yet, the film remains an interesting statement about the ethics of the press and politicians on the eve of American participation in World War II.[6]

A heroic portrayal of newspaper reporters as honorable, shoe-leather-pounding-the-pavement-for-truth-and-justice citizens is *Call Northside 777* (1948). The film stars Jimmy Stewart as P. J. "Jim" McNeal, an honest and dogged Chicago reporter who ultimately exonerates an innocent man sentenced to death for the murder of a policeman. McNeal is initially skeptical of the incarcerated man's innocence and for much of the film believes the sentenced man is guilty. Can he find out what really happened and free an innocent man before the parole board's deadline? Proof that this "ethical journalist in a race-against-time" plotline continues to periodically pop up in screenplays is Clint Eastwood's tepidly received *True Crime* (1999), in which the Hollywood icon plays a washed-up reporter who is assigned to cover the execution of an innocent man. Like Stewart's indefatigable character in *Northside*, Eastwood puts the pieces of the murder puzzle together in just the nick of time.

The Heroic Press and a Corrupt Government: Watergate and *All the President's Men*

As films moved into the latter part of the twentieth century—especially in the Vietnam and Watergate era—they became much more pessimistic about the press and politics. Made in the same year as *Network* (1976), a scathing criticism of the media, *All the President's Men* chronicles *Washington Post* reporters Carl Bernstein (Dustin Hoffman) and Bob Woodward (Robert Redford) as they uncover the political scandal known as Watergate. The film follows their investigative reporting exploits from the break-in at the Democratic National Committee Headquarters at the Watergate office building in June 1972, and the arrest of the burglars, to the eventual resignation of President Richard Nixon in August 1974. Indeed, on more than one occasion, the crusty, sage editor of the *Post*, Ben Bradlee (Jason Robards), hounds "Woodstein" (his nickname for Woodward and Bernstein) for more sources and refuses to run some of their Watergate articles. Bradlee demands multiple sources, as he does not want the veracity and ethics of the paper to be challenged. As he tells his ace reporters, "There's nothing at stake here except the Constitution and the Presidency of the United States." Simply put, this is serious, serious business, and since the media can have an overwhelming effect on public opinion and political institutions, the press must go the extra mile for accuracy and the public interest.

What Was Watergate?

Almost every American political scandal since the mid-1970s has adopted a title that includes "gate" at the end of the title (for example, Iran-Contra-gate, Whitewater-gate, etc.). These are all references back to the original "gate"—Watergate. The scandal and cover-up that came to be known as Watergate was the most significant political and constitutional scandal in the United States during the twentieth century.

The term "Watergate" refers to the hotel/apartment complex along the Potomac River in Washington, D.C., where an infamous crime took place. On June 17, 1972, a group of Republican operatives, led by G. Gordon Liddy, broke into Democratic National Headquarters located in the Watergate complex to steal sensitive information about the election campaign of the party's nominee, Senator George McGovern, and to install listening devices. Liddy and his cohorts were funded and paid by the Committee to Re-Elect the President (CREEP), a Republican campaign apparatus chaired by Attorney General John Mitchell and determined to help facilitate the reelection of President Richard Nixon.

Initially the White House denied all knowledge and dismissed the incident; however, as Bob Woodward and Carl Bernstein began to investigate the incident, it became clear that many people working in the White House had knowledge of and sanctioned the break-in. President Nixon would go on to win the 1972 president election in a landslide. Yet, as the cover-up began to unravel, the question around Washington was, "What did the president know and when did he know it?"

Congressional hearings continued to bring pressure on the White House and President Nixon, specifically. Evidence continued to mount that the White House used the FBI to spy on Democrats in the run-up to the election, which amounted to an abuse of power. Further, there was evidence to suggest that the White House was using the various agencies of the federal government to help win elections. It became increasingly clear to many that the White House had engaged in a cover-up about the crime. If this was true, people in the White House, and perhaps even the president himself, were guilty of conspiracy and obstruction of justice.

With support for the president evaporating, and the Congress on the verge of impeaching him, a group of Republican senators went to the White House to counsel President Nixon to step down. On August 9, 1974, Richard M. Nixon became the first president in American history to resign. Soon after assuming the presidency, Gerald Ford pardoned Nixon for all crimes related to the Watergate scandal in a move he believed would help to heal growing national discord and distrust of political institutions and politics. The move effectively ended the scandal in terms of the formal legal and political process in Washington. Yet, the saga of Watergate and the role, motives, and psychological dimensions of the man at the center of the storm remain fertile terrain for scholars and filmmakers.

In addition to *All the President's Men,* there are a number of films that examine Watergate and the aftereffects. For a psychological profile of Nixon from childhood through Watergate, see Oliver Stone's controversial and remarkably sympathetic presidential psychohistory *Nixon* (1995), starring Anthony Hopkins as Nixon. For a comedic, over-the-top, and purposely absurd retelling of Watergate—from the point of view of innocent teens unexpectedly caught up in the imbroglio (Kirstin Dunst and Michelle Williams)—see Dan Hedaya as Richard Nixon in the lighthearted *Dick* (1999). The saga of Watergate and Richard Nixon's lengthy postpresidential interviews with British journalist David Frost are examined in the Tony Award–winning play and later the major motion picture *Frost/Nixon* (2008), featuring Frank Langella as the embattled thirty-seventh president. Finally, for fans of sophisticated animated comedy, Nixon and Watergate are satirized in the *Futurama* episode "A Head in the Polls" (1999).

Angry Prophets + Angry Shows = Profits: *Network*

In contrast to the heroic portrayal of Woodward and Bernstein—and the institution of the press in general—*All the President's Men* portrays the government, politicians, and political players in a very dark and shadowy light. For example, the pressroom at the *Post* is perpetually bathed in brightness, whereas the corridors of power and national monuments in Washington, D.C., are almost always shot in the dark. Thus, the government is frequently presented as an ominous institution where no one can be trusted and the depth of corruption is unimaginable. In contrast, the reporters are saviors, shedding light on corruption and exposing the illegal chicanery and dirty tricks at the heart of Watergate.[7] Here we see responsible media clearly acting in the public interest—a far cry from the irresponsible cutthroat greed and corporate madness of *Network* (1976).

There could not be more dramatic difference in how the media are portrayed in *Network* and *All the President's Men*. While *All the President's Men* presents dogged, ethical reporters who are overly concerned with arriving at the truth and getting verification of their story, *Network* depicts the media as increasingly controlled by dominant, ruthless, profit-driven corporations unconcerned with truth or the public interest, as evidenced by the surrealistic, unscripted commentary from former news anchor and now "mad prophet of the airwaves" Howard Beale:

> Ladies and gentlemen, I would like at this moment to announce that I will be retiring in two weeks' time because of poor ratings . . . and since this show is the only thing I had going for me in my life, I have decided to kill myself. I'm going to blow my brains out right on this program a week from today. So tune in next Tuesday. That'll give the public relations people a week to promote the show. That ought to get a hell of a rating, a fifty share easy.[8]

Sidney Lumet's classic, acerbic tale of television journalism and media ethics gone mad (and we mean, *really, really mad*), *Network* chronicles the descent of responsible, enlightened television journalism into the revolting, obnoxious swamp of entertainment, titillation, violence, ratings, and greed. The deterioration of a once-venerated institution has been triggered—and accelerated—by the mergers of giant multinational corporations hell-bent on maximizing profits, no matter the cost to civility, truth, public discourse, or even the well-being of its own employees. Whatever will increase ratings and generate advertising dollars—whether it is ranting lunatics, live terrorism, or palm readers—is what will go on the air. Long gone are the halcyon days when corporations' news divisions—staffed by serious, professional journalists—were allowed and expected to run deficits in order to provide the range and quality of coverage and expertise necessary to inform the populace. Now the news, much like the game shows and sitcoms with their explicit corporate sponsors and steady advertising revenue, must reach ratings nirvana, enhancing the bottom line rather than the public interest.

Paddy Chayefsky's prophetic screenplay, winner of the 1977 Academy Award, brilliantly satirizes the brave new world of international mega-corporate television and those who make it tick. In *Network*, the chief villains who turn the news division of UBS (United Broadcasting System) upside down in the hunt for a ratings winner and deeper profits are UBS vice president of programming Diana Christensen (Faye Dunaway) and Frank Hackett, UBS executive senior vice president and chairman of the board (Robert Duvall). Although he has become emotionally unhinged and now spends his time ranting and raving, urging everyone to go to their window and yell, "I'm as mad as hell, and I'm not going to take it anymore!" Howard Beale is somewhat of a hero here, as, even in his state of dementia, he understands the inordinate power of television in this modern age. In his new role as "mad prophet of the airwaves" on his own show, *The Howard Beale Show*, Beale articulates the danger of relying on television for reality, deeper truths, and meaning:

> There is a whole and entire generation right now who never knew anything that didn't come out of this tube. This tube is the gospel. This tube is the ultimate revelation. This tube can make or break presidents, popes, and prime ministers. This tube is the most awesome goddam force in the whole godless world! And woe is us if it ever falls in the hands of the wrong people. . . . Television is not the truth! Television is a goddamned amusement park. Television is a circus, a carnival, a traveling troupe of acrobats and story-tellers, singers and dancers, jugglers, sideshow freaks, lion-tamers and football players. We're in the boredom-killing business! If you want truth go to God, go to your guru, go to yourself because that's the only place you'll ever find any real truth. But man, you're never going to get any truth from us. We'll tell you anything you want to hear. We lie like hell![9]

Chayefsky's over-the-top, in-your-face critique of television ratings obsession, profit maximization, media monopolies, and the mega-multinational conglomerate Wizards of Oz[10] presents us with a sobering and depressing dilemma in a political system such as ours. To be informed, enlightened citizens and voters, we must rely on vigilant, responsible media with some sense of the public interest to give us the tools to participate and make thoughtful decisions. But what if the media have little to no interest in the public interest? What if the quest for private profits substantially outweighs any concern for the accuracy or the health of democracy? Do we live in a world of reality shows, and entertaining and ideologically driven "shout shows" on cable television, that all too often pass for deliberative cultural and political discussions? The question is: How do we further the public interest and inform, rather than merely entertain, the citizenry? In the final analysis, the ranting, hyperactive, unhinged Howard Beale of *Network* just may be prescient. But an "amusement park" is hardly a solid foundation on which to build an informed, engaged citizenry and a robust democracy.

Paddy Chayefsky's assessment and dissection of news, ratings, and corporate reality in *Network* also inform a contemporary examination of the world of 24-hour cable news networks—namely, CNN, Fox, and MSNBC—and the degree to which they offer commentary rather actual, meaningful news. Journalist and media scholar Terry McDermott argues that while much is made of the fairly obvious adherence to a particular viewpoint, the real story is the shocking dearth of actual news reporting. Rather than using their omnipresent status to inform via the substantive *reporting* of news stories, the cable news networks tend to *comment* on stories and political figures, oftentimes doing so via incoherent, quirky conversations between popular personalities, with an emphasis on performance and ideological certainty. But what are they actually talk *about*? McDermott suggests that what most cable news offers is not news but, rather, a constant barrage of ideological bluster and tactical considerations, and accusations and pontifications about who the news is good for, or who is selling out the country. In a stunning indictment, McDermott concludes that news hosts and pundits are little more than modern-day Howard Beales from *Network*.[11]

It is clear that cable news networks play a vital role in the political socialization process, galvanizing partisans through the repetition of specific story lines, frames, and commentary. Alexandra Pelosi's documentary *Right America: Feeling Wronged* (2009), for example, illustrates the significant role of cable news media outlets in shaping a slice of the electorate's perceptions of major political, economic, and cultural issues. In the film, Pelosi travels to twenty-seven states during the 2008 presidential election between John McCain and Barack Obama, interviewing activist, rally-attending, door-knocking conservative supporters of the McCain–Palin ticket to discern their primary objections to the Obama candidacy. One of the dynamics that emerges is the singular prominence and influence of Fox News in providing conservative citizens with their news. At McCain and Palin rallies, Sean Hannity, conservative Fox News personality and also a popular radio host, is treated as royalty by the legions of attendees. Although they still differ somewhat in tone and content, in recent years, it is clear that MSNBC has emerged as an ideological counterweight to Fox News, devoting a number of hours, primarily in the evenings, to liberal commentary and opinion programs, with hosts such as Chris Matthews, Lawrence O'Donnell, Rachel Maddow, and Ed Shultz offering opinion and analysis of current events.

Local television news knows that covering murders and violent crimes is profitable. Thus, producers choose stories based on the aphorism "if it bleeds, it leads."[12] This phenomenon, and its effects on Americans' psyche, is addressed by sociologist Barry Glassner in his book *The Culture of Fear*.[13] The widespread consequences of this fear lie at the heart of Michael Moore's *Bowling for Columbine* (2002), Academy Award winner for best documentary feature. Posing the question, "Are we a nation of gun nuts. . .or are we just nuts?" Moore examines the root causes of America's fear-driven culture, identifying the ways in which rampant anxiety shapes our lives. While supportive of gun control measures, Moore posits that it is more than *just* lax gun laws and easy access to firearms that lead to America's deadly rates of gun violence. Specifically, the film argues that our obsession with cutthroat capitalism and fear of the other (whether black men or African bees), along with a series of other suspicions and worries driven by media stereotypes and the drive for profit, create a climate in which citizens are conditioned to react violently.

Although accelerated in recent times, the tension between profit and public service is not all that new. In *Good Night, and Good Luck* (2005), which tells the true story of Edward R. Murrow's battle with Senator Joseph McCarthy in the 1950s over the House Un-American Activities Committee (HUAC) hearings, we find similar concerns. Murrow (David Strathairn) and his colleagues, especially CBS boss Fred Friendly (George Clooney), are more interested and motivated by news stories that affect the lives of Americans. However, the television network on which Murrow appears, CBS, is interested in entertainment stories that will not make sponsors (those who advertise) uncomfortable. Murrow was forced to do interviews with celebrities (in the film, Murrow's vapid interview with Liberace is juxtaposed with the threat to free speech) in order to conduct his investigative claims of the notorious Senator Joseph McCarthy, who falsely accused a variety of government officials of being communists. He was pressured to conduct four celebrity interviews for every news program. By the end, McCarthy is exposed as a charlatan and his claims are discredited; however, it comes with a tinge of regret because such civic-minded yet less monetarily profitable journalistic efforts will become more difficult in the future. It is perhaps instructive that at the end of the day it is the news stories that have a lasting impact. Today, Murrow is remembered for his wartime broadcasts from London and his investigation and commentary about McCarthyism rather than his celebrity interviews.[14]

Soft News and Modern Journalism: *Broadcast News*

I watched your six o'clock news today. It's straight tabloid. You had a minute and
a half on that lady riding a bike naked in Central Park. On the other hand, you
had less than a minute of hard national and international news. It was all sex, scandal, brutal crimes, sports, children with incurable diseases and lost puppies. So I
don't think I'll listen to any protestations of high standards of journalism. You're
right down the street soliciting audiences like the rest of us. All I'm saying is, if
you're going to hustle, at least do it right.

—DIANA CHRISTENSEN (FAYE DUNAWAY), *NETWORK* (1976)[15]

Critics claim that television news has descended into an abyss of soft news,
something that might entertain the public but does not inform. Moreover,
media and politics scholars have also noted that, even when the subject is
apparent hard news or crucial current events, the media often approach it
from either an entertaining, conflict-driven framework or shortchange serious
matters through the overuse of narratives.[16] Soft news, therefore, is information
about celebrities, popular culture, and human interest that does not help maintain the democratic balance within a society.[17] In the quest for higher ratings,
and thus more advertisers, news outlets have increasingly turned to softer news
to draw viewers.[18]

Criticism of how corporate news media serve the public is nothing new. The
trend in late twentieth-century news was to move away from public service to
ensuring that the news division of a network was making a profit (see, for example, the aforementioned *Network* and *Good Night, and Good Luck*).[19] These
concerns are addressed by the James L. Brooks film *Broadcast News* (1987).
Although a romantic comedy, *Broadcast News* delves into some of the moral and
ethical dilemmas facing broadcast journalism. The film is eerily prescient as it
follows the Washington news bureau of a major television network. Jane (Holly
Hunter) is a super-organized news producer who is best friends with Aaron
(Albert Brooks), an energetic and smart reporter. After putting together a
piece on returning veterans that wins accolades from their colleagues, Jane gives
a speech to broadcast journalists in which she decries the movement towards
looks over substances. When the camera pans over the audience, it is comprised
primarily of well-tanned blondes who are bored with the speech. When audience members begin leaving the talk, Jane jumps to a video clip to illustrate her
point. All three networks carried a story of a massive domino fall in an Asian
country, which, while entertaining, is not news. As Jane explains the trouble
with passing such items off as news, the audience becomes transfixed by the

dominos falling and applauds at the completion of the tape. Jane feels like a failure.

At the same time she meets her news colleague and potential love inter-est Tom (William Hurt), who is, incidentally, blonde and good looking. He liked her speech and message but confesses not to understand the news he is reporting. Tom is assigned to the Washington bureau and during a crisis is tapped to anchor a breaking news story, while Aaron is completely cut out, even though he has the contacts and is knowledgeable about the situation. In the run-up to airtime, Jane and the news team are busy preparing the special report; Aaron calls the bureau to offer background and contacts, while Tom concerns himself with which shirt and tie he will wear on the air.

The special report is a success; however, it is the *news team* rather than the anchor that has pulled it off. Aaron rhetorically asks, "What is the next step . . . lip synching?" When Tom does produce his own story, it manages to pull at the heartstrings of everyone, with the exception of the hard-boiled journal-istic Aaron, who views the report as less news than social issue. Tom manages a few tears to demonstrate his concern. Historically, reporters showing their emotions while reporting a story has been frowned upon; reporters are supposed to hold their emotions in check and to report facts to the public. It was con-sidered significant when the king of news anchors Walter Cronkite showed emotion during a report. Famously, Cronkite showed significant emotion on two dramatic occasions: reporting on the assassination of President Kennedy in 1963 and on the landing of the first men on the moon in 1969. Today, news anchors and commentators regularly display emotion, presumably to garner higher ratings.

The success of the special report means Tom is in line to eventually be net-work news anchor. Traditionally, the news anchor is not only the face of the network but also serves as managing editor, essentially the top reporter of the network. In the film, while all of this is going on, the network is facing major budget cuts, a situation that was, and is, all too real.[20] All the people who helped to make the special report a success, the behind-the-scenes reporters and tech-nical help, are subject to losing their jobs. When the network anchor (Jack Nicholson) visits the Washington bureau as a sign of solidarity, one executive half-jokingly comments that if he were to take a pay cut of a million a year, then they could save most of the jobs, a suggestion that is not taken to be funny.

As the love story culminates, so does the professional story. Aaron cautions Jane about Tom. In reality it is a warning to the audience. He says that Tom is a nice guy but that he is not worthy of Jane (and by extension, the public). Tom is not smart, he is not knowledgeable; he is a good-looking empty suit that does not understand the words coming out of his mouth. The screenplay, written by James L. Brooks, does not mince words with the implications:

> Please don't take it wrong when I tell you that I believe that Tom, while a very nice guy, is the Devil. . . . What do you think the Devil is going to look like if he's around? Nobody is going to be taken in if he has a long, red, pointy tail. No. I'm semi-serious here. He will look attractive and he will be nice and helpful and he will get a job where he influences a great God-fearing nation and he will never do an evil thing, he will just bit by little bit lower standards where they are important. Just coax along flash over substance, just a tiny bit. And he will talk about all of us really being salesmen. (Pause.) And he'll get all the great women. (James L. Brooks, *Broadcast News*, New York, Vintage Books, 1988, page 139.)

While the indictment of television news is devastating, there is more below the surface we should consider. Jane rejects the staging of events, yet she asks a soldier to put on boots, for dramatic effect, so that the camera crew can film it (just a wee bit of lowering of standards). Yet, when the scene wins her praise, she gladly accepts the accolades and presumably engages in more of it. When Aaron seeks a promotion to news anchor, he goes to Tom for advice on how to dress and enunciate. By contract, Tom recognizes that he is not very informed and freely acknowledges those who work to make him look good on screen.

Different Channels, Different Truths: *Control Room*

All too often, our perspective of particular political events is shaped by the nature of our connection to the story. If an audience is not directly tied to the story, it is not news.[21] In the case of the documentary *Control Room* (2004), the audience impacted is the Iraqi people, and the event is the American invasion. The film chronicles how a global television news organization, the Arab-language satellite channel Al-Jazeera, covers the American invasion of Iraq in 2003. The network is very popular in the Arab world because it covers Arab news and focuses on Arab perspectives (as opposed to Western perspectives carried by CNN or the BBC). *Control Room* follows several employees of Al-Jazeera from the beginning of the war to the end of major combat operations as announced by President George W. Bush on May 1, 2003. What emerges in the film is a picture of war, how governments want it covered by the press, the dangers journalists face, and the struggle to remain objective in the face devastating events and images in the Arab world. The filmmakers are less interested in the organizational particulars of Al-Jazeera and more concerned about the story of journalists in wartime.

Al-Jazeera is famous (or infamous) for its reporting of the Iraq War from an Arab perspective. During the course of the war, then–secretary of defense Donald Rumsfeld labeled the network as a propaganda mouthpiece for the regime of Saddam Hussein because it told the Iraqi side of the war. Al-Jazeera came under heavy criticism and even faced threats when the network broad-cast images of dead American soldiers and prisoners of war (POWs). Rumsfeld decried the displaying of such images as contrary to the rules of war as estab-lished by the Geneva Conventions.[22] As the filmmakers point out, a few days earlier Western television networks broadcast images of dead Iraqi soldiers. An American lieutenant responsible for media relations admits in the film that when he saw the images of dead Iraqi soldiers it did not affect him as much as when he saw the images of dead Americans. Because Al-Jazeera was covering the news from the Arab perspective the focus was on how the war affected Iraqis (Arabs), not Americans.

Interestingly, although Al-Jazeera came under heavy criticism from the United States during the war and the building that housed Al-Jazeera was struck by American missiles, killing a correspondent, the network was condemned by Arab governments as well. Al-Jazeera regularly invites American officials on their interview programs to explain Americans policies. At one point, the Iraqi Minister for Information demanded Al-Jazeera stop "broadcasting American propaganda" (the opposite of what American officials demanded). *Control Room* provides an excellent demonstration of how various media out-lets might cover a story differently. What is impressive is that it is also an object lesson on how people might understand a situation or problem from a differ-ent perspective. At the same time, *Control Room* helps to demonstrate how humans are the same. Those who work for Al-Jazeera do their best to cover the story and want good things for the families, perhaps even the American dream itself. Politics and the way media cover politics, especially during wartime, can be very complex, and this film helps to demonstrate how and why people might draw very different lessons from the same events.[23]

The Rally to Restore Sanity and/or Fear: Stewart, Colbert, and 200,000 Friends Go to Washington

The Death Star was an outside job, and so was 9/11.

The Voices In my HEAD SAY CHOOSE SANITY

We're all in this together. Let's act like it.

Legalize Gay Marriage They have the right to regret their decisions too!

WTF, I thought I voted for a Muslim?!

A festival-like atmosphere permeated the nation's capital on October 30, 2010, when comedians Jon Stewart and Stephen Colbert hosted an afternoon of political satire, music, and media criticism on the National Mall. Encouraged to bring homemade signs, legions of fans obliged, sporting deliberately nonideological, irreverent, and humorous posters. At the close of the rally, Stewart emphasized the need for media responsibility and civility in our political discourse.

Satire and Media: *The Daily Show with Jon Stewart*
The 24-Hour Media Circus Meets a Mighty
(and Eloquent) "New Form of Desperation"

I think of myself as a comedian who has the pleasure of writing jokes about things
that I actually care about. And that's really it.
—JON STEWART (2003)[24]

The Daily Show with Jon Stewart has become a staple of American late night
television and an indispensable component of contemporary popular culture,
media, and political criticism. In a poll conducted by *Time* magazine after the
death of legendary CBS news anchor Walter Cronkite, Stewart was named the
most trusted news anchor in America, winning with a resounding "44% of the
vote, beating out Brian Williams, Charlie Gibson and Katie Couric."[25] Stewart
has, since he began hosting the Comedy Central show in 1999, cultivated a
loyal and attentive following. His status as a media critic gained legendary status when he appeared on the now-defunct *Crossfire* in October 2004, a longtime staple of cable news' combative, two-sides-to-all issues opinion program.
Stewart's critical assessment of the show's format—which he believed accen-
tuated differences to the detriment of civil discourse—went "viral" on the
Internet and beyond, and as the show's ratings continued to plummet, *Crossfire*
was cancelled three months after Stewart's appearance. It is significant to note
that, when asked about the show's demise, the president of CNN, Jonathan
Klein, noted that Stewart offered legitimate criticism of the program, and that
the show did "nothing to illuminate the issues of the day."[26] As Theodore
Hamm, an associate professor of urban studies and author of *The New Blue
Media* (2008), has noted, Stewart's official self-designation as a comedian,
rather than allowing himself to be pigeonholed as *solely* a media or a political
critic, "removes the intellectual burdens that go along with" such labels, and
liberates the prescient satirist from having to "explain his positions or advocate
specific ideas."[27]

Stewart's role as trusted satirist-jester-commentator was especially apparent when, in the weeks leading up to the 2010 midterm elections, he and his
faux-conservative blowhard nemesis Stephen Colbert, host of *The Colbert
Report*, organized a "Rally to Restore Sanity and/or Fear."[28] Attracting an estimated 215,000 to the National Mall on October 30, 2010, the satirists combined music, sketches, catharsis, and media analysis to produce an eclectic,
timely assessment of an unnecessarily fractured and polarized media and political landscape.[29] Towards the end of the rally, laughter gave way to a critique

of not only the news media but the culture of bitter partisan bickering. It is significant that in his concluding speech at the rally Stewart changed into a suit and tie to make a plea for civility, and to highlight his point that most people in the United States work together (unlike the politicians in Washington or pundits and ideologues on 24-hour cable news).[30] Addressing various criticisms and pundit pontifications regarding the mission of the rally, and the supposed proper role of comedians in public discourse, Stewart brought the rousing rally to a close with an extended moment of candor and eloquence:

> I can't control what people think this was. I can only tell you my intentions. This was not a rally to ridicule people of faith or people of activism or to look down our noses at the heartland or at passionate argument or to suggest that times are not difficult and that we have nothing to fear. . . . The press can hold its magnifying glass up to our problems bringing them into focus, illuminating issues heretofore unseen or they can use that magnifying glass to light ants on fire and then perhaps host a week of shows on the sudden, unexpected dangerous flaming ant epidemic. If we amplify everything, we hear nothing.[31]

Jon Stewart is clearly a satirist, and an erudite one at that. His frequent comedic critiques of the occasional coziness, laziness, and self-importance of the Washington establishment, and hyperbolic media outlets that frequently "light ants on fire" rather than bring clarity and context to our problems, reveal a media oftentimes focused on celebrity, noise, conflict, and ratings at the expense of an informed, reasoned citizenry. Rather than being vigilant watchdogs acting in the public interest, enlightening citizens on the most vital issues of the day, all too often the cable news machine (along with its ideologically rigid brethren of the blogosphere) advances pre-ordained narratives that eschew reason and nuance, to the detriment of a civil society.

As noted by Theodore Hamm, during a lengthy interview Stewart conducted with Bill Moyers, journalist, commentator, and former aide to President Lyndon Johnson, when Moyers suggested that Stewart's *The Daily Show* was an astute, vital, and powerful mixture of *journalism* and satire—"I do not know whether you are practicing an old form of parody and satire. . .or a new form of journalism"—Stewart acknowledged that the program was engaged in the media and political-criticism business but perhaps as a matter of necessity and desperation:

> Well then that either speaks to the sad state of comedy or the sad state of news. I can't figure out which one. I think, honestly, we're practicing a new form of desperation. We are just so inundated with mixed messages from the media and from politicians that we're just trying to sort it out for ourselves.[32]

In essence what Stewart and Colbert are expressing, night after night, is frustration, outrage, and sadness over a media universe and political climate that have become so toxic in recent years that one prominent media analyst has called journalism a "blood sport," designed to enrage and entertain rather than inform the public.[33]

At the same time, Stewart's fundamental frustration—he has occasionally asked, "Did I mention that I give up?" after showing segments of especially egregious media and political malfeasance—has not deterred the court jester from taking on the more serious role of public policy advocate when deemed necessary. Perhaps the most direct example of this is Stewart's passionate devotion of two episodes of The Daily Show to the plight of September 11th first responders, individuals who faced life-threatening illnesses as a result of their exposure to myriad hazardous materials during cleanup efforts at Ground Zero. After the Senate failed yet again to pass a measure to fund medical care for the first responders, and the media neglected to cover it substantively, if at all— Stewart decided to show the country the face and struggles of several severely ill individuals who continued to face uncertainty due to the lack of medical treatment. Much of the U.S. media as well as partisanship were abandoning the responders, so Stewart used his platform to illustrate the human costs of inaction. On The Daily Show, Ground Zero workers with cancer, cardiac problems, and severe respiratory conditions told their stories. Several days later, legislation that was blocked for months would pass, establishing a fund for September 11th first responders' medical care. Many media outlets and several elected officials credited Stewart's efforts with the bill's passage.[34]

In the final analysis, no matter the media performance, there is one constant ingredient in the Daily Show's cocktail of satire and silliness. As a profile in the New York Times asserted, Stewart stands as a "sane voice in a noisy red-blue echo chamber" and "displays an impatience with the platitudes of both the right and the left and a disdain for commentators who parrot party-line talking points and engage in knee-jerk shouting matches."[35]

Conclusion

After an opening sequence in which a Fox News helicopter, emblazoned with the slogan, "Fox News: Not Racist, But #1 with Racists," careens to the ground ("We're not fair, we're not balanced!" is heard from the frantic cockpit), The Simpsons episode "The Fool Monty" (2010) commenced with a media confab of leading network programmers and executives. Here, we see the money-grubbing elites ponder ways to drum up fake epidemics (or other manufactured calamities!) in order to scare the dickens out of the American public and, thus, capture higher ratings and profits.[36] The fictional corporate media honchos featured in animated form are more interested in private profit than advancing the public interest, and their chief vehicle to reach this destination is fear.

This satirical, over-the-top send-up of the motives and tactics of large media conglomerates is not new. As we have indicated, Paddy Chayefsky's *Network* covered this terrain in vivid detail, and Michael Moore's *Bowling for Columbine* revisited this perspective via the program COPS as well as warped local news coverage centered on violence and anxiety out of sync with reality. Yet in the age of *The Daily Show* and *The Colbert Report*, this animated critique of the economic bottom line and pervasive media infotainment may resonate more than some media executives might appreciate. The incongruity of media responsibility and the public interest vs. corporate profits that produces stories meant to engender fear is perhaps best, or at least most consistently, communicated by the faux-conservative TV talk show host Stephen Colbert. He gleefully "works" to scare viewers on a nightly basis (or at least, most Mondays–Thursdays), whether via bear or bee. Colbert's satirical indictment of media *and* political figures and forces is clear: fear sells, and this has a deleterious effect on the citizenry.

Whether considering the advent of so-called soft news, the rush for ratings and comfort in once-sacred, civic-minded, profitless news divisions (recall Edward Murrow's warnings of a lazy, content Fourth Estate as presented in *Good Night, and Good Luck*), or the prevalence of formulaic and often ideologically driven cable news, the heart of the matter for students and consumers of media—in other words, all of us—is: *To what extent do the images, stories, and messages we are exposed to reflect socioeconomic, cultural, and political realities, and to what degree are they presented in order to entertain rather than inform? Are we educating and informing with attention to context, facts, and nuance, or are we lighting ants on fire?*

Notes

1. Terry McDermott, "Dumb Like a Fox," *Columbia Journalism Review*, March/April 2010, pp. 26–32.
2. For example, in 2004 one faux news correspondent signed off on a VNR with the tagline, "This is Kelly Ryan reporting from Washington." The reporter in actuality was a public relations executive employed by the Department of Education.

3. Consider, for example the Bush administration's use of video news releases (VNR) to promote their Medicare prescription drug plan and a tutoring program that was part of the No Child Left Behind education legislation. These particular VNRs were produced by the administration and then replayed on nationwide newscasts, even on CNN, giving the appearance that the reports were the product of independent journalism, when in reality the tutoring program VNR "was narrated by a PR executive posing as a journalist." This is but one example of an official governmental use of a VNR. See Zachary Roth, "Video News Releases: They're Everywhere!" *Columbia Journalism Review*, October 13, 2004: http://www.cjr.org/behind_the_news/video_news_releases_theyre_eve.php.

4. For more information, see Frank Luther Mott, *American Journalism: A History of Newspapers in the United States through 250 Years, 1690–1940* (New York: Macmillan, 1941), esp. 538–41; and W. Joseph Campbell, *Yellow Journalism: Puncturing the Myths, Defining the Legacies* (Westport, CT: Praeger, 2001).

5. Upton Sinclair, *The Jungle* (New York: Doubleday, Jabber and Co., 1906).

6. George Toles provides an analysis of *Meet John Doe* in "Believing in Gary Cooper," *Criticism* 45, no. 1 (Winter 2003): 31–52.

7. For more on the light (press) vs. dark (politicians and government) aspect of *All the President's Men* as well as criticism of the film, see William E. Leuchtenburg, "All the President's Men," in *Past Imperfect: History According to the Movies*, ed. Mark C. Carnes (New York: Owl Books, 1996), 292–95.

8. Paddy Chayefsky, *The Collected Works of Paddy Chayefsky: The Screenplays*, vol. 2 (New York: Applause Books, 1995), 125–26.

9. Chayefsky, *The Collected Works*, 2:183.

10. This is a reference to the stories of Oz by Frank L. Baum and the film *The Wizard of Oz* (1939), in which the wizard is nothing more than a charlatan behind the curtain conjuring fancy tricks.

11. McDermott, "Dumb Like a Fox," pp. 30–32.

12. See, for example, the PBS series *Local News: One Station Fights the Odds* (2001) for additional insight regarding local news practices and the propensity to favor violence and sensationalism: http://www.pbs.org/wnet/insidelocalnews/about.html.

13. Barry Glassner, *The Culture of Fear: Why Americans Are Afraid of the Wrong Things* (New York: Basic Books, 2000). An updated, revised, tenth anniversary edition version was released in 2010.

14. For more information about Edward R. Murrow, see Bob Edwards, *Edward R. Murrow and the Birth of Broadcast Journalism* (Hoboken, NJ: John Wiley & Sons, 2004).

15. Chayefsky, *The Collected Works*, 2:159.

16. A number of insightful pieces of scholarship lend credence to the shortcomings of the mainstream media in terms of their lack of pursuit of the public interest and/or serious oversight of government. For example, James M. Fallows, *Breaking the News: How the Media Undermine Democracy* (New York: Pantheon, 1996); and Kathleen Hall Jamieson and Paul Waldman, *The Press Effect: Politicians, Journalists, and the Stories That Shape the Political World* (Oxford: Oxford University Press, 2002) are just two of the texts that deal with these issues. Fallows, a former speechwriter for President Jimmy Carter, editor at *U.S. News & World Report*, and currently at *The Atlantic*, examines the insider culture of Washington and the profitable,

entertainment-, conflict-, and pundit-driven talk shows of the era (*The McLaughlin Group, Crossfire*, etc.), while Jamieson, dean at the Annenberg School of Communication at the University of Pennsylvania, and one of the nation's most perceptive and prolific media analysts, illustrates how—via the example of the 2000 Al Gore–George W. Bush election coverage—the media frame presidential campaigns, often making events, stories, or candidate idiosyncrasies fit into an established narrative or predetermined candidate caricature.

17. For more background about soft news and its impacts, see David K. Scott and R. H. Gobetz, "Hard News/Soft News," *Journalism Quarterly* 69 (1992): 412–26; and Matthew A. Baum, *Soft News Goes to War: Public Opinion and American Foreign Policy in the New Media Age* (Princeton: Princeton University Press, 2003), 1–8.

18. These are trends that are becoming more prevalent today. For example, Alison Dagnes examines the effects of a continuous, 24-hour news cycle on the media's coverage of American politics, arguing that the quality and quantity of the resultant reporting undermine Americans' faith in their political institutions and politicians. See Alison Dagnes, *Politics on Demand: The Effect of 24-Hour News on American Politics* (Santa Barbara, CA: Praeger, 2010). Likewise, Jamieson and Waldman's aforementioned *The Press Effect* (2002) also sheds light on how campaign coverage reinforces negative or exaggerated stereotypes of candidates, to the detriment of American democracy.

19. There are several books examining the construction of news media empires. For example, see David Halberstam, *The Powers That Be* (New York: Knopf, 1979); and Matthew A. Baum, *Soft News Goes to War* (Princeton: Princeton University Press, 2003).

20. See, for example, Penn Kimball, *Downsizing the News: Network Cutbacks in the Nation's Capital* (Washington, DC: Woodrow Wilson Center Press, 1994), esp. p. 54; Brian Stelter and Bill Call, "ABC News to Cut Hundreds of Staff," *New York Times*, February 23, 2010, p. B5; and Sam Schenchner, "Cuts at TV-News Divisions Signal Leaner Approach," *Wall Street Journal*, February 26, 2010.

21. Benedict Anderson illustrates how a public's relationship to news events creates communities and/or nations in his *Imagine Communities: Reflections on the Origins and Spread of Nationalism* (New York: Verso, 1991), esp. chaps. 3 and 4.

22. For background and the text to the various Geneva Conventions, which cover the laws of war, see the International Committee of the Red Cross's website: http://www.icrc.org/eng-/war-and-law/treaties-customary-law/geneva-conventions/index.jsp.

23. A concern of some has been the ideological rigidity of, or increased political polarization engendered by, various media outlets in the United States. During the George W. Bush administration (2001–2009), many acknowledged that Fox News—whose founder and president, Roger Ailes, served as a political operative and media guru to Richard Nixon, George H. W. Bush, among other prominent Republicans—was the media outlet sympathetic to conservative and Republican politics, and, by end of Bush's second term, MSNBC's evening opinion programming was increasingly sympathetic to liberal and Democratic politics. Documentaries, such as Robert Greenwald's *Outfoxed: Rupert Murdoch's War on Journalism* (2004), were made to counter claims that Fox News was actually "fair and balanced." For Brave New Films' *Outfoxed*, see: http://www.outfoxed.org/.

24. Theodore Hamm, *The New Blue Media* (New York: The New Press, 2008), 160–61. See also the transcript of Bill Moyers's 2003 interview with Jon Stewart: http://www.pbs.org/now/transcript/transcript_stewart.html.

25. "Jon Stewart named America's Most Trusted News Caster," July 22, 2009, Comedy Central website: http://ccinsider.comedycentral.com/2009/07/22/jon-stewart-voted-americas-most-trusted-newscaster/. Stewart also fared well in a 2007 survey conducted by the Pew Center for Press and the People, when he was tied for fourth as the "most trusted person in America." See Michiko Kakutani, "Is Jon Stewart the Most Trusted Man in America?" *New York Times*, August 17, 2008, p. AR1: http://www.nytimes.com/2008/08/17/arts/television/17kaku.html?_r=1.

26. Howard Kurtz, "Carlson & 'Crossfire,' Exit Stage Left and Right," *Washington Post*, January 6, 2005, p. C1.

27. Hamm, *The New Blue Media*, p. 161.

28. It should be noted, however, that the movement for a Stephen Colbert "Rally to Restore Truthiness" began on the social networking site Facebook in the late summer of 2010, and a specific Facebook page/online petition was developed to promote the idea. A few weeks later, Stewart and Colbert announced their joint venture during their respective programs.

29. The 215,000 estimate for the Rally to Restore Sanity comes from a study commissioned by CBS News. See "Jon Stewart Rally Attracts Estimated 215,000," October 30, 2010: http://www.politico.com/news/stories/1110/45032.html. According to CBS News, "The company AirPhotosLive.com based the attendance at the 'Rally to Restore Sanity and/or Fear' on aerial pictures it took over the rally, which took place on the Mall in Washington. It has a margin of error of plus or minus 10 percent." As is the case with all rallies and marches on the National Mall, estimates vary widely, as the National Park Service ceased making official estimates after the 1995 Million Man March.

30. Jessica Horowitz, Melissa Hesse, and Dan Zak, "Stewart, Stephen Colbert Host Rally to Restore Sanity and/or Fear on Mall," *Washington Post*, October 31, 2010: http://www.washingtonpost.com/wp-dyn/content/article/2010/10/30/AR2010103001573.html.

31. The text of Stewart's final comments at the Rally to Restore Sanity is from Greg Mitchell, "Jon Stewart's Closing Statement at Rally, 'From the Heart,'" *The Nation*, October 30, 2010: http://www.thenation.com/blog/155692/jon-stewarts-closing-statement-rally-heart.

32. Hamm, *The New Blue Media*, p. 160.

33. Howard Kurtz, "In Journalism's Crossfire Culture, Everyone Gets Hurt," *Washington Post*, August 2, 2010.

34. Brian Stelter, "Jon Stewart, the Advocate, on the 9/11 Health Bill," *New York Times*, December 17, 2010: http://mediadecoder.blogs.nytimes.com/2010/12/17/jon-stewart-the-advocate-on-the-911-health-bill/?ref=jonstewart; Christopher Beam, "By Pushing for the 9/11 First Responders Health Bill, Stewart Steps onto the Political Playing Field," *Slate*, December 20, 2010: http://www.slate.com/id/2278625/; Ari Shapiro, "John Stewart's Latest Act: Sept. 11 Responders Bill," NPR's *Weekend Edition*, December 26, 2010: http://www.npr.org/2010/12/26/132310870/jon-stewarts-latest-act-sept-11-responders-bill.

35. See the updated *New York Times* profile of Stewart, December 28, 2010: http://topics.nytimes.com/top/reference/timestopics/people/s/jon_stewart/index.html.

36. This critique of Fox was briefly featured by Fox commentator Bill O'Reilly during his popular "O'Reilly Factor" program; he called the forces behind the show "pinheads" for their dig at the network. For more on this and *The Simpsons'* many playful jabs at, and ongoing "good-natured feud" with, their parent network, Fox, see Dave Itzkoff, "Friendly Enemies on Fox: 'Simpsons' and O'Reilly," *The New York Times*, November 30, 2010:

http://www.nytimes.com/2010/12/01/arts/television/01simpsons.html. *Simpsons'* producer Al Jean indicated that the back-and-forth between Fox personalities and the show, and the ability to place topical material in the opening sequences, allows for greater impact, Internet chatter, and interest. Said Jean:

> Both ends of it benefit the ultimate News Corp. agenda. . . . We're happy to have a little feud with Bill O'Reilly. That's a very entertaining thing for us. . . .
>
> We've really entered this new era . . . where even a show like us, that's produced so far in advance, turns into a sort of daily show, where you do something, you can throw something in that gets immediately around the Internet. It gets a response. It's mostly just us trying to do our humor in the new way that humor is done.

·SECTION 3·

THE INTERNATIONAL DIMENSION

· 8 ·

WAR AND TERRORISM

Introduction

War—and the prevention of war—is the most serious and demanding duty of any country. The primary responsibility of any country is the survival and protection of its population. Thus, war is, and always has been, a primary concern of international leaders. Because the very survival of the country could be at stake, citizens who fight in state-sponsored, organized armed conflicts are considered selfless and thus honored by their countrymen and women. As humanity has progressed and the economic, psychological, and physical costs of war have been more fully considered, preventing war has been seen as both noble and necessary. Given the enormous implications, war stories are both compelling and relevant.

This chapter briefly explores how films have portrayed war over the past one hundred years. Before examining these films, we will discuss a few political science concepts that are important in understanding international relations theory in general: the *security dilemma, anarchy,* and the theoretical divide between *realists* and *pluralists* in international relations theory. The chapter then explores how film has been portrayed historically—specifically, war as necessary and war as destructive and senseless. Next, the text will examine the change the introduction of nuclear weapons has brought to films. Finally, we will end our examination of war and film with the post–Cold War emphasis on ethnic conflict. Along the way, the chapter considers wars in Iraq and Afghanistan.

Concepts

Understanding war in modern world politics depends on an understanding of key concepts. A fundamental characteristic of the international system has been the notion of *sovereignty*.[1] The international system understands that each state has the right to decide its own internal matters without interference from the outside. Sovereignty has been understood as virtual political independence, but in reality the term is more of a concept that implies equality and freedom from meddling in domestic politics from outside actors. This is, arguably, the most important characteristic of the modern state. At the same time, another important characteristic of the international system is *anarchy*: the absence of higher authority in the international system. In an anarchical system, there is no entity that can enforce rules or laws; each state must look after its own interests. Note that this does not mean that the system is in chaos; actually the system is fairly orderly. Yet, if a state decides to step outside the agreed behavior of states, there is nothing to stop its actions, except maybe the coordinated actions of other states.

For scholars, the likelihood of war or peace in international politics depends on how one views the *security dilemma* and how likely the dilemma can be solved. The security dilemma can be defined as the situation where one state feels so insecure that it builds its military defenses in order to address its insecurity. Because the international system is anarchic, meaning that the state has to rely on itself to defend its own interests, the state often sees this as its only option. The state's neighbors, seeing this increase in defenses, respond to this increase in arms by doing likewise. Because of these actions, the security of the first state is once again diminished. History has seen several examples of what appears to be the security dilemma.[2]

Demonstrating abstract ideas, such as the security dilemma, is difficult; however, it is a staple of the mid-twentieth-century animated shorts of the Warner Brothers Studio. One of the most enjoyable cartoons of the studio is *The Rabbit of Seville* (1950). The cartoon is a parody of Rossini's opera *Il Barbiere di Siviglia* and captures some of the sense of humor that was present at the Termite Terrace (the studio for animation at Warner Bros.) throughout the

1930s, 1940s, and 1950s.[3] The premise, if you can call what occurs in the cartoon a premise, has Bugs Bunny being chased onto a stage being readied for a performance of *The Barber of Seville* by Bugs's arch-nemesis, the hunter Elmer Fudd. What follows is an imaginative reworking of the opera to reflect the ongoing battles between Bugs and Elmer.

When viewing this Mel Blanc–voiced Bugs Bunny treasure, pay particular attention to the sequence that begins about six and a half minutes into the film. The scene begins with Bugs applying hair tonic and fertilizer to Elmer's bald head. At first Elmer is excited as what is seemingly hair sprouts from his head, but then becomes quite upset as poppies begin to emerge from the spouts. Bugs runs away from the scene as Elmer chases him with a hatchet. The dastardly "wabbit" then responds by running offscreen to retrieve an axe, with which he begins to chase Elmer, and Elmer responds by running offscreen to retrieve a pistol to resume the chase. The scene continues with upgrades to weaponry through rifles and various sizes of cannons until Bugs brings Elmer flowers, candy, and an engagement ring. The scene culminates (along with the short) in a "marriage" of Bugs Bunny and Elmer Fudd (in a wedding dress), after which Bugs drops Elmer from a dizzying height onto a huge wedding cake scripted with "Marriage of Figaro." Of course, the cartoon does not end like we expect the security dilemma to end in the international community. Instead of ending in a marriage proposal, most of the time we expect two states engaged in the security dilemma to find some method of settling their dispute or to go to war.

The reason that the security dilemma is vexing is because countries are participating in an international system that is in anarchy. If each state has sovereignty, then the world, by definition, does not have any government and is in anarchy. There is no higher power or authority that can enforce the rules and laws of the system. Hence, states are on their own in protecting their interests. One of the best examples of how anarchy operates can be demonstrated in the comedy classic *It's a Mad Mad Mad Mad World* (1963). The film of three hours and eight minutes includes almost every imaginable comedian of the era, including Milton Berle, Jonathan Winters, the Three Stooges, and several unbilled celebrity cameos. Because the film is so long, and some of the comedy sequences are zany—but not pertinent to the political discussion—it is sufficient to limit the discussion to the first half hour or so.

The film opens with a car driving recklessly and dangerously passing cars in the California desert. On one particularly bad turn, the reckless car cannot make the turn and runs off the road over a small cliff and down a ravine. The car is badly damaged and the occupant, Smiler Grogan (played by Jimmy Durante), is thrown from the car and lies dying in the sun. Four cars stop to view the crash scene, and the five men from the cars go down to the crash scene to see if they can render assistance. They quickly realize that Smiler is in bad shape, but he is still alive, and barely conscious. Smiler tells the men that he was on the way to pick up $350,000, stolen money that he insists he has paid for every day of his life. He knows that he is not going to make it, but someone should enjoy the money. Smiler says that he is giving it to them and that it is buried in Santa Rosita Park under a big W. The prospect of acquiring a vast amount of money (one could say security) is very tantalizing. But *how* the money would be divided is a problem; there are eight people in four cars, but not all the cars (countries) have the same population.

One motorist (Sid Caesar) eventually devises a plan to create twenty-five shares; eight shares for each person, four shares for each vehicle, five shares for each person who went to the accident scene, and eight shares for each person in each vehicle. It all becomes too complicated. Slowly the group comes to the conclusion that there was only one way to decide about the money: every person for themselves. What ensues for the rest of the film is an incredible chase film, which has been imitated several times, but rarely lives up to the original. Along the way, each person makes side deals with the others, increasing the number of people who are in pursuit of the money under the big W. In the end, the money goes to *none* of the pursuers, and *each* one of them winds up in the hospital with various ailments from the chaotic climactic scene.

It's a Mad Mad Mad Mad World represents how the international system appears to some. None of the characters can trust anyone in their pursuit of the prize. Temporary alliances may appear, but ultimately these alliances fall apart when individuals have interests that differ. Scholars who come from a *realist* perspective will argue that this is the way the international system looks.[4] Other scholars, such as *liberals*, will argue that anarchy does not have such dire consequences for world politics. Liberals will argue that other factors, including ethnic and religious differences, perceptions and misperceptions, and the amount of interdependence among states, determine the likelihood of cooperation, war, and peace between states. Whether humans are essentially prone to aggression and violence is a philosophical and theological debate unlikely to be resolved anytime soon. It takes a great deal of effort to convince people to fight in wars.[5] As we will see, films and popular culture have been used to convince people to kill one another whether as a part of war or, even more sinister, as a violation of human rights.

Movies tend to be a personal medium that tells stories of individuals. Therefore, theoretical debates are often not well suited to narrative films. On the one hand, one danger to keep in mind is that films might give too much agency to individuals, meaning that in the fictional world of film humans can do more than they could in real life. On the other hand, non-narrative films can sometimes help in exploring why countries go to war, even if we consider the film an example of propaganda. Frank Capra made a series of films during World War II on behalf of the United States government entitled *Why We Fight*. In the second film of the series, *The Nazis Strike* (1943), Capra explores German aggression as a method of fulfilling geopolitical aspirations. Capra juxtaposes the need for world domination as seen by the Nazi leadership with American notions of democratic values and fundamental freedoms.[6]

In *The Nazis Strike*, the film seems to present two different reasons as to what led to German expansionism. First, the film presents the idea that Germany was expansionistic because of primordial reasons. The sense of being German meant that the population was militaristic and expansionistic. The opening sequence of the film asserts that German ambitions for world domination date back to 1863, and that while the symbols and leaders have changed, the German desire to rule the world has been constant for the previous seventy-five years.

According to the film, the second reason for German militarism and expansionism can be found in the ideology of the regime. The film points out that the Nazis were particularly impressed with the writings of Karl Haushofer, who modified the geopolitical theories of H. J. Mackinder, to develop a conception and plan of world domination.[7] Haushofer argued that the world was comprised of two commodities, labor and raw material. Land, which constituted only a quarter of the world's surface, was where all the natural resources laid. Furthermore, he argued that the world's land masses could be divided into two main territories, the West Hemisphere and the World Island. The World Island, composed of Asia, Europe, and Africa, had the majority of the world's resources and seven-eights of the world's population. Thus, a theory of world domination, employed by the Nazis, argued that if you conquered Eastern Europe, then you dominated the heartland of the World Island. If you conquered the heartland, then you dominated the World Island. If you conquered the World Island, then you dominated the world.

The film goes on to refute some of the arguments made by the Nazis. First, it points to a number of German Americans who did not agree with the militarism of Germany. Second, it argues that democracy is inherently more peaceful and just than the ideology of National Socialism. Finally, the film argues that the only thing the German command had to fear in the attempt to accomplish world domination was collective action. If, the film argues, states worked together, then the Nazis could never carry out their plans. The film attempts to juxtapose the ideas expressed by the Nazis with the ideas of liberal democracies in an attempt to demonstrate why democracies were more peaceful and why war against the German regime was necessary.

What *The Nazis Strike* explores, as well as other films in the *Why We Fight* series, is the motivation behind World War II. Obviously, the film is not an unbiased examination of prewar politics in Europe but rather a propagandistic justification and explanation of the United States' participation in the war. Still, we should not underestimate the reasoning and motivation of the American government in its participation. The film clearly argues that there is a reluctance among democracies to go to war, and motivating a democratic population for war is more difficult because democratic regimes are held to a standard of truth and popular will. More subtle, though, is a notion that no country should be allowed to gain too much power in the international system. The argument for opposing German expansion is one of opposing the concentration of too much power in Central Europe, an argument made by political realists.

Because it is difficult to portray theoretical debates in terms of narrative films, the next two sections examine war along different classifications. The following section uses film to explore the premise that war is sometimes necessary. Following that, the next section examines films that suggest that wars are destructive and should be (and can be) avoided at all costs.

Wars Are Sometimes Necessary

Especially in more recent times, films that glorify battle without a serious consideration of the implications of war, such as *The Charge of the Light Brigade* (1912), are rare. Even if wars are considered destructive and vile, they might still be considered unavoidable. Thus some films, like *The Red Badge of Courage* (1951), acknowledge war is horrible but sometimes necessary. The Soviet film *Alexandr Nevsky* (1938) used history to argue that war between the Germans and the Slavs was inevitable because the Germans (Teutonic Knights) were bent on religious conquest and militarism. The film was made on the eve of the Second World War; at the time it seemed that war had been avoided because of the Molotov-Ribbentrop Pact in 1939, in which Germany and the Soviet Union secretly divided Poland. Nevertheless, the film seems to be prophetic;

the Germans proved to be untrustworthy in their treaty obligations and attacked the Soviet Union in June 1941.

In the film, the people of Novgorod debate their reaction to invading Teutonic (German) forces. The city is divided over what should be done; some citizens want to fight for their freedom while others are less inclined to do so and would prefer to submit to German rule. Some in the crowd argue that the rich merchants are less inclined to defend Russia than are the poor (an allusion to communist ideology). Meanwhile in Pskov, the German invasion force has destroyed the town. The knights burn the citizens (even infants) who refuse to submit, saying that anyone who does not submit to the Church of Rome must be destroyed (a critique of both Germany and the Roman Catholic Church).

The citizens of Novgorod are persuaded to join the battle after hearing arguments that patriotism is more important than profit. Even women suit up in armor to join the fight against the Germans. The climactic battle occurred on April 5, 1242; the scene in the film is considered a milestone in film history. Nevertheless, *Alexandr Nevsky* alternates between excitement and tedium at times. Certainly the scenes in which the Germans are committing atrocities in Pskov, and the battle on the ice, lead to some very exciting sequences; at other times, though, the narrative of the film drags at an agonizing pace.[8]

The depiction of a particular war often depends on whether a country won or lost the war. This Chambersburg, Pennsylvania, monument is dedicated to the men who died during World War I. In much the same way, films about wars that were won are more likely to have positive portrayals of the conflict than wars that were lost or particularly costly.

During World War II, American films also reflected a sense that sometimes war was necessary, primarily because one had to defeat the enemies of peace and democracy. Certainly, *Sergeant York* (1941) and *Casablanca* (1943) fall into this category. On the surface, *Casablanca* is a love story, perhaps one of the greatest love stories of the American screen. But on a deeper level, the film is about the place of the United States in the world and a commentary on American foreign policy.

The film opens with the latest news to hit Casablanca: two German couriers have been murdered, and the local French administration, which is run by Vichy France (a puppet government that was loyal to the Germans), is "rounding up the usual suspects." The couriers had been carrying two letters of transit, which would allow the holder to escape Casablanca without any questions. The letters fall into the hands of an American, Rick Blaine (Humphrey Bogart), who runs the most popular nightclub in Casablanca. Rick is reclusive and cynical; when asked to help a leader of the resistance, he explains, "The problems of the world are not in my department."

One of the most evocative scenes in *Casablanca*, or in film generally, is a scene in which German soldiers, singing a rousing patriotic anthem, "Die Wacht am Rhein" ("The Watch on the Rhine"), interrupt the festivities. Everyone in the nightclub looks downtrodden and hopeless, staring impassively at the Germans singing triumphantly. The leader of the resistance, Victor Laszlo, goes to the bandstand and demands that they play "La Marseillaise" (the French national anthem). As the band strikes the first few notes, the entire club comes to their feet to join in the singing. In the emotional high point, the Germans are eventually shouted down and forced to cease their singing, over the patriotic fervor of "La Marseillaise." The song ends with shouts of "Vive la France!" from several of the patrons.

Rick's reluctance to get involved is complicated by his love for an old girlfriend, Victor's wife, Ilsa (Ingrid Bergman). Ultimately moved by the situation, the work of Victor Laszlo, his love for a woman, and the brutality of the Nazis, Rick is moved to action. In the climactic airport scene, Rick explains to Ilsa: "I'm no good at being noble, but it doesn't take much to see that the problems of three little people don't amount to a hill of beans in this crazy world. Someday you'll understand that."

Casablanca is a plea for American involvement in the war in Europe. The film is full of allegorical references: "Casablanca" is Spanish for "white house," seen as support for the Roosevelt administration's policy of aiding Europe.[9] Most film historians agree that Rick represents the United States; Renault, occupied

France; Major Stroesser, Germany; and the various patrons of the bar as different countries of Europe. Victor and Ilsa Laszlo represent either the future or the world. Throughout the film Rick astutely stays completely neutral, despite hearing several stories of hardship and deprivation, as did the United States before its entry into the war. Rick's customers and employees are compelled to come to him to explain their problems; however, Rick remains aloof and noncommittal. In many ways, despite his protestations, Rick is seen as someone who can provide hope if only he can be reached. Even some of the nuances of American behavior can be seen in Rick. In the film, Rick helps a young Bulgarian couple to obtain enough money at the roulette wheel to purchase an exit visa by fixing the game. However, after the couple win he denies and underplays his involvement, saying they had a lucky break. This can be seen as a parallel to American behavior of tacitly supporting the Allies prior to December 1941 but wanting to maintain a façade of neutrality.

Singing in Rick's Café

In Rick's Café, the German officers are having a good time singing patriotic songs.[10] This scene causes great anguish and despondency among the other patrons of the café. It is at this point that Victor Laszlo tries to rally the spirits of the patrons against German domination. The two songs that are sung are of note here: The Germans are singing "Die Wacht am Rhein," while Laszlo and the patrons counter with the French national anthem, "La Marseillaise."

There is a similar scene in the anitwar film *The Grand Illusion* (*La grande illusion*, 1937). Set in German prisoner-of-war camps during the First World War, the film explores aspects of war and identity. In one scene, word comes that the Germans have captured the town of Douaumont. This sparks a celebration among the Germans, who sing "Die Wacht am Rhein." During a stage production put on by prisoners, word comes that the French have once again captured the town of Douaumont, which results in the French breaking into "La Marseillaise." The town remains in the news as both sides fight and temporarily gain control over it. However, the news sends the prisoners on an emotional roller coaster, prompting a captive to the verge of a nervous breakdown, shouting unintelligibly at his German captors. One of

the German guards asks another, "Why did he shout like that?"
The reply is, "The war is lasting too long."

Popular culture, in the form of song, reflects participation in politics. Both songs have patriotic meanings, and both are dependent on war images. Compare the translation of both songs:

"Die Wacht am Rhein"
(The Watch on the Rhine)

A call flies like thunder
Like clanging of swords and noise of waves
To the Rhine, to the Rhine, to the German
    Rhine
Who will be the guardian of the stream?
    Beloved Fatherland, you may be calm
    Firm and loyal stands the watch on the Rhine

Through hundreds of thousands it flashes
And all eyes are flashing light
The German youth, pious and strong
Protects the holy borderland
    Beloved Fatherland, you may be calm
    Firm and loyal stands the watch on the Rhine

He looks up, where the sky is blue
Where Father Arminius looks down
And he pledges with proud desire to fight
"Ya, Rhein, will remain German as my chest!"
    Beloved Fatherland, you may be calm
    Firm and loyal stands the watch on the Rhine

"And though my heart breaks in death
You will not become a (Frenchman)
As rich as you are of water
Germany is of heroes' blood"
    Beloved Fatherland, you may be calm
    Firm and loyal stands the watch on the Rhine

"As long as there is one drop of blood left
And one fist draws the sword
And one arm cocks the gun
No Frenchman will step on you shore"
    Beloved Fatherland, you may be calm
    Firm and loyal stands the watch on the Rhine

The pledge resounds, the wave rolls,
The flags are flying in the wind
One the Rhine, on the Rhine, on the German
    Rhine
We will all be guardians
    Beloved Fatherland, you may be calm
    Firm and loyal stands the watch on the Rhine

"La Marseillaise"
(The Song of the Marseillaise)

Ye sons of France, awake to glory!
Hark! Hark! the people bid you rise!
Your children, wives, and grandsires hoary
Behold their tears and hear their cries!

Shall hateful tyrants, mischief breeding,
With hireling hosts a ruffian band
Affright and desolate the land
While peace and liberty lie bleeding?

To arms, to arms, ye brave!
The avenging sword unsheathe!
March on, march on, all hearts resolved
On liberty or death.

Oh liberty can man resign thee,
Once having felt thy generous flame?
Can dungeons, bolts, and bars confine thee?
Or whips thy noble spirit tame?

Too long the world has wept bewailing
That falsehood's dagger tyrants wield;
But freedom is our sword and shield
And all their arts are unavailing.

The film *Sergeant York* (1941) follows the real-life exploits of Alvin C. York (Gary Cooper), the most decorated American during the First World War. York, who hailed from rural Tennessee, initially resisted combat service based on religious grounds. He believed that the biblical proscription "Thou shalt not kill"[11] prevented observant Christians from actively participating in combat. The film follows his evolution, with the help of American officers, to the notion that war is extremely distasteful, but in order to preserve rights, such as religious freedom, was sometimes necessary.[12]

Alfred Hitchcock's contribution to the war effort during the Second World War followed many of the same ideas. In *Lifeboat* (1944), one of the overriding themes is that there is a need for cooperation in order to defeat the enemy. An assumed message is that there are enemies and sometimes, although distasteful, war is necessary. The story is about a small group of people escaping a sinking ship after a German submarine has torpedoed it. One by one, people come to, or are rescued by, the lifeboat. The passengers represent different walks of life and allowed Hitchcock to explore issues including morality and racism. One of the rescued is a German sailor, Willy (Walter Slezak), and the group must decide whether to kill him or to allow him to stay on the lifeboat.

Over the course of the story it becomes clear that Willy is not an innocent German sailor but rather the captain of the U-boat that sank their boat and is, in fact, undermining the survivors. Willy uses deception to kill other passengers and to slowly turn the situation to his favor. When he is found out the others kill him. It becomes increasingly obvious that the only way the passengers will survive is by their mutual cooperation.[13] Towards the end of the film, another German is rescued. The members of the lifeboat tend to his wounds. The German asks if the group is not going to kill him, and the character Kovac (John Hodiak), the acting skipper of the lifeboat, presents the rhetorical question, "What do you do with people like that?" The film contains several messages, not the least of which is the necessity of war in the face of brutality. But note also the diversity of the lifeboat and the sense that all had to sacrifice for their mutual survival.

Each of the World War II films discussed above, *Alexandr Nevsky*, *Casablanca*, *Sergeant York*, and *Lifeboat*, presents reasons why involvement in a war against Germany was necessary. Both *Nevsky* and *Casablanca* worry about a militaristic ideology, and all four tout the need for cooperation among those who opposed the Nazis. Each film examines different factors that might inhibit cooperation. In *Alexandr Nevsky*, cooperation is threatened by class differences. Initially, the merchant class of Novgorod is reluctant to join the resistance to the Germans because of a decline in their profits. Similarly, in *Lifeboat* there is an element of class struggle as well. However, the barriers to cooperation are a little more complex in *Lifeboat*. The existence of a racial divide is evidenced by how the survivors treat Joe (an African American survivor). Finally, cooperation in *Casablanca* is difficult because of various reasons. In the love story, Rick's feelings of betrayal prevent him from cooperating against the Germans. In the more allegorical story, it is only when the United States cooperates with the rest of the Allies that the Germans can be defeated. Despite these difficulties, war as an institution is not questioned. It is seen as a necessity, particularly against very difficult foes.

Wars Are Evil and Destructive

The alternative idea that war must be avoided at all costs first gained currency during the early years of cinema. Films concerned with the First World War became synonymous with the idea of the futility of war. One of the earliest antiwar films was Thomas Ince's film *Civilization* (1916). The film uses a moralistic overtone to tell the story of Christ returning to the earth to prevent a massive conflict, which mirrors the First World War. Films throughout the 1920s expressed an abhorrence of war because of the seemingly senseless slaughter of millions of young men in the fields, trenches, cities, and seas of Europe. Famous American silent films such as *The Big Parade* (1925) and *Wings* (1927)[14] expressed the idea that while some ideas were worth fighting for, the end result was the death of a number of innocents and a decline in moral stature. *The Big Parade* sends American troops off to war with patriotism and flag-waving jubilation. It spends nearly ninety minutes showing recruits being "trained" for battle but then thrown into a situation in which the protagonists are never prepared.[15] The combatants come home often damaged, either physically or psychologically; sons, husbands, and brothers return having seen horrors unimaginable to civilians and leaving comrades behind buried in faraway places.

Also taking place during World War I, Stanley Kubrick's stirring anitwar film *Paths of Glory* (1957), set in France and starring Kirk Douglas as the heroic, steadfast Colonel Dax, is a devastating condemnation of the selfish machinations of elite, glory-seeking, cowardly generals, who, for vanity, political favor, and private gain send their brave men to fight unwinnable battles under hellish conditions. Based on the novel of the same name by Italian-born, Canadian World War I veteran Humphrey Cobb, the film follows the courage and moral outrage of Colonel Dax as he stands up for his soldiers against General Mireau (George Macready), after his men disobey the general's orders by refusing to follow his suicidal battle commands in the trenches.[16] Here, the principled soldier lions resist the corrupt commanding lambs, and we see the folly, tragedy, and inhumanity of war. The grunts on the front lines are sent to die while the masters of war live in relative luxury, ensconced in arrogance. Though Colonel Dax's courage ultimately wins the battle for justice, the over-all message about the horrors of war is unmistakable.

Set during the First World War, *The Grand Illusion* (1937) was a plea against war and an acknowledgment of the changing politics in Europe. The story is set in 1916, prior to the entry of the United States into the war. Three French pilots are shot down over German territory and become prisoners of war. Before they are transferred to a prisoner-of-war camp, their German counter-parts treat the French prisoners to a magnificent dinner. As the group of com-batants talk they find out that each has ties to the other side: one of the French pilots has a cousin in Berlin, one of the German pilots worked in Lyon, and so on.[17]

The Grand Illusion uses World War I as a warning of what might be com-ing; the growing clouds of the Second World War certainly factoring into the film. It is such a powerful film that when historian J. M. Winter asked World War I veterans what should be in a museum of the war, several cited this film.[18] *The Grand Illusion* explores factors that might prevent cooperation between individuals. Issues such as economic class, religion, and nationality are all explored as potential roadblocks to cooperation. While these factors are vex-ing over the course of the film, each is seemingly overcome. With *The Grand Illusion* the main focus is on the effects of the war on individuals. Even though the French prisoners of war are living in better conditions than their German captors, their confinement is ultimately dehumanizing and they are willing to do almost anything to escape. While nationality seems important, the soldiers on each side find they have more in common than they might otherwise sus-pect. All of this drives the idea that war should and can be prevented.

With war clouds gathering in the late 1930s, some films, like *The Grand Illusion,* continued to look back at the First World War and warn of the con-sequences. Another antiwar film of the era was Charles Chaplin's *The Great Dictator* (1940). Millions of people, for more than a generation, had loved Chaplin's silent films. This would be his first sound film and revives his tram-plike character. Although the film is a sound film and dialogue is important, there are long sequences of pantomime that occasionally take away from the

This monument in Ostend, Belgium, is subdued and focuses on the sacrifices that war brings rather than a triumphalism that might be depicted elsewhere. Because Belgium was occupied in both the First and Second World Wars, conflicts are depicted less glamorously.

momentum of the film. Nevertheless, the film is an important statement for democratic values prior to World War II.

The film opens with a prologue set during the First World War. Chaplin plays a Jewish barber who is assigned to the artillery division of the army of the mythical country Tomania (a not-too-subtle reference to Germany). With the war going badly for Tomania, all troops, including the inept Chaplin, are sent to the front. The Tomanian forces are being overrun everywhere. Chaplin comes across a wounded pilot, Schultz, who is sure that he can get his information to his superiors, and that Tomania might still win the war. Schultz is grateful that the Jewish barber has saved his life, but their efforts have been in vain—Tomania has lost the war.

During the intervening years, Tomania suffers from economic depression, riots, and the rise of a dictator, Adenoid Hynkel, who looks remarkably like Adolf Hitler. Hynkel (also played by Chaplin) is self-important, yet paranoid at the same time. His dictatorship, of the "double cross" (read, swastika) is based on megalomania and intimidation of the population. Meanwhile, the Jewish barber has never really recovered from his injuries suffered during the airplane crash. While physically he is fine, he believes that he has only been in the infirmary for a couple of weeks. He believes that he will return to his barbershop in the ghetto in a couple of days, not realizing that two decades have passed.

In an effort to distract the population from the economic troubles at home, the Hynkel regime has sought to blame the Jewish population. The film moves back and forth between two stories: one, centered in the ghetto of the Jewish population; the other in the palace of Adenoid Hynkel. When the Jewish barber leaves the infirmary and makes his way back to the ghetto, he takes down the boards that have covered his shop windows, and he finds that storm troopers have painted JEW across the glass. When he goes out to protest, he gets in a scuffle with the storm troopers. Major Schultz recognizes the Jewish barber as the one who had saved his life back in 1918. Schultz orders the storm troopers to leave the barber and his friend alone, thus repaying the barber by saving his life.

Predictably, the film moves toward a case of mistaken identity between the Jewish barber and Hynkel. The story is full of allusions to the politics of Europe in the 1930s. For example, the dictator of Bacteria, Napaloni, bears a remarkable resemblance to Benito Mussolini, fascist dictator of Italy. At the end of the film the Jewish barber, dressed as the dictator of Tomania, addresses the crowd. The speech becomes Chaplin's stirring commentary on European politics of the late 1930s.[19] In it, Chaplin calls for democracy and a struggle against fascism, but rather than one of the characters in the movie, Chaplin becomes *himself*, in a last ditch effort to save the continent and the world from war. The speech is rich in religiosity and morality, and it ends with Chaplin pleading:

> Dictators free themselves but they enslave the people. Now let us fight to free the world! To do away with national barriers! To do away with greed, with hate and intolerance! Let us fight for a world of reason, a world where science and progress will lead to the happiness of us all. Soldiers, in the name of democracy, let us unite!

The film, which was financed almost entirely by Chaplin himself, was unsuccessful at the box office, and later in his career Chaplin's loyalties were questioned. Eventually, Chaplin would leave the United States during the communist scare of the 1950s and subsequently would be persona non grata. Chaplin would only be invited back to the United States for a special Academy Award in 1977.

The Great Dictator, like *The Grand Illusion*, examines the effects of war and militarism on the civilian population. The hospital where the Jewish barber spends twenty years is one of the minor scenes of the film, but it is a potent reminder of the effects of war on the general population. The film also comments on the use of part of the population, such as Jews, as scapegoats.[20] The people in the Jewish ghetto are tempted to support Hynkel once he lifts the harsh restrictions he had placed on them. Ultimately, it is Hynkel's military obsessions that require the population to sacrifice economically and also require a scapegoat to blame. Chaplin's call to avoid the Second World War was not heeded, and in later years he regretted the film in light of the genocide that unfolded in Central Europe.[21] Nevertheless, the film argues that people did not want wars, but wars served the interests of dictators and strongmen.

Revisiting the Antiwar Film: Vietnam

The American experience during the Vietnam War prompted a reassessment of war in a number of films and television shows on the subject. During the 1940s and 1950s war films typically focused on the needs to confront a substantial German or Japanese enemy during the Second World War; the films of the red scare focused on a potential communist enemy. During the Vietnam War, however, the United States would eventually experience a number of protests and massive demonstrations against America's involvement in the military conflict. The war's effects on the United States were profound. At its height, more than 500,000 American troops were fighting in the war; over 58,000

Americans would lose their lives; an estimated two and half million Vietnamese civilians were killed; and American citizens' confidence in their government generally, and in successive presidencies specifically, was severely shaken. Former Department of Defense and RAND Corporation military analyst Daniel Ellsberg, who facilitated the controversial release of the Pentagon Papers in 1971—highly classified documents which revealed deception and flawed strategies in the execution of the war during previous presidential administrations— became, according to the Nixon administration, "The Most Dangerous Man in America."[22] Though it can be argued that the most *directly* critical commercial films would not arrive until a few years *after* the Vietnam War ended—according to poet Samuel Hazo, "a decade late and safely critical"—the scope of the divisive conflict in Southeast Asia stirred up antiwar sentiments both in the United States and around the world, and these were eventually reflected in the films produced by Hollywood.[23]

Nevertheless, others (inside and outside Hollywood) not only believed war to be necessary but that actors and the motion picture industry had a responsibility to promote the justness of a war. In this vein, "The Duke," Hollywood legend John Wayne, used his political and artistic capital to gain the explicit and necessary support of the Pentagon in order to make his pro–Vietnam War film, the borderline propagandistic *The Green Berets* (1968). Against a backdrop of increasing opposition to the conflict in Southeast Asia, Wayne sought to make a movie to answer the war's critics. Writing President Lyndon Johnson on December 28, 1966, Wayne noted that the most "effective way" to gain public support for the war in Vietnam was through the medium of film, and that it was time to build support for the U.S. involvement in Vietnam—both at home and abroad—via an unabashedly pro-military, pro–Vietnam War motion picture.[24]

Antiwar films after the Vietnam War, such as *The Deer Hunter* (1978), *Coming Home* (1978), and *Platoon* (1986), would revisit the theme of war and the specific impacts on different segments of the population, from those deep in the battle and those waiting at home for their loved ones to return. The movie and television show *M*A*S*H* (1970; 1972–1983) and the films *Born on the Fourth of July* (1989) and *When We Were Soldiers* (2002) examined the effects of the Vietnam War on individuals as well. Although *M*A*S*H* was set in the Korean War, it was clearly an indictment against American involvement in the Vietnam War. *Born on the Fourth of July*, which told the story of Vietnam veteran Ron Kovic, who was paralyzed in the war, and *When We Were Soldiers* (2002), which told the personal stories of the soldiers who fought the first major engagement of the war—Ia Drang—examined both the personal and psychological impact that Vietnam had on those who served.[25] Kovic's experiences in Vietnam led him to become an outspoken opponent of not only the Vietnam War but U.S. military intervention in other parts of the world as well, even opposing the 1990–1991 Persian Gulf War by entering some early Democratic Party primaries in 1992 as a candidate of conscience. The devastating impact of the Vietnam War on both the United States and Vietnam—from soldiers and families to lovers and innocent civilians—is a theme that has been at the heart of several films by *Born on the Fourth of July* director, and Vietnam veteran, Oliver Stone. Stanley Kubrick's *Full Metal Jacket* (1987) delves deep beneath the surface of a soldier's psychological makeup, from the consequences of the rugged culture of boot camp at Paris Island to the jungles and cafés of Vietnam.

Vietnam also touched a raw spot in American politics. Gone was a consensus of ideas that war was noble and glorious. Popular culture in general mobilized against the war and the aftermath. The song "War" (1969), written by Norman Whitfield and Barrett Strong, is a classic example. The song was popularized by Edwin Starr, whose version was a number one hit. The lyrics repeatedly ask, "War, What is it good for?" with the answer coming emphatically, "absolutely nothing!" Yet, as the long and storied history of protest music illustrates, songs of dissent and social unrest are not limited to pithy slogans and jingoistic logic. For example, Bruce Springsteen's "Born in the U.S.A." at first listen sounds like an unqualified celebration of being an American; however, a careful listen to the lyrics reveals a more critical comment on the lives of working Americans and the struggles of returning veterans. This is a point that has been lost on many—including some high-profile politicians—and the song continues to be utilized during patriotic ceremonies and flag-waving public events, from popular sporting events to presidential rallies.[26] In a poignant moment of the song the singer notes the apparent futility of war, "I had a brother at Khe Sahn / Fighting off the Viet Cong / They're still there, he's all gone." Post-1980s, Springsteen frequently performed the song in its original spare and raw, purely acoustic form, as it was when he first cut the demo during the sessions for his album *Nebraska* (1982), an unflinching and bleak examination of the American economic, social, and political landscape of the early 1980s.

Many other performers have expressed sentiments that may cut a bit closer to the bone. Crosby, Stills, Nash and Young (CSNY) bitterly mourned the deaths of four student protesters who died at Kent State University in the song "Ohio" (1970), repeatedly lamenting, "How many more?" over clanging guitars. Bob Dylan, who helped build upon the legacy of the protest tradition through his own sensibility, revisited the human costs of the Vietnam War in the early 1980s. His song "Clean-Cut Kid" (1985) follows the downward slide of an All-American boy who was transformed into a killer.[27]

Conflicts in the Aftermath of September 11th: Iraq and Afghanistan

While there have been a few films produced specifically concerned with the execution of American wars in Iraq and Afghanistan, a fairly diverse cadre of films exists that deal more broadly with post-9/11 military matters and national security policy, as well as the psychological and physical costs of war. Of these films, some have been critically acclaimed, but none has done particularly well at the box office.

The films about Iraq have typically focused on the effect of the war on individuals. For instance, *In the Valley of Elah* (2007) tells the story of a father (Tommy Lee Jones) trying to understand why his son has gone AWOL after returning from Iraq. It is clear that the war has had a devastating psychological effect on his son and other veterans. In *Stop-Loss* (2008), the effects of the war are explored by examining those who have returned home and have difficulty adjusting to civilian life, and face the prospect of returning to Iraq for another tour of duty.[28] The storyline of *Brothers* (2009), starring Jake Gyllenhaal, Sam Shepard, and Natalie Portman, centers around the inability of an Afghanistan veteran (Tobey Maguire) to adjust to civilian life after enduring one of the more psychologically damaging and disturbing scenarios in modern war film. The post-traumatic stress disorder (PTSD) struggles of veterans—well chronicled in crises in mental health treatment and higher suicide rates[29]—lie at the heart of this film, and several others. Even as Maguire's character has been to hell and back, the film ends on a potentially positive, if somewhat ambiguous, note. Similarly, the PBS *Frontline* documentary *The Wounded Platoon* (2010) involves harrowing tales of psychological struggle, detailing the real-life story of Iraq War veterans and an often-violent, anti-social nightmare of zombie-like prescription drug use, depression, PTSD, and, tragically, murder in Colorado.[30]

Restrepo (2010), an Afghanistan War documentary, presents a soldier's perspective of the war.[31] Covering military service in the violent Korengal Valley over a period of several months, the film, made by war correspondents Sebastian Junger (journalist) and Tim Hetherington (photographer), was designed to "capture the experience of combat, boredom and fear through the eyes of the soldiers themselves."[32] As such, the film shares some common cinematic and thematic traits with the Iraq War documentary *Gunner Palace* (2004), which provides a "ground-level . . . messy and immediate" perspective of the day-to-day life and military missions of American soldiers of the 2/3 Field Artillery, stationed in a partially decimated palace of Saddam Hussein.[33]

The critically acclaimed *The Messenger* (2009), directed by screenwriter and Israeli veteran of the first Lebanon War Oren Moverman, follows two casualty notification officers (Ben Foster and Woody Harrelson)—one, an Iraq War vet, and the other, a veteran of the Persian Gulf War—as they inform military families of their loved ones' deaths. The film follows their emotional fallout from PTSD, recurrent alcoholism, depression, and persistent physical ailments.[34] Unlike a few of the more prominent films of the Iraq–Afghanistan era, such as Michael Moore's anti–Iraq War box office hit *Fahrenheit 9/11* (2004), John Cusack's powerful performance in *Grace Is Gone* (2007) avoids polemics and politics entirely and offers a quiet, introspective—if no less painful— examination of coping with the loss of a loved one in a war. In the understated *Grace*, the soft-spoken, devoted midwestern suburban father (Cusack) struggles for a way to tell his two children that their mother, Grace, died in Iraq. Unable to tell his daughters, he takes them on a trip to a theme park in the hope that at some point the words and strength will arrive, and he can reveal the loss.

Probably the most high-profile film on the war in Iraq is the film that won the 2010 Academy Award for best picture, *The Hurt Locker* (2009). The film follows soldiers who have the task of disabling improvised explosive devices (IEDs). The film focuses on the consequences of the war on individuals; the soldiers witness brutal acts and lose friends and comrades. The war has different effects on different soldiers, and while some cannot wait to leave the military to try to start a normal civilian life, others become addicted to the excitement of the situation, knowing full well it might mean death. Adrenaline arrives in spades in the Paul Greengrass–directed *Green Zone* (2010), with Matt Damon (Miller) as a dedicated soldier under the direction of the CPA (Coalition Provisional Authority) searching, to no avail, for elusive WMDs (weapons of mass destruction) in Iraq after the American invasion in 2003 and the fall of Saddam Hussein. The film is based on real-life events—famously chronicled in Rajiv Chandrasekaran's widely praised book *Imperial Life in the Emerald City: Inside Iraq's Green Zone* (2006).[35] The film exposes the disconnect between the "Green Zone" safe haven and the more chaotic reality raging outside. Moreover, the film is a sharp critique of the alleged miscalculation, mismanagement, and, most significant, faulty intelligence that many believe characterized this crucial period after the U.S. invasion of Iraq. In the final analysis, no WMDs were located, and Damon's loyal soldier learns of the CPA's deception and American reliance on the at-best questionable intelligence sources.

Critical and disturbing entries in the documentary field include several highly regarded films that examine different degrees of government malfeasance and cover-up during war. In Alex Gibney's exceptional *Taxi to the Dark Side* (2007), the Academy Award winner for best documentary feature, and *Ghosts of Abu Ghraib* (2007), from Rory Kennedy's Moxie-Firecracker Productions, we find critical and in-depth analyses of U.S. treatment of prisoners of war, "enemy combatants," and even innocent civilians—from Iraq to Afghanistan to Guantanamo Bay. The films consider the political, legal, and cultural antecedents and consequences of U.S. interrogation techniques and treatment of prisoners.

Amir Bar-Lev's "sorrowful, devastating . . . clear-sighted, emotionally steady" documentary *The Tillman Story* (2010), narrated by Josh Brolin, chronicles the life and friendly fire death of former iconoclastic safety for the Arizona Cardinals, Pat Tillman.[36] Tillman, who had voluntarily left his lucrative football career behind to serve in the U.S. Army (he was an Army Ranger) in the months after September 11, 2001, was eventually sent to Iraq, a war, we learn through acquaintances and family members, he fundamentally disagreed with. Later stationed in Afghanistan after refusing to have his army stint shortened due to his star status as an athlete, Tillman was killed on a mountainside in Afghanistan, under assault from a barrage of gunfire. While the military brass stated that Tillman had died heroically, protecting his fellow soldiers during an ambush from the Taliban, the Tillman family—and indeed the country— would later learn that he was killed by his own men. The Tillman family—led by Pat's indefatigable mother, Mary, investigate the matter, probing, questioning, sifting through thousands of pages of redacted military documents, and, eventually, in the case of Pat's fellow soldier brother, Kevin, even testifying before Congress. The case of Pat Tillman stands as both a cautionary tale of a military willing to exploit the death of high-profile soldiers for propagandistic purposes, and the story of a dogged, intellectual, fiercely patriotic, truth-seeking family who deserve to know what happened to their son and brother.

There have been numerous documentaries and television specials about the war in Iraq, as well as works which address this specific conflict within the larger context of the consequences and realities of war generally. The documentary film *Control Room* (2004), discussed in Chapter 7, examines the beginning of the war in Iraq from the perspective of the Arab television channel Al-Jazeera. And centered on the ideological and systemic dynamics driving the George W. Bush administration's decision to go to war in Iraq, Eugene Jarecki's *Why We Fight* (2005), discussed in the conclusion of this chapter, explores U.S. motivations to engage in military action from the Eisenhower era onward, focusing on the central concept of the military-industrial complex. The uneven but biting dark comedy *War, Inc.* (2008), starring John Cusack and written by the actor along with Jeremy Pikser and Mark Leyner, serves as a critical commentary on the power of private military contractors—in this case, one that occupies a fictional Middle Eastern country (Turaqistan) and is led by a former vice president. Obviously this is a not-so-veiled critique of Vice President Dick Cheney and companies such as Halliburton and Blackwater.[37] The aforementioned *Frontline* (PBS) film *The Wounded Platoon* (2010) examines the severe mental health crisis facing returning soldiers and the deadly related events that transpired in Colorado Springs, Colorado, in 2007.

War in Iraq and Afghanistan: A Selected Filmography

2004	*Control Room*		*Alive Day Memories: Home*
	Fahrenheit 9/11		*from Iraq*
	Gunner Palace		
		2008	*Stop-Loss*
2005	*Operation Dreamland*		*The Hurt Locker*
			War, Inc.
2006	*Baghdad ER*		
		2009	*Brothers*
2007	*Ghosts of Abu Ghraib*		*The Messenger*
	In the Valley of Elah		
	Lions for Lambs	2010	*The Ghost Writer*
	No End in Sight		*Green Zone*
	Redacted		*Restrepo*
	Taxi to the Dark Side		*The Tillman Story*
	Grace Is Gone		*War Torn: 1861–2010*
	Rendition		*The Wounded Platoon*

Nuclear War

The debate about whether war is sometimes useful took on new urgency with the advent of nuclear weaponry in 1945. The prospects of mass devastation, or even the elimination of human life from Earth, greatly change the calculus of using war to achieve an end. While people like nineteenth-century military thinker Carl von Clausewitz suggested that war is an extension of politics,[38] nuclear weapons changed the equation. The possession of nuclear weapons by both sides means that there is little difference between winning and losing.

Films have reflected the growing awareness of the destructive potential of nuclear weaponry. Early on, films in the sci-fi genre, particularly low-budget films, did not take the destructive power as a necessary threat but instead used the weapons as a force to conduct good or its aftermath to create new heroes.[39] Films of the genre did present other views of nuclear weapons but were not as serious as later films. The sci-fi genre during the early part of the nuclear age warned of the impact of nuclear radiation. However, none of these films could really be taken seriously. In *Them!* (1954), radiation causes ants to be mutated into giant ants; in *The Beginning of the End* (1957), radiation causes grasshoppers to grow to an enormous size; and in *Godzilla* (1956), nuclear tests cause the awakening of an ancient monster that goes on a rampage in downtown Tokyo.

Despite the fun and frivolity of these films, the subject of nuclear war and nuclear weaponry took on more serious dimensions as the Cold War progressed. During the 1940s and 1950s, the U.S. government produced a number of films that touted the benefits of nuclear weaponry. The films often downplayed the effects of radiation on the human body. Also, the films often showed U.S. government officials extolling the potential peaceful uses of nuclear weapons as a reason for test detonations. These short subjects seem naïve and antiquated by today's standards. However, they served as the primary source of information about nuclear weapons and power for an entire generation of Americans before the dawn of television. An early, but important, exploration of the effects of a potential nuclear war was the 1959 film *On the Beach*. Based on the novel of the same name by Nevil Shute, the story is set in the aftermath of a nuclear war in 1964.[40] An American submarine surfaces in Australia to find what are, apparently, the last people alive on Earth.

On the Beach depicts the horrors of a potential nuclear war, without showing any violence or destruction. Through the course of the film normal Australians go through their lives waiting for death from radiation poisoning. While people desperately look for love, satisfaction, and meaning in their final days, the overriding theme of the film seems to be the wastefulness of war in a nuclear age. The end of the film is a shot of a cautionary banner from a religious revival, which has a second meaning for the audience, "There is still time."

The difficulty of war in a nuclear age is that it is unlikely that anyone could survive a total war to make a film afterwards.

Other films in this genre capture very well the paranoia of a nuclear war as well as the potentially devastating effects of nuclear war. *The Missiles of October* (1974) captures the struggle in the Kennedy administration of trying to avoid nuclear war during the Cuban Missile Crisis of 1962. Adapted from Robert Kennedy's book *Thirteen Days*, the film reflects the struggle within the administration to understand and respond to the crisis.[41] *The Missiles of October* depicts the problems of securing and understanding information during a crisis situation. While there was initial support among administration officials for a military strike to destroy the missiles, the realization that those strikes might trigger a nuclear response from the Soviet Union dampened the appeal of that course of action.[42]

The events of October 1962 were revisited in the popular 2000 film *Thirteen Days*, which incorporated a great deal of information about the events that was declassified following the end of the Cold War. Starring Kevin Costner as Special Assistant to the President Kenny O'Donnell, Bruce Greenwood as President John F. Kennedy, and Steven Culp as Attorney General Robert F. Kennedy, *Thirteen Days* provides a mostly accurate account of the Kennedy administration's extensive (and secret) deliberations over how to respond to Soviet missiles in Cuba.[43] In the process, we learn of the views of key EXCOM players, including Dean Acheson, Adlai Stevenson, Robert McNamara, McGeorge Bundy, Maxwell Taylor, and Curtis LeMay. The film also does an exemplary job of detailing President Kennedy, Robert Kennedy, and General-Secretary Khrushchev's back-channel negotiations, diplomatic overtures, and political and strategic concessions used to defuse the crisis. Yet, the film was not without its critics. One concern articulated by some historians and students of politics was that the film substantially overplayed the significance of Kennedy aide Kenny O'Donnell, who, alongside JFK and RFK, is clearly the star of the film. Another criticism lodged by some was that the hawks in the military brass—namely, Curtis LeMay—were portrayed in an overly negative light. Lastly, another complaint concerned the fact that O'Donnell's son Kevin, an Earthlink millionaire, was an investor in the company of *Thirteen Days* producer Armyan Bernstein, thus raising the issue of conflict of interest and the inflation of Kenny O'Donnell's role in the film and the real-life crisis.[44] These legitimate complaints aside, however, the film is refreshingly accurate in its depiction of most of the aspects of the military, political, and diplomatic history of the Cuban Missile Crisis.[45]

The Cuban Missile Crisis drew the United States and the Soviet Union probably as close as they ever came to a nuclear confrontation. The prospects had a sobering effect on policy makers and citizens alike. One could almost say that a preoccupation and paranoia began to creep into the minds of many concerning the potential effects of a nuclear war. Films like *Dr. Strangelove* (1964) and *Fail-Safe* (1964) continued an examination of the preoccupation with paranoia and imminent destruction. *Dr. Strangelove, Or How I Learned to Stop Worrying and Love the Bomb* (the official satirical and long-winded title), Stanley Kubrick's classic dark comedy, uses absurdity to laugh our collective way through an accidental nuclear Armageddon. The director employs hilariously demented, selfish, and frequently sex-crazed presidents, generals, and nuclear physicists to drive home his argument that the arms race and nuclear deterrence theory were the height of irrationality. The overall message is clear: the dominant theory of nuclear deterrence, MAD (mutually assured destruction)— which was based on human rationality and assumed that a state would not strike first because world destruction was assured when the other state responded with its own nuclear attack—was itself "mad." Those in charge of nuclear weapons in *Dr. Strangelove* are hardly rational actors.

Kubrick's landmark movie tells the story of General Jack D. Ripper (Sterling Hayden), commander of the Strategic Air Command, who launches a first strike on the Soviet Union. Ripper believes that the Soviets are responsible for his sexual dysfunction, and also sees the fluoridation of water as a vast communist conspiracy. He takes it upon himself to give the order to attack the Soviets, bypassing the president of the United States and the seemingly established chain of command. Along the way, a number of characters sweeten the plot with their belligerence, bullheadedness, and testosterone, among them General "Buck" Turgidson (George C. Scott) and Major T. J. "King" Kong (Slim Pickens). Other key political actors in the film determining the fate of mankind are just plain dim-witted (Keenan Wynn as Colonel "Bat" Guano) or just too darn calm, egg-headed, or intellectual, given the tense circumstances (Peter Sellers as both U.S. president Merkin Muffley and British group captain Lionel Mandrake). Dr. Strangelove (Peter Sellers, in his *third* role in the film!) is a nuclear physicist and former Nazi who now advises the Pentagon on U.S. nuclear policy.[46]

The character "Dr. Strangelove" represents a clear connection between history and Hollywood, as the character is a composite of three vital players in Cold War politics and nuclear deterrence: Henry Kissinger, Edward Teller, and Wernher von Braun.[47] Kissinger, author of the realist-driven treatises

Nuclear Weapons and Foreign Policy (1957) and *The Necessity for Choice* (1961), among others, was Richard Nixon's top foreign policy adviser, and one of the chief architects of U.S. nuclear strategy from the late 1950s through the 1970s, serving as Nixon's National Security Advisor, and, later, as Secretary of State in the Ford administration. Teller oversaw the development and testing of the first hydrogen bomb in 1952 at the University of California's Lawrence Livermore Radiation Laboratory and used his clout to push for the unimpeded expansion of the United States' nuclear arsenal. In addition, he fiercely opposed the Limited Nuclear Test Ban Treaty of 1963. Von Braun was a rocket technician for Hitler's Nazi Germany and later worked for the United States, where he was eventually stationed in Huntsville, Alabama, "directing more than one hundred German scientists and engineers with whom he had worked in Hitler's day."[48] But that is not the end of the real-world political parallels of the film. The bizarre, impotent, and paranoid Gen. Ripper is patterned after the renowned hawk and onetime head of the Strategic Air Command Curtis LeMay.[49] During the Cuban Missile Crisis in October 1962, LeMay promoted a preemptive air strike against the missile sites followed by a full-scale invasion. Running as George Wallace's vice presidential nominee on the American Independent Party ticket in 1968, LeMay suggested that he would "bomb North Vietnam back to the Stone Age" if elected.[50]

The topic—and conclusion—of the film may be the senseless annihilation of the world at the hands of delusional, irrational men, but Kubrick's sardonic take on Cold War superpower strategies provides a way to both critique the dominant theories shaping foreign policy and laugh at the absurdity of the irrational human condition. As great mushroom clouds encompass the globe after Slim Pickens's Major "King" Kong guides and rides (yes, rides) a nuclear missile to its final destination, we hear Vera Lynn's sugary, comforting crooning of the standard "We'll Meet Again"—"a 1939 song indelibly associated with England's heroic stand during World War II."[51] *Dr. Strangelove* is both a political statement *and* a way to laugh through the omnipresent fear and madness of a nuclear doomsday . . . what more could one possibly hope for in a film?

Fail-Safe, however, is a much more serious examination of a potential unintentional nuclear war. While both *Fail-Safe* and *Dr. Strangelove* are based on the same nuclear war novel—Peter George's *Two Hours to Doom* (published in Britain under the pseudonym Peter Bryant)—and deal with inadvertent nuclear holocaust, their similarities end there.[52] In the film *Fail-Safe*, through a series of computer and human errors, as well as miscalculations, the United

States mistakenly launches a nuclear attack against the Soviet Union. Before the situation can be rectified, the bombers on their way to Moscow have crossed the fail-safe line and cannot be called back. The Soviets, of course, have no choice but to retaliate, even if they are convinced that the attack is a mistake. Moral questions abound, but one of the most poignant is, "Can you trade New York for Moscow?" In the end, the two sides cannot solve the problem, and each is forced into attempting to destroy the other side.

Despite the effectiveness of both *Dr. Strangelove* and *Fail-Safe*, when it comes to depicting the overwhelming horror of nuclear war, these commercial films pale in comparison to a British film made about the same time. The film *The War Game* (1965) describes the effects of a nuclear attack on a typical English town. So devastating and disturbing were the scenes in the film that the film was never shown on television as it was meant to be, and played on a limited number of screens. The film, running a mere forty-five minutes, is shot as if it were a documentary. It draws on the experiences of Hiroshima and Nagasaki, as places that were destroyed by nuclear weapons, and also cities like Dresden and Hamburg, which suffered from severe firebombing, to project what an attack on Britain would look like. In describing the probable aftermath of a nuclear attack, the filmmakers do not pull away from some of the most gruesome events. Children are shown with burnt retinas, firefighters are pulled into conflagrations by the winds of one hundred miles per hour in a firestorm, individuals with severe burns who have no chance of recovery are shot rather than allowed to suffer without medicine, and food riots break out among the survivors. In the end, *The War Game* is perhaps one of the most memorable and frightening films ever made. The film does not shy away from raising questions about the public's ignorance, nor does it dress up the potential horrors of a nuclear war to allay the fears of a middle-class audience.

As the antinuclear movement gained momentum in the 1980s, the motion picture industry reflected the sentiment. A subtler commentary on nuclear weaponry is found in the documentary film *Atomic Café* (1982). This film used archival footage juxtaposed to American propaganda films and newsreels with no commentary to chronicle the history and development of nuclear weaponry in the 1940s and 1950s. The film begins with the first four nuclear detonations of atomic bombs: the Trinity Test in New Mexico; the bombings of Hiroshima and Nagasaki, Japan; and the test at Bikini Atoll in the South Pacific. U.S. Army information films describe the test at Bikini Atoll as a test to determine the effects of the weapon. The inhabitants of Bikini Atoll were relocated from the island by the U.S. government, and the film "records" the meeting at which the move is discussed. The scene, however, uses the actual footage to reveal that the meeting was staged for the cameras.

Later, the film examines the dangers of radiation after a detonation. U.S. government films assure soldiers that the radiation after a blast is of minimal danger and that it is perfectly safe to conduct maneuvers in the wake of an atomic blast. The audience sees soldiers talking about getting a mouth full of dust as the concussion shock washes over their bunkers. The residents of a small town in Utah receive a dose of radiation as wind directions change after a test. The residents are told to stay inside for one hour and the danger will pass. The point of the film and newsreels is to downplay the risk of radiation. However the next scene shows the effect of radiation on pigs exposed to a blast. Pigs are deformed, burned, and suffer from other debilitating effects. Taken as a whole, the clips compiled in *Atomic Café* paint a picture of ignorance among the mass population about the effect of nuclear weapons, and the film serves as a cautionary tale about relying solely on governmental information about issues that have an important impact on society.

The most famous of the films during this period was the TV movie *The Day After* (1983). The film hypothetically explored the effects of a nuclear attack on Lawrence, Kansas. Unfortunately, the message of the film seems to get lost in some of the sentimental contrivances of the story. Incidentally, *The Day After* is said to have had a profound effect on President Reagan when he saw the film and helped to convince him to pursue a more conciliatory stance with the Soviet Union.[53] The British counterpart to *The Day After* was *Threads* (1984). *Threads* examined the long-term effects of an attack on a northern English town. The film follows generations following the war and emphasizes the environmental impact and genetic mutations that are a result of radiation. Other films during the period, such as *War Games* (1983) and *When the Wind Blows* (1986), reflected similar concerns. While this type of film reached a climax in the mid-1980s, the elevation of Mikhail Gorbachev to General-Secretary of the Communist Party in the Soviet Union dramatically changed world politics. The end of the Cold War greatly reduced the attention that the potential of a nuclear war received.

Nuclear weapons, and the possibility of nuclear war, faded into the background somewhat after the end of the Cold War. *The Sum of All Fears* (2002), based on the 1991 novel by Tom Clancy, raises the specter of nuclear weapons in a post–Cold War world. Following the exploits of Clancy hero Jack Ryan (played by Ben Affleck), the story examines the possibility of a terrorist attack using nuclear weapons on the homeland of the United States. The plot of the movie, which has been widely criticized as impossible,[54] has the United States and Russia duped by a neo-fascist terrorist into confronting each other in a nuclear war. The premise is that a reemergent fascist state in Europe would survive after the two superpowers take each other out. The mysterious fascist, played by Alan Bates, is able to acquire a nuclear weapon after it had been found in a forgotten Israeli jet crash from the Yom Kippur War in 1973. This is another point of contention, because most analysts doubt whether Israel would have left a missing nuclear weapon buried in the sand for thirty years.

Despite the dubious plot of *The Sum of All Fears*, the story does remind us that, although the Cold War may be over, the problems and challenges of nuclear weapons remain with us. This is the premise of *Countdown to Zero* (2010), a documentary directed by Lucy Walker. The film examines how easy it is to acquire fissionable material and the likely effect of a detonation on cities. It demonstrates that although arms control treaties have reduced the threat of a nuclear exchange, the threat from nuclear weapons has not completely vanished.

Civil and Ethnic Conflicts

As some scholars have pointed out, wars between major powers since the Second World War have virtually ceased. In fact, no wars between major powers have occurred since 1945. Interstate wars are seemingly on the decline as well. Of the 185 wars that occurred between 1946 and 1999, only about 25 percent were interstate wars.[55] What has been on the rise is the number of civil conflicts, oftentimes centered on ethnic, religious, or racial politics. The civil conflicts during the late twentieth and early twenty-first centuries have proved to be complicated and in some cases particularly brutal. Ethnic conflicts between Hutus and Tutsis in Rwanda during the spring of 1994 cost an estimated 800,000 to 1,000,000 persons their lives. Countries such as Angola and Guatemala have experienced civil conflicts that lasted for decades. While these types of conflict are not new, their predomination of the international system puts strains on mechanisms and institutions that were designed to prevent interstate conflicts rather than intrastate conflicts.

During the 1990s the United States conducted two air campaigns in an effort to have some effect on the wars in Bosnia and Kosovo. The effects of ethnic strife and the problems of the intermixing of ethnic groups, which are cast as ancient rivalries, remain a problem in that region. The film *Before the Rain* (1994) is told in circular dramatic form, so that the audience comes into the story and is taken around the narrative, which in this film begins and ends in Macedonia. The impression is that the director, Milcho Manchevski, is making a statement that ethnic conflict transcends time and place and affects individuals not even directly related to the conflict. The film is dramatic and, at times, disturbing.

The story is told in three chapters, which are interrelated stories taking place at different places and times. The film explores how the war in Macedonia impacts people, communities, friendships, and the world. One of the most striking messages of the film is to understand how the ethnic lines in a community become more stringent once the conflict begins. At first, the Macedonian and Serb communities live side by side and often intermarry. Yet, when trouble between the two groups breaks out, every little argument, whether it is between a waiter and a customer or a family dispute, is cast in the light of ethnic division.

The difficulty in the film, and in ethnic conflicts, is that there are people who want to do the right thing—they want to be neighbors with others. Events begin to overtake goodwill: old friendships are cast aside for fear that one will be perceived as selling out their own ethnic group. One of the clever points about *Before the Rain* is that the story makes some subtle allusions to the conflict in Northern Ireland while the majority of the story is about Macedonia and the conflict in the former Yugoslavia. It is a reminder that many ethnic conflicts follow the same pattern of behavior, the same insults, the same provocations, and, ultimately, the same outcomes.

Many of the films about the wars in the former Yugoslavia have employed a circular storytelling style, similar to *Before the Rain*, to describe the violence in the Balkans. *Cabaret Balkan* (*Bure baruta*; or *The Powder Keg*, 1988), a film from Serbia, uses a similar storytelling method. In this very disturbing film, the narrative relies on the ramblings of a cabaret performer to link the stories together. The performer discusses those who live outside of the Balkans as looking down on those who live in the Balkans, while commenting on the absurdity of life and the beauty of death. The depiction of life in Belgrade on a winter night in the mid-1990s has all of the characters on edge and ready to explode, as depicted in the film's original title, *The Powder Keg*. The only comedy in the film is black, and the film exudes a negative and dark energy.

The film *Bloody Sunday* (2002) examines the events of January 30, 1972, in Derry, Northern Ireland, which would come to be known as "Bloody Sunday." On that day, Catholic protestors gathered to protest the new British policy of detaining Roman Catholics in the province of Northern Ireland without trial. Before the day was over, there was a confrontation between some of the marchers and British paratroopers. The confrontation resulted in thirteen marchers killed, and fourteen hospitalized (one would later die). Although no British soldiers were killed, an official inquiry later stated that the soldiers had returned the fire of the protestors. The event became a galvanizing episode in the conflict between the Catholics and the Protestants in Northern Ireland. In June 2010, a report issued by the British government found that the shootings were "unjustified."[56]

The film examines the events of that day in a documentary style. The camera appears to be at the scene, moving within the crowd and capturing the events as they actually happen. To that extent, some of the camera angles are unconventional, and not all the conversations are heard clearly, as if the audience were a part of the event. One of the unfortunate parts of the film is that it does not provide a context to the violence; instead it focuses on the events of those twenty-four hours. However, it is an excellent examination of how sectarian violence comes about. Ethnic conflict can escalate into much more serious problems, such as civil war and even genocide (which is addressed in the chapter in this book on human rights, Chapter 9).

Ethnic conflict is something that is not usually found in American narrative films. Films like *Billy Jack* (1971) and Spike Lee's *Do the Right Thing* (1989) deal with race and ethnicity in a sense but do not get at the heart of what communities locked in hatred and violence mean when genocide is attempted. The films of Spike Lee, director of *Do the Right Thing*, do address the issue of race. The film *C.S.A.: The Confederate States of America* (2004), produced by Lee, imagines the United States in modern times if the South had won the civil war. The film uses the perspective of a fake British documentary to illustrate how race was and is a key topic in contemporary American life. One American film that does deal with the wars in former Yugoslavia is *Welcome to Sarajevo* (1997), which depicts the horrors of the war in Bosnia, much in the same way *Before the Rain* deals with the complexity of ethnic relations in Macedonia. However, most American films that deal with ethnic conflicts tend to focus on genocide rather than the interplay of ethnic identities.

Terrorism

The horrific events of September 11, 2001, may demonstrate a new level of unconventional political violence. In an event that has had a transforming effect on American society, the brutality and random violence that are associated with terrorism were brought home to American soil. Four jet planes were hijacked: two of them were flown into the World Trade Center in New York City, destroying the seemingly invincible towers of steel and international commerce; one was smashed into the nerve center of the American defense establishment, the Pentagon; and another, also en route to Washington, D.C., crashed in Shanksville, Pennsylvania, just outside of Pittsburgh. Over 2,800 people lost their lives. The events spawned a number of films including the well-received *United 93* (2006), which is a film shot in real time and tells the story of the plane that crashed in Pennsylvania. Two documentaries, *National Geographic: Inside 9/11* (2005) and *Inside the Twin Towers* (2006), recounted the events of the attacks and both garnered Emmys. Other movies and television shows were, directly or indirectly, inspired by the events of that day, such as Oliver Stone's *World Trade Center* (2006) and the very popular television series *24* (2001–2010).

Of course this was not the first time a major terrorist bombing had occurred on American soil. On April 19, 1995, the Alfred P. Murrah Federal Building in Oklahoma City was destroyed by a truck bomb, killing 168 people. Timothy McVeigh, a Gulf War veteran and associate of the Michigan Militia, was ultimately convicted of the crime. Terry Nichols, an associate of McVeigh's, was also connected to the terrorist attack and convicted. That attack was a case of domestic terrorism, but the events of September 11, 2001, represent a case of international terrorism. Regardless of the distinction between domestic and international terrorism, the results are the same: innocents are killed, and in the aftermath of the event, questions are raised about the nature of society and the strategies used to prevent such cataclysmic acts.

Terrorism has been far more frequent in other parts of the globe. A 2002 State Department report suggests that the region of the world most prone to terrorist attacks has been Latin America[57]; however, global media and popular culture lead people to believe otherwise. There are very few films that explore terrorism outside the context of the Middle East. Films such as *Munich* (2005) and *The Sum of All Fears* (2002) help to keep the use of terrorism in the Middle East in the minds of film viewers, while world events might suggest that there are other areas of the world that might be more dangerous or prone to terrorism. Consider films from India, for example: *Theeviravaathi: The Terrorist* (1999), a film that follows a young woman who has volunteered to become a suicide bomber; *Black Friday* (2004), which chronicles the 1993 bombing in Mumbai (Bombay) that utilized thirteen car bombs; and *Red Alert: The Enemy Within* (2009), a film about Maoist rebels in India. While these films are not widely known in North America, they are a clear indication of the importance of terrorism in Indian political life.

Of course, terrorism is in no way a new phenomenon. Some authors have claimed that as far back as the first century, terrorism has been used to create a situation where no one felt safe.[58] It has not been in the too-distant past that some may have even considered terrorism an acceptable form of political violence. Even President Ronald Reagan, in 1981, in discussing the Contras of Nicaragua, argued, "One man's terrorist is another man's freedom fighter."[59] The problem is some acts are seen as "justified," while they can be seen by others as terrorism.[60]

Even popular American films have championed the cause of rebels and saboteurs. The original *Star Wars* trilogy, comprised of *Star Wars* (1977), *The Empire Strikes Back* (1980), and *The Return of the Jedi* (1983), is one of the most famous and popular series in the history of the movies. In the trilogy, the audience roots for the exploits of Luke Skywalker, Princess Leia, and Han Solo in their fight against the imperial government and its number one henchman, Darth Vader. To be sure, the imperial government does not hold the moral high ground in the story; in fact, early on the government destroys the entire planet of Alderaan. Yet, the trio, along with their allies, use sabotage, ambush, and surprise attacks to try to wrest the power of the galaxy away from the imperial government. Interesting historical parallels can be drawn between them and freedom fighters in the past. There is no question that most would prefer the ideals of many freedom fighters over oppressive governments. There seems to be general agreement among people as to what constitutes terrorism and what constitutes legitimate resistance. However, how to definitively draw the line between the two is a problem. Scholars have had just as difficult a time defining terrorism as policy makers have, but one definition that many people have accepted is by George Rosie, who defines terrorism as violence intended to have a target group meet the political demands of the group (or people) who commit the terrorist act.[61]

The goal of terrorism is not necessarily to kill enough people to gain a political end, but to use death and violence to scare (or terrorize) the target population into an action. Hence the effectiveness of terrorism is found in the ability to get people to do things with as little action as possible. What this means is that the battle with terrorists often portrayed in such movies as *Invasion U.S.A.* (1985) and *Air Force One* (1997) does not capture the psychological pressure target populations experience. This psychological pressure can lead to societies beginning to question their core values.

Perhaps one of the best depictions of how fear and terror lead a community to reassess the basic notions of society is contained in one of the most famous episodes of the classic television program *The Twilight Zone* (1959–1964). In the half-hour drama "The Monsters Are Due on Maple Street" (1960), the story opens on Maple Street, in a quiet unnamed suburban town, on a late-afternoon Saturday. The scene mirrors the perceived stereotypes of Americana at the time. People are washing their cars and mowing the grass, while children are playing baseball. Suddenly something passes over the sky and grabs the attention of everyone on the street. The camera remains focused on the street and the reactions of the residents. Thus, the audience cannot evaluate for itself what has flown over in the sky. The viewer relies on the interpretations of the people on Maple Street for the rest of the story.

The initial assumption of the residents is that the object was a meteor. However, if it was a meteor, then it was one with special properties. After it passes over, most of the conveniences of modern life cease to work. Various residents report that electricity, telephones, radios, automobiles, and lawnmowers have stopped working. This causes great consternation among the residents, because while they understand that the electricity or telephones may have been knocked out, it seems to make no sense that the automobiles or portable radios would stop working as well. One resident, Pete van Horn, goes over to Floral Street to see if he can find out anything.

Meanwhile, the residents gather to decide what should be done. Steve (Claude Akins) emerges as a leader, and he suggests that he and Charlie walk downtown to see if the police know what is happening. Before they can leave, Steve and Charlie are warned by one of the teenagers not to go. In every story that he has ever read, the "monsters" who come from outer space want the people to stay where they are. Initially people are dismissive of the teenager's story, but when he starts telling them how the monsters always send a few in advance to pose as humans to prepare the way for an invasion, the residents of Maple Street begin to eye each other suspiciously. No one is allowed to leave the area except the people that were sent down ahead.

Les, who has not come out to see the meteor, comes out to get in his car but it does not start. He comes toward the group, but then an automobile which belongs to Les starts on its own, and people begin to suspect him. Les is considered a real oddball, because he spends some nights in his yard looking up at the stars (as if he is waiting for someone). He claims that he has insomnia. Night falls and people are still suspicious of Les, but suspicions shift as people find out that Steve uses a ham radio (questions of who he is talking to are raised).

As the residents trade suspicions and accusations, a shadowy figure begins walking up Maple Street toward the residents. Someone yells, "It's the monster!" Charlie grabs a gun and shoots the figure, which falls to the ground. The residents run down to get a good look at the monster only to find that Charlie has shot Pete van Horn, who had gone over to Floral Street to see if they had any power there. Charlie is accused by the group, which is fast becoming a mob, of preventing Pete from telling the residents what was going on or warning them who the monster was. Mayhem ensues. The final scenes of the show have the residents fighting and killing one another. As the camera pans up from a Maple Street littered with bodies and debris, the camera has in the foreground two figures standing on a hillside overlooking the rioting:

FIGURE 1:   Understand the procedure now? Just stop a few of their machines, and radios, and telephones, or lawnmowers. . . . Throw them into darkness for a few hours and then sit back and watch the pattern.
FIGURE 2:   And this pattern is always the same?
FIGURE 1:   With few variations, they pick the most dangerous enemy they can find, and it's themselves. All we need do is sit back and watch.
FIGURE 2:   Then I take it this place, this Maple Street, is not unique?
FIGURE 1:   By no means. Their world is full of Maple Streets. And we'll go from one to another and let them destroy themselves.

One of the hallmarks of *The Twilight Zone* was the commentary offered at the end of the program by the show's creator, Rod Serling. Serling, who also wrote the episode, offered the following commentary:

The tools of conquest do not necessarily come from bombs and explosives and fallout. There are weapons that are simply thoughts, attitudes, prejudices to be found only in the minds of men. For the record, prejudices can kill, and suspicion can destroy, and the thoughtless, frightened search for a scapegoat has a fallout all of its own . . . for the children and the children yet unborn. And the pity of it is that these things cannot be confined to the Twilight Zone.

Perhaps one of the casualties of any society that has suffered a terrorist attack is its self-confidence. The task is to resist the temptation of undermining the fundamental values of a society. It is a difficult task, but part of surviving and persevering through a terrorist attack is to maintain one's way of life and one's values.[62]

Conclusions: Why *Do* We Fight?

Understanding the reasons for war is a theoretical debate that has vexed humans for centuries. Is war part of human nature, like the realists believe, or is it a learned trait, in accordance with pluralist thinking? At first glance wars seem to happen all the time. News broadcasts often lead with international violence somewhere in the world; however, the news media do not report how many countries are at peace (e.g., "Today New Zealand and Australia are not at war"). This skews our perception of how frequently wars occur. Yet, the salient question persists: Why do we fight?

Opening with President Dwight Eisenhower's farewell address in January 1961, Eugene Jarecki's documentary *Why We Fight* (2005) examines the question of what causes the United States to engage in military actions overseas, making a direct connection to Frank Capra's series of informational (or perhaps more accurately, propaganda) films made during World War II and discussed earlier in this chapter. [63] After serving as a five-star general, Supreme Allied Commander during the Second World War, and two terms as the thirty-fourth president of the United States, Eisenhower warned that private economic interests (defense industry contractors) should not be allowed to drive policy, for a society that depended too much on armaments for economic growth would never be able to afford peace. He believed that unwarranted and dangerous power was held by three core components: Congress, the military establishment (i.e., the Pentagon), and the aforementioned defense corporations. Eisenhower named this phenomenon the military-industrial complex. [64]

The documentary *Why We Fight* traces the American invasion of Iraq in 2003 and the political and economic role of companies that make weapons. In the film, Senator John McCain, a leading voice on foreign policy and a decorated veteran, voices concern about military allocation and money spent on weapons. [65] Yet arms control expert Joseph Cirincione observes that any politician who even appears to be in opposition to military spending is considered suspect, naïve, or less-than patriotic. Through data and testimony from congressional experts and military defense industry insiders, Jarecki asserts that the perpetual need for jobs across the country means that members of Congress will fight to fund the defense industry projects in their districts, thus perpetuating the cycle of sweeping defense appropriations. The film makes the case that the armaments industry deliberately disperses their work in myriad House districts throughout the country, thus avoiding being only a regional political force. The shrewd scattering of the projects assures adequate distribution of political power around the country.[66]

Other scholars, however, believe that it is our differences that cause war. Different cultures, religions, or ideologies can create suspicions, which eventually manifest themselves in war. From this point of view, films and popular culture can help to create or perpetuate hostile characterizations of others.[67] Of course, the opposite can be true as well: shared films and popular culture can help to bridge differences and create understanding. Still other scholars take a more dim view of human nature and believe war is inevitable because humans are essentially violent.

Perhaps the best way to frame our understanding of war is through the imperfect, compromised vision that initiates and executes it. Such is the perspective provided by documentarian Errol Morris's Academy Award–winning film *The Fog of War: Eleven Lessons from the Life of Robert S. McNamara* (2003), released in the midst of debate over the invasion of Iraq. In the film, McNamara, who was Secretary of Defense in the 1960s and directed the American participation in the Vietnam War, provides a startling account of that war, his service in World War II, and armed conflict in general. He concludes, among other things, that war is so complex, and there are so many variables, that it is beyond the comprehension of humans, thus the phrase "the fog of war." As a counterbalance, many filmmakers would argue that films help to cut through the fog of war and illustrate complex and divergent issues for viewers.

Regardless of perspective, war films can be essential tools in understanding international politics. This does pose challenging questions: *Do war films promote war or do they dissuade people from engaging in it? What motivation does a filmmaker have to accurately portray war? Is the filmmaker's primary intent to entertain, advocate policy, or . . . both?* Understanding how filmmakers answer these questions is essential to understanding the effects war films might have on a society. Foreign and domestic movies, from dramas and documentaries to cartoons and comedies, reveal a number of vital concepts and theories in international relations. In addition to shedding light on these fundamental ideas, the movies reviewed in this chapter illustrate how different wars in different times shape our view of the nature and effect of war itself. How war has been portrayed over the past one hundred years is, in part, a reflection of international politics and the realities of specific eras.

Notes

1. Sovereignty has traditionally been associated with the Peace of Westphalia (1648), which ended the Thirty Years War, a war between Catholics and Protestants in Europe. As part of the agreement, it was decided that the leader of each country would determine the religion of that country—essentially that the rulers of a country can make the rules. In actuality, the history of sovereignty is a little more involved. For further readings, see Alan James, *Sovereign Statehood* (London: Allen & Unwin, 1986); and Daniel Philpott, "Sovereignty: An Introduction and Brief History," *Journal of International Affairs* 48, no. 2 (1995): 353–68.

2. Prior to the First World War, Germany decided that the best way to become a major power was to make itself a predominant naval power. The move to create a substantial navy provoked a response from Great Britain to increase its naval capabilities. Both countries engaged in an arms race. Similarly, during the early years of the Cold War, there was an insistence that the United States have more missiles than the Soviet Union in order to ensure its own security. U.S. presidential candidates, especially John Kennedy in 1960, warned of the dangerous consequences of a real or perceived "missile gap" with the Soviet Union. During this period, each superpower's increase in the size of its nuclear arsenal or new missile technology led to a similar reaction from the other.

3. See Martha Sigall, *Living Life Inside the Lines: Tales from the Golden Age of Animation* (Jackson: University Press of Mississippi, 2005); and Kevin S. Sandler, *Reading the Rabbit: Explorations in Warner Bros. Animation* (New Brunswick, NJ: Rutgers University Press, 1998).

4. Mark Sachleben, "Realism 101," in *International Relations Theory 101*, ed. Eric Leonard (Lanham, MD: Rowman and Littlefield, 2011).

5. The divide in the discipline is often expressed in the dynamic between the history of the international system as being one of peace punctuated by conflicts, as opposed to the view that the history of the international system is one of war punctuated with moments of peace. Central to this understanding is the idea that war is inevitable, or that war is preventable, if we know what the causes of war are. Some scholars argue that states must sometimes demonstrate their ability and resolve to protect themselves. States are insecure and therefore their insecurity will lead them to actions that will inevitably clash with other states. Traditionally, studies of war have focused on what factors make wars more likely.

   Pluralists often seek to explain what factors might cause wars to occur. Scholars have examined factors such as a leader's perception of the enemy, regime type, the amount of interdependence in the world, and other factors to explain war and peace in the international system. One of the most promising lines of research has been the effect of regime type on war and peace in international politics. With a theory popularly known as democratic peace, scholars such as Bruce Russett and Michael W. Doyle have argued that democracies do not fight other democracies. See Bruce Russett, *Grasping the Democratic Peace: Principles for a Post–Cold War World* (Princeton: Princeton University Press, 1993); and Michael W. Doyle, "Liberalism and World Politics," *American Political Science Review* 80, no. 4 (December 1986): 1151–69. If, as people like Francis Fukuyama have speculated, there is a spread of democracy among states around the world, then there would be a corresponding spread of international peace as well. See Francis Fukuyama, "The End of History," *The*

National Interest (Summer 1989), and Francis Fukuyama, *The End of History and the Last Man* (New York: Free Press, 1992).

6. Similarly, in the final installment of the series, *War Comes to America* (1945), Capra reminds Americans how our sacred secular documents, shared values, superior political system, rising wealth, and immigrant melting pot form the strength of our economic and political institutions and our unity of purpose. When these institutions are threatened and physically attacked—such as the Japanese raid on Pearl Harbor on December 7, 1941—there is no rational alternative but to unite in defense of our way of life.

7. Catherine Lovatt, "Europe: What Are East and West?" *Central European Review* 23 (1999): http://www.ce-review.rg/99/23/lovatt23.html.

8. Jay Leyda, *Kino: A History of the Russian and Soviet Film* (New York: Macmillan, 1960), 350. A careful study of the dialogue reveals interesting details about the debate within Russian and communist ideology in practice. The vision presented by Eisenstein is unique and important. The film also resonated with the Soviet population as well since it was the most popular film during the Second World War. In the film, the knights are presented as almost inhuman and definitely sinister (a reference to the Nazis). Notice that the helmets of the Teutonic Knights allow only for a slit for the eyes. Also there is an attempt to divide the population prior to the invasion of the city. All of this is allegorical to the situation in Europe in the late 1930s.

9. For a discussion of *Casablanca* as political allegory, see Aljean Harmetz, *Round Up the Usual Suspects: The Making of Casablanca—Bogart, Bergman, and the World* (New York: Hyperion, 1992).

10. The authors would like to thank Oliver Schulze-Nahrup for his translation of "Die Wacht am Rhein."

11. Part of the Ten Commandments, found in Exodus 20:2–17.

12. For more about the life of Alvin C. York, see David D. Lee, *Sergeant York: An American Hero* (Lexington: University Press of Kentucky, 1985).

13. François Truffaut, *Hitchcock* (New York: Simon & Schuster, 1967), 112–14. For those interested in the work of Alfred Hitchcock, Truffaut's conversation with him is a fantastic opportunity to see the thought process of the master director. One might also consider Donald Spiro, *The Dark Side of Genius: The Life of Alfred Hitchcock* (Boston: Little, Brown, 1983). For interpretations of the work of Alfred Hitchcock, see Marshall Deutelbaum and Leland Poague, eds., *A Hitchcock Reader* (Ames: Iowa State University Press, 1986).

    Hitchcock did receive some criticism based on the character of Willy. As the one who represents the Nazis, Willy is strong, smart, and able to manipulate the others. Critics thought Hitchcock was portraying the democracies as weak and the only way the Nazis could be defeated was through their coordinated efforts.

14. *Wings* (1927) was the first film to win an Academy Award for best picture; the story juxtaposes a love story with the emotion of losing comrades during battle. It is the only silent film to win the Academy Award for best picture.

15. William K. Everson, *American Silent Film* (New York: Oxford University Press, 1978), 292.

16. Humphrey Cobb's (1899–1944) novel was first released in 1935. A new paperback Penguin Classics edition was published in 2010, featuring a foreword by HBO's *The Wire* creator, David Simon, and an introduction from retired U.S. Air Force Lt. Col. James H. Meredith. Humphrey Cobb, *Paths of Glory* (New York: Penguin Classics, 2010).

17. The three prisoners, Boeldieu (an aristocrat), Rosenthal (a Jew), and Maréchal (a laborer), represent different segments of society. The film also explores the relationship between Boeldieu and von Rauffenstein, as aristocrats. They have an affinity with each other and spend many hours discussing the future of politics. Von Rauffenstein laments the advent of democracy in Europe because it brings people like Maréchal and Rosenthal (laborers and Jews, or the lower classes) into politics. Even though there is a general mistrust between Jews and laborers (represented by Rosenthal and Maréchal), their mutual plight begins to develop acceptance, trust, and admiration between the two men. The film's director, Jean Renoir, tries to demonstrate that it is the aristocratic governments of Europe that repeatedly lead the continent to war. Renoir reminds us that it is the lower classes that suffer the most during the war.

18. J. M. Winter, *Remembering War: The Great War between Memory and History in the Twentieth Century* (New Haven: Yale University Press, 2006).

19. Chaplin was clearly pleased by the speech and the reception it received. In his autobiography, he mentions many of the comments he received about the film and especially the ending speech. He reprints the entire speech, as well, in Charlie Chaplin, *My Autobiography* (New York: Simon & Schuster, 1964), 397–400.

20. This is an issue explored in Chapter 9, "Human Rights."

21. Chaplin, *My Autobiography*, pp. 392–93, 404–5; David Robinson, *Chaplin, His Life and Art* (New York: McGraw-Hill, 1985), 485.

22. The full title of the Pentagon Papers was "United States–Vietnam Relations, 1945–1967: A Study Prepared by the Department of Defense." Ellsberg, a military analyst with the RAND corporation and, formerly, with Robert McNamara's Department of Defense, decided that his conscience would not allow him to remain silent about the Johnson administration's years of public and congressional deception on the war in Vietnam, and he first leaked the highly classified documents to the *New York Times* and later to several other newspapers and elected officials. The highly regarded and Oscar-nominated documentary *The Most Dangerous Man in America: Daniel Ellsberg and the Pentagon Papers* was released in 2009. The film chronicles Ellsberg's work leading up to the release of the Pentagon Papers, his shifting views on the Vietnam War, the wide-ranging political and legal impact of the release of the classified documents, and the Nixon administration's vigorous attempts to discredit Ellsberg and the *New York Times*. The documentary premiered nationwide on PBS's *Independent Lens* in October 2010. The film's website is: http://www.mostdangerousman.org/.

23. From the poem "Vietnam," which is in Samuel Hazo, *The Past Won't Stay Behind You* (Fayetteville: University of Arkansas Press, 1993), 47–48. Hazo was the founder, and served as director (1966–2009), of the International Poetry Forum. He was selected as Pennsylvania's first State Poet by Gov. Robert Casey in 1993, and is a retired professor emeritus at Duquesne University.

24. Journalist David L. Robb has written extensively and eye-openingly about the Department of Defense's long-standing ability to force minor-to-substantial changes in a film's tone, dialogue, and even plot in exchange for the Pentagon's cooperation and assistance in the making of the film—such as the use of military bases, weapons, aircraft, etc. See David L. Robb, *Operation Hollywood: How the Pentagon Shapes and Censors the Movies* (New York: Prometheus Books, 2004).

For John Wayne's letter to LBJ (actually, via Johnson assistant Bill Moyers), see Robb, "The Propaganda Value of Film," pp. 277–84. Seeking Pentagon assistance and approval in making a fiercely pro–Vietnam War film, Wayne wrote President Johnson, "We are fighting a war in Vietnam. Though I personally support the administration's policy there, I know it is not a popular war, and I think it is extremely important that not only the people of the United States, but all over the world, should know why it is necessary for us to be there. . . . The most effective way to accomplish this is through the motion picture medium. Some day soon a motion picture will be made about Vietnam. Let's make sure it's the kind of picture that will help our cause throughout the world" (Robb, 281).

25. The film *We Were Soldiers* was based on the bestseller by Harold G. Moore and Joseph L. Galloway, *We Were Soldiers Once . . . and Young* (New York: Random House, 1992).

26. President Reagan's reelection campaign in 1984 used the refrain of "Born in the U.S.A." at many of his campaign stops without the campaign realizing that the song was a blistering critique of socioeconomic conditions in the United States, and in particular, its treatment of veterans. See Jefferson Cowie and Lauren Boehm, "Dead Man's Town: 'Born in the U.S.A.,' Social History, and Working Class Identity," *American Quarterly* 58, no. 2 (2006): 353–78. See also Karlstad University (Sweden) media professor Christian Christenson's "Springsteen's 'Born in the U.S.A.' Turns 25, a 25-Year Misunderstanding," March 19, 2009: http://springsteeninformationcenter.wordpress.com/category/born-in-the-usa/. Conservative columnist George Will also mistakenly praised the song as an example of patriotic Republican values, writing of Springsteen, "He is no whiner, and the recitation of closed factories and other problems always seems punctuated by a grand, cheerful affirmation: 'Born in the USA!'" See George Will, "Bruce Springsteen's USA," *Washington Post,* September 13, 1984. Twenty-six years later the controversy about the meaning and intention of the song was briefly resurrected when pundit and activist Glenn Beck accused the song of being un-patriotic and Springsteen anti-American. See *The Glenn Beck Program,* March 11, 2010 (Premiere Radio Networks). From the World Wrestling Federation of the 1980s—where stock patriotic "All American" tag-team champions Barry Windham and Mike Rotundo routinely entered the ring to the rousing opening chords of "Born in the U.S.A" (they defeated the Russian–Iranian tag-team combo of Nikolai Volkoff and the Iron Sheik in 1985, at Wrestlemania, for the tag-team title)—to the start of NFL games in 2010, Springsteen's song continues to be used in celebratory and patriotic contexts oddly out of sync with the song's message of pain, desperation, and disillusionment.

27. Dylan briefly discussed his song "Clean-Cut Kid" from the album *Empire Burlesque* (Columbia Records, 1985) and American military involvement in an interview with Mikal Gilmore in the July 17, 1986, issue of *Rolling Stone*. The interview is reprinted in its entirety in Jonathan Cott, ed., *Bob Dylan: The Essential Interviews* (New York: Wenner Books, 2006), 333–46. The specific "Clean-Cut Kid" references can be found on pages 342–43.

28. The film's title, *Stop-Loss*, refers to the policy of the American military indefinitely and involuntarily extending a soldier's tour of duty beyond their enlistment agreement because of military combat missions. See "New Stop-Loss Policy," *Army* 53, no. 4 (2003): 56–57.

29. "Military, VA Confront Rising Suicide Rates Among Troops," PBS's *NewsHour with Jim Lehrer,* November 10, 2008: http://www.pbs.org/newshour/bb/health/july-dec08/suicides_11-10.html/. From the *NewsHour* report: "The Army says suicides among its active-duty

personnel have doubled in recent years, with almost 700 since the year 2000. If current trends continue, suicide will eventually surpass the civilian rate of 19 suicides per 100,000 people. Other alarming statistics: Attempted suicides and self-injuries have quadrupled over the past six years."

30. *The Wounded Platoon*, PBS's *Frontline* film, May 18, 2010: http://www.pbs.org/wgbh/pages/frontline/woundedplatoon/view/.

31. Philip Kennicot, "In 'Restrepo,' the Afghan War's Brutality as Viewed through the Soldier's Scope," *Washington Post*, June 27, 2010: http://www.washingtonpost.com/wpdyn/content/article/2010/06/24/AR2010062406891.html. The title (Restrepo) refers to a remote outpost in Afghanistan's Korengal Valley, which is named after a the platoon's medic who was killed in action.

32. Ibid.

33. Roger Ebert, "Gunner Palace," *Chicago Sun-Times*, March 11, 2005: http://rogerebert.suntimes.com/apps/pbcs.dll/article?AID=/20050310/REVIEWS/50301002/1023.

34. Naomi Pfefferman, "Oren Moverman's 'The Messenger': The Unseen Casualties of War," Jewishjournal.com, November 29, 2009: http://www.jewishjournal.com/hollywood_jew/article/oren_movermans_the_messenger_the_unseen_casualties_of_war_20091120/.

35. The book was re-released in 2010, in paperback, to correspond with the release of the film. The new title of Chandrasekaran's book is, not surprisingly, just *Green Zone*, and features Matt Damon (from the film) on the cover.

36. Stephen Holden, "When Heroism Means Finding Truth," *New York Times*, August 19, 2010: http://movies.nytimes.com/2010/08/20/movies/20tillman.html.

37. A number of scholars have studied the politics and legal-moral ramifications of privatized military operations. One of the most exhaustive (and very critical) examinations of the founding and influence of the security firm/military contractor Blackwater (later renamed Xe Services for public relations purposes) and its CEO Erik Prince is Jeremy Scahill's *Blackwater: The Rise of the World's Most Powerful Mercenary Army* (New York: Nation Books, 2007). Other texts that detail the power of and dilemmas posed by private armies in contemporary warfare include: P.W. Singer, *Corporate Warriors: The Rise of the Privatized Military Industry* (Ithaca: Cornell University Press, 2003); Suzanne Simmons, *Masters of War: Blackwater USA's Erik Prince and the Business of War* (New York: Harper Paperbacks, 2009); and Robert Young Pelton, *Licensed to Kill: Hired Guns in the War on Terror* (New York: Broadway Books, 2007).

38. Carl von Clausewitz, *On War*, ed. and trans. Michael Howard and Peter Paret (Princeton: Princeton University Press, 1976).

39. Take, for example, the 1955 film *King Dinosaur*. In the not-too-distant future, explorers from Earth travel to the newly discovered Planet Nova. The humans travel to a planet where they find a group of dinosaurs, including a Tyrannosaurus Rex, inhabiting the island. After "harrowing" experiences, the explorers escape the island, leaving a nuclear device to destroy it. One of the characters comments, "It was the only thing to do."

40. Nevil Shute, *On the Beach* (London: Heinemann, 1957). Nevil Shute was the pen name of Nevil Shute Norway.

41. Robert F. Kennedy, *Thirteen Days: A Memoir of the Cuban Missile Crisis* (New York: W. W. Norton, 1971).

42. Although the film is somewhat inaccurate, it is useful to demonstrate the complexity and difficulty the Kennedy administration faced in the midst of the crisis.

43. Don Munton and David A. Welch, *The Cuban Missile Crisis: A Concise History* (New York: Oxford University Press, 2007), 110–12.

44. See Roger Ebert's three-star review of *Thirteen Days*, *Chicago Sun-Times*, January 12, 2001.

45. In addition, it is worth noting the several worthwhile features that are contained in the DVD release of *Thirteen Days*. Among the indispensable items for those who are interested in the Cuban Missile Crisis are a timeline of key events, biographies of the political and military players in the real-life drama ("Historical Figures Biographical Gallery"), and an excellent documentary film, *Roots of the Cuban Missile Crisis*, which provides valuable, essential political and historical context by covering U.S.-Soviet relations from the Second World War through 1962. And, it does so in slightly under an hour.

46. Actually, Sellers was supposed to play a *fourth* character, the jingoistic American bomber pilot Kong, made immortal by western film (and *Blazing Saddles*) legend Slim Pickens, but Sellers suffered an injury on the set and the rest is, as they say, history.

47. Paul Boyer, "Dr. Strangelove," in *Past Imperfect: History According to the Movies*, ed. Mark C. Carnes (New York: Owl Books, 1996), 266–69.

48. Ibid., 267.

49. His views earned him the nickname "Bombs-Away LeMay."

50. Boyer, "Dr. Strangelove," 266.

51. Ibid., 269.

52. Ibid., 266.

53. Beth A Fischer, *The Reagan Reversal: Foreign Policy and the End of the Cold War* (Columbia: University of Missouri Press, 1997), 115–22; Robert Brent Toplin, *Ronald Reagan and the Day the Earth Stood Still*, History News Network, December 29, 2008: http://hnn.us/articles/58928.html. See also the audio and transcript "The Day After: 20 Years Later," NPR's *All Things Considered*, November 20, 2003: http://www.npr.org/templates/story/story.php?storyId=1514779.

54. Chris Cobb, "A Tragedy Coming to the Western World," *Ottawa Citizen*, June 2, 2002, p. A9.

55. Nils Petter Gleditsch, Håvard Strand, Mikael Eriksson, Margareta Sollenberg, and Peter Wallensteen, "Armed Conflict 1946–99: A New Dataset," paper presented at the 42nd Annual Convention of the International Studies Association, Chicago, Illinois, February 20–24, 2001: http://www.isanet.org/achive/ngp.html.

56. The official website for the inquiry into the events of Bloody Sunday can be found at: http://www.bloody-sunday-inquiry.org.uk. The complete report, the Report of the Bloody Sunday Inquiry (Lord Saville Report), is available at: http://report.bloody-sunday-inquiry.org/. See also Gerry Moriarity, "Relief and Vindication in Derry at Findings in 5,000-page Report," *The Irish Times*, June 16, 2010.

57. United States Department of State, "Patterns of Global Terrorism," 2002: http://www.state.gov/s/ct/rls/crt/2002/pdf/index.htm.

58. Sean Anderson and Stephen Sloan, *Historical Dictionary of Terrorism* (London: Scarecrow Press, 1995).

59. Barry James, "International Terrorism Expected to Worsen in the 1980s," *United Press International*, August 12, 1981.

60. See, for example, the vote at the United Nations to postpone work on the Comprehensive Convention Against Terrorism following the September 11th attacks when diplomats found it difficult to find common ground on how to define terrorism. News reports can be found at "Terrorism Convention: Fresh Talks in January," *The Hindu*, November 23, 2001; and "U.N. Deadlocked on Anti-Terrorism Treaty," Inter Press Service World News: http://www.oneworld.net/ips2/oct01/01_13_005.html.

61. George Rosie, *Directory of International Terrorism* (Edinburgh: Mainstream Publishing, 1996).

62. In 2003, "The Monsters Are Due on Maple Street" was remade for a new version of *The Twilight Zone*. In the reincarnation, terrorism is more explicitly reinforced as the topic at hand, and rather than aliens watching the accusatory, paranoid, fear-ridden suburban neighbors turning on each other, it is the government watching over the state of affairs (and knocking the power off) to see how Americans would react in case of a terrorist attack.

63. President Eisenhower's farewell address can be viewed at: http://video.google.com/videoplay?docid=-2465144342633379864#. For a link, see: www.seeingthebiggerpicture.net.

64. For background to Eisenhower's claim and the military-industrial complex, see William D. Hartung, "Eisenhower's Warning," *World Policy Journal* 18, no. 1 (Spring 2001): 39–44. The novel and film *Seven Days in May* (1964), which told the story about a military coup in the United States directed against a president who signed a peace treaty with the Soviet Union, was based on the fear of a growing military-industrial complex. See James Fallows, "The Military-Industrial Complex," *Foreign Policy* 133 (November–December 2002): 46–48. In the original draft of Eisenhower's farewell address, he was more explicit about the collusion between the defense establishment and armaments industries; he called the powerful relationship the "Military-Industrial-Congressional Complex." See the section of Eugene Jarecki's film *Why We Fight* (2005) entitled "the Missing C." For a link to watch President Eisenhower's farewell address, visit: www.seeingthebiggerpicture.net.

65. For example, an expensive second engine was developed for the F-35 Joint Strike Fighter. The American Department of Defense decided it was unnecessary. Nevertheless, Congress voted to approve the project over the objection of the Defense Department. Subsequently, several people in Congress were found to have received campaign donations from the contractors who made the aircraft. See Herb Jackson, "Defense Contractors Remember Their N.J. Friends in Congress," *North Jersey Record*, May 4, 2010: http://www.northjersey.com/news/politics/95593349_Defense_contractors_remember_their_N_J__friends_in_Congress.html; and Christopher Drew, "Panel Seen Approving F-35 Engine, Risking Veto," *The New York Times*, July 26, 2010.

66. Jarecki expands on some of these ideas in his larger examination of post–World War II American militarism and the forces that facilitate it in Eugene Jarecki, *The American Way of War: Guided Missles, Misguided Men, and a Republic in Peril* (New York: Free Press, 2008). Ultimately, Jarecki's provocative examination of forces driving American military involvement in the post–World War II era adds a new and troubling contemporary element to Ike's notion of the military-industrial complex: the synergetic, and largely unaccountable, rise and force of think tanks and their media allies. Specifically, *Why We Fight* spotlights the influence of the neoconservative Project for a New American Century, a highly influential think tank comprised of former government officials and neoconservative intellectu-

als, which exerted tremendous influence on the George W. Bush presidency and foreign policy generally, and the war in Iraq in particular.

67. Consider films such as *Japoteurs* (1942), *Bugs Bunny Nips the Nips* (1944), and *The Kaiser: The Beast of Berlin* (1918).

· 9 ·

HUMAN RIGHTS

The universal, ever-salient quest to ensure basic human rights, regardless of the political-economic system, dominant religion, or cultural order, remains a matter that film and popular culture explore on a persistent basis. Popular music has been especially persistent in this regard, addressing the struggle for human rights across the globe over many decades and across myriad cultures and musical styles. With penetrating, provocative works from diverse artists and genres, songs and popular music have given voice to the voiceless and shed light on infringements of human rights. Popular performances include:

- Billie Holiday's landmark rendition of Abe Meeropol's "Strange Fruit" in 1939, which became an anti-lynching anthem;
- The socially conscious, civil rights movement–inspired folk music revival of the 1950s–1960s, such as Bob Dylan's "Blowin' in the Wind" and Pete Seeger's "If I Had a Hammer," both popularized by Peter, Paul and Mary;
- Soul pioneer Sam Cooke's "A Change Is Gonna Come";
- International performers in less-developed countries such as Bob Marley who sang for political and social rights, including the reggae classic "Get Up, Stand Up";

- The anti-Apartheid movement, which sparked interest in the music of native South Africans like legendary civil rights activist Miriam Makeba (1932–2008), Johnny Clegg and Savuka, and Ladysmith Black Mambazo, and inspired the Steven Van Zandt all-star benefit record *Sun City* by Artists United Against Apartheid;
- Amnesty's International's concert tour on the twenty-fifth anniversary of the United Nations' Universal Declaration of Human Rights, featuring the likes of Bruce Springsteen, Sting, Tracy Chapman, and Youssou N'Dour; and
- Numerous benefit concerts calling for the release of human rights activists, like Nelson Mandela (1988) and Aung San Suu Kyi (2009–2010).

There are seemingly endless examples of musicians and singers employing their trade to examine the consequences of human rights abuses and humanitarian crises resulting from national disasters and political upheaval.

This chapter will use the simple definition that human rights are those conditions that allow a human to live a life of dignity.[1] Generally, the portrayal of human rights violations is particularly effective on film. First, a discussion of human rights violations lends itself to film because it is dramatic. Second, human rights violations also leave a record that is visual, particularly when that violation is something like torture or genocide. Whatever the case, there is a plethora of films that explore the topic of human rights. However, our discussion here is limited to emphasizing the vital human rights concerns raised by a small but representative sampling of films in the human rights genre.

The idea of sovereignty suggests that the internal decision-making process, or politics of a country, is not the concern of other states. Because the principle of sovereignty has been a particularly relevant force in the international system since the Treaty of Westphalia in 1648, human rights have not typically been a concern of states prior to the Second World War. That is not to say that there were not domestic considerations. In fact, several films in the United States dealt with human rights violations as a justification for entering World War I. In *Hearts of the World* (1918), famed silent-film director D. W. Griffith depicts a French town occupied by the Germans where torture is commonplace. A highly propagandized film, *Kaiser, the Beast of Berlin* (1918) focused on the alleged depravities of the German regime during the war. Even Mary Pickford, America's sweetheart, in *The Little American* (1917), is the target of an attempted rape by Germans. Films would often use factual cases to bolster the idea that crimes of great magnitude were being committed by Germans, such as the case of Edith Cavell, the British nurse who was executed by the Germans as a spy and for helping a couple hundred Allied soldiers to escape.[2]

The slaughter of six million Jews and several million others during the Second World War prompted the international community to take up the discussion of human rights in international forums. The newly formed United Nations in 1948 adopted two instruments that attempted to address the subject of human rights. The first was a resolution designed as a guide for the formulation of human rights conventions in the future. Former First Lady Eleanor Roosevelt—an outspoken advocate for human rights at home and abroad—chaired the UN committee charged with drafting a worldwide declaration of human rights.[3] Known as the Universal Declaration of Human Rights, the document laid out thirty articles that delineated what constitutes fundamental human rights in the international community. Among its thirty articles, the Universal Declaration calls for guaranteeing all individuals vital human rights, including "the right to life, liberty and the security of person," freedom from slavery, protection from discrimination, the prevention of torture or "cruel, inhuman or degrading treatment or punishment," and other basic social, political, and economic rights.

A Brief Summary of the Universal Declaration of Human Rights (adopted December 10, 1948)

Article 1: All humans are born free and equal
Article 2: Everyone is entitled to the rights contained in the Declaration, without distinction (such as race, sex, language, religion, or political opinion)
Article 3: The right to life, liberty and the security of person
Article 4: Prohibition of slavery
Article 5: Prohibition of torture
Article 6: Recognition before the law
Article 7: Equality before the law
Article 8: Effective remedy for violation of fundamental rights
Article 9: Prohibition of arbitrary arrest
Article 10: Fair trial
Article 11: Guarantee of presumed innocence until proven guilty
Article 12: Guarantee of privacy
Article 13: Freedom of movement
Article 14: Guarantee to seek asylum from persecution

Article 15: Nationality
Article 16: Marriage and family
Article 17: Own property
Article 18: Freedom of thought, conscience and marriage
Article 19: Freedom of opinion, and expression
Article 20: Peaceful assembly and association
Article 21: Participation in government
Article 22: Social security
Article 23: Work
Article 24: Rest and leisure
Article 25: Adequate standard of living
Article 26: Education
Article 27: Participation in cultural life
Article 28: Social and international order (in order so that the above rights can be realized)
Article 29: Everyone has duties in the community so that the rights can be achieved
Article 30: Insures that nothing in the Declaration can be construed as destroying the rights enumerated in the document

For a link to the complete text, see www.seeingthebigger picture.net.

A second document adopted by the United Nations in 1948, which more directly confronts some of the problems arising from the Second World War, is the Convention on the Prevention and Punishment of the Crime of Genocide. This is an attempt to prevent and punish one of the most pernicious problems of the twentieth century. Genocide is defined in the Convention as the attempt "to destroy, in whole or in part, a national, ethnical, racial or religious group."[4] Looking back on the events in Europe during the 1930s and 1940s, the international community was outraged at the attempts of the Nazi regime to eradicate particularly Jews, but also Gypsies and homosexuals as well. As horrific as what was to become known as "the Holocaust" was, it was neither the first nor last time the complete destruction of a group was attempted. We are familiar with some of the most egregious of cases, but other examples often tend to be underreported.

The remainder of this chapter will discuss films that examine human rights broadly by utilizing different techniques. The aim of filmmakers who develop films about human rights is to raise the issues depicted in their films. This chapter explores the various techniques one could employ. Following this we will explore how films have been used to perpetrate human rights violations. The chapter will conclude with a debate about the use of the death penalty (particularly in the United States) and whether its use constitutes a human rights violation.

Films about Human Rights

A daunting challenge is to select a few films about human rights to discuss in this chapter—the number of human rights documentaries alone is staggering. Every year the human rights group Amnesty International sponsors a film festival for documentaries about human rights. There are many methods of storytelling in which filmmakers can relay their concern about a particular topic in human rights. This section examines examples of films from four types of storytelling: documentary films in which participants give a testimony about what they did or saw; documentary films in which academics and experts give context to the events; narrative films that reenact events; and narrative films that use fictional events to make a point. Each of these methods has strengths and weaknesses. By exploring different examples, we hope to demonstrate a broad cross section of films about human rights.

Documentary films in which participants give a testimony provide the viewer with access to people who witnessed or experienced human rights violations. The 1985 documentary *Shoah* uses firsthand accounts of witnesses, survivors, and participants to help tell the story. At over nine hours, the film can be overwhelming. Released forty years after the end of the Second World War, the film provides an all-encompassing panorama of the Holocaust, not just as unplanned violence but as a premeditated act designed to eliminate an entire group of people from Europe and the world. Perhaps one of the stunning aspects of the film is the number of people who simply stood by and did or said nothing as the crimes were committed.

Shoah relies primarily on testimonials to tell the events of the Holocaust. For example, there is the testimony of Filip Müller, a Czech Jew, who describes his experiences on "special detail" at Auschwitz. The description of his experiences focuses on the taking of prisoners from the trains to the gas chambers, and then, once dead, the bodies were taken to the crematoriums. Müller describes the conflicts of those who were on the special detail as to whether those who were going to the gas chambers should be told of their impending deaths. Another example is a segment that describes how the Jews of Corfu were rounded up and shipped to Auschwitz. Of the 1,700 people who reported when summoned, only 122 returned after the war. The film does not rely solely on the testimonials of victims, though; Walton Stier, former head of the Reich Railways Department, supervised the coordination of the so-called special trains, which transported the Jews of Eastern Europe to the concentration camp of Auschwitz. Over the course of the testimonial Stier denies that he knew what awaited the Jews when they arrived at Auschwitz, despite the overwhelming evidence and that there were no trains filled with people ever leaving the camp.[5]

A recurring theme among this type of film is that eyewitness accounts humanize human rights violations and allow a better understanding of the brutality and violence of war. Instead of reading a dispassionate account of human rights violations, films that relay a victim's testimonial, or an account from a witness, allow the viewer to consider the humanity of the victims. Relying on an overview of the events, like statistics, perpetuates an emotional distance from particularly horrific crimes. As powerful as this type of film might be, the drawback to this approach is that one must be familiar with the precise actions and incidents in question. Without knowing who the people are, what happened, or why the severe violence and abrogation of human rights occurred, it is sometimes difficult to make sense of testimonials that usually focus on a specific event rather than giving a broader perspective.

One way to combat the potential weakness of this well-intentioned format and bridge the gap between dispassionate data and emotional testimonials, and the all-too-real significance of the exact human rights violations in question, is to use documentary films rich in historical background and analysis. Thus, documentaries in which academics and experts give context to the events try to address the knowledge gap of potential audience members. For example, the PBS *Frontline* special film *The Triumph of Evil* documents the Rwandan genocide of 1994 and the failure of Western countries to act.[6] Moreover, on the tenth anniversary of the Rwandan genocide, *Frontline* revisited the tragic consequences of international inaction that led to over 800,000 Rwandans being slaughtered in 100 days with an updated version of this landmark documentary, *Ghosts of Rwanda* (2004). A companion website adds even more information, with a timeline of events, analysis, interviews, and a section on the state of contemporary Rwanda.[7] Director of the International Crisis Group Gareth Evans argued forcefully that the international community must have a coherent, effective plan in place to confront genocide and humanitarian crises such as those that transpired in the 1990s–2000s in Rwanda, the Balkans, Haiti, Somalia, Sudan, Sierra Leone, East Timor, and elsewhere: "Reacting to these situations in the ad hoc, usually ineffective and often counter-productive way that we have in the past is no longer the kind of luxury we can afford as inter-dependent global neighbours."[8]

For those who study genocide, one of the issues about Rwanda is that very few people know what happened. *The Triumph of Evil* methodically, but suc-cinctly, relays the story of Rwanda to the audience. It mixes the comments of scholars, diplomats, and victims to help the audience understand what hap-pened in 1994.[9] The landing of Western countries' troops only to evacuate Western diplomats (not even those Rwandans who worked for the Western embassies) and the Clinton administration's refusal to call the events at the time a genocide rarely fail to promote anguish among viewers.

Similarly, the four-part documentary *The Genocide Factor* (2000) chroni-cles the history of genocide.[10] The film depicts the dehumanization process and the attempt to find scapegoats, and it is successful in educating the viewer about the problems of dehumanizing victims.[11] The film concludes that factors like the lack of democracy and extreme nationalism contribute to the possibility that genocide might occur, but it leaves open the question of the rationalization of an individual to torture, maim, and desecrate other human beings. The film, in graphic and uncomfortable detail, documents the effects of genocide in a number of different settings. Film and still photography of some of the most egregious events of crimes against humanity are displayed.

While many Americans are cognizant of the attempt of the Nazis to erad-icate the Jews, *The Genocide Factor* (2000) asks the audience to move beyond the one incident and see the larger picture of the history of genocide. Included in the discussion of genocide is the Soviet-orchestrated famine in Ukraine dur-ing the 1930s, the reign of terror in Cambodia under Pol Pot (which also is depicted in the 1984 film *The Killing Fields*), the Japanese invasion of Nanking, the 1923 massacre in Rosewood, Florida (which also is depicted in the 1997 film *Rosewood*), and the numerous wars in the Balkans and Sub-Saharan Africa dur-ing the 1990s. Particularly disturbing and moving are the scenes of Rwandan amputees holding their limbs. A story common to many survivors was that they witnessed their families brutally killed before their eyes.

There is no doubt that scenes in films like this are difficult, at best, to watch and to comprehend on an emotional basis. These films do not sentimentalize;

the images are not dressed up to make them artistic. The drawback to such films is that the number of people who might see a documentary film about human rights violations is substantially lower than the number who would see a narrative film on the same topic. On the one hand, the message and information the filmmakers are trying to disseminate might not reach a wide audience. On the other hand, documentary films provide and contextualize information that is helpful in understanding mass human rights violations.

To help reach a broader audience a filmmaker might choose to make a narrative film that reenacts events. Such films attempt to give the audience an overview about a topic or incident through a dramatic retelling that appeals to the average moviegoer. Because filmmakers must be more concerned with storytelling than accuracy, one of the drawbacks to this genre of film is that they may be less rigorous historically than documentary films. Nonetheless, these films have the ability to reach mass audiences.

For many people in Europe and North America, we are far removed from a world where human rights violations occur on a regular basis. Perhaps some of the most interesting and dramatic stories that are told are when people are faced with the terror of living in fear of severe human rights violations. One of the best films for capturing this nightmare is *Missing* (1982). Starring Jack Lemmon, the film is based on the real-life experiences of Ed Horman, whose son disappeared after a military coup in Chile. Ed's son, Charles, is a writer and political activist, living and working in Chile with his wife, Beth. During the September 1973 *coup d'état* of General Augusto Pinochet,[12] Charles Horman was picked up, taken to a soccer stadium along with other students, writers, and activists, and was beaten, tortured, and, finally, executed the week following the coup.

In the film, Ed Horman flies to Chile at the behest of his daughter-in-law, Beth, to help search for Charles. Ed's political leanings are the opposite of his son's; Ed is a conservative who believes that any American involvement in Chile was more than likely justified. His first assumption is that Charles has done something wrong and has been arrested by the police for some crime. As the film progresses Ed begins to understand that his son's only crime was that he might have had prior knowledge of the coup.

The movie finds Ed frustrated by a number of barriers. As he makes the rounds to the police and American officials in Santiago, Ed is stonewalled, delayed, and sent to other officials. Gradually, Ed comes to the realization that even the U.S. government is lying to him. When Charles's body is returned to the family, it is badly decomposed, making it difficult to tell whether or not

Charles had suffered from torture. Years later, after repeated efforts by many activists, the CIA released some documents surrounding the death of Charles Horman. In one document, dated August 1976, the State Department admitted that American intelligence officials might have played "an unfortunate part" in Charles Horman's death.[13]

Missing won the Academy Award for best screenplay and the film was nominated for best picture.[14] An interesting contradiction about the film is that the audience becomes entranced about the death of a single American in Chile, which is depicted as tragic, but the film pays little attention to the approximately 1,500 Chileans who died during the aftermath of the *coup d' état*. A film such as *The Official Story* (*La historia oficial*, 1985), made in Argentina about the aftermath of that country's "Dirty War," helps to fill in the gaps.[15] The film is about a middle-class family who adopts a young girl whose parents have "disappeared" (a euphemism for been killed) as a result of opposing government policies. The *Official Story* points to the widespread and lasting implications of human rights violations by examining the effects on a single family.

A combination of documentary and strategic reenactments forms the foundation of director Anders Østergaard's exposé of pervasive human rights abuses in Myanmar (Burma), *Burma VJ: Reporting from a Closed Country*. Nominated for best documentary feature yet reaching its widest American audience through cable television's HBO in 2009–2010, *Burma VJ* employs raw, disturbing, smuggled video footage of rampant violence and harassment engineered against citizens by the country's military junta. Captured by critics of the government and sent clandestinely to sympathizers and contacts in Thailand and later Denmark, the film follows the uprisings of pro-democracy forces against the backdrop of the authoritarian government's repression and detention (house arrest) of human rights activist and Nobel Peace Prize Laureate Aung San Suu Kyi. The growing support of the pro-democracy movement is reflected in the actions of many of the nation's Buddhist monks, who, in one of the most dramatic scenes in the film, march in solidarity with the dissidents after yet another brutal crackdown on anti-government demonstrations. Yet even these revered religious leaders, who in many ways undergird the culture's spiritual and moral center, find that they are not spared the wrath of the military and police. It is this display of official governmental violence against a notoriously peaceful population that shocked many Burmese citizens and outraged many throughout the world.

The genre of narrative films that reenact events also help to educate people by making them more interested in a subject. Many times when the word "genocide" is mentioned the first reaction is often to think about the events of Central Europe in the 1930s and 1940s. Unfortunately, although the term "genocide" was not coined until after World War II, the phenomenon has occurred many times before and since. Films that have mass distribution help to keep these stories alive.

One event of mass starvation and killing of Armenians (1915–1918) still generates a great deal of controversy as to whether or not the event was actually a genocide.[16] Only fragments of a silent film *Ravished Armenia* (1919) exist, but it is one of the first films that makes the claim of genocide.[17]

During the 1970s one of the most popular genres in American television was the mini-series. The first and most famous of these mini-series was *Roots* (1977), based on Alex Haley's novel, which told the story of slavery in the United States through the experiences of generations of an African American family. Another major mini-series was *Holocaust* (1978),[18] which followed the trials and tribulations of each member of the Weiss family, who were Jewish, and compare them with the Dorf family, who were German, during the Nazi regime in Germany. For four nights in April 1978, Americans watched as the Weiss family was stripped of their jobs, honor, citizenships, and, eventually for most of them, their lives. It is difficult to sum up the story of a film that takes 475 minutes to screen on television, but the audience is educated, nonetheless, in a general history of the major events of European Jewry during the 1930s and 1940s.

While the audience sees the plight of the Jewish Weiss family, the viewer also is asked to consider the plight of other Germans who are not Jewish. Erik Dorf is an out-of-work lawyer, who joins the SS to support his family. As the film progresses, Erik becomes more and more aligned with the movement and identifies with the objective of "saving Western civilization from the Jews." Other Germans in the story have difficult choices to make, as their lives are intertwined with the lives of Jews. In the end, the film forces the audience into a dilemma: Given the same situation what would we do? Options are rather limited and depressing. Ultimately, people become the persecutors or the persecuted.

Some television critics have complained that the story is too contrived at points. It is rather hard to imagine that such a small number of people were witnesses to so many events during the war, including *Kristallnacht*, the uprising in the Warsaw Ghetto, and the "Final Solution" at Auschwitz.[19] Even some Holocaust survivors (most notably Elie Wiesel) thought that by portraying a fictional family in the midst of such horrific events cheapened and diminished what had actually happened during those fateful years.[20]

Nevertheless, *Holocaust* was an important event in U.S. television history. The mini-series raised consciousness about the crimes of Nazi Germany and the effects of genocide. When the mini-series was shown in West Germany the following January, the impact on public opinion was dramatic. The entertainment trade journal *Variety* reported that among teenagers in West Germany, seven in ten reported that they had learned more by watching the mini-series than they had in all their studies of West German history.[21] Other documentaries have addressed the horrors of the Holocaust, as well as the post–World War II struggle of Jewish refugees en route to the creation of the state of Israel in 1948. Such is the focus of the Academy Award winner for best documentary *The Long Way Home* (1997), narrated by Oscar-winner Morgan Freeman, and featuring the voiceover contributions of a range of award-winning actors, including Martin Landau, Ed Asner, and David Paymer. The vigilant search for Nazi war criminals and the ongoing international educational and legal efforts to keep the horrors of the Holocaust fresh in the minds of citizens lie at the heart of the powerful biographical documentary of Holocaust survivor Simon Wiesenthal, *I Have Never Forgotten You: The Life and Legacy of Simon Wiesenthal* (2007). Moreover, Hollywood's reluctance to address pervasive anti-Semitism generally, and the destruction of human rights during Nazism specifically—and thus, confront Hitler's regime directly—is explored in Daniel Anker's provocative *Imaginary Witness: Hollywood and the Holocaust* (2004). Yet *Imaginary Witness* is significant in that it also reveals the incredible power and positive lasting effects of the moving image, as U.S. Army films from concentration camps and a host of postwar movies from Hollywood serve as a clarion call to arms, galvanizing a once-reluctant industry and ill-informed American public to rise up, using its art and enlightened outrage to inform and mobilize the public so that the evils perpetrated by Adolf Hitler and his minions will, one hopes, never occur again.

Some films are more popular and influential than others. Steven Spielberg's acclaimed *Schindler's List* (1993) recounts the true story of the efforts of Oskar Schindler to save Jews in Poland. Schindler used his position as an industrialist to save thousands of Jewish lives by employing them at his factory. Spielberg would win the Academy Award for best picture and best director for this film, which many consider one of the best films of the 1990s. The film is at once moving and, at the same time, an in-depth exploration of humanity. *Hotel Rwanda*, while less well known than *Schindler's List*, helped to raise awareness about the 1994 genocide in Rwanda. Some examples of lesser-known, but very good, films about the genocide include *100 Days* (2001) and *Sometimes in*

April (2005). Both films effectively capture the immense tragedy of the Rwandan genocide without the ostentation that is often associated with big-budget Hollywood films. The film *The Killing Fields* (1984) re-creates the actual murder of millions of individuals in Cambodia and the plight of one man trying to escape the Khmer Rouge. While it is an excellent film, *The Killing Fields* assumes a great deal of knowledge about Cambodia and the politics of Southeast Asia in the 1970s, and although the story is compelling, it might be difficult to follow the political story that triggered the events.

An important aspect of genocide that is often underappreciated is that the act is not spontaneous violence but is a well-planned attempt to eliminate a group of people. Gregory Stanton, president of Genocide Watch, points out that a genocidal event goes through several stages, including organization and preparation.[22] The film *Wannsee Conference* (*Wannseekonferenz*, 1984) is a real-time (85 minutes) recounting of the actual meeting where the Nazis ultimately decided to undertake the Final Solution in 1942. The German film transfixes the viewer because most of the participants are rather glib and jovial over their decision to murder six million Jews. Another version of the film, the American-made *Conspiracy* (2001), provides an interesting perspective to the meeting. The film juxtaposes the opulent setting of a Nazi meeting, complete with crystal and fine china, with the grim reality of murdering millions of people.

Sometimes the concepts and points a filmmaker wants to make are very complex and abstract. Thus a filmmaker might decide to make a narrative film that uses fictional events to tell a story. For example, Roberto Benigni cowrote and directed the 1999 Academy Award winner for best foreign-language film, *Life Is Beautiful* (*La Vita è Bella*, 1997). The film, which was immensely successful for a foreign-language film in the United States, starts out as a comedy with Benigni playing a fanciful Jewish man who falls in love. But as the film progresses and Benigni raises his family, he is first deprived of his home, then sent to a concentration camp, and ultimately sacrifices himself to save his son. Similarly, the Czech film *Divided We Fall* (*Musíme si pomáhat*, 2000) also uses some humor to address the seriousness of the Holocaust. Set in Prague during the war, a childless couple hides the son of their former employer, who is Jewish, for the better part of the German occupation. The original title, which translates as *We Must Help One Another*, explains the situation of the characters. The tragic *The Boy in the Striped Pajamas* (2008) uses a fictional story of a friendship between a German and a Jewish boy to demonstrate the symbols and labels adults apply to others. The film leaves the audience with the message that children are all the same, regardless of ethnicity and religion. *Jacob the Liar* (*Jakob*, *der Lügner*, 1975), an East German film remade in the United States as *Jakob the Liar* (1999), highlights heroism inside concentration camps. Because so few survived the camps it is difficult to procure a factual or true story; authors have tried to re-create dramatic stories of what it must have been like.

On the one hand, the drawback to films that use a fictional story is that the stories are fictional; thus, the story can undermine the very serious human rights claims made by victims. On the other hand, such stories can highlight real issues and dilemmas that prompt the audience to think and engage in research. Such stories also invite comparisons. One reason why stories about the Holocaust (the genocide of Central Europe in the 1930s and 1940s) continue to resonate with audiences is that they invite comparisons to today's world. The methods used to dehumanize people are still used today. Thus, reminders of what happened in the past are a way of motivating the viewer to think about human rights today.

As mentioned elsewhere in this book, propaganda films are used to give an account of events by distorting information without a serious counterargument. Propaganda films can be used to facilitate human rights abuses by denying the victims his or her humanity. Films from the Nazi era are very effective in demonstrating the dehumanization process that is essential to genocidal events. However, a film such as *Jud Süß* (1940) is so vile, vitriolic, and manipulative that it is difficult to justify its viewing. The film concocts a fictitious story to demonstrate how manipulative Jews were according to the Nazi regime.[23] Like another (in)famous film of the Nazi period, *The Eternal Jew* (*Der Ewige Jude*, 1940), *Jud Süß* is an attempt to equate the target of genocidal violence with the worst of society's ills, including the disease and theft that were designed to generate genocidal hatred among the viewers. Despite being rather clumsy in their depictions, these films can serve to reinforce stereotypes and mislead those whose knowledge is limited.

Summing up Films about Human Rights

Films serve a useful purpose to those who are interested in human rights. If these events of horror are to be prevented from happening in the future, we, as engaged and informed citizens of the world, must be cognizant of what people are capable of doing to one another. In that effort, there are a number of international bodies determined to keep citizens informed and the past from repeating itself. In addition to international governmental organizations (IGOs) dedicated to monitoring the state of human rights across the globe—such as the

United Nations Human Rights Commission—there are nongovernmental organizations (NGOs) that devote their efforts on behalf of human rights worldwide, among them, Amnesty International and Human Rights Watch. The good news is that the mission, history, and work of these groups can be readily accessed and digested within mere minutes: extensive information on these IGOs and NGOs—and the state of human rights around the world—can be found on their home pages on the Internet, just a few clicks away.

Human Rights Organizations and References

There are several international human rights organizations around the world. We have chosen a few prominent advocacy organizations to highlight the advancement of international human rights around the world.

Nongovernmental Organizations (NGOs)

Amnesty International: http://www.amnesty.org

Perhaps the most well known of the international human rights organizations, Amnesty is famous for getting citizens involved in letter-writing campaigns to raise attention about the plight of the victims of human rights abuses. Amnesty International was founded in 1961 and today has over one million members. Currently, the organization operates in over 140 countries and is considered independent from any government, religious persuasion, or political ideology. Its fundamental driving force is the Universal Declaration of Human Rights, a document signed by every government in the world in 1948, which guarantees every human being basic political, social, and economic rights, regardless of race, religion, or the political system under which they live.

Human Rights Watch: http://www.hrw.org

Another independent human rights organization is Human Rights Watch, which is based in New York but has offices around the world. Founded in 1978, HRW was originally founded to help monitor Eastern European governments' compliance with the Helsinki Accords. The organization seeks to publish human rights abuses as a way to raise consciousness about severe international human rights violations.

Medecins sans Frontieres: http://www.msf.org

Actually less of a human rights organization and more of a humanitarian relief organization, Doctors Without Borders is a French-based organization that helps provide medical assistance to populations that are in danger. Operating in over 80 countries, MSF works to rebuild medical services, instigate vaccination programs, and to provide clean water and food.

Information and Resources

In addition to the organizations listed above you might want to consider consulting these Internet resources

- Committee to Protect Journalists: http://www.cpj.org
- Freedom House: http://www.freedomhouse.org
- Genocide Watch: http://www.genocidewatch.org
- Human Rights Web Resources: http://www.hrweb.org
- Lawyer's Committee for Human Rights: http://www.lchr.org
- Physicians for Human Rights: http://www.phrusa.org
- UN High Commissioner for Human Rights: http://www.unhchr.ch
- United Nations Human Rights Page: http://www.un.org/rights/

The Debate about the Death Penalty in the United States

One of the most vexing and intellectually challenging debates in American society today is the necessity, legality, and morality of the death penalty. There is a long history, in many societies, of executing people who have committed the most heinous of crimes. Many are quite familiar with the notion of "an eye for an eye, a life for a life." However, for years voices have been raised over the issue of the death penalty in a civilized society. Does society have the right to kill? Should society, as a whole, stoop to the level of those who committed the crime? Are there proper safeguards to insure the fairness of the trial and the quality of the lawyers? Does the administration of the death penalty constitute "cruel and unusual" punishment? Passionate voices on both sides of the issue attempt to answer these questions as they raise other intriguing and difficult issues.

Since the Supreme Court ruled the death penalty constitutional in 1976, thirty-eight states and the federal government have reinstated capital punishment. A 2009 poll by Gallup indicated that roughly two-thirds of Americans, or 65 percent, support the death penalty for individuals convicted of murder.[24] At first glance most Americans would not consider this a topic under human rights; however, for many people the issue of the death penalty is considered a matter of human rights in the international community. The Second Optional Protocol to the International Covenant on Civil and Political Rights,[25] an international treaty designed to eliminate the use of the death penalty worldwide, states that abolition would contribute "to enhancement of human dignity and progress." Because the United States has not signed or ratified the treaty, its provisions are not binding on the United States. Nevertheless, the use of the death penalty in the United States is scrutinized and followed closely in the international media.[26]

In 1972, in the case of *Furman v. Georgia*, the United States Supreme Court struck down state death penalties, finding the application of capital punishment to be "arbitrary and capricious." Specifically, the Court struck down the Georgia and Texas death penalty procedures and set aside *all* death sentences imposed under existing state and federal law. However, in 1976, with the Court's decision in *Gregg v. Georgia*, the death penalty was reinstated after new measures were adopted by the states to guarantee proper legal procedures. From 1976 until 1988, there was no federal death penalty until Congress adopted similar measures. Since that time, however, the federal government has continually expanded its death penalty jurisdiction, making a number of criminal offenses federal crimes punishable by death. The federal government also has pursued the death penalty in a number of cases, perhaps most notably the 1995 Oklahoma City bombing. The U.S. government sought and achieved the death sentence for Timothy McVeigh, the man convicted of killing 168 people in the bombing of the Alfred P. Murrah Federal Building.

What makes the death penalty all the more difficult is the finality of the punishment. If an innocent person is convicted of a crime and sentenced to jail, then that person's freedom could be reinstated. However, if an innocent person is convicted of a crime and sentenced to death, then that person's life cannot be reinstated. Questions such as these prompted then-Governor George

Ryan to suspend the use of the death penalty in Illinois in the year 2000. Between the years 1977 and 2000, Illinois executed twelve people on Death Row; yet by employing new DNA techniques, Illinois had freed thirteen people sentenced to death, finding them innocent of the crimes for which they were convicted, thus raising concerns about imperfections in the legal process and the irrevocable nature of a death sentence. Governor Ryan was stunned that more people had been exonerated than had been executed from Death Row and concluded that the system was fatally flawed.[27] As Ryan left office in January 2003, he commuted the death sentences of everyone on Death Row in Illinois. Indictments of the Illinois criminal justice system generally and the state's death penalty process in particular are the main themes of the Katy Chevigny and Kirsten Johnson's documentary *Deadline* (2004), which chronicled these aforementioned dynamics and actions in Illinois in the 1990s.[28] Praised as "enlightening . . . engrossing" and an "example of social activism at its best" by the *Hollywood Reporter*, the activist documentary *Deadline* raises serious questions about the moral and legal implications of implementing the death penalty in the United States.[29] Yet it is not just documentaries such as *Deadline*, or Liz Garbus's 2002 examination of the death penalty in Oklahoma, *The Execution of Wanda Jean* (see the call-out "Debating the Death Penalty in the United States"), that present criticism of capital punishment in the United States. A fictionalized Hollywood treatment of capital punishment occurs in the vehemently anti–death penalty film, set in contemporary Texas, *The Life of David Gale* (2003), starring Kevin Spacey and Laura Linney. It is worth noting that the film was not very successful commercially, and even some who may have been predisposed to oppose capital punishment offered blistering assessments of the film. For example, the liberal-leaning online magazine *Slate* found the film to be so "ham-fisted" and nonsensical as to be wholly ineffective.[30]

However, debate over the death penalty is certainly not limited to the United States. Concern about the death penalty takes on a worldwide dimension. Advocates for the abolition of the death penalty call on countries that impose *Sharia* law to rethink their punishments. For countries that aspire to become part of the European Union, they must first, among other things, abolish the death penalty. Listed below are death penalty–related films, television segments, and websites that address many of the ethical, moral, and legal dimensions surrounding this controversial and emotional issue. In addition, the following call-out provides a brief review of seminal Supreme Court cases that deal with the administration and constitutionality of the death penalty in the United States. As we provide links to the full decisions of these cases from the

Internet database of Court decisions provided by the Legal Information Institute at Cornell University, we urge you to consult these cases, some of which are narrow 5–4 decisions and assess the evolving legal consensus on capital punishment as it relates to the mentally disabled and adolescents. Do you find yourself in agreement with these cases? Why or why not?

Debating the Death Penalty in the United States

For an excellent informative overview of films that provide critical analysis of the existence and implementation of the death penalty in the United States, see Amnesty International: Films on the Death Penalty: http://www.amnestyusa.org/faithinaction/II DiscussionAction/2FilmDiscussionGuides/FilmsontheDeathPenalty .pdf.

The Death Penalty in the United States in Film and Television

- *The Thin Blue Line* (1988): Directed by Errol Morris; documentary; setting: Texas
- *Dead Man Walking* (1995): Directed by Tim Robbins; commercial film; setting: Louisiana
- *The Green Mile* (1999): Directed by Frank Darabont; setting: the American South
- *The Execution of Wanda Jean* (2002): Directed by Liz Garbus; documentary; setting: Oklahoma
- *The Awful Truth* (television, 1999–2000): "Sibling Rivalry" (2002); setting: Texas and Florida
- *Monster* (2003): Directed by Patty Jenkins; setting: Florida
- *The Life of David Gale* (2003): Directed by Alan Parker; setting: Texas
- *Deadline* (2004): Directed by Katy Chevigny and Kirsten Johnson; setting: Illinois

After Viewing the Above Films, Consider These Questions for Discussion and Debate:

- Does the death penalty constitute "cruel and unusual punishment", and thus, violate the Constitution's Eighth Amendment protections?

- Is the death penalty a deterrent?
- Should the United States execute the mentally retarded?
- Should the United States execute juveniles?
- What do U.S. law and international law have to say about capital punishment?

Supreme Court Decisions

Legal Information Institute at Cornell University
Cornell University's Archive of Supreme Court Decisions
http://supct.law.cornell.edu/supct/

Pro-Death Penalty Internet Resources

http://www.prodeathpenalty.com/
The Death Penalty: A Defense
Swedish author David Anderson defends the death penalty.
http://w1.155.telia.com/~u15509119/ny_sida_1.htm
Death Penalty Links
Steven D. Stewart, prosecuting attorney of Clark County, Indiana, and advocate of the death penalty, provides over 1,000 links to articles and statistics concerning capital punishment in the United States.
http://www.clarkprosecutor.org/html/death/death.htm

Anti–Death Penalty Internet Resources

Amnesty International
"The Death Penalty in the United States of America"
http://www.amnestyusa.org/rightsforall/dp/index.html
Death Penalty Information Center
Provides state-by-state information on executions and a history of the death penalty; it also looks at issues such as mental retardation, race, innocence, and deterrence.
http://www.deathpenaltyinfo.org/dpicmr.html
Human Rights Watch
"The Death Penalty in the United States of America"
http://www.hrw.org/campaigns/deathpenalty/
"Beyond Reason: The Death Penalty and Offenders with Mental Retardation"
http://www.hrw.org/reports/2001/ustat/
The Justice Project: Campaign for Criminal Justice Reform (www.CJReform.org)
"A Broken System: Error Rates in Capital Cases, 1973–1995"

James S. Lineman, Simon H. Rifling Professor of Law, Columbia University School of Law; Jeffrey Fagan, Professor, Joseph Mailman School of Public Health, Visiting Professor, Columbia University School of Law; Valerie West, Doctoral Candidate, Department of Sociology, New York University
http://justice.policy.net/jpreport/

A Sampling of Prominent Supreme Court Death Penalty Cases

Furman v. Georgia (1972)

The Court held that the imposition of the death penalty is a discretionary process not guided by legislatively defined standards, and as such, is a violation of the Eighth and Fourteenth Amendments. The Court struck down the Georgia and Texas death penalty procedures and set aside *all* death sentences imposed under existing state and federal law.

Gregg v. Georgia (1976)

The Court upheld new state death penalty statutes; at the same time it held that a constitutional violation could be established if a plaintiff demonstrated a "pattern of arbitrary and capricious sentencing."[32]

McCleskey v. Kemp (1987)

The Court rejected a Fourteenth Amendment Equal Protection Clause challenge to Georgia capital sentencing laws and procedures, despite a statistical study—the Baldus Study—which "revealed significant disparities in the imposition of the death sentence based on the race of the victim."[33]

Thompson v. Oklahoma (1988)

The Court held that the implementation of a death sentence on a person who is fifteen years old at the time of the offense was outside the parameters of "evolving standards of decency" at home and, especially, abroad. In his dissent, Justice Scalia posits that the international standards evoked by the majority were irrelevant when interpreting the U.S. Constitution.[34]

Stanford v. Kentucky (1989)

The Court ruled constitutional the execution of Kevin Stanford, who was seventeen years old at the time he committed murder.[35]

Atkins v. Virginia (2002)

The Court held that executions of mentally retarded criminals are "cruel and unusual punishments" prohibited by the Eighth Amendment.[36]

Ring v. Arizona (2002)

The Court held that, based on the Sixth Amendment's guarantee of a fair, impartial jury trial, a jury, not a judge, must determine whether a capital defendant gets the death penalty. The ruling invalidated the death penalty procedures in Arizona and four other states.[37]

Roper v. Simmons (2005)

In a 5–4 decision the Supreme Court held that the Eighth and Fourteenth Amendments forbid the "execution of offenders who were under the age of eighteen when their crimes were committed"; "the Court reasoned that the rejection of the juvenile death penalty in the majority of states, the infrequent use of the punishment even where it remains on the books, and the consistent trend toward abolition of the juvenile death penalty demonstrated a national consensus against the practice."[38]

Kennedy v. Louisiana (2008)

In a case involving the rape of an eight-year-old child, which did not result in murder, the Court ruled (in a 5–4 decision) that the Eighth Amendment's protection against cruel and unusual punishment bars Louisiana from "imposing the death penalty for the rape of a child where the crime did not result, and was not intended to result, in the victim's death."[39]

Conclusion

The case of the death penalty in the United States, and whether it is a question of individuals' fundamental rights, is but one example of the different approaches to, and understandings of, what constitutes human rights around the world. Yet the issue of the death penalty does invite challenging questions: *What do you think about the legality, necessity, and morality of the death penalty? What recent films have addressed the myriad issues that surround the death penalty, and do such films merely reinforce your fundamental views, or do they challenge your perspectives?* Many observers have noted that there is a tendency toward cultural relevance when it comes to human rights, meaning that people will argue that such rights are not universal but might vary from culture to culture. Critics of this approach will say that this is just an excuse to allow continued human rights violations under the guise of cultural practices. This raises interesting and vexing questions about human rights around the world: *What should our attitude be toward practices that we think are violations of human rights yet are justified as being part of long-standing cultural or religious practices?* You might also consider the importance of popular culture and film in this process: *Does seeking to explain how people might see this as a human rights issue, or, alternatively, a cultural practice, help to achieve a life of dignity for all?* Regardless, the use of film helps the viewer to empathize and appreciate the complexity of human rights in the modern world.

Notes

1. The concept and definition of human rights are highly debatable among practitioners and academics. For an overview of these debates, consult David P. Forsythe, *Human Rights in International Relations* (New York: Cambridge University Press, 2000), 28–52; William F. Schulz, *In Our Own Best Interest: How Defending Human Rights Benefits Us All* (Boston: Beacon Press, 2001), 1–37; and Jack Donnelly, *Universal Human Rights in Theory and Practice*, 2nd ed. (Ithaca: Cornell University Press, 2003).
2. Films such as *Nurse and Martyr* (1915) and *Nurse Cavell* (1916) played on the idea that the Germans were so barbaric that they would execute a woman. It is no accident that people would remind the public of Cavell in the days leading up to the Second World War. For example, the film *Nurse Edith Cavell* (1939) was released coincidentally on the day the Germans invaded Poland to start the Second World War.
3. Mary Ann Glendon, *A World Made New: Eleanor Roosevelt and the Universal Declaration of Human Rights* (New York: Random House, 2001).
4. Convention on the Prevention and Punishment of the Crime of Genocide (adopted by the United Nations General Assembly, December 9, 1948; entered into force, January 12,

1951). For a link to the Convention, see: www.seeingthebiggerpicture.net.

5. The testimonials from the film were transcribed into book form. See Claude Lanzmann, *Shoah: An Oral History of the Holocaust; The Complete Text of the Film* (New York: Pantheon Books, 1985).

6. A transcript of the entire program is available online at: http://www.pbs.org/wgbh/pages/ frontline/shows/evil/etc/script.html.

7. For *Ghosts of Rwanda* (2004), PBS's *Frontline* film, see: http://www.pbs.org/wgbh/pages/front-line/shows/ghosts/.

8. See: http://www.pbs.org/wgbh/pages/frontline/shows/ghosts/etc/protect.html. The online resources also included a topical essay, "Banishing the Rwanda Nightmare: The Responsibility to Protect," by a former co-chair of the International Commission on Intervention and State Sovereignty (ICISS). ICISS, "a group which has laid out for the world community a new framework and new ground rules on when to intervene in human-itarian crises," released a report, "The Responsibility to Protect," which articulated a pre-cise structure and agenda for combating future catastrophes. The December 2001 ICISS report "The Responsibility to Protect" can be found online at: http://www.iciss.ca/report-en.asp.

9. For an overview of the Rwandan genocide, see Philip Gourevitch, *We Wish to Inform You That Tomorrow We Will Be Killed with Our Families: Stories from Rwanda* (New York: Farrar, Straus and Giroux, 1998); and Linda Melvern, *A People Betrayed: The Role of the West in Rwanda's Genocide* (New York: Zed Books, 2000).

10. For the film's official website, see: http://www.genocidefactor.com/.

11. For examples of dehumanization, see Howard Ball, *Prosecuting War Crimes and Genocide: The Twentieth-Century Experience* (Lawrence: University Press of Kansas, 1999), 220.

12. For more information about the *coup d'état* in Chile and its aftermath, see Carlos Huneeus, *The Pinochet Regime* (Boulder, CO: Lynne Rienner, 2007); Heraldo Muñoz, *The Dictator's Shadow: Life under Augusto Pinochet* (New York: Basic Books, 2008); and Róbinson Rojas, *The Murder of Allende and the End of the Chilean Way of Socialism* (New York: Harper & Row, 1976). There have been some questions about the efforts of the CIA to effect change in Chile as well. See Kristian Gustafson, *Hostile Intent: U.S. Covert Operations in Chile, 1964–1976* (Washington, DC: Potomac Books, 2007).

13. Mary Dejevsky, "U.S. Implicated in 'Missing' Death," *The Independent*, October 9, 1999, p. 6; Ben Macintyre, "Papers Suggest CIA Role in Chile Killings," *The Times*, February 14, 2000; Diana Jean Schemo, "F.B.I. Watched an American Who Was Killed in Chile Coup," *New York Times*, July 1, 2000, p. A6.

14. Jack Lemmon and Sissy Spacek were both nominated for the Academy Award for lead actor and actress, respectively, for their performances.

15. Another insightful film about Argentina's Dirty War is *Funny Dirty Little War* (*No habrá más penas ni olvido*, 1983), which examines how people in a small village turn on one another. For background to the Dirty War, consult Donald E. Hodges, *Argentina's "Dirty War": An Intellectual Bibliography* (Austin: University of Texas Press, 1991).

16. The national legislatures of many countries have declared the events of 1915–1918 as genocide despite protests and consternation by the Turkish government. For a list of par-liaments that have recognized the event as genocide, see: http://www.armeniaforeign ministry.com/fr/genocide/current_status.html.

17. The Canadian film *Ararat* (2002) examines the events of Armenia from a modern-day perspective.

18. For an examination of the impact of *Holocaust* on television history, see the Museum of Broadcast History web page on the mini-series at: http://www.museum.tv/archives/etv/H/htmlH/holocaust/holocaust.htm.

19. See James Lardner, "Making History," *New Republic*, May 13, 1978; and Lance Morrow, "Television and the Holocaust," *Time* (New York), May 1, 1978.

20. Elie Wiesel, "Trivializing the Holocaust: Semi-Fact and Semi-Fiction," *New York Times*, April 16, 1978.

21. Judith Doneson, *The Holocaust in American Film*, 2ⁿᵈ ed. (Syracuse: Syracuse University Press, 2002), 192–94; Anne Monely, "Holocaust," in *Encyclopedia of Television*, 2ⁿᵈ ed., ed. Horace Newcomb (New York: Fitzroy Dearborn/Museum of Broadcast Communications, 2004), 1112–13.

22. Stanton identifies eight stages of genocide: classification, symbolization, dehumanization, organization, polarization, preparation, extermination, and denial. Gregory H. Stanton's State Department briefing paper on the Eight Stages of Genocide can be accessed at: http://www.genocidewatch.org/images/8StagesBriefingpaper.pdf.

23. The title is taken from the 1925 novel *Jud Süss* by Lion Feuchtwanger. The novel was, ironically, concerned with anti-Semitism and was the basis of the 1934 British film *Jew Süss*.

24. Frank Newport, "In U.S., Two-Thirds Continue to Support the Death Penalty," *Gallup*, October 13, 2009: http://www.deathpenaltyinfo.org/documents/GallupPoll1009.pdf.

25. A link to the treaty of the Second Optional Protocol to the International Covenant on Civil and Political Rights, aiming at the abolition of the death penalty, can be found at: www.seeingthebiggerpicture.net.

26. For example, the British newspaper *The Guardian* regularly covers stories about American executions on its front page. See its web page for details of executions and related stories: http://www.guardian.co.uk/world/capital-punishment.

27. The Illinois case sparked a great deal of controversy and debate. For a review of the events leading up to the suspension, see Maureen O'Donnell, "Illinois to Stop Executions: Ryan Panel to Study 13 Wrongful Convictions," *Chicago Sun-Times*, January 31, 2000, p. 3; and Dirk Johnson, "Illinois, Citing Faulty Verdicts, Bars Executions," *New York Times*, February 1, 2000, p. A1. While some argued that this evidence was a call for fundamentally reconsidering the death penalty, others argued that this was not the case. See David Frum, "The Justice Americans Demand," *New York Times*, February 4, 2000, p. A29.

28. For more on *Deadline*, see: http://deadlinethemovie.com/about_the_film/about_deadline.php.

29. A blurb from James Greenberg's review in the *Hollywood Reporter* is listed on the film's website: http://deadlinethemovie.com/about_the_film/about_deadline.php.

30. David Edelstein, "Flip the Switch: The Life of David Gale Makes the Electric Chair Seem Humane," *Slate*, March 3, 2003: http://www.slate.com/id/2079505/.

31. For *Furman v. Georgia* (1972), see: http://www.law.cornell.edu/supct/search/display.html?terms=furman%20v.%20georgia&url=/supct/html/historics/USSC_CR_0408_0238_ZO.html.

32. To see more on *Gregg v. Georgia* (1976), go to: http://www.law.cornell.edu/supct/html/historics/USSC_CR_0428_0153_ZS.html.

33. For *McCleskey v. Kemp* (1987), visit: http://www.law.cornell.edu/supct/html/historics/USSC_CR_0481_0279_ZO.html.
34. To see more on *Thompson v. Oklahoma* (1988), go to: http://www.law.cornell.edu/supct/html/historics/USSC_CR_0487_0815_ZS.html.
35. For *Stanford v. Kentucky* (1989), visit: http://www.law.cornell.edu/supct/html/historics/USSC_CR_0492_0361_ZS.html.
36. To see *Atkins v. Virginia* (2002), go to: http://www.law.cornell.edu/supct/html/00–8452.ZS.html.
37. For *Ring v. Arizona* (2002), see: http://www.law.cornell.edu/supct/html/01–488.ZS.html.
38. For the three standards applied by the Court cited in the text for *Roper v. Simmons* (2005), see the Death Penalty Information Center: http://www.deathpenaltyinfo.org/u-s-supreme-court-roper-v-simmons-no-03–633. For the complete Court decision, see: http://www.law.cornell.edu/supct/html/03–633.ZS.html.
39. To see *Kennedy v. Louisiana* (2008), go to: http://www.law.cornell.edu/supct/html/07–343.ZS.html.

· 1 0 ·

ENVIRONMENTAL POLITICS

Released during the holidays of 2009, *Avatar*, the epic written, directed, and produced by James Cameron, became a mega-blockbuster, setting a record for the top grossing box office film. The message of the film, which is a warning about the destruction of habitats and the environment and callous disregard for indigenous populations, was enhanced by the use of cutting-edge special effects. Perhaps lost in the hype about *Avatar* was that the movie's phenomenal commercial success provided clear evidence that films about the environment had become mainstream fare accepted by the general moviegoing audience. While receiving some criticism, particularly from conservatives,[1] the film nevertheless managed to attract large audiences and only passing mentions in the mainstream media about any controversy over its message. Also of note when considering *Avatar* and its overt political messages is Cameron's extensive, and, at times, controversial, consultative work on a contemporary environmental disaster in the Gulf of Mexico.[2]

It has only been in the last generation that mainstream public attention has recognized the issue of the environment. In the 1970s it was common for motorists to simply throw their trash out the window. Public awareness began to be raised primarily over the beauty and aesthetics of the environment. This concern led to one of the most famous and effective public service announcements (PSAs) ever broadcast on American television. In a spot entitled "Crying Indian," a Native American, portrayed by Iron Eyes Cody, paddles up a polluted stream, past smokestacks pouring out polluted air, and watches as cars on an interstate throw trash out their windows. As the Native American turns towards the camera, he has a single tear running down his face. A voiceover tells the viewer, "People start pollution . . . people can stop it." This PSA probably remains one of the most memorable in American television history. *The Simpsons*, that seemingly omnipresent purveyor of pop culture and political commentary, parodied the spot almost a quarter of a century later, in their 1998 environmentally themed (and 200th) episode "The Trash of the Titans," when Homer runs for Springfield Sanitation Commissioner.[3]

Of course environmental concerns are more complex than just simply litter. In the years since the beginning of the modern environmental movement, the big screen has addressed a broader range of issues, including overpopulation, industrial waste, nuclear power, and nature preservation. One of the persistent problems in dealing with such issues is that they tend to be interrelated. For example, one of the best ways to deal with high population growth is by encouraging industrial development. Increasing industrial development, though, also boosts the output of industrial pollution. Also, an escalating population requires more land, both for people to live on and for the growing of food to feed an ever-increasing population. Because of the often complex interaction between these environmental and economic development issues, narrative feature films have had a difficult time portraying stories that adequately cover the myriad problems associated with these dynamics. Popular films usually focus on a single storyline rather than complex interactions between multiple narratives. Some of the more recent effective films that have had an impact on the public's conscience have been documentaries; however, a number of feature films have addressed environmental concerns as well.[4]

The Early Environmental Movement and Films

The modern environmental movement began the late 1960s and early 1970s and was reflected in various expressions of popular culture.[5] The publication of the *Whole Earth Catalog* in 1968 and the celebration of the first Earth Day in 1970—which was founded and championed in large part by the vocal and legislative support of longtime conservationist and U.S. Senator Gaylord Nelson of Wisconsin—demonstrated that a new movement was at hand.[6] Popular songs, such as Joni Mitchell's "Big Yellow Taxi" (originally released in 1970), which featured the lyrics, "They paved paradise and put up a parking lot" and "They took all the trees / Put 'em in a tree museum," reflected this emerging sensibility.[7] Similarly, the environmental devastation wrought by rampant coal mining along the Green River in Muhlenberg County, Kentucky, was catalogued by the Midwestern singer-songwriter John Prine, in his 1971 classic "Paradise."[8] Films of the late 1960s and early 1970s did address environmental issues but frequently did so in a heavy-handed or didactic way, often without adequate attention to, or appreciation of, the sheer complexity and full range of relevant issues.

One film that at least attempted to make allusions to the intricacies of the problems is *Silent Running* (1972). The film takes place completely in outer space. Several ships are in orbit around the planet Saturn loaded with what remains of Earth's trees (a tree museum!). One scientist, Freeman Lowell (Bruce Dern), is committed to the preservation of these environmental assets. Lowell's two companions and coworkers are less committed; in fact, they are contemptuous of the project, arguing that trees are no longer necessary. Everyone on Earth has a job, there is plenty of food, and the global temperature is at a constant 75 degrees. Lowell thinks life on Earth is bland; while he enjoys fresh fruits and vegetables, his colleagues are content to eat preprocessed wafers that serve as their sustenance.

Lowell mutinies when officials on Earth order the project's termination and destruction. In an attempt to protect the trees, Lowell sacrifices himself and his colleagues. In many ways *Silent Running* may prove dated to contemporary audiences. When folksinger Joan Baez sings "Earth between my toes and a flower in my hair / That's what I was wearing when we laid among the ferns" in the middle of the film, modern audiences may snicker or roll their eyes. Yet, *Silent Running* remains a cautionary tale calling the audience's attention to the need for biodiversity. Bruce Dern's character, Lowell, wants to prevent the extinction of everything in the forest. The film sets up an interesting conundrum for the audience. Most arguments about saving the environment are constructed around having enough food, or some kind of economic benefit, or provide a certain quality of life. *Silent Running* takes these issues off of the table for us. One character argues in the film that people on Earth all have a job, everyone has more than enough food, the planet is comfortable, and there is plenty of food. By protecting the environment some argue that environmental concerns come at the expense of jobs and much-needed economic development. The film isolates those concerns and asks us if trees, fresh food, and beauty are reasons enough to protect the environment. In other words: Are we so concerned with progress and technology that we are willing to jettison the necessities provided by the forest?

Soylent Green (1973) is another film made in this period that addresses the problems of overpopulation and pollution. Set in the year 2022, one of the key features of the film is the constant examination of how overpopulation affects the lives of the individuals in the film. One of the key points is that the over-population has created an upper class that is far removed from the plight of everyday people. Against this background, Detective Robert Thorn (Charleston Heston) is sent to investigate the murder, or assassination, of a leading execu-tive of the Soylent Corporation. Thorn returns to his own apartment, where he shares his booty of goods with his roommate, Sol Roth (Edward G. Robinson), an elderly researcher who remembers a time when the earth was still beautiful and food was still plentiful. Sol uncovers the shocking secret of the Soylent Corporation, and rather than facing the consequences of the news, Sol elects to be euthanized. Before he dies, Thorn manages to reach Sol and he reveals the great, ghoulish cover-up that has led to so much anguish: Soylent Green is made out of people! The sad, grotesque truth is now upon us: with the decline of food stocks and the oceans dying, the Soylent Corporation is forced to rely on the bodies of humans to feed the living.

The film Soylent Green was based on the novel Make Room! Make Room! by Harry Harrison.[9] The dire warnings of Soylent Green are very interesting, especially in the increasingly globalized world we now inhabit, where unchecked pollution and population growth have the capability of unleashing enormous negative consequences on society. Not only will this impact be in terms of massive degradation for substantial numbers of people—and an unde-sirable quality of life in developed countries—but it also creates a widening gap between haves and have-nots and may ultimately lead to the commoditization of humans. In the film the upper class enjoys a life of privilege; yet such an absolute, persistent, and wholly impenetrable stratification of wealth does not seem to have come to pass. At the same time, some activists would encourage us to think about the world differently, to consider the real and potential long-term consequences of our population growth as well as the consumption of food, water, and energy. There is no evidence that we are anywhere close to a world where some people must practice cannibalism to live, but as fish stocks collapse, many populations increasingly live on marginal food sources.

Many people are surprised that Charlton Heston, perhaps better known in his later years for his outspoken conservative politics and his presidency of the National Rifle Association, would be committed to a film with such a seemingly liberal message. Yet Heston is said to have loved the novel, and wanted to bring an adaptation to the screen. He also starred in the futuristic 1968 sci-fi classic *The Planet of the Apes*, which was ultimately about the dangers of nuclear weapons. What the Heston, *Soylent Green*, and *Planet of the Apes* examples illustrate is that concern for environmental policies (and nuclear proliferation) need not be confined to people who embrace any single viewpoint on the political spectrum. Solutions to these vexing concerns—and thus, the proper role of government in addressing these dynamics—will undoubtedly involve some adherence to ideology; yet an underlying acknowledgment of environmental dangers is not necessarily limited to the province of any one distinct political view. Moreover, and perhaps more important, one cannot discount the lure of starring in a production with a provocative story and entertaining action sequences. The movie business is a *business*, after all, and there is a special career boost that can emanate from participation in a highly successful major motion picture.

Environmental Films Grow Up: Adapting Real-Life Stories

Since the bourgeoning crop of environmental films of the early 1970s, one of the more significant changes has been an increased focus on specific issues, struggles, personalities, and consequences rather than all-encompassing epics. An oft-repeated theme that has emerged in the past few decades is the role of regular citizens and stressed out yet noble lawyers faced with impossible odds while seeking recompense from irresponsible environmental actors, many of whom are corporations. With the tagline, "She brought a small town to its feet and a huge corporation to its knees," the box office smash and Oscar-nominated *Erin Brockovich* (2000), starring Julia Roberts, is an example of this genre. The film, based on a true story, follows the crusading efforts of a down-on-her-luck single mother of three, Erin Brockovich, who in 1993 battled a behemoth California power company, Pacific Gas & Electric, over their alleged environmental malfeasance, specifically, the polluting of the groundwater in Hinckley, California, and the repercussions for local families' health.

Working for a crusty-but-lovable lawyer, Ed Masry (Albert Finney), Brockovich begins to learn of the contamination of the small town's water supply, and the debilitating effects it has had on the health of the local, working-class residents. Dogged, determined, and willing to sacrifice in order to discover the truth, the screen version of Brockovich also selectively employs her physical attributes (particularly her cleavage) to uncover the sordid details surrounding toxic waste and local health concerns. These tactics, combined with shrewd maneuvering and creative investigative work, aid her efforts to demonstrate that PG&E was guilty of dumping the lethal toxic waste hexavalent chromium (or chromium-6) into the water supply of Hinckley. Through her tenacious investigative work and the support of Masry, Brockovich helps secure a $333 million settlement for the families (and the law firm), a sizable dividend in one of the largest class action lawsuits in American history. In the end, justice was served; contrary to what many would have believed possible, the small-town lawyer and the everywoman Brockovich won, and PG&E was held accountable for polluting the environment.

The overwhelming success of *Erin Brockovich* demonstrated that, backed by the star power of Julia Roberts, a compelling tale based on real-life events, skillful marketing, and some cinematic clichés, political films about environmental concerns can perform very well at the box office. Clearly, many explicitly political films do not, or cannot, offer the budget, entertainment amenities, or eye candy of an *Erin Brockovich*. Yet some critics found the David vs. Goliath tale of environmental justice to be a "loose and funny *Norma Rae*" and praised the script for getting "to the engrossing bare bones of Erin's search for justice."[10] Roberts's sassy performance and revealing outfits, combined with a compelling tale of pollution, corporate abuse, and citizen empowerment, helped *Erin Brockovich* gross over $125 million in the United States and an additional $258 million around the world.[11] In addition to earning Julia Roberts an Oscar for best actress, *Erin Brockovich* garnered Academy Award nominations for Albert Finney (best supporting actor) and Steven Soderbergh (director), as well as for best picture, among other accolades.

Moreover, illustrative of the long-standing intersection of public affairs, the political process, and popular culture is the real-life Erin Brockovich's role in environmental and political advocacy in the aftermath of the film's success. Most notably, Brockovich briefly served as a surrogate for Vice President Al Gore's presidential campaign in 2000, appearing in post-debate analysis in "the spin room," the post-debate media circus where supporters gather to advance the merits of their candidate's performance. She also hosted the ABC television series *Challenge America with Erin Brockovich*, served at consulting firms focusing on class action cases, and continued acting on behalf of citizens seeking environmental justice. Such work included a fact-finding trip to four states along the Gulf Coast in 2010 in the aftermath of BP's Deepwater Horizon oil rig explosion and catastrophic oil spill, the largest environmental accident of its kind in U.S. history.[12]

Another film based on a similar situation—claims of corporate malfeasance amid charges of pollution and deleterious health effects—is the 1998 film *A Civil Action*. Released on Christmas Day 1998 and directed by Steven Zaillian, the film, named by the Political Film Society as the best film on human rights for 1998, was adapted from the 1995 book by Jonathan Harr, which won the National Book Critics Circle Award for nonfiction.[13] Previous Oscar nominees Robert Duvall, John Travolta, and William H. Macy added their legendary acting chops to the cinematic effort, and the project also featured James Gandolfini, a year before he hit the big time as New Jersey "family man" Tony Soprano in HBO's cultural phenomenon *The Sopranos*.[14]

In *A Civil Action*, the scene of the crime is not working-class California but the working-class Boston suburb of Woburn, Massachusetts. While *Erin Brockovich* features a ragtag amateur sleuth–single mom as a crusader, the righteous cause in *A Civil Action* is taken up by a wealthy, hotshot, high-profile personal injury lawyer named Jan Schlichtmann (Travolta). Here, in working-class New England, the environmental malady that struck the town had a direct and devastating effect on its citizens. In Woburn, over a period of fourteen years, twelve children had died from leukemia linked to tap water contaminated by toxic chemicals. Investigations soon indicated that a major well near factories was contaminated by the industrial solvent trichloroethylene (TCE), which the Environmental Protection Agency (EPA) lists as a carcinogen. The film asks: Is the TCE to blame for the leukemia? Should the corporations who allegedly polluted the well with TCE be held liable for the illness, death, and environmental cleanup?

Eight families in 1981, with the help of attorney Schlichtmann and his small firm, sued the corporate powers—W. R. Grace and Beatrice Foods—in a case known as *Anne Anderson et al. v. W. R. Grace & Co. et al.*[15] The hard-nosed, erudite Jerome Facher (Robert Duvall) provides the chief legal representation for W. R. Grace, and proves to be a master tactician and superior legal mind who skillfully defends his corporate clients. Schlichtmann and his firm go into enormous debt to finance their investigation, which endures a number of setbacks and legal obstacles.

In the end, *A Civil Action* is a sober, well-paced film that does not offer a purely clichéd, good vs. evil, fist-pumping courtroom climax that results in an unequivocal slam-dunk for the grieving Woburn families or a massive financial windfall for Schlichtmann. There *is* no immediate multimillion dollar settlement for the families or Schlichtmann's law film. Rather, justice eventually comes down the road in the form of environmental cleanup after EPA action against the corporations, Schlichtmann does not gain back all of the millions lost after years of litigation. As the film's tagline notes, "Justice has its price." It is also worth noting that the lawyer-underdog-protagonist in this struggle, Schlichtmann, is hardly a stock hero who is driven solely by a sincere passion for justice and a clean environment. It is very clear at the outset that he is a Porsche-driving ambulance chaser who relies on major settlements to fund his fledgling firm and expensive suits.

What transpires in *A Civil Action*, therefore, can really be characterized as three major dynamics: the potentially devastating effects of pollution on the health and well-being of regular, hardworking, and often powerless, citizens; a careful review of the twists, turns, challenges, and injustices of civil litigation; and a spiritual awakening for Schlichtmann. Along the way, the cynical Schlichtmann, who loses money, his car, his firm, and nearly his sanity, gains a sense of right and wrong. He—and the viewers—learns a vital lesson: Justice is a long, difficult road, and it is not necessarily paved with immediate monetary gain. It is through his lengthy investigation that the EPA gains the appropriate information to take action to clean up the mess in Woburn. Schlichtmann, in the meantime, has since devoted his efforts to other cases and causes, including an environmental justice case in Tom's River, New Jersey, where federal and state health officials concluded that there was a link between "prenatal exposure" to water and air pollution and "unusually high levels of" leukemia in girls.[16]

Yet, unlike the far more formulaic, sexy, and predictable *Erin Brockovich*, *A Civil Action* did not perform very well at the box office—at least by Hollywood's standards. Despite the bona fide star power of *A Civil Action*, which also included the talents of John Lithgow and Sydney Pollack, and a fair amount of critical praise, the U.S. gross for *A Civil Action* was only a modest $56.7 million, a paltry sum when compared to a film like *Brockovich*. Apparently not all true tales of injustice and dirty water—and Davids vs. Goliaths—are equal in the minds of American consumers. This suggests a rather persistent puzzle for those interested in making this type of serious, factual, and intellectual film: Should filmmakers interested in environmental or other political issues dress up a story with romantic subplots and generic formulaic story lines in order to entice more people to watch, or should they focus on portraying an accurate depiction of the facts at hand, knowing full well that fewer people are likely to see the film? It is a difficult and important decision for filmmakers to consider. Accuracy, art, and commerce do not always mix successfully, and, as ever, moviemaking is a market-driven, moneymaking, bottom-line enterprise. Such

is the conundrum that has bedeviled many a politically minded, socially relevant motion picture over the past century.[17]

Documentaries: Trying to Make Sense of Complicated Issues

The first decade of the twenty-first century saw an increasing number of documentary films designed to raise public consciousness about the plight of environmental concerns. Without a doubt the most significant of these has been
An Inconvenient Truth (2006), which features former Vice President Al Gore
and addresses the dangers of climate change. The film, directed by Davis
Guggenheim, follows Gore on the lecture circuit as he presents the evidence
of human-induced climate change, providing interesting insight into not only
the scientific evidence that supports this theory but Gore himself: the person,
the politician, and the intellectual and spiritual antecedents of his ecological
awakening and intense focus on climate change.

Perhaps not surprising given the narrator's extremely high-profile position
in the American political system, *An Inconvenient Truth* was not without controversy. Many who doubt the veracity of claims in the film labeled it as propaganda.[18] After the film was shown in schools in England, Scotland, and
Wales, a school governor tried to ban the film on grounds that it presented an
inaccurate picture of the reasons for climate change. A British High Court
found in 2007 that there were nine inaccuracies or overstatements of facts in
the film, but the central thesis of the film was upheld, namely, that climate
change was occurring because of human activity.[19]

The controversies gave credence to those who deny the effects of human-
induced climate change.[20] While most scientists agree with the premise that
humans are having an effect on the climate, the way in which it is presented
in the press leaves doubts in the minds of some people. Typically, when there
is a debate about climate change in the press (whether in a newspaper article,
or on television, and especially cable television), it is pitched as an intellectually and academically equal debate between those who believe that climate
change is happening versus those who do not. Yet the actual debate among scientists is usually about the *degree* of impact of human activity on the climate
rather than if humans are having an impact. The science involved is complex
and difficult for people to comprehend. But because there are two sides presented as equally valid, it has been argued that the public gets a false impression that
there is a real scientific debate that climate change is occurring.[21] Nevertheless,
in 2007, the Intergovernmental Panel on Climate Change concluded that
there was unequivocal evidence that climate change was occurring.[22]

Despite debates over An Inconvenient Truth, the film garnered numerous accolades and awards, including the Academy Award for best documentary film and a screening at the Cannes Film Festival. Al Gore would eventually win the 2007 Nobel Peace Prize for his work in highlighting the issue of climate change in the world. In the final analysis, the importance of the film is probably less about the scientific points than the conversation that it has provoked. There is no doubt that An Inconvenient Truth has sparked an important dialogue about a host of related environmental issues both here in the United States and across the globe, including ongoing debates about the precise prescriptions for combating climate change. The film's credits—as well as the promotional campaign accompanying its release—emphasized a number of actions that citizens could take to make a difference. Indeed, as patrons entered movie theaters across the country to watch An Inconvenient Truth, flyers in the theater lobbies identified "Ten Things You Can Do To Help Solve the Climate Crisis," and the film's web page, operated by Participant Media, cited "Five Things You Can Do Now" to combat global warming.[23] Melissa Etheridge's song "I Need to Wake Up," written specially for the film and meant as a clarion call to civic engagement to combat climate change, plays at the documentary's conclusion and over the credits, where the list of suggested actions and environmental-political resources are displayed.

At the same time, pivoting from conversations, individual actions, and "Things You Can Do" lists to unified governmental action can be a Herculean task. Finding substantive common ground—or at least, a filibuster-proof consensus—as to the proper national policy prescriptions for combating climate change remains elusive in the fragmented and persistently polarized American political system, where competing and powerful interest groups, the structure and rules of the Senate, and the traditional fossil fuel economy can stymie concerted, coherent, and significant paths forward.[24]

We can see a continuation of these environmental themes with another important, but lesser known, film, The 11th Hour (2007). Narrated and produced by Leonardo DiCaprio, the documentary takes a more direct approach to the issue of climate change than does An Inconvenient Truth. Whereas An Inconvenient Truth uses the personality, intellectual journey, and humor of former Vice President Gore to draw the audience into the subject of climate change, The 11th Hour makes a more straightforward appeal to the audience by focusing solely on the mountain of scientific evidence. This might have an initial dampening effect on the audience, but the film turns explicitly towards solutions before it ends. The strength of the film is that, compared to An

Inconvenient Truth, it provides a more comprehensive list of solutions that individual audience members can adopt to help alleviate the problems of climate change. Rather than leaving the film feeling overwhelmed by the sheer magnitude of the environmental crisis, *The 11th Hour* may well provide the audience with a greater chance to feel empowered and motivated.

One should not get the impression that all environmentally oriented films deal solely with climate change. During the 1980s growing concerns about the loss of species prompted numerous documentaries and even a few feature films. Television programs, such as those produced by public television in the United States and the BBC in the United Kingdom, have highlighted environmental concerns. Television series such as *Nova* (1974–), *Nature* (1982–), *Journey to Planet Earth* (2003) and several *National Geographic Specials* (1964–), which regularly air on PBS in the United States, combine educational information about wildlife and science with concerns about the environment and conservation. The highly acclaimed British series *Planet Earth* (2006) was a popular tour de force about the wide variety of animal life mixed with a message about the need for conservation and habitat protection. The visually stunning *Earth* (2007) and *Oceans* (2009) continued in the vein, emphasizing similar perspectives. There have also been very successful feature documentaries, such as *Winged Migration* (2001), *Microcosmos* (1996), and *The National Parks: America's Best Idea* (2009), which highlight the wonders of the natural world while simultaneously calling for vigilant environmentalism. On the fictional side, even the venerable *Star Trek* movie franchise explored the importance of species protection; in *Star Trek IV: The Voyage Home* (1986), the crew travels back in time to rescue humpback whales.

Perhaps most dramatic and arresting among habitat protection films is the groundbreaking thriller–meets–environmental activism movie *The Cove* (2009), an Academy Award winner for best documentary. The film, which exposes the abuse, exploitation, sale, and wanton slaughter of dolphins, follows former dolphin trainer Ric O'Barry (who worked on the 1960s television show *Flipper* before he devoted his life to dolphin protection) and his band of devoted dolphin advocates and fearless technological wizards as they infiltrate a notorious dolphin cove near Taijii, Japan. What O'Barry and his team find is that not only are the Japanese at the forefront of the global sale and exploitation of dolphins, but that dolphins are deliberately led to a peaceful cove where they are trapped and brutally killed. Indeed, their mercury-ridden, toxic meat is provided to unwitting students throughout the Japanese school system as well as consumers throughout the country. The startling and unsettling revelations, and the jarring footage documenting them, are nothing short of riveting. O'Barry's crew uses an amazing array of determination, disguises, hidden microphones, and night and underwater cameras to document the dolphin massacre and the incredible lengths to which the Japanese business and government officials go to hide their actions. The film methodically documents the intimidation and detainment of those seeking the truth about what really happens to dolphins in *The Cove*.[25]

Many documentaries of the first decade of the twenty-first century have highlighted several issues that are not necessarily focused on the environment per se, but point out the environmental impact of these specific concerns. For example, the film *Wal-Mart: The High Cost of Low Price* (2005), from Robert Greenwald's liberal-leaning Brave New Films, examines the effect of Wal-Mart on the economy of small towns but also addresses the environmental impact of Wal-Mart stores in local communities. Among other environmental consequences of the retail giant, the film cites Wal-Mart's violations of the Clean Water Act in seventeen locations in Texas, New Mexico, Oklahoma, and Massachusetts.[26]

Similarly, the exposé of modern corporate farming and food production *Food Inc.* (2008) demonstrates how modern farming techniques have a deleterious effect on the environment, and, by extension, the health of the population.[27] Similar themes are examined in two other documentaries of this era: Morgan Spurlock's commercially successful and critically praised film documenting his one-month McDonald's-only diet, *Super Size Me* (2004), and Aaron Woolf's *King Corn* (2007). Despite slightly different approaches and narratives, all of these films consider these fundamental questions: Where does our food come from (and why), and how does this affect our health? These provocative films reveal that much of our diet derives from cheap, sweet, fattening, and genetically modified corn and soybeans. As the aforementioned movies demonstrate, as the environmental movement has matured so have environmental films. Today, rather than the environment being isolated as a special topic, it is integrated into a web of complex and interrelated socioeconomic, health, and political issues that demand the public's attention.

Meanwhile, in the era of exponential growth in bottled water—brought to us by Coke and Pepsi (and other corporate behemoths, such as Nestlé)—some powerful contemporary films and books have focused their energies on the precious water side of the human survival equation. Asserting that "water is a basic human right, the right to survive," the cautionary documentary *Blue Gold: World Water Wars* (2008), directed by the first-time filmmaker Sam Bozzo and

King Corn (2007): "Two Friends, One Acre of Corn, and the Subsidized Crop That Drives Our Fast-Food Nation"[28]

King Corn (2007), *an environmental road trip of sorts featuring East Coast college pals Ian Cheney and Curt Ellis, examines the primacy of corn in the mass production of food products in the United States, tracing the centrality of corn from its genetically modified seeds to our grocery shelves, restaurants, and dinner tables.*

narrated by *A Clockwork Orange* star Malcolm McDowell, and based on the book *Blue Gold: The Fight to Stop the Corporate Theft of the World's Water Supply* (2003), warn of the negative, nay catastrophic, consequences of the rampant privatization of public water sources across the globe. As such, the scarcity of clean, plentiful and necessary "blue gold" may very well define the pressing social-political-economic crises in the future. From the United States to Africa, the film documents citizens' work to reclaim uncontaminated water for their families, farms, and future.[29]

Awarded a special jury prize at the Sundance Film Festival and a LennonOno Grant for Peace award by Yoko Ono in Iceland, the documentary *Gasland* (2010) chronicles one man's journey across several states to examine the health and environmental hazards of a form of natural gas extraction called hydraulic fracturing, or "fracking"—a process of using pressurized water and chemicals to dislodge the gas from rock deep beneath the surface.[30] The man in question, filmmaker and narrator Josh Fox, after being offered a signing bonus to allow gas extraction on his family's property along the Delaware River in eastern Pennsylvania, soon finds nearby residents complaining of water degradation and illnesses. Fox asserts the fracking process has been excluded from certain federal environmental regulations via 2005 energy legislation favored by Vice President Dick Cheney and the energy industry, and journeys across the country to highlight the trials and tribulations of everyday Americans seeking environmental justice.

Though *Gasland* has been widely praised as, among other things, "artful and disturbing," and "mesmerizing and thorough," it has faced criticism.[31] The film has been an instrumental tool in grassroots environmental awareness and advocacy related to natural gas extraction; New York, for example, imposed a moratorium on the practice of fracking until further environmental impact studies were completed (actor Mark Ruffalo has been an especially active voice in that state), and, like a swath of municipal governments in western Pennsylvania, Pittsburgh's City Council banned natural gas drilling within city limits.[32] Others, especially in but not limited to the natural gas industry, have heavily criticized the film as propaganda. They met Josh Fox's ambitious schedule of free screenings, college campus visits, and talk-back sessions with a veritable avalanche of press releases and articles challenging claims made in the film.[33] Meanwhile, nonpartisan civic associations, such as the League of Women Voters, have entered the policy fray, hosting screenings of the film and conducting community discussions about the impact of natural gas drilling. Whether one favors, opposes, or continues to gather data regarding the environmental and health impact of the fracking process, *Gasland* stands as an excellent example of how film can be an influential tool for civic discourse and political action.

Using Fictional Stories to Raise Concerns about the Environment

By the early twenty-first century, films about the environment had moved into the mainstream; no longer were such stories solely the purview of science fiction. Environmental stories had become commonplace, perhaps even routine. The long-awaited *The Simpsons Movie* (2007) used an environmentally themed story to advance its story line. In the film, Lake Springfield becomes so polluted that the residents of Springfield and the federal government must

Gasland Comes to a Community Near You: Don't Frack with Pittsburgh

Film as an educational, advocacy, and grassroots mobilization tool: Here, a local business displays a sign promoting a screening and discussion of the documentary Gasland (2010), which chronicles allegations of environmental and health hazards, and regulatory malfeasance, associated with a form of natural gas extraction known as hydraulic fracturing, or "fracking." Josh Fox's provocative film has been widely praised by environmental organizations and local government officials, and the League of Women Voters has even hosted screenings. At the same time, the documentary has been met with suspicion, ridicule, and outrage by many within the energy industry, which has developed detailed websites and fact sheets to challenge many of the film's claims.

take drastic action. Lisa Simpson, the one character consistently concerned with environmental issues through the run of the television series, holds a meeting that is homage to *An Inconvenient Truth*. Lisa's lecture to the town meeting is entitled "An Irritating Truth" and uses a scissor lift just as Al Gore did in his lecture. When the warnings are not heeded, the effects of polluting Lake Springfield are devastating and have dire consequences for the town of Springfield; thus, the federal government places a dome over the town so that it cannot export its pollution to its neighbors.[34] Even when the Simpson family temporarily moves to Alaska, the film makes sly comments about environmental and political issues. For example, the family, upon arriving in Alaska, is given their annual stipend from the "Alaska Permanent Fund." In the movie, the fund is characterized as payment from the oil companies to allow them to plunder the natural beauty of the state.

Another popular animated feature that uses the environment as a starting point is *Wall-E* (2008). The film is ostensibly a children's film set in the distant future. A small robot (Wall-E) is left to clean up the mess left by humans because they have consumed so much and left mountains of trash behind. Humans have temporarily migrated to space to escape the garbage (because "there is plenty of space in space"), while robots clean up and prepare Earth for the return of humans. As the film progresses it becomes clear that the devastation of the earth has been so complete that it is doubtful that Earth can be rehabilitated. One of the primary commentaries of the film is that the lifestyle of humans, one of overconsumption, lack of activity, and trivial gadgetry, leads to environmental problems.

Even though *The Simpsons Movie* and *Wall-E* were enormously successful at the box office, it is debatable whether either film had a significant impact on the national conversation about environmental issues. Ultimately, in both films, the environmental drama of the plotline gives way to more traditional concerns of American motion pictures—friendship and family ties. In *The Simpsons Movie*, Homer's lesson is that he must consider others, including his family and neighbors, in his daily life. The relationship between a boy and his father is also prominent in the film, much as it has been on the television show during its more than two-decade run. Similarly, *Wall-E* focuses on the importance of friendship and loyalty. One wonders if the environmental message of the films becomes submerged under these more traditional themes.

The plots of a few other films that contain elements of environmental catastrophe probably do not advance an environmental agenda very well either. For instance, *The Day After Tomorrow* (2004) is really a disaster movie masquerading as an environmental film. The plot creates a scenario in which increased greenhouse gases lead to a devastating chain of events culminating in a new ice age that engulfs North America. The plot was so far-fetched and unbelievable that there is considerable doubt about its educational value in shaping public understanding about the real dangers of climate change. Officials from NASA backed away from officially commenting on the film and used the opportunity to present data and real projections to the public.[35]

The Day the Earth Stood Still (2008), which is a remake of an antinuclear film from 1951, brings the alien Klaatu (Keanu Reeves) to Earth to usher the destruction of humans in order to preserve other forms of live on Earth. His reasoning is that humans are so destructive that the earth needs to be protected from human qualities; however, the plot descends into almost incomprehensible reasoning and action. It is difficult to believe that the cause of environmentalism is actually served by films like *The Day After Tomorrow* and *The Day the Earth Stood Still*. Nevertheless, we must accept that some films fare much better at the box office than others. Big budget films with action sequences and unbelievable special effects are typically more popular than films that rely on scientifically based information.

Conclusion

> All economic activity is dependent upon that environment and its underlying resource base of forests, water, air, soil, and minerals. When the environment is finally forced to file for bankruptcy because its resource base has been polluted, degraded, dissipated, and irretrievably compromised, the economy goes into bankruptcy with it.
>
> —U.S. SENATOR GAYLORD NELSON, 1992[36]

Whether or not one embraces the views of Gaylord Nelson, former Governor and Senator from Wisconsin, and founder of Earth Day, awareness of the problems of pollution, environmental degradation, and conservation has been raised in the minds of a large portion of the population over the past generation. Film and music, among other forms of popular culture, have played a role in advancing our national conversation about economic development, overpopulation, and air and water pollution, among a slew of other salient matters. In some cases, documentaries have even been part of the framing of policy choices. Notwithstanding the controversy over human-induced climate change, there is a general recognition of the importance of environmental issues. In the early 1990s, the Turner Broadcasting network even broadcasted a half-hour animation series about a group of five teenagers who battle to save the planet from environmental harm called *Captain Planet and the Planeteers* (1990–1996). However, the environment remains a difficult dilemma to represent on the screen. The sheer scale and complexity of the problems associated with it make it difficult to address. What is the proper balance between the need for economic development and the need to protect the environment? In a broader sense, can the environment afford any significant development from the Third World? If it cannot, can people in the developed world in good conscience say that the planet cannot afford the development of the Third World?

What the films in this section demonstrated is that the problems associated with environmental degradation have only begun to scratch the surface of the problems. Movies typically focus on a single issue rather than a complex set of dynamics. As such, the difficulty in discussing the interrelatedness of these realities means that big budget movies are likely not well suited to nuance, context, and serious examination of environmental matters. At the same time, however, the increasingly accessible documentary format (via cable television, the Internet, as well as traditional theaters) may fare much better in providing a more serious, sober, and real-world context for understanding and debating environmental issues. Yet major releases such as *Erin Brockovich* and *A Civil Action* remind us that failure to address matters of pollution and injustice in our communities might lead to health and environmental catastrophes. And controversial and provocative documentaries such as *Gasland* and *An Inconvenient Truth* illustrate that films can help drive issue advocacy, policy discussions, and grassroots political mobilization. Films and human beings may be imperfect vessels, after all, but on the journey to seeing the bigger picture, having all hands on deck may be a useful, noble, and necessary enterprise.

Notes

1. See Huma Khan, "The Politics of 'Avatar:' Conservatives Attack Movie's Political Messaging," ABC News, January 6, 2010: http://abcnews.go.com/Politics/Movies/politics-avatar-conservatives-attack-movies-political-messaging/story?id=9484885; and Ross Douthat, "Heaven and Nature," *New York Times*, December 21, 2009, p. A31.
2. By the time an expanded version of the film was later re-released in 2010, Cameron, who had a background with deep water robotics, consulted directly with oil giant BP and numerous public agencies over the 2010 Deep Water Horizon oil rig explosion and resultant oil spill. Working with a team of engineers and experts to provide advice on how to proceed in the Gulf of Mexico, Cameron and his team produced a 25-page report offering summary and conclusions to the Department of Energy, the EPA (Environmental Protection

Agency), the Coast Guard, and NOAA (the National Oceanic and Atmospheric Administration). Jen Chaney, "James Cameron on the Special Edition of 'Avatar,' Eco-conscious DVDs and BP," *Washington Post*, August 27, 2010. In the interview, several exchanges illustrate Cameron's attention to (1) environmental policy within the context of energy consumption in the entertainment industry and beyond, and (2) the politics and science of climate change, public policy, and renewable sources of energy. Here are two relevant excerpts:

Honestly, the truth is, we have to revisit almost every part of our lives and our existence over the next few years. Energy consumption, I think, being the biggest one. Energy and global warming are interlinked issues obviously, and global warming is going to take us out long before plastic pollution. Don't get me started on that. I just got back from a two-day renewable energy conference in Aspen and it's grim trying to get the needle of policy to move. . . .

When the oil and coal industries are being subsidized at a level much higher than renewable energy, the people who try to do utility-scale renewable projects, they're not competitive. They have to be competitive. And the only way to make it competitive is to price carbon accurately. And the only way that's going to happen is for people to realize that carbon is a pollutant and it's a pollutant that's going to affect, not only the quality of our lives, but it will cause the destruction of 50 percent of all species on this planet by the end of the century. And people need to wake up to that.

3. A link to the original Ad Council public service announcement can be viewed at: http://www.seeingthebiggerpiecture.net. For *The Simpsons* episode that includes the homage to the PSA, see "The Trash of the Titans," original airdate April 26, 1998.
4. PBS's ambitious and richly detailed *American Experience* film *Earth Days* (2010) chronicles the rise of the modern environmentalist (or Green) movement in the United States. The trailer for this exceptional film can be viewed at: http://www.youtube.com/watch?v= FwRNj0Op61I; and the film itself can be viewed in its entirety at: http://www.pbs.org/wgbh/americanexperience/films/earthdays/player/.
5. Barry Commoner, *Making Peace with the Planet* (New York: Pantheon, 1975, 1990).
6. Sen. Gaylord Nelson (1916–2005), Democrat from Wisconsin, was a longtime conservationist and liberal reformer. He served in the U.S. Senate from 1963 to 1981. For additional information about Nelson and Earth Day, see, among others, The Nelson Institute for Environmental Studies at the University of Wisconsin, "Gaylord Nelson and Earth Day: The Making of the Modern Environmental Movement": http://www.nelsonearthday.net/; and Bill Christofferson, *The Man from Clear Lake: Earth Day Founder Senator Gaylord Nelson* (Madison: University of Wisconsin Press, 2004).
7. The song has been remade by several artists, including successful recent editions by the Counting Crows and Amy Grant.
8. For more on John Prine—songs, lyrics, albums, tour dates, etc.—see the John Prine Shrine fan site: http://www.jpshrine.org/; and the singer's record label, Oh Boy! Records: http://www.ohboy.com/. In "Paradise," Prine laments the loss of Kentucky's pristine beauty, enjoyed by his family for generations, at the hands of "Mr. Peabody's coal train." In 2003,

as the issue of mountainside removal mining gained increasing public attention, the CD *Coal Country Music* was released, with all proceeds benefiting The Alliance for Appalachia, a coalition of groups opposed to mountaintop removal mining. Prine, along with over a dozen prominent folk artists, was featured on the release.

9. Harry Harrison, *Make Room! Make Room!* (New York: Berkley Publishing Co., 1967).

10. Wesley Morris's review from the *San Francisco Examiner*, March 17, 2000: http://www.sfgate. com/cgi-bin/article.cgi?f=/e/a/2000/03/17/WEEKEND6120.dtl. Other critics sneered at the over-the-top cleavage shots, skimpy clothing, and formulaic romantic subplot that ran alongside the battle against corporate polluters. One prominent film critic, for example, characterized the screenplay as having the "depth and insight of a cable-TV docudrama." See Roger Ebert's review of *Erin Brockovich*: http://www.suntimes.com/ebert/ebert_reviews/ 2000/03/031703.html.

11. See: http://www.the-numbers.com/movies/2000/ERINB.html.

12. "Erin Brockovich Joins Forces with Weitz & Luxenberg, P.C. to Assist Victims of BP Oil Spill," *JD Journal*, May 6, 2010: http://www.jdjournal.com/2010/05/06/erin-brockovich-joins-forces-with-weitz-luxenberg-p-c-to-assist-victims-of-bp-oil-spill/. Concerning the BP oil spill in the Gulf of Mexico and its potential deleterious effects on citizens' health and livelihood, Brockovich stated, "People want to know, 'What will happen to the ecosystem, the fish and wildlife? Who can help local commercial fishermen, property owners whose land has been ruined, and families worried about the spill's impact on their food and health?'" On a personal level, she even experienced a phenomenon affecting other American home-owners: the health risks posed by toxic mold. This particular virulent form of mold can, according to some industrial hygienists, cause "runny nose, runny eyes, headaches, sinus con-gestion, cough, fatigue, and neurological problems." See "Silent Killers: Toxic Mold," CBS's *48 Hours*, September 5, 2001: http://www.cbsnews.com/stories/2001/09/05/48hours/ main309720.shtml.

13. For *A Civil Action* and the Political Film Society's best human rights award for 1998, January 1, 1999, see: http://www.polfilms.com/issue32.html; and http://www.polfilms.com/ brockovich.html.

14. Jonathan Harr, *A Civil Action* (New York: Random House, 1995).

15. For a summary of the case, see "Science in the Classroom: The Woburn Toxic Trial": http://serc.carleton.edu/woburn/Case_summary.html.

16. Tom Avril, "Study Links Tom's River, N.J., Cancers to Pollution," *Philadelphia Enquirer*, December 19, 2001. Regarding the conclusions of state and federal health officials in this Tom's River case, the article states, "The findings, released days after dozens of families set-tled their claims against three companies for an undisclosed amount, stopped short of declaring that contaminants caused the girls' cancer. The researchers said pure chance could not be ruled out as an explanation. No associations were found between the pollution and cancer in boys. Nor were links found for other cancers, such as those of the brain or ner-vous system, that also are unusually high in the area."

17. Daniel P. Franklin's excellent *Politics and Film: The Political Culture and Film in the United States* (Lanham, MD: Rowman & Littlefield, 2006) does an outstanding job of highlight-ing the evolution of the political economy of Hollywood and points out that, in many ways, consumerism and the ability for studios to successfully market niche films—in the era he calls the "Marketization of Hollywood"—are what drives the content and themes of film.

We buy tickets to the films we want to see, and the industry is there, ready, willing, and able to provide us with whatever product we desire (for better or worse, of course). Of the slew of Iraq–Afghanistan and post-9/11 films, very few performed well at the box office. Most notably, *The Hurt Locker* (2009), the Academy Award winner for the best picture in 2010, which cost roughly $11 million to make, earned a mere $12.6 million in its commercial release (pre-DVD sales).

18. Proponents of the film and the cause had their cause hurt in the climate e-mail scandal. For more information see Matthew Weaver, "Climategate emails report due today," *The Guardian*, July 7, 2010, http://www.guardian.co.uk/environment/2010/jul/07/climategate-emails-report-handed-down and the webpage dedicated to the controversy, http://www.guardian.co.uk/environment/series/climate-wars-hacked-emails

19. To see more on the *Dimmock v. Secretary of State for Education and Skills* case, visit "Gore's Climate Film's Nine 'Errors,'" BBC News, October 11, 2007: http://news.bbc.co.uk/2/hi/uk_news/education/7037671.stm.

20. For more about the politics behind the climate change debate, see Eric Pooley, *The Climate War: True Believers, Power Brokers and the Fight to Save the Earth* (New York: Hyperion, 2010). Some independent filmmakers created films to counter Gore's arguments, such as the films *Apocalypse No* (2008) and *The Great Global Warming Swindle* (2007): http://www.garagetv.be/videogalerij/blancostemrecht/The_Great_Global_Warming_Swindle_Documentary_Film.aspx. See also: http://www.greatglobalwarmingswindle.co.uk/.

21. See Ross Gelbspan, *Boiling Point: How Politicians, Big Oil and Coal, Journalists, and Activists Have Fueled the Climate Crisis—And What We Can Do to Avert Disaster* (New York: Basic Books, 2004), chap. 4, "Bad Press," pp. 67–85.

22. Intergovernmental Panel on Climate Change, 2007: http://www.ipcc.ch/.

23. For "Ten Things You Can Do" adopted from the film, see: http://images.rodale.com/read-thetruth/pdfs/readthetruth-checklist.pdf. For "Five Things You Can Do Now," see Participant Media's website for *An Inconvenient Truth*: http://www.takepart.com/anincon-venienttruth.

24. In the first legislative session of President Barack Obama's tenure (2009–2011), the markedly more liberal Democratic House passed comprehensive environmental legislation aimed at lowering carbon emissions and investing in alternative energies. A "cap and trade" element was a central part of this package. Conversely, the significantly more moderate-conservative Senate, while ostensibly in Democratic control, could not muster the requisite votes to pass legislation resembling the more progressive House version. As such, nothing passed in the Senate, so there was no legislation to go to conference for negotiation, let alone make it to the desk of President Obama. A few key Democratic senators in oil- and gas-producing states, combined with near-unanimous Republican opposition to Democratic environmental measures in the Senate, provided huge obstacles to passing comprehensive legislation limiting carbon emissions during this time.

25. Moreover, to further promote the cause of freeing dolphins from captivity, and to raise awareness of the dolphin slaughter in Taijji, a visit to the film's website finds a PSA from a veritable who's who of contemporary cinema and pop culture figures: Jennifer Aniston, Woody Harrelson, Naomi Watts, Paul Rudd, Robin Williams, Ben Stiller, Courteney Cox, Russell Simmons, and James Gandolfini, among others. "The Cove PSA—My Friend Is . . . ," featuring the numerous actors and artists cited, can be found at:

http://www.thecovemovie.com/.

26. EPA Press Release, "U.S. Reaches Water Pollution Settlement with Wal-Mart," June 7, 2001: http://yosemite.epa.gov/opa/admpress.nsf/b1ab9f485b098972852562e7004dc686/dfc27e3cc459534d85256a64005f9dd2?OpenDocument#. Also see the film's website for supporting documentation: http://www.walmartmovie.com/facts.php.

27. Similarly, *King Corn* (2007) examines the primacy of corn and its government subsidies in the mass production of food products in the United States, tracing the centrality of corn from its genetically modified seeds to the dinner table (and breakfast and lunch and everything in between). See: http://www.pbs.org/independentlens/kingcorn/. The film *Fast Food Nation* (2006), based on Eric Schlosser's bestseller of the same name (HarperPerennial, 2001, 2005), tangentially deals with some of the environmental hazards and work conditions in chicken and beef processing plants.

28. For part of the documentary's official summary from the filmmakers, see, for example: http://www.imdb.com/title/tt1112115/plotsummary.

29. *Blue Gold*'s tagline is from the film's web page: http://www.bluegold-worldwaterwars.com/actionplan/index.html. Bozzo's documentary *Blue Gold* is based on Maude Barlow and Tony Clarke's *Blue Gold: The Fight to Stop the Corporate Theft of the World's Water* (New Press, 2003). Barlow is the chair of the public advocacy group the Council of Canadians; Clarke serves as the director of the Polaris Institute of Canada. Connected to this exploration of the siphoning of public water for private enrichment is the matter of increased plastic waste in the oceans. Obviously this is not due to merely the bottling of water, but the increase of everyday use of plastics across the globe. The exponential growth in plastic waste, and the threat to marine and mammal life in the Pacific—namely, the "Great Pacific Garbage Dump," twice the size of Texas—is chronicled in Kitt Doucette, "An Ocean of Plastic," *Rolling Stone*, October 29, 2009, pp. 54–57.

30. "David Browne, "Lennon's 70th Birthday Marked by Reissues, Concerts, Movies," *Rolling Stone*, October 14, 2010, p. 18. Director Josh Fox was presented with the LennonOno Grant for Peace award alongside authors Michael Pollan and Alice Walker and public-health advocate Barbara Kowalcyk.

31. Quotes from Hank Stuever, "On HBO, One Man's Journey into a Natural Gas Crisis," *Washington Post*, June 21, 2010. Wrote Stuever: "Mesmerizing and thorough as it is, 'Gasland' is one of those documentaries that will send you into the Google quagmire in search of some answers, which, I can report after a few hopeless hours of looking, you won't easily get." And the League of Women Voters of Arkansas responded to an attack on *Gasland* from the Arkansas Chamber of Commerce, August 19, 2009: http://www.facebook.com/note.php?note_id=151692471514953&comments.

32. "The Region's Top 10 News Stories of 2010," *Pittsburgh Post-Gazette*, January 2, 2010: http://www.post-gazette.com/pg/11002/1114801-455.stm?cmpid=news.xml. Mark Ruffalo's outspoken opposition to fracking in New York can be found in a number of videos, including: http://www.youtube.com/watch?v=3_g1_hJ0iaA, http://www.youtube.com/watch?v=brzYG-7t4GU&feature=related.

33. For additional insight on fracking and *Gasland*, see Josh Fox's interview on PBS's *Now*, March 26, 2010: http://www.pbs.org/now/shows/613/index.html; "The Price of Gas: A Need to Know Investigation," August 27, 2010: http://www.pbs.org/wnet/need-to-know/environment/the-price-of-gas-a-need-to-know-investigation/3170/; and

"Awash in Natural Gas?" on PBS's, *Need to Know*, August 26, 2010: http://www.pbs.org/wnet/need-to-know/voices/awash-in-natural-gas/2912/. Democrats in the 111th Congress sponsored the FRAC (Fracturing Responsibility and Awareness of Chemicals Act) to create transparency regarding the chemicals used in fracking fluids; this legislation, sponsored by U.S. Senator Robert Casey (D-PA), can be found at: h t t p : / / w w w . g o v t r a c k . u s / c o n g r e s s / bill.xpd?bill=s111–1215. There is extensive natural gas and oil industry criticism of *Gasland*. One of the most prominent of these industry-sponsored clearinghouses for articles and point-by-point challenges to Fox's claims is the website for the group Energy in Depth: http://www.energyindepth.org/tag/gasland/.

34. This is not dissimilar from the plot offered in the original *The Day the Earth Stood Still* (1951), where the people of Earth were told that they would not be allowed to export their violent behavior to other planets.

35. NASA created a website that used information from the film to help determine what was the actual science and what was Hollywood hyperbole: http://nsidc.org/news/press/day_after/. Initially, the Bush administration, which was the target of the filmmakers, prevented NASA scientists from commenting on the film, which led to a debate about the government's role in climate change data and information. See Scott Bowles, "'The Day After Tomorrow' Heats Up a Political Debate," *USA Today*, May 26, 2004; and Michael Coren, "Climate Flick Favors Fantasy over Fact," CNN, May 20, 2004: http://www.cnn.com/2004/TECH/science/05/27/weather.movie/.

36. Sen. Gaylord Nelson's quote is taken from the University of Wisconsin's web page for *Beyond Earth Day: Fulfilling the Promise*, by Gaylord Nelson, with Susan Campbell and Paul Wozniak (Madison: University of Wisconsin Press, 2002): http://uwpress.wisc.edu/books/2095.htm.

·SECTION 4·

FINISHING UP

· 1 1 ·

CONCLUSIONS

This book is a labor of love for both authors; it combines two of our favorite passions in life, namely, politics and popular culture, especially film. If there are new socially relevant, provocative films in the multiplex, at a film festival, or on cable television, we aim to somehow, sometime, somewhere find the occasion to view them. The same goes for satire that occasionally drifts across our television and computer screens, even if the art form is not as grandiose or the cinematography is lacking. Why? Much like humorist David Sedaris feels most at home in the dark (movie theaters) in the City of Light (Paris), the authors find similar solace in the power of film.[1] We are each in our own way, to borrow the title of Jan Troell's quiet-yet-profound Swedish film set in the early twentieth century, searching for those "everlasting moments," those images that help capture some essence of our existence, illuminating profound aspects of the human condition that may educate, inspire, unsettle, or challenge the way we think about the great issues of the day, or even the very meaning of the past.[2] These moments, on the big and small screen alike, can help bridge the gap between political science theory and reality; aid in the application of these ideas to the debates that consume our world; and give greater meaning to these concepts and challenges that might at first appear abstract or elusive.

No doubt, as you might have already deduced, the authors come at politics and popular culture from very different perspectives: one author focuses on the international aspect, the other concentrates a little more on domestic American politics; one on film and popular culture as a driving force in current political discussion, the other on film and popular culture as a cultural-historical phenomenon. We believe that this is one of the strengths of the book. Regardless of the approach, what we have hoped to demonstrate in this book is how film and popular culture go a long way to help explain the theory, practice, and relevance of politics. Whether we discuss pop culture icons, catch-phrases, *Food, Inc.*, *South Park*, *The Simpsons*, or Czech New Wave films around the water cooler or in the grocery store, we are creating crucial frames of reference through which we interpret politics.

One trend impacting the intersection of politics and popular culture that is especially evident in our media age is the democratization of film. In short, what we mean by this is there is now greater access to politically relevant foreign and domestic films (or any films for that matter) than ever before. Long gone are the days where *only* single-screen art house theaters in major cities or university film series displayed socially conscious documentaries and foreign and independent films (those generated from outside of the studio system) for the intelligentsia. With the readily accessible rental and purchase of films over the Internet; the low-cost distribution of advocacy films through organizations with a clear viewpoint (such as Robert Greenwald's progressive Brave New Films); the ability for professionals *and* engaged citizens to make their own politically minded films with available software on their laptops; and our nation's treasure of community and university library systems, featuring a great diversity of film, there is now a greater ability for more students and citizens to access a cornucopia of previously unattainable or cost-prohibitive films.

In our discussions, films and popular culture can be used a number of different ways. For brevity's sake we have divided these into three categories. First, films and popular culture can be used as advocacy. We have seen a diverse array of writers, actors, and directors attempt to change viewers' political stances or actions based on the evidence that the filmmakers present. Certainly, there are examples in each chapter; however, films covering topics like social justice and human rights are prone to this form of explicit "message" filmmaking. The most overt films in this category are documentary films. The films of Michael Moore, and his critics, for example, are attempts to sway public opinion, as are a number of the environment-themed works we cited.[3] But this category is not limited to documentary films. Some narrative films, such as *Missing* (1982) and

Wall-E (2008), are designed to tell a story that leads to a change in the public's political philosophy. This category is perhaps the most common way the
majority of people identify the relationship between films and politics, but it
is not the only one.

Second, films and popular culture, much like the educational system, help
to pass along cultural information, historical perspectives, and societal norms
to the population at large. As such, these films do not try to change people's
minds, instead they try to reinforce ideas that the society broadly shares already.
Take, for example, the classic film *Mr. Smith Goes to Washington* (1939). The
goal of this film is certainly to entertain. On a deeper level, however, it is meant
to reinforce the basic premises of American democracy. Of course, in the film
and in real life, there are those who will try to circumvent or use the system to
their own advantage, but in the long run it does not work. *Mr. Smith* argues that
the system can withstand nefarious people, and ultimately, American democracy will compensate and come through better and stronger. Similarly, historical films, such as *Young Mr. Lincoln* (1939) and *Truman* (1995), attempt to
educate and inform the public about political and social values that are broadly held in society.

Finally, films can simply be entertainment; however, the subtle or covert
messages that are carried within the film help us appreciate the understanding
of our political and cultural realities. This is not a concept that was emphasized
as much in this book, but it is present nonetheless. There are visual clues
about how a society operates just by observing the norms within a film. Consider
a few American television programs. In *The Simpsons* nearly everyone goes to
church on Sundays[4]; in *The Gilmore Girls* nearly everyone participates in town
meetings; and in *Friends* different ethnicities and religions are not only friends,
but frequently the characters date and marry across ethnic-religious lines. This
says a great deal about what people believe about the political culture of the
United States (mainly the ideas of the importance of civil society and mass participation, regardless of religion or ethnicity) without directly discussing politics.

The study of film and popular culture is an excellent and fertile field of
exploration and research. A word of warning before we finish: To believe that
watching a film will substitute for reading and research is simply fallacious.
There is a growing consensus among political scientists about the role of film
and popular culture in politics. Nevertheless, as demonstrated several times in
this book, filmmakers often leave out events, motivation, crucial context, and
nuance for the sake of drama, time and budget constraints, and frankly because
it does not fit their ideological preconceptions. Reading and research are an

integral part of understanding and analysis. We encourage you to do your own investigation and critical thinking when it comes to film and politics; by no means have we (or any other author) cornered the market on the full range of understandings and interpretations. Remember: Viewing a film may introduce you to a new ideological framework or alter the way you think about a particular event, issue, or public policy; that in itself is certainly not a negative development. But it is imperative that you do the heavy lifting of enlightened citizenship—namely, reading and research—so that you can make the most informed conclusion that incorporates data, appreciates history, and considers a variety of relevant perspectives.

One of the great challenges of writing a book like this is to decide which films to discuss and what aspect of politics to highlight. This is certainly not the definitive book about film and politics (much less, popular culture and politics). Nonetheless, we hope that you will look at films a little more critically and think about their impact on the political world a little more carefully after reading *Seeing the Bigger Picture*. For this edition, we have created a website to continue the conversation. We look forward to responding to your insights and inquiries and hope you will take the opportunity to engage with others who might be interested in film, popular culture, and politics.

See www.seeingthebiggerpicture.net.

Notes

1. David Sedaris, "The City of Light in the Dark," in *Me Talk Pretty One Day* (New York: Back Bay Books, 2001).
2. *Everlasting Moments* (2008), directed by Jan Troell.
3. And it is worth noting that, on several occasions, Moore has deemed his documentaries failures, in the sense that he was unable to impact events and effect change as he had hoped. *Roger & Me* did not stem the tide of deindustrialization in the American heartland in the 1990s; *Bowling for Columbine* (2002) did not lead to either the greater regulation of firearms (such as the closing of gun show loopholes) or to a sustained examination of the role of contemporary capitalism in feeding our fears and anxiety; and *Fahrenheit 9/11*, released in the summer of 2004, despite shattering all box office records for a documentary, did not prevent President George W. Bush from winning a second term in the fall.
4. For more about the role of religion in *The Simpsons*, consult: Mark I. Pinsky, *The Gospel*

According to the Simpsons: The Spiritual Life of the World's Most Animated Family (Louisville, KY: Westminster John Knox Press, 2001).

· 1 2 ·

SELECTED FILMOGRAPHY

Seeing the Bigger Picture

Air Force One
1997 United States / Germany
Director: Wolfgang Petersen
Subjects: presidency, terrorism, foreign policy, Twenty-fifth Amendment (presidential health and disability)

Alexandr Nevsky
1938 Soviet Union
Directors: Sergei M. Eisenstein and Dmitri Vasilyev
Subjects: communism, war, rebellion

All the President's Men
1976 United States
Director: Alan J. Pakula
Subjects: presidency, Watergate, media (newspapers), corruption

American Dream
1990 United States / United Kingdom
Director: Barbara Kopple
Subjects: labor struggles, capitalism, meatpacking/processing industry

The American President
1995 United States
Director: Rob Reiner
Subjects: presidency, elections, media, American politics

American Standoff
2002 United States
Director: Kristi Jacobson
Subjects: labor struggles, trucking industry

Amistad
1997 United States
Director: Steven Spielberg
Subjects: presidency, slavery

Apocalypse Now
1979 United States
Director: Francis Ford Coppola
Subject: Vietnam War

Armageddon
1998 United States
Director: Michael Bay
Subjects: presidency, nuclear weapons

Atomic Café
1982 United States
Directors: Jayne Loader and Kevin Rafferty
Subject: nuclear war

Avatar
2009 United States
Director: James Cameron
Subject: environment

Baghdad ER
2006 United States
Directors: Jon Alpert and Matthew O'Neill
Subjects: war, Iraq War

Before the Rain
1994 Macedonia / France / United Kingdom
Director: Milcho Manchevski
Subjects: ethnic conflicts, war

The Best Man
1964 United States
Director: Franklin J. Schaffner
Subjects: presidency, campaign, elections, homosexuality, civil rights

Big Jim McLain
1952 United States
Director: Edward Ludwig
Subjects: communism, red scare

The Big One
1997 United States / United Kingdom
Director: Michael Moore
Subjects: capitalism, globalization, labor struggles, elections

The Big Parade
1925 United States
Director: King Vidor
Subject: war

The Birth of a Nation
1915 United States
Director: D. W. Griffith
Subjects: democracy, civil rights, racism, war

Black Friday
2004 India
Director: Anurag Kashyap
Subjects: terrorism, human rights

Bloody Sunday
2002 United Kingdom / Ireland
Director: Paul Greengrass
Subject: ethnic conflict

Blue Gold: World Water Wars
2008 United States
Director: Sam Bozzo
Subjects: capitalism, environment, natural resources

Bob Roberts
1992 United States / United Kingdom
Director: Tim Robbins
Subjects: campaigns, corruption, media, ideology

Born on the Fourth of July
1989 United States
Director: Oliver Stone
Subjects: war, human rights, physical and mental disabilities, PTSD (post-traumatic stress disorder)

Bowling for Columbine
2002 Canada / United States
Director: Michael Moore
Subjects: media, gun control, capitalism, social and economic justice

The Boy in the Striped Pajamas
2008 United Kingdom / United States
Director: Mark Herman
Subjects: human rights, genocide

The Brave One
1956 United States
Director: Irving Rapper
Subject: red scare

Broadcast News
1987 United States
Director: James L. Brooks
Subject: media

Brothers
2009 United States
Director: Jim Sheridan
Subjects: war, PTSD (post-traumatic stress disorder)

Bulworth
1998 United States
Director: Warren Beatty
Subjects: elections, political corruption, media, race relations

C.S.A.: The Confederate States of America
2004 United States
Director: Kevin Willmott
Subject: civil rights

Call Northside 777
1948 United States
Director: Henry Hathaway
Subject: media

Can Mr. Smith Get to Washington Anymore?
2006 United States
Director: Frank Popper
Subjects: campaign, elections, media

Canadian Bacon
1994 United States
Director: Michael Moore
Subjects: presidency, media, foreign policy, war, capitalism

The Candidate
1972 United States
Director: Michael Ritchie
Subjects: campaigns, elections, media

Capitalism: A Love Story
2009 United States
Director: Michael Moore
Subjects: capitalism, democracy

Casablanca
1943 United States
Director: Michael Curtiz
Subjects: war, democracy, fascism

The Celluloid Closet
1995 United States / United Kingdom / France / Germany
Directors: Rob Epstein and Jeffrey Friedman
Subjects: homosexuality, social justice, censorship

Citizen Kane
1941 United States
Director: Orson Welles
Subjects: campaign, elections, media

A Civil Action
1998 United States
Director: Steven Zaillian
Subjects: environment, legal system

Clear and Present Danger
1994 United States
Director: Philip Noyce
Subjects: presidency, terrorism, national security, corruption

Coming Home
1978 United States
Director: Hal Ashby
Subject: war

Conspiracy
2001 United States
Director: Frank Pierson
Subjects: genocide, war

Control Room
2004 United States
Director: Jehane Noujaim
Subjects: war, Iraq

Countdown to Zero
2010 United States
Director: Lucy Walker
Subjects: nuclear weapons, war

The Cove
2009 United States
Director: Louie Psihoyos
Subjects: environment, animal cruelty and species depletion, food safety

Cradle Will Rock
1999 United States
Director: Tim Robbins
Subjects: red scare, labor struggles

Crash
2004 United States
Director: Paul Haggis
Subjects: racial and ethnic conflict, immigration

Crossfire
1947 United States
Director: Edward Dmytryk
Subjects: anti-Semitism, social justice

Dave
1993 United States
Director: Ivan Reitman
Subjects: presidency, elections, political corruption

The Day After
1983 United States
Director: Nicholas Meyer
Subject: nuclear war

The Day After Tomorrow
2004 United States
Director: Roland Emmerich
Subject: environment

The Day the Earth Stood Still
1951 United States
Director: Robert Wise
Subjects: war, nuclear weapons

Dead Man Walking
1995 United States / United Kingdom
Director: Tim Robbins
Subject: death penalty

Deadline
2004 United States
Directors: Katy Chevigny and Kirsten Johnson
Subject: death penalty

Deadline U.S.A.
1952 United States
Director: Richard Brooks
Subject: media

Death Wish
1974 United States
Director: Michael Winner
Subjects: crime and deviance, vigilantism

Deep Impact
1998 United States
Director: Mimi Leder
Subjects: presidency, military

The Deer Hunter
1978 United States
Director: Michael Cimino
Subject: Vietnam War

The Defiant Ones
1958 United States
Director: Stanley Kramer
Subjects: racism, ethnic conflict

Divided We Fall
Musíme si pomáhat
2000 Czech Republic
Director: Jan Hrebejk
Subjects: genocide, human rights

Do the Right Thing
1989 United States
Director: Spike Lee
Subjects: racism, ethnic conflict

Dr. Strangelove
Or, How I Learned to Stop Worrying and Love the Bomb
1964 United Kingdom
Director: Stanley Kubrick
Subjects: war, nuclear weapons

Earth
2007 United Kingdom / Germany / United States
Directors: Alastair Fothergill and Mark Linfield
Subject: environment

Earth Days
2009 United States
Director: Robert Stone
Subject: environment

The 11ᵗʰ Hour
2007 United States
Directors: Leila Conners Petersen and Nadia Conners
Subject: Environment

Enemy of the State
1998 United States
Director: Tony Scott
Subjects: presidency, national security, intelligence

Erin Brockovich
2000 United States
Director: Steven Soderbergh
Subjects: environment, legal system

The Execution of Wanda Jean
2002 United States
Director: Liz Garbus
Subjects: death penalty, legal system, civil rights, racism

Fahrenheit 9/11
2004 United States
Director: Michael Moore
Subjects: war, media, propaganda, terrorism, Iraq, presidency

Fail-Safe
1964 United States
Director: Sidney Lumet
Subjects: presidency, national security, war, nuclear weapons

The Fall of the Romanov Dynasty
Padeniye dinastij Romanovykh
1927 Soviet Union
Director: Esfir Shub
Subjects: communism, war

Fantastic Planet
La planète sauvage
1973 France / Czechoslovakia
Director: René Laloux
Subject: communism

Fast Food Nation
2006 United States
Director: Richard Linklater
Subject: environment

Fight Club
1999 United States
Director: David Fincher
Subjects: capitalism, fascism

The Firemen's Ball
Horí má panenko
1967 Czechoslovakia / Italy
Director: Miloš Forman
Subject: communism

The Fog of War: Eleven Lessons from the Life of Robert S. McNamara
2003 United States
Director: Errol Morris
Subjects: war, nuclear deterrence, cold war, realism

Food Inc.
2008 United States
Director: Robert Kenner
Subjects: environment, capitalism, food safety

For Whom the Bell Tolls
1943 United States
Director: Sam Wood
Subjects: fascism, war, Spanish Civil War

4 Little Girls
1997 United States
Director: Spike Lee
Subjects: civil rights movement, racism in the American South

The Front
1976 United States
Director: Martin Ritt
Subjects: communism, red scare, democracy

Frost/Nixon
2008 United States / United Kingdom / France
Director: Ron Howard
Subjects: presidency, media, Watergate

Frozen River
2008 United States
Director: Courtney Hunt
Subjects: capitalism, immigration, ethnic conflict

Full Metal Jacket
1987 United States
Director: Stanley Kubrick
Subjects: war, Vietnam, psychological effects

Gabriel over the White House
1933 United States
Director: Gregory La Cava
Subjects: democracy, fascism, presidency

Gasland
2010 United States
Director: Josh Fox
Subjects: environment, capitalism, natural gas industry

The Genocide Factor
2000 United States
Director: Robert J. Emery
Subject: genocide

Gentleman's Agreement
1947 United States
Director: Elia Kazan
Subjects: anti-Semitism, social justice

George Wallace
1997 United States
Director: John Frankenheimer
Subjects: racism, ethnic relations

George Wallace: Settin' the Woods on Fire
2000 United States
Directors: Daniel McCabe and Paul Stekler
Subjects: racism, civil rights movement, political power, electoral politics

The Ghost Writer
2010 United Kingdom
Director: Roman Polanski
Subjects: Iraq war, war crimes

Ghosts of Abu Ghraib
2007 United States
Director: Rory Kennedy
Subjects: war, human rights

Ghosts of Mississippi
1996 United States
Director: Rob Reiner
Subjects: civil rights, racism, legal system

Ghosts of Rwanda
2004 United States
Director: Greg Barker
Subjects: genocide, war, human rights

The Gods Must Be Crazy
1980 Botswana
Director: Jamie Uys
Subjects: race relations, capitalism

Good Night, and Good Luck
2005 United States / France / United Kingdom / Japan
Director: George Clooney
Subjects: media, red scare

Goodbye Lenin!
2003 Germany
Director: Wolfgang Becker
Subjects: communism, capitalism

Grace Is Gone
2007 United States
Director: James C. Strouse
Subject: war

Gran Torino
2008 United States / Germany
Director: Clint Eastwood
Subjects: ethnic conflict, racism, identity

The Grand Illusion
La grande illusion
1937 France
Director: Jean Renoir
Subjects: war, nationalism, class relations

The Great Dictator
1940 United States
Director: Charles Chaplin
Subject: war, anti-Semitism

The Green Berets
1968 United States
Directors: Ray Kellogg and John Wayne
Subjects: war, Vietnam

The Green Mile
1999 United States
Director: Frank Darabont
Subject: death penalty

Green Zone
2010 United States
Director: Paul Greengrass
Subjects: war, Iraq

Guilty by Suspicion
1991 United States / France
Director: Irwin Winkler
Subjects: red scare, civil liberties, communism

Gunner Palace
2005 United States
Directors: Petra Epperlein and Michael Tucker
Subjects: war, Iraq

Hair
1979 United States
Director: Miloš Forman
Subjects: individual freedom

The Handmaid's Tale
1990 United States
Director: Volker Schlöndorff
Subjects: ideology, religion

Harlan County, USA
1976 United States
Director: Barbara Kopple
Subjects: labor struggles, capitalism

His Girl Friday
1940 United States
Director: Howard Hawks
Subject: media

Holocaust
1978 United States
Director: Marvin J. Chomsky
Subjects: genocide, anti-Semitism

Hotel Rwanda
2004 United Kingdom / United States / Italy / South Africa
Director: Terry George
Subject: genocide

The Hurt Locker
2009 United States
Director: Kathryn Bigelow
Subjects: war, Iraq

I Was a Communist for the FBI
1951 United States
Director: Gordon Douglas
Subjects: red scare, communism

I'm on the Ballot
2000 United States
Director: Al Ward
Subjects: third parties, campaigns, elections, media, presidency

Imaginary Witness: Hollywood and the Holocaust
2004 United States
Director: Daniel Anker
Subjects: genocide, anti-Semitism

In the Valley of Elah
2007 United States
Director: Paul Haggis
Subjects: war, Iraq, PTSD (post-traumatic stress disorder)

An Inconvenient Truth
2006 United States
Director: Davis Guggenheim
Subjects: environment, climate change

Independence Day
1996 United States
Director: Roland Emmerich
Subjects: presidency, national security, conspiracy theory

Inside the Twin Towers (2006)
2006 United States
Director: Richard Dale
Subject: terrorism

Invasion of the Body Snatchers
1956 United States
Director: Don Siegel
Subjects: red scare, communism, cold war conformity

The Iron Curtain
1948 United States
Director: William A. Wellman
Subject: communism

It Happened One Night
1934 United States
Director: Frank Capra
Subject: media

Jacob the Liar
Jakob, der Lügner
1975 German Democratic Republic (East Germany)
Director: Frank Beyer
Subject: genocide

JFK
1991 United States / France
Director: Oliver Stone
Subjects: presidency, conspiracy theories, military, foreign policy, assassination

Journeys with George
2002 United States
Directors: Aaron Lubarsky and Alexandra Pelosi
Subjects: campaigns, media, presidency

Judgment at Nuremberg
1961 United States
Director: Stanley Kramer
Subjects: war crimes, genocide

The Killing Fields
1984 United Kingdom
Director: Roland Joffe
Subject: genocide

King Corn
2007 United States
Director: Aaron Woolf
Subjects: environment, capitalism

The Laramie Project
2002 United States
Director: Moisés Kaufman
Subjects: homosexuality, hate crimes, social justice

The Last Hurrah
1958 United States
Director: John Ford
Subjects: elections, campaigns, political machines

The Last Truck: Closing of a GM Plant
2009 United States
Directors: Steven Bognar and Julia Reichert
Subjects: capitalism, auto industry, economic and social justice

Life Is Beautiful
La Vita è Bella
1997 Italy
Director: Roberto Benigni
Subjects: genocide, anti-Semitism

The Life of David Gale
2003 United States / Germany / United Kingdom
Director: Alan Parker
Subject: death penalty

Lifeboat
1944 United States
Director: Alfred Hitchcock
Subjects: war, democracy

The Lives of Others
Das Leben der Anderen
2006 Germany
Director: Florian Henckel von Donnersmarck
Subjects: communism, civil liberties

Love Actually
2003 United Kingdom
Director: Richard Curtis
Subjects: presidency, foreign policy

Loves of a Blonde
1965 Czechoslovakia
Director: Miloš Forman
Subject: communism

The Man Who Wasn't There
2001 United States
Directors: Joel Coen and Ethan Coen
Subject: existentialism

The Manchurian Candidate
1962 United States
Director: John Frankenheimer
Subjects: fascism, red scare, political assassination, communism

Manufacturing Dissent
2007 Canada
Director: Rick Caine and Debbie Melnyk
Subjects: Michael Moore, propaganda

Matewan
1987 United States
Director: John Sayles
Subjects: labor struggles, race relations, entrenched economic power

Meet John Doe
1941 United States
Director: Frank Capra
Subject: media

Metropolis
1927 Germany
Director: Fritz Lang
Subjects: democracy, labor relations

Michael & Me
2004 United States
Director: Larry Elder
Subject: Second Amendment

Michael Moore Hates America
2004 United States
Director: Michael Wilson
Subject: criticism of filmmaker Michael Moore

Milk
2008 United States
Director: Gus Van Sant
Subjects: democracy, LGBT (lesbian, gay, bisexual, and transgendered) rights

Minority Report
2002 United States
Director: Steven Spielberg
Subjects: democracy, fascism, civil liberties

The Missiles of October
1974 United States
Director: Anthony Page
Subject: war

Missing
1982 United States
Director: Constantin Costa-Gavras
Subjects: human rights, democracy

Mission to Moscow
1943 United States
Director: Michael Curtiz
Subjects: fascism, communism

Mississippi Burning
1988 United States
Director: Alan Parker
Subjects: racism, civil rights

Monster
2003 United States / Germany
Director: Patty Jenkins
Subjects: death penalty, human sexuality

Monster's Ball
2001 United States
Director: Marc Forster
Subjects: racism, death penalty

Monty Python and the Holy Grail
1975 United Kingdom
Directors: Terry Gilliam and Terry Jones
Subject: democracy

Mr. Conservative: Goldwater on Goldwater
2006 United States
Director: Julie Anderson
Subjects: conservatism, democracy, ideology

Mr. Smith Goes to Washington
1939 United States
Director: Frank Capra
Subjects: democracy, political machines

Munich
2005 United States / Canada / France
Director: Steven Spielberg
Subject: terrorism

Murder at 1600
1997 United States
Director: Dwight H. Little
Subjects: presidency, national security

Murder on a Sunday Morning
Un coupable ideal
2001 France / United States
Director: Jean-Xavier de Lestrade
Subject: racial profiling, justice system, civil rights

My Fellow Americans
1996 United States
Director: Peter Segal
Subjects: presidency, corruption, conspiracy

My Son John
1952 United States
Director: Leo McCarey
Subjects: red scare, communism

Naked Gun 21/2: The Smell of Fear
1991 United States
Director: David Zucker
Subjects: presidency, conspiracy

National Geographic: Inside 9/11
2005 United States
Subject: terrorism

The National Parks: America's Best Idea
2009 United States
Director: Ken Burns
Subject: environment

Network
1976 United States
Director: Sidney Lumet
Subjects: media, capitalism, globalization

Nixon
1995 United States
Director: Oliver Stone
Subjects: presidency, Watergate, war

No Country for Old Men
2007 United States
Directors: Ethan Coen and Joel Coen
Subjects: drug trafficking, capitalism

No End in Sight
2007 United States
Director: Charles Ferguson
Subjects: war, Iraq

Nothing Sacred
1937 United States
Director: William A. Wellman
Subject: media

O Brother, Where Art Thou?
2000 United States
Director: Joel Coen
Subjects: racism, civil rights

Oceans
Océans
2009 France / Switzerland / Spain
Directors: Jacques Perrin and Jacques Cluzaud
Subject: environment

The Official Story
La historia oficial
1985 Argentina
Director: Luis Puenzo
Subjects: human rights, torture

On the Beach
1959 United States
Director: Stanley Kramer
Subject: nuclear war

Operation: Dreamland
2005 United States
Directors: Ian Olds and Garrett Scott
Subjects: war, Iraq

Out in the Silence
2009 United States
Directors: Dean Hamer and Joe Wilson
Subjects: social justice, LGBT (lesbian, gay, bisexual, and transgendered) rights

Outfoxed: Rupert Murdoch's War on Journalism
2004 United States
Director: Robert Greenwald
Subjects: media, capitalism

Paths of Glory
1957 United States
Director: Stanley Kubrick
Subject: war

The Pelican Brief
1994 United States
Director: Alan J. Pakula
Subject: presidency

The People vs. Larry Flynt
1996 United States
Director: Miloš Forman
Subject: civil liberties

A Perfect Candidate
1996 United States
Directors: R. J. Cutler and David Van Taylor
Subjects: campaigns, elections, media

Planet Earth
2006 United Kingdom
Subject: environment

The Planet of the Apes
1968 United States
Director: Franklin J. Schaffner
Subject: nuclear war

Platoon
1986 United States
Director: Oliver Stone
Subject: war

Potemkin
Bronenosets Potyomkin
1925 Soviet Union
Directors: Sergei Eisenstein and Grigori Aleksandrov
Subjects: war, communism

Primary Colors
1998 United States
Director: Mike Nichols
Subjects: presidency, campaigns, elections

The Rabbit of Seville
1950 United States
Director: Chuck Jones
Subjects: war, security dilemma

Red Alert: The Enemy Within
2009 India
Director: Anant Mahadevan
Subject: terrorism

Red Badge of Courage
1951 United States
Director: John Huston
Subject: war

The Red Menace
1949 United States
Director: R. G. Springsteen
Subjects: red scare, communism

Redacted
2007 United States / Canada
Director: Brian De Palma
Subjects: war, human rights, media

Reel Injun
2010 United States
Directors: Neil Diamond, Catherine Bainbridge, and Jeremiah Hayes
Subjects: racism, ethnic conflict, human rights

Rendition
2007 United States
Director: Gavin Hood
Subjects: war, terrorism, human rights

A Report on the Party and the Guest
O slavnosti a hostech
1966 Czechoslovakia
Director: Jan Němec
Subject: communism

Right America: Feeling Wronged
2009 United States
Director: Alexandra Pelosi
Subjects: media, ideology

Roger & Me
1989 United States
Director: Michael Moore
Subjects: capitalism, labor struggles

Roots
1977 United States
Directors: Marvin J. Chomsky, John Erman, David Greene, and Gilbert Moses
Subjects: slavery, human rights

Rosewood
1997 United States
Director: John Singleton
Subjects: racism, genocide, human rights

Salt of the Earth
1954 United States
Director: Herbert J. Biberman
Subjects: ethnic conflict, labor relations, red scare

Schindler's List
1993 United States
Director: Steven Spielberg
Subjects: genocide, anti-Semitism

Sergeant York
1941 United States
Director: Howard Hawks
Subject: war

Seven Days in May
1964 United States
Director: John Frankenheimer
Subjects: presidency, national security, foreign policy

Shadow Conspiracy
1997 United States
Director: George P. Cosmatos
Subject: presidency, conspiracy, political assassination

Shoah
1985 France
Director: Claude Lanzmann
Subjects: genocide, anti-Semitism

Silent Running
1972 United States
Director: Douglas Trumbull
Subject: environment

The Simpsons Movie
2007 United States
Director: David Silverman
Subjects: environment, democracy

Soldiers of Salamina
Soldados de Salamina
2003 Spain
Director: David Trueba
Subjects: war, fascism, media

Sometimes in April
2005 France / United States
Director: Raoul Peck
Subject: genocide

Soylent Green
1973 United States
Director: Richard Fleischer
Subject: environment, overpopulation, food supply

The Spanish Earth
1937 United States
Director: Joris Iven
Subjects: war, fascism, Spanish Civil War

Star Trek IV: The Voyage Home
1986 United States
Director: Leonard Nimoy
Subject: environment

**Star Wars: A New Hope / Star Wars: The Empire Strikes Back /
    Star Wars: The Return of the Jedi**
1977 / 1980 / 1983 United States
Director: George Lucas
Subjects: terrorism, war

Starship Troopers
1997 United States
Director: Paul Verhoeven
Subjects: war, fascism

State of the Union
1948 United States
Director: Frank Capra
Subjects: democracy, media, campaigns, elections, presidency

Stop-Loss
2008 United States
Director: Kimberly Pierce
Subjects: war, Iraq

Store Wars
2001 United States
Director: Micha X. Peled
Subjects: capitalism, democracy

Strange Fruit
2002 United States
Director: Joel Katz
Subjects: racism, civil rights

Street Fight
2005 United States
Director: Marshall Curry
Subjects: campaign, elections, racial identity

The Sum of All Fears
2002 United States
Director: Phil Alden Robinson
Subjects: terrorism, nuclear weapons, presidency

Taxi to the Dark Side
2007 United States
Director: Alex Gibney
Subjects: war, Iraq, Afghanistan, human rights

Team America: World Police
2004 United States
Director: Trey Parker
Subjects: war, terrorism, ideology

Tender Comrade
1943 United States
Director: Edward Dmytryk
Subjects: communism, democracy

Theeviravaathi: The Terrorist
1999 United States
Director: Santosh Sivan
Subject: terrorism

The Thin Blue Line
1988 United States
Director: Errol Morris
Subject: death penalty

Thirteen Days
2000 United States
Director: Roger Donaldson
Subjects: war, nuclear weapons

Threads
1984 United Kingdom
Director: Mick Jackson
Subject: nuclear war

The Tillman Story
2010 United States
Director: Amir Bar-Lev
Subject: war

To Kill a Mockingbird
1962 United States
Director: Robert Mulligan
Subjects: racism, legal system, civil rights

Triumph of the Will
Triumph des Willens
1935 Germany
Director: Leni Riefenstahl
Subject: fascism

Truman
1995 United States
Director: Frank Pierson
Subjects: presidency, foreign policy, campaigns, elections

Trumbo
2007 United States
Director: Peter Askin
Subjects: red scare, communism

The Unbearable Lightness of Being
1988 United States
Director: Philip Kaufman
Subject: communism

United 93
2006 United States
Director: Paul Greengrass
Subjects: terrorism

Up in the Air
2009 United States
Director: Jason Reitman
Subject: capitalism

Vote for Me: Politics in America
1996 United States
Directors: Louis Alvarez, Andy Kolker, and Paul Stekler
Subjects: campaigns, elections

W
2008 United States
Director: Oliver Stone
Subjects: presidency, war

Wag the Dog
1997 United States
Director: Barry Levinson
Subjects: presidency, political corruption, war

Wall-E
2008 United States
Director: Andrew Stanton
Subject: environment

Wal-Mart: The High Cost of Low Price
2005 United States
Director: Robert Greenwald
Subjects: capitalism, environment, labor relations

The Wannsee Conference
Die Wannseekonferenz
1984 Austria / Germany (West)
Director: Heinz Schirk
Subject: genocide

War Game
1965 United Kingdom
Director: Peter Watkins
Subject: nuclear war

WarGames
1983 United States
Director: John Badham
Subject: nuclear war

The War Room
1993 United States
Directors: Chris Hegedus and D. A. Pennebaker
Subjects: media, campaigns, elections, presidency, political parties

We Shall Remain
2009 United States
Director: Ric Burns
Subjects: civil rights, ethnic conflict, genocide

When the Wind Blows
1986 United Kingdom
Director: Jimmy I. Murakami
Subject: nuclear war

When We Were Soldiers
2002 United States
Director: Randall Wallace
Subjects: war, Vietnam

Why We Fight
2005 United States
Director: Eugene Jarecki
Subjects: war, military-industrial complex, media

Why We Fight: The Nazis Strike
1943 United States
Director: Frank Capra
Subjects: war, democracy, fascism

Why We Fight: War Comes to America
1945 United States
Director: Frank Capra
Subjects: war, capitalism

Winter's Bone
2010 United States
Director: Debra Granik
Subject: capitalism

World Trade Center
2006 United States
Director: Oliver Stone
Subject: terrorism

Yankee Doodle Dandy
1942 United States
Director: Michael Curtiz
Subjects: presidency, patriotism

Young Mr. Lincoln
1939 United States
Director: John Ford
Subject: presidency

Television

There are many television programs mentioned in the text; listed below are specific episodes of television series and televised films discussed in *Seeing the Bigger Picture*.

The Awful Truth
1999–2000 United Kingdom / United States
Director: Michael Moore
Subjects: civil rights, racism, labor struggles, death penalty, campaign, elections, abortion

Boardwalk Empire
2010 United States
Subjects: women's suffrage, temperance movement, organized crime, campaigns

Frontline
1996 *Why Americans Hate the Press*
Subjects: media, campaigns, elections
1998 *The Triumph of Evil*
Subjects: genocide, human rights, war
2004 *Ghosts of Rwanda*
Subjects: genocide, human rights, war
2010 *The Wounded Platoon*
Subject: war, PTSD (post-traumatic stress disorder)

Futurama
1999 "A Head in the Polls"
Subjects: presidency, Watergate

Journey to Planet Earth
2003 "On the Brink"
Subjects: environment, immigration, poverty

Simpsons The
1990 "Two Cars in Every Garage and Three Eyes on Every Fish"
1991 "Mr. Lisa Goes to Washington"
1994 "Sideshow Bob Roberts"
1996 "Treehouse of Horror VII: Citizen Kang"
1998 "Trash of the Titans"
Subjects: campaigns, elections, presidency, environment, democracy

Six Feet Under
2000–2005 The United States
Subjects: homosexuality, civil rights, capitalism

TV Nation
1993–1995 United States / United Kingdom
Subjects: civil rights, racism, labor struggle, media

The Twilight Zone
1960 "The Monsters Are Due on Maple Street"
Subject: terrorism

The West Wing
1999 "A Proportional Response"
1999 "The Short List"
1999 "Mr. Willis of Ohio"
2001 "Two Cathedrals"
2002 "College Kids"
2002 "20 Hours in America"
2006 "Tomorrow"
Subjects: democracy, presidency, elections, civil liberties, civil rights

INDEX

N

O